THE DRUM

A History

Matt Dean

THE SCARECROW PRESS, INC.
Lanham • Toronto • Plymouth, UK
2012

Published by Scarecrow Press, Inc.
A wholly owned subsidiary of The Rowman & Littlefield Publishing Group, Inc.
4501 Forbes Boulevard, Suite 200, Lanham, Maryland 20706
http://www.scarecrowpress.com

Estover Road, Plymouth PL6 7PY, United Kingdom

British Library Cataloguing in Publication Information Available

Library of Congress Cataloging-in-Publication Data

Dean, Matt, 1980–
    The drum : a history / Matt Dean.
        p. cm.
    Includes bibliographical references and index.
    ISBN 978-0-8108-8170-9 (cloth : alk. paper) — ISBN 978-0-8108-8171-6
(ebook)
    1. Drum. I. Title.
    ML1035.D43 2012
    786.909—dc23   2011028905

Contents

iii

Preface

The drum is indispensable in primitive life; no instrument has so many ritual tasks, no instrument is held
more sacred.

—Curt Sachs, 1940

THE DRUM HAS BEEN A POWERFUL, awe-inspiring, and emotive instrument from ancient history until today. So many of us are drawn to
it when we hear the rhythm, the heartbeat of the drum, as if it had
some kind of supernatural power beyond the level of our understanding. It has certainly held me spellbound for the majority of my
life. But why does the world need a book about its history?

For me, this is the written record of my findings in answer to
an ongoing quest, namely to find out how the modern drums that I
play today evolved and from where they came.

As a musician, I have come to realize that my knowledge of the
drum, drumming, and their histories is as important as my technical
ability to strike the drum. For all the lightning-fast notes I am able
to play, the decision of what to play, and when, is just as pertinent.

By listening to the rich recorded musical catalog available, we
learn that which helps us make informed decisions when we play
our instrument. But having a deeper understanding of the instrument and its history can also aid in one's development as a drummer and even in one's evolution as a listener.

Emulating our favorite drummers is commonly the starting point for those who drum, and from this platform we then leap off into the unknown as we forge our individual musical paths. The more we learn about these past masters and the instrument itself, the larger, richer, more creative, and more inspiring this platform becomes.

Looking back at who and what came before underscores the geographical, religious, political, social, and emotional influences and traditions that resulted in the modern drum (or "drum kit"). The raw, primal, and often divine power that this instrument possesses ensured its importance among many cultures. That power is still felt to this day in our experience of the drum.

This quest has been occurring for years without my realizing it. It is the fruit of the many countries I have visited over the years and masses of research I have collated in my head, on my computers, in notebooks, on videos and CDs, in magazines and books and even manuscripts. After so long an immersion, now seemed the time to make some structured sense of all to which I had been exposed. This book is the product of that immersion. It is my Columbus's voyage of discovery, my attempt to map how the drum evolved through the ages and across the planet into what we know today.

Along this often-solitary journey, I married, bought a house, and witnessed the birth of my first son, Oliver. And accompanying each of these major events was my earnest effort to finish this book, which at times seemed to have no end. But as I finish its writing, I still have a wife, a house, and a son, and that is largely due to the understanding and selflessness of my spouse, Hannah. To her, I say: I am eternally grateful, and I gladly promise all of my time to you and Oliver—until the next drum-related project takes hold.

Let me, of course, also thank my parents. My father introduced me to so much great music, sparked my passion, and provided me with the foundation of knowledge I have today—not to mention my first paid performance with his band. And, of course, alongside him was his wife, my mother, who turned inadvertent bigamist when she learned that she had married a man and his bass guitar. Their patience, support, and encouragement allowed me to follow my dreams as a drummer and as a writer.

Let me also acknowledge Bill Bruford, who, possibly unwittingly, carried my interest in musical history beyond what I learned from my father and who is ultimately responsible for triggering the many questions in my head mainly along the lines of "how did that facet of music come to be?"

I also should tip my hat to the many, many musical friends, educators, colleagues, and acquaintances who all contributed to this journey and helped me in the quest for answers. You are too numerous to mention by name, so I only hope I have thanked you sufficiently in person.

I hope this book answers many of the questions you have, as I once had about how the drum came to be the instrument we know today. At the very least, I hope it will prove an interesting read. Dare I write that beyond this book there are many more questions I have yet to answer. But one book allows only so many answers, and so my quest continues.

Chapter One

———————————◯———————————

What Is a Drum?

WE ARE ALL FAMILIAR WITH THE DRUM, and the word surely conjures up various different images in each reader's head depending on nationality, country of residence, age, most recent experience with drums, and a host of other factors. But in general the image will consist of a resonating chamber with at least one membrane, be it animal or synthetic, stretched tight across an opening, which is then beaten with a body part or a stick—resulting in a noise.

The *Collins English Dictionary*, third edition (1991), entry is "A percussion instrument sounded by striking a membrane stretched across the opening of a hollow cylinder or hemisphere."

Of course the drum is actually found in many different shapes and forms beyond this definition, as people over thousands of years across the face of the earth have been inspired to create weird and wonderful drums on which to create rhythm. The membranes themselves can be held taut with nails, pegs, lacing of many different materials, and metal screws in more modern examples, and they can be attached to shells of wood, metal pottery, and anything else that sounds or looks appealing.

I should mention that this book will follow the Sachs-Hornbostel musical instrument classification system.[1] Although it contains many subdivisions of instrument groupings, it is based on four main categories: chordophones, aerophones, idiophones, and membranophones. A membranophone is defined as containing a

1

membrane stretched across a shell and struck to make a sound. Most drums are membranophones.

This book seeks to chart the origin of the simple, humble, yet incredibly powerful and emotive membranophone to discover how it developed into the many different forms with as many different uses that we enjoy today.

NOTE

1. E. Hornbostel and C. Sachs, *Classification of musical instruments* (*The Galpin Society Journal*, 14 March 1961), 3–29.

Chapter Two

─────────○─────────

Drum History

THE ANIMALS

DRUMS HAVE BECOME COMMONPLACE in the modern world as the key rhythmic factor in artistic expression. We use drums and rhythm in general to synchronize performances for our own, and the audience's, listening pleasure. Thousands of radio stations, TV channels, Internet sites, and books supply a constant source of drumming material, which we enjoy, study, and emulate to create a multimillion-dollar industry. Drummers strive in a competitive race to be the most stylish, original, fastest, and best players in their field.

It wasn't always like this, however. Throughout their history, drums have given the human race many more functional and practical uses, necessary for survival. Cultures have ascribed strong sexual symbolism to drums, whether it's attaching gender to different drumsticks, helping girls through their first menstrual cycle, or marking the rites of passage through circumcision with rhythm.

We can speculate that our distant ancestors may have originally used music in religious ceremony, hunting calls, courtship, battle, or social bonding, but it will always be speculation. Early man may have struck two objects together and accidentally stumbled across a pleasing resonance that compelled him to repeat the action. It would only take several strikes at a consistent speed for a rhythm to

Various frame drums. Courtesy of the author and www.rhythmuseum .com.

be created. It seems impossible to imagine this intelligent life form not using rhythm in some way; after all, our ability and desire for artistic expression is one of the factors that set us apart from all other species. Our need to express emotion through motion is inherent, such as dancing, a common by-product of which is stamping feet or body slapping and therefore audible rhythm.

We can, however, see rhythm in other areas of nature, such as certain mammals that drum their feet to advertise residence and ward off competitors, "In Taï forest, wild chimpanzees seem to use drumming on buttressed trees to convey information and changes of travel direction."[1] These African chimpanzees with their drumming language may suggest that as humans evolved, they could have communicated through drumming languages before spoken language was created. This is speculation, but surely it must have been impossible for any human ancestor with a pulse to ignore the lure of rhythm, which, even in its simplest form, moves people irresistibly.

ANTIQUITY

Scientists speculate about evidence of Neanderthal man using musical instruments such as a 35,000-year-old bone flute, which was discovered in the late 20th century. It is possible to play full modern-day scales on the "instrument" by covering the holes and blowing into it, but some argue that this is coincidence, and scratches indicate that the holes were made by a carnivore's teeth.

Earlier still is evidence from as long as 70,000 years ago. Paleolithic tools were discovered in Belgium along with a mammoth bone engraved with parallel lines. It is believed that this was a rasp or skiffle. These are basic idiophones similar to the guiro.

However, a Neanderthal site in the Crimea has offered us clues from as long as 100,000 years ago in the form of whistles made from saiga antelope bones. If these surviving objects really are instruments, then we can guess that these people would have used some form of drums. Unfortunately it is left to guesswork, as the wood and animal hide often used for drums would have perished thousands of years ago, leaving only the bone flute and whistle instruments as evidence.

Certainly it can be proven that the people from the late Paleolithic Age around 32,000 years ago had artistic tendencies, as shown in the caves of Europe. The painted buffalo shaman in Les Trois-Frères, southern France, appears to be dancing and playing an instrument. If these pictorial references show purpose-made instruments, surely they had also crafted percussive instruments. Could they have possibly danced without rhythm? Drums from early times were symbolic, ritualistic, and possibly perceived to contain powers. This magical power may have been responsible for the Shaman dancers' seemingly trancelike state.

Although Europe is famous for these paintings, such records of earlier civilizations are known throughout the world, such as the rock paintings found in the Tassili-n-Ajjer plateau of Algeria by the French ethnologist Henri Lhote in 1956. These depict exciting dance scenes dating back to the Neolithic hunters of 6,000 to 4,000 BCE and are perhaps the earliest evidence of African music and dance.

We can see that music, and indeed percussion, can be traced back as far as almost any other aspect of civilization, but although drums are often carelessly talked about as the earliest instrument, this is unlikely. There is a big leap from scratching out an animal bone for a whistle to stretching a prepared animal skin over a hollowed shell and securing it in that position with adequate tension to make a satisfying sound.

However, the origin of the drum may have taken a different, simpler form. This can be traced back to the stamped pit, which consisted of a hole dug into the ground and covered with planks of wood. These were then jumped up and down upon, creating a percussive sound with the hollow pit providing the resonance to produce a pleasing tone. These have existed in many cultures, including the Solomon Islands, Indonesia, and Malaysia, and might loosely fall into the category of membranophone.

There is also similar evidence from the dawn of Hinduism, when the Vedic texts speak of the bhumi dundubhi. This is a pit covered with ox hide. The skin was nailed to the earth around it and either a wooden stick or the tail, which was sometimes left on the hide, was used as a beater.

Even simpler than these is the drum of the earth as used in New Guinea, India, and Ethiopia. This consists of two holes of different depths, each dug into a cone shape in the earth, the opening of which is slapped with the palm of the hand, also making use of the resonance of the cavity.

This constitutes the drum (although with no membrane, not a membranophone) in its simplest form and therefore, quite possibly its oldest form too.

Similar uses are numerous in African domestic work, where tribes of people pound stone pestles into stone troughs. Sexual symbolism is attached, with the pestle as the penis of a spirit and the trough as the vulva. This strong sexual significance was commonplace among early civilizations and often connected with percussion instruments.

The advances of the drum have to be viewed with an element of guesswork until the time of Mesopotamia and Egypt, when writing developed. They also took items to the afterlife via their tombs, which has helped many musical artifacts survive decomposition. Thanks to the civilizations of these areas and their excellent record keeping, we have evidence from as early as 3000 BCE depicting a variety of drums and other instruments such as harps, flutes, bells,

** PURCHASE **

Panda Express #1284
Batavia, IL
(630)482-9867

8/5/2019   1:16:01 PM   -Drive Thru-
Order: 408870   Server: Emanuel A

1 Bigger Plate	9.20

    CHOW MEIN-1/2
    CHOW MEIN-1/2
    ORANGE CKN
    BROCCOLI BEEF
    VEG SPRING ROLLS

SubTotal	9.20
TAX	0.74
Total	**9.94**
Master Card	**9.94**

Acct:XXXXXXXX1335
AuthCode:06776B

```
***************************************
*        FREE ENTREE ITEM!            *
*    Tell us about your visit and     *
*  receive a free entree item on us.  *
*          See back for details.      *
*                                     *
*          Survey Code:               *
*    1509-0887-4840-0128-0313-07      *
***************************************
```

Questions or Comments?
pandaexpress.com/connect

FREE ENTREE ITEM!

1. Within 2 days visit us online at
   pandaexpress.com/feedback
   or call **1-855-51-PANDA**

2. Write redemption code below:

3. Bring this receipt to a Panda
   Express to receive a free entree
   item with purchase of a Plate
   (2 entree plate)

Good Fortune is Best Shared.
PANDAEXPRESS.COM/CAREERS

and cymbals. Drums of this time were shown to involve the sacrificing of certain symbolic animals for their hide to make drums to appease the gods with their music.

But the identity of the person who created the first membranophone remains a mystery. It must have existed before the time of any surviving evidence, so the exact origin of this mighty concept is likely to remain a mystery forever.

Many early membranophones involved shells so similar to household objects, such as cooking pots, that it seems impossible to ignore the likelihood that these drums derived from such domestic objects. A fish, reptile, or animal skin over a pot or even a hole in the ground could have easily been stretched while it was being dried and, while it was held taut, somebody may have casually struck it when passing, only to be stopped in their tracks by the surprisingly pleasing resonance. The Swazi tribe of South Africa use such a method with the intambula. One man holds the skin taut over the end of a clay pot while another man beats it with a stick. From here, the taut skin just needs to be secured over the shell and we have our first purpose-made membranophone. The drums created in many of these tribal environments have changed little over time, so it is to other civilizations that we must look for further evolution of the drum. As reptile and fish skins were replaced by animal hides of greater durability, sticks replaced bare hands as beaters, creating greater volume and different sounds. However, in some cultures such as parts of East Africa, the drumstick was a phallic symbol in contrast to the feminine connotations sometimes held by the vessel or drum shell itself, and therefore only used by men to play the drum. In a few cases the sticks used for particular ritualistic playing are actually human leg bones.

By Mesopotamian times (around 4,000 to 5,000 years ago), purpose-made drums with specifically designed shells and carefully prepared and fixed skins existed. Social classes and labor divisions had elevated the musical instrument from one that any old soul could have a go at, to a skilled art that required professional musicians to perform to the highest standard. Of course, just as it is today, anyone can still play an instrument at some level, but the existence of professionals certainly helped to increase the development of the drum as those professionals embarked on the never-ending search for superior sound and playing quality.

One of these drums was the frame drum. A frame drum usually has a single head, the diameter of which is greater than its depth. In many cases the frame simply consists of a thin strip of bent wood. It is the most geographically widespread drum in history and is still popular today all around the world.

Other popular shapes across the various cultures were barrel drums, whose middle was wider than the heads, and hourglass drums, in which the middle was narrower than the heads.

These drums developed in design and usage, yielding many interesting, innovative, and beautiful designs from the tiniest drum to huge drums 6 feet in diameter. The world was given drums with handles, straps, carved feet, and those set on a frame. They were played vertically and horizontally, with hands or sticks. The skins were glued, neck-laced, buttoned, braced, and nailed onto the shells. They were single and double headed and made from all manner of woods and ceramics, some even containing bells or jingles within the shell, similar to a modern tambourine. Many of these drums have remained largely unchanged for hundreds of years. However, it was Western Asia that provided excellent early information and advances before influencing the Western civilization, and in particular Europe, where the membranophone was to see dramatic changes leading us to the drums that are available today.

NOTE

1. Christophe Boesch, "Symbolic communication in wild chimpanzees," *Human Evolution*, 6:1 (1991): 81.

Chapter Three

———————◯———————

Western Asia

FRAME DRUM GRIPS

WITH THE POPULARITY OF THE FRAME DRUM in so many parts of the world, unsurprisingly, different peoples have used different techniques to strike the drums. Sometimes sticks were used, but often these remained as hand drums. Larger frame drums would be used in a seated position with the drum resting on the legs, but smaller drums afforded different options. The two most-often-seen grips in artwork from around the world have become known as the Oriental grip (traditional grip) and the European grip (new grip). The Oriental grip was used throughout Western Asia, as observed in many paintings. This involved the weaker hand holding the drum at the bottom with the skin pointing away from the player. The fingers of the holding hand wrap around to play the front of the skin, and the dominant hand is free to reach over and employ a number of different techniques across the whole surface of the skin. The European grip involves the weaker hand holding the drum with the skin facing skyward, allowing the right hand to play the drum. This is more limited than the Oriental grip because the weak hand is less able to contribute any notes.

THE BIBLE

It is possible to learn about drums from thousands of years ago through excavation findings and pictorial and literary evidence. As a result, one of our best resources from Western Asia is the Bible. As it details the times before Jesus was born, we can easily observe that in the thousand years before Christ's birth people used hand drums known as tofs and cymbals known as meziltayim, as well as pitched instruments such as the lyre, woodwind instruments, shakers, trumpets, and harps. This collection of instruments was likely amassed over the period in which the Hebrews were settled in Canaan (roughly the site of modern Israel and surrounding areas) from around the 13th century BCE following the exodus from Egypt.

References to musical instruments are spread liberally throughout the Old Testament, and often the use of percussion is mentioned. Such mentions include this passage from Psalm 68:24–25: "They have seen thy goings, O God; even the goings of my God, my king, in the sanctuary. The singers went before, the players on instruments followed after; among them were the damsels playing with timbrels."

In Genesis 31:27 we can see, "Wherefore didst thou flee away secretly, and steal away from me; and didst not tell me, that I might have sent thee away with mirth, and with songs, with taberet, and with a harp."

Taken from Psalm 150:3–4 is, "Praise Him with the sound of the trumpet: praise Him with the psaltery and harp. Praise Him with the timbrel and dance: praise Him with stringed instruments and organs."

These are just three examples of the many that exist, and they all create excellent evidence of the drum's use in ceremony, celebration, worship, and praise, often accompanied by such instruments as a harp, psaltery, trumpet, or pipe. The examples above are consistent with most references that demonstrate use of the timbrel or taberet. The timbrel or taberet was also known as the tof by the ancient Hebrews (as the original Hebrew Bible would have written it), the daff or duff by Muslims, the dafik by the Kurdish, the def by Bosnians and Albanians, and the adufe by Portuguese and Spanish.

The tof also pertains to a gruesome connection with the hellish area of Tophet in Jerusalem in which children were sacrificed to the god Moloch in burning fires while drums were beaten to disguise their screams. This alleged connection is referenced by Mudge: "To drown the cries of the poor innocents, large drums were beaten: hence the place became, the valley of Tophet, or a drum, with allusion to its rites of torture and of death."[1]

Aside from these accounts, archaeological sites in Israel such as Tel Shikmona and Achzib have helped confirm the Bible stories by yielding clay figurines, which clearly depict females playing frame drums.

But just as words can be written to fit the author's own needs or views, artistic works might also be distorted through lack of artistic ability or the use of artistic license to portray the image as desired. This makes it more difficult to accurately determine drum sizes and applications, but these different sources make it irrefutable that frame drums were an important part of ancient Hebrew life and that women were often the performers.

The tof was in fact the main percussive instrument used by the Israelites. It was essentially the instrument that we call a tambourine, having been introduced to European culture via the Crusades, and may have been used in Israel both as a head stretched over a wooden frame and also with attached metallic jingles.

Prior to their great exodus to Israel, many Hebrews had been enslaved in Egypt and therefore were heavily influenced by Egyptian as well as Mesopotamian music.

Interestingly the New Testament, which was written from the 1st century CE, has no reference to drums and very little to musical instruments at all, save for sparse mention of such instruments as the harp. This has led to continual debates regarding the modern use of instruments in the church, which often declare drums to be of the old Hebrew law and not relevant in the new law of Christianity.

ISLAM

Islam is distributed widely today, but the center of the religion is Mecca, Saudi Arabia, so the Qur'an offers an excellent Western

Asian insight, although it is significantly more recent than the Old Testament. To a non-Muslim, the message regarding drumming in the Qur'an seems confusing. And indeed, upon conversation with several Muslims, the general consensus is still uncertain.

There is a reference in the Qur'an in Surah 62—Al-Jumua (Madina): Verse 11, which translates as, "But when they spy some merchandise or pastime they break away to it and leave thee standing. Say: That which Allah hath is better than pastime and than merchandise, and Allah is the Best of providers. And when they see merchandise or sport they break up for it, and leave you standing. Say: What is with Allah is better than sport and (better) than merchandise, and Allah is the best of Sustainers."[2]

Some have interpreted such scripts to mean that music is forbidden. This passage alludes to the message that pastime, entertainment, and leisure activities are bad, as they cause a distraction from more holy pursuits. It suggests that Allah can provide all that is needed and frivolous activities are not necessary, although it is hardly compelling evidence against the use of music.

There is evidence beyond the Qur'an, however, appearing in greater measure through the many Hadiths, which are narratives of the words of Muhammad told through other sources of varying repute. These are not as important as the Qur'an in Islam but are considered significant sources. These could be interpreted to paint a very negative stance toward drumming and indeed, musical instruments in general. An example of such opinion is found in Sunan Abu-Dawud, Book 26, Number 3677: Narrated Abdullah ibn Amr ibn al-'As. It says, "The Prophet (PBUH) forbade wine, game of chance, drum (kubah), and wine made from millet, saying: Every intoxicant is forbidden."[3]

This looks bleak for Muslim drummers' opportunities, but even worse than that are the words found in Sahih Bukhari, Volume 7, Book 69, Number 494v: Narrated Abu 'Amir or Abu Malik Al-Ash'ari, which says, "That he heard the Prophet saying, 'From among my followers there will be some people who will consider illegal sexual intercourse, the wearing of silk, the drinking of alcoholic drinks and the use of musical instruments, as lawful. And there will be some people who will stay near the side of a mountain and in the evening their shepherd will come to them with their sheep and ask them for something, but they will say to him, 'Return to us tomorrow.' Allah will destroy them during the night and will let the mountain fall on them, and He will transform the rest of them into monkeys and pigs and they will remain so till the Day of Resurrection.'"[4]

There is Hadith evidence to the contrary with a show of leniency in The Two Festivals (Eids) Volume 2, Book 15, Number 103, which reads, "On the days of Mina (11th, 12th, and 13th of Dhul-Hijjah), Abu Bakr came to her while two young girls were beating the tambourine and the Prophet was lying covered with his clothes. Abu Bakr scolded them and the Prophet uncovered his face and said to Abu Bakr, 'Leave them, for these days are the days of 'Id and the days of Mina.'"[5]

The lack of clear guidance in the Qur'an and the argued reliability of any Hadith reference leaves severe doubt as to whether musical instruments really were considered as Haraam. There were occasions when drums were allowed, such as to announce Nikah, which is a Muslim marriage, where the beating of the duff was customary. This suggests that a particular type of drum used for a halal (permissible) function was allowed, but music as an art form was forbidden, as the ecstasy that it might induce was impure or against Allah's interests.

Despite this there is evidence of Muslim music, and in the early years of Islam around the 8th and 9th centuries, Ibrahim Al-Mausili was a famous Persian musician who was celebrated by the caliphs (Islamic religious leaders) of the time, as was his son Ishaq. Furthermore, we know of Islamic theoreticians, one of the most famous of whom is Al-Kindí, also a highly regarded mathematician and philosopher who expanded on Greek musical theory and developed instrument design.

So we know that music existed within Islam. We know it was played, enjoyed, and studied, although it may or may not have been forbidden. This paradoxical approach to drumming in Islamic history has meant that, although music and dance were enjoyed throughout the ages on many levels and by all classes, it has also been scorned upon as a result of religious interpretations and therefore, scholars may have been less willing to describe in depth any technical details. Although some written records do exist, the music tradition was largely an oral one. However, the debate regarding the legitimacy of drumming in Islam is not the subject of this book, but rather the drums that existed and how they were used throughout history. And on that level, we do know about other instruments from Western Asia long before the Qur'an was revealed to the Islamic prophet Muhammad and back to the time of the Old Testament.

MESOPOTAMIA

In Mesopotamia, a region now largely encompassed by Iraq, the earliest form of writing developed within the Sumerian empire. Subsequently the region became widely considered the cradle of civilization. In this region, music was a very important part of daily life both socially and religiously and as such, every temple or palace employed its own professional musicians.

In this early language the Sumerians used the name *ub* for the drum, as it roughly translates as open container, in this case a drum shell. They also used the prefix su-, which translates roughly as the skin. Therefore the word su-ub represents a membranophone, while ub-tur meant "little drum." Pictorial evidence from this period is often found on perforated plaques and cylinder seals amid banquet scenes, while written evidence is found on cuneiform tablets. Just as with the Hebrews, the frame drum was prevalent, and it often held spiritual meaning. Timbrels can be seen on Mesopotamian artwork as early as 2700 BCE in round and rectangular versions. The rectangular version was known as the adapu and possibly had metal jingles, as it accompanied hymns and liturgies in religious ceremonies. This was the forerunner to the Arabic duff or adufe.

The round sibling of the adapu was the mezu, which had a single head and enjoyed more extensive use because, while still used for liturgy accompaniment, it was also being included in celebratory events with other instruments. In fact, from the early 2nd century BCE, evidence of these drums has been found buried with

Naked woman with tambourine, Mesopotamia, 2340–1500 BCE, Louvre. Courtesy of the author.

Mesopotamia, 8th to 5th century BCE terracotta statuettes
with tambourine, Louvre. Courtesy of the author.

the corpses of people of high social standing. More adapu evidence lies upon an unfinished kudurru at the Musée du Louvre in Paris from the Kassite era around the early 12th century BCE, which depicts a procession of gods carrying weapons and playing lutes who are followed by a goddess playing a tambourine and dancing. Sumerian figurines from around 2000 BCE also show us females playing frame drums, as at the British Museum, where a baked clay plaque from the Diqdiqqa region near Ur shows a nude female holding a tambour. And as mentioned in chapter 13, literature also exists that tells of the priestess Lipushiau, who played the balag-di.

Mesopotamian kudurru, Kassite era 1186–1172 BCE, Louvre. Courtesy of the author.

Possible Mesopotamian lilissu depiction, Louvre. Courtesy of the author.

The balag may have been a generic word for a drum and was often seen as an hourglass double-headed instrument used as the sole accompaniment for religious chants or song and to help lift the audience's mood. Along with its smaller brother, balag-tur, it was played by the hands, possibly even subjected to advanced techniques such as thumb rolls, which involves the (sometimes moistened) thumb pressing around the drum rim to facilitate fast bounces and an interesting sound effect. The drum was most likely constructed from cedarwood with wooden pegs to hold the membrane. The balag-di was a frame drum.

Increasing in size, we get to the su-ala, a big drum of around 6 feet in diameter suspended from a frame positioned in front of temples in the late 3rd century BCE. Pictorial evidence exists of the su-ala, such as on the stele of Ur-Nammu of 2270 BCE, which shows the drum as tall as the player.

Another very large and very important drum was one that the Mesopotamian Kalu-priest possessed in the form of a large bronze version known as the lilissu drum. It was essentially a kettledrum with a domed foot to support it, giving the whole instrument a goblet shape. The large shell was only to be covered with the hide from a black bull that was free from blemishes. In fact by Sumerian times, the bull archetype had evolved from that of the shaman to be symbolic of kings, and "the striking of the drum covered with that specific bull hide was meant as a contact with heaven at its most significant point, and in the age of Taurus (c. 4000–2000 BC) this was also explicitly said to represent Anu, now casually identified as 'God of heaven.'"[6]

The method of skinning the drum was also very symbolic and ritualistic, with a certain protocol followed during the killing of the animal before it was skinned and the hide treated with substances such as wine, beer, grease, and flour. The wet hide was then stretched over the shell and wooden pegs hammered through it into predrilled holes. The skin would then dry in position and become taut.

Other evidence of larger drums can be seen at the British Museum upon a baked clay plaque from around 2000 BCE, which was found in the Senkereh region of modern-day southern Iraq. It shows boxers fighting while one figure plays clappers and another beats a drum that is taller than their waists. The drum is of goblet shape with a large, bowl-like shell and smaller support foot: a possible representation of a form of lilissu drum.

And so, in essence, the highly cultured Mesopotamians relied on three main types of drum with the frame drum, the hourglass drum, and the kettledrum.

ARABIA

Due to the close political and geographical relationship of the Mesopotamian empires, they shared many of the same musical values and instruments. One example concerning drums is the Sumerian balag, which was known in Assyria as a ballagu or pallaga. As the power of Mesopotamia dispersed and the people of the southern Arabian peninsula migrated north to occupy it, they also inherited the highly advanced cultures of those lands. This migration occurred in the early years of Christianity, although it was only really at the dawn of Islam that this cultural richness began to flourish with the Arabs.

As a result we can find similarities in names from the different cultures. The Babylonian-Assyrian general name for drum was ṭabbalu, which is then later seen in Arabia as ṭabl, just as the Babylonian frame drum, adapu, is then seen as evolved into the Arabic duff. The specific Persian/Arabic name for a tambourine with jingles was riqq.

Where the ṭabl and duff very first appeared is uncertain, but clues from the Bible and then Arabic interpretations of such stories offer one idea. We find words in the Old Testament that describe the descendants of Adam and Eve with Jubal, son of Lamech, as the one who introduced the harp and organ. Genesis 4:19–22, "And Lamech took unto him two wives: the name of the one was Adah, and the name of the other was Zillah. And Adah bare Jabal: he was the father of such as dwell in tents, and of such as have cattle. And his brother's name was Jubal: he was the father of all such as handle the harp and organ. And Zillah, she also bare Tubal-cain, an instructor of every artificer in brass and iron: and the sister of Tubal-cain was Naamah."

Arabian culture also recognizes Tubal but gives the family greater musical significance, as this metalsmith Tubal Cain, or the Arabic Tūbal bin Lamak, "is credited with having introduced the ṭabl (drum) and duff (tambourine)," into Arabian culture.[7]

As Islam spread, their culture grew rich, but they still relied on three types of drums: frame drums, bowl drums, and cylindrical drums. Thanks to an encyclopedia of Arabic music known as the Kitāb al-aghānī, detailed information regarding performers, techniques, and the music that they played is available from the 10th century CE. We know that the use of such drums as dabdāb (a kettledrum) and the qaṣ'a (a shallow kettledrum) had become very popular in martial music. To be granted the privilege of such drums was an honor bestowed only upon those deemed worthy by the Caliph, which at this time was of the Abbasids Caliphates. These drums were often advanced, with metal shells and tension-adjustable cords to tighten the skins. Another name for the dabdāb was ṭabl-al markhab or naqqāra, which found its way into Europe

Arabic-style naqqāra. Courtesy of the author.

during the Crusades and gave rise to the nakers. Pictorial evidence
shows these types of drums used in pairs hung from horses or cam-
els upon which the player rode. Across Western Asia every region
had similar drums with their own variations of size, shape, usage,
and name. For example, the Persian name for a type of small copper
kettledrum at this time was Tás.

    As well as the dabdāb and the qaṣ'a, the Arabians possessed
the Kūsāt or Kūs, which was an enormous kettledrum. The big
Arabian kettledrums began with flat bottoms as possibly derived
from cooking pots and gradually evolved into a hemispherical
shape. The metallic shells began to be seen grouped together in
combinations of different sizes for varying pitches.

    We know that by the 7th century CE cities such as Mecca and
Al-Medína were producing high standards in music, and rhythm
had evolved to a high state with a small group of modes as the main-
stay of Arabic rhythm. The Arabic word for these rhythmic modes
was īqā, the plural being īqā'āt, and by the 7th century six core īqā'āt

were in use, known as the khafīf thaqīl, hazaj, thaqīl awwal, thaqīl thānī, ramal ṭubūrī, and ramal.

These developed beyond those six and could become very complex before even considering the various melodic modes for accompanying instruments. In fact, a highly respected 10th-century Arabic mathematician named Abū'l-Wafā' al-Buzjānī actually wrote his *Mukhtaṣar fī fann al-īqā'*, which was a compendium on the science of rhythm.

These rhythmic modes were each a series of notes and pauses, or naqareh, which formed a cycle. A naqurāt (plural naqareh) is a measurement comparable to a Western note value such as a quaver. A number of naqareh combined form an īqā. The īqā'āt form the rhythmic cycles on which Arabic music is based. These cycles did not adhere to evenly counted measures as are so common in Western cultures. They were equally likely to be in an odd time, as they were even and they could last for many notes before resolving.

Furthermore, notation of these cycles fails to capture the nuances of rhythm. The feel of traditional Western Asian drummers may consist of certain idiosyncrasies such as slight delay of certain beats within the phrase. It is much less mechanical than Western rhythm.

The notes in each mode vary between different types of sounds that can be played on a drum by using different parts of the instrument and with different parts of the hand. These different sounds help to create strong and weak beats, which add emphasis to certain notes within the cycle. The melody's rhythmic stresses may not relate to the percussion's rhythmic stresses, and so the two may not be obviously in synchronization to the listener, although over a longer period of music, the measures might interact more clearly. Harmony, in a Western sense, was not prevalent, and the music was often monophonic, relying more on the connection between the melody's rhythm and that of the percussion to create interest.

These rhythmic cycles are documented inconsistently between different sources as were often passed orally down the generations, inevitably evolving slightly between different localities. Furthermore, "There is no explicit border between the Arabic and Persian cycles in these old sources . . . there is no way to explicitly separate the past music cultures of the areas with today's political borders of Iran, Iraq, Syria, Turkey and so forth."⁸ The early Arabic rhythms were based on poetic meter and taught onomatopoeically. Different syllables were assigned to different sounds with a long syllable representing two units of time and a short syllable representing one unit of time. Two such examples are the dum sounds, which are strong beats, while the tak sounds are weak. Persians share this method, although a third Arabic stroke, which sounds as kah, is omitted from the Persian culture. Beyond these sounds, we find various finger rolls, dampening effects, and resonant slap techniques, which mold the sounds to create vast possibilities and nuances.

The popularity in martial music necessitated military bands, which were known as a ṭabl-khāna, an ensemble that held great prestige in 10th-century Arabia. Such privileged rulers to be allowed the ṭabl-khāna boasted performances of great extravagance with large groups of more than thirty drums, decorated with gold and pearls, and sometimes carried upon chariots.

Over time, contact with other cultures brought new diversity to Western Asia, causing drums and rhythms to evolve. In the 19th century, Arabic and Persian artwork increasingly depicts another drum. Here we find the lilissu to have shrunk and evolved, retaining the goblet shape but with a drum shell that has vastly decreased in size and is less rounded. The Arabic doumbek and Persian tonbak had emerged. The doumbek was a single-headed goblet drum from Western Asia and North Africa, which came with many other possible names due to regional variations such as derbocka, dumbec, darabukka, and dumbelek. These names may have derived from other words in existence in various languages or may be onomatopoeic as a result of the different sounds achieved such as the deeper dum sound from the center of the drumhead and the staccato slap of the fingers, which creates a bek sound.

Although widespread by the 19th century within many regions under different names and uses, there is much earlier evidence of the kūba, also known as ṭabl-mukhannath, which was an hourglass-shaped drum and may have been the forerunner to the doumbek. This was "forbidden to be used by Muslims, as early as 'Abd Allāh b. 'Umar (d. 639). It is condemned by several legists including Ibn

Arabic doumbek, www.
rhythmuseum.com.

Abi 'l-Dunyā (d. 894) because of its association with people of low character."[9]

The doumbek was made from clay, wood, or metal and comes in a number of sizes. All have a single head usually of goat skin and are traditionally played under the arm. The membrane is glued or nailed to the wider upper opening of the sound chamber above a narrower throat, which joins it to the splayed base. The fact that it has an open base is evidence that it was purpose made for drumming, because a domestic vessel would have necessitated a closed container to contain liquid or food. Ancient examples also have lugs or brackets built into the shell around the top, which appear ideal for attaching a membrane.

Doumbek performances utilized complex drumming patterns involving fast rolls of the fingers, finger slaps, and low notes with the heel of the hand. It was usually played across the lap, strapped over the shoulder for processional performance, or held under the arm of the less-dominant hand.

NOTES

1. William Mudge, *Tabernacle of Moses* (Whitefish, MT: Kessinger Publishing, [1842] 2003), 312.

2. University of Southern California's Center for Muslim-Jewish Engagement. http://www.usc.edu/schools/college/crcc/engagement/resources/texts/muslim/quran/062.qmt.html (23 Aug. 2010).

3. University of Southern California's Center for Muslim-Jewish Engagement. Sunan Abu-Dawud. *Book 26, Number 3677*. Narrated Abdullah ibn Amr ibn al-'As: http://www.usc.edu/schools/college/crcc/engagement/resources/texts/muslim/hadith/abudawud/026.sat.html (23 Aug. 2010).

4. University of Southern California's Center for Muslim-Jewish Engagement. Sahih Bukhari. *Volume 7, Book 69, Number 494v*: http://www.usc.edu/schools/college/crcc/engagement/resources/texts/muslim/hadith/bukhari/069.sbt.html (23 Aug. 2010).

5. University of Southern California's Center for Muslim-Jewish Engagement. Translation of Sahih Bukhari: The Two Festivals (Eids) Volume 2, Book 15, Number 103: Narrated 'Urwa on the authority of 'Aisha: http://www.usc.edu/schools/college/crcc/engagement/resources/texts/muslim/hadith/bukhari/015.sbt.html (23 Aug. 2010).

6. Hertha Von Dechend and Giorgio De Santillana, *Hamlet's mill: An essay investigating the origins of human knowledge and its transmission through myth* (Jaffrey, NH: David R. Godine, Publisher, Inc, 1977), 124–125.

7. Henry George Farmer, *A History of Arabian music* (New Delhi, India: Goodword Books, 2001 [1929]), 6–7.

8. Mohammad Reza Azadehfar, *Rhythmic structure in Iranian music* (Tehran, Iran: Tehran Art University Press, 2006), 76.

9. M. TH. Houtsma and A. J. Wensinck, *E. J. Brill's first encyclopaedia of Islam 1913-1936* (Leiden: The Netherlands: E. J. Brill, 1993), 216.

Chapter Four

---○---

Africa

THE WESTERN WORLD ASSOCIATES DRUMS with the African continent more than any other instrument, and their rich polyrhythmic culture is enjoyed globally. In fact, as mentioned in chapter 2, Algerian rock paintings from 6000 to 4000 BCE are perhaps the earliest evidence of African music and dance.

Rhythm, song, and dance are integral to life on much of this continent, but drums have huge significance, well beyond entertainment. They contain great power and divinity and are often considered more than just inanimate objects, having names and genders.

They were often considered spiritual and therefore had very special purposes in ceremonies or events. Once Christianity had arrived, the drums would also take the place of church bells to call worshippers to service.

The power of drumming is also sought after for its ability to heal, by purging the body of any disease, evil spirit, or impurity through the monotonous, hypnotic repetition of rhythm. Rituals to facilitate this process often have the healer himself playing the drum.

Another use was that of royal drums, which were often purpose built by drum builders specifically tasked to create the instruments throughout a number of ceremonies to ensure the successful reign of the new monarch. The monarch might have in excess of a thousand such drums with particular names and purposes assigned to the drum batteries, all elaborately decorated with beads and cowry shells. The drums could be played with hands, wooden sticks, or even the bones of the deceased as they welcomed in a new monarch, mourned a dead member of royalty, or simply added pomp to a ceremonious occasion. Drums might also be beaten when the king rose in the morning and set down for the night in a display of his authority and power.

This usage is interwoven so deeply into the fabric of life that children become active from a very young age. Bebey states, "The average African child reveals a natural aptitude for music at a very early age. He is already making his own musical instruments at three or four; an empty tin becomes a rattle, an old window frame and a piece of animal hide make a drum."[1]

Beyond the uses mentioned above, every tribal group would have its own set rhythmic pattern to identify its clan, almost serving as the equivalent of a national anthem. Upon the playing of this rhythm on the large drums, the clan could be instantly identified. Drums were also used as an alarm or call to arms. Different drum patterns may also call the men together to work on a project. Maybe a bridge needs repairing and the beat goes out requesting the men to collect their tools and gather for this communal task. The use of drums for communication was expanded further through creation of a drum language, which enabled messages to be conveyed over several miles via the beating of a drum.

Generally these drum languages are specific to each group and thus are only understood by those people. Communications could to this end be sent secretly in some cases, almost like coded messages. In more modern times this can backfire. Take an incident in 1947 told by a Bete chief of how "a French tax collector shot a drummer after realising he had warned surrounding villages of the collector's imminent arrival. To avoid tax paying, the men who had understood the drummed message had fled the villages."[2]

And so the many drums in existence throughout Africa were, and still are, integral to everyday life and survival, as well as the perfect accompaniment to any good celebration. Many of the drums are common throughout the continent in one form or another, but some aspects are specific to that particular region.

As with most cultures, frame drums are common across Africa, appearing with many forms and uses. One such drum is the Egyptian tar, which is a round frame drum of about 12 to 16 inches and is played using the Oriental grip. The adufe is also found in Egypt. This double-headed square frame drum, which is roughly the same size as the tar, may have bells attached inside the drum for varying timbres. The Egyptians also possessed the mazhar, which is a tambourine with large brass jingles and can therefore be struck or shaken. Other northern frame drums include the Algerian duf, which is a utilitarian square frame drum of around 8 inches in diameter. The more elaborate bendir of Tunisia and Morocco often features a snare strand across the skin to add a buzz to the sound. It is usually 10 to 16 inches in diameter. Tunisian frame drums can also be seen with the earth-mother goddess Cybele, such as on a statue currently held at the Carthage Museum, which originates in the 5th to 3rd century BCE. In fact, depictions of Cybele with frame drums are numerous, often also involving her seated with lions. Such image content was so popular that it even appeared on Roman coins.

Going south of the Sahara, in the West the jújù drums of Nigeria are their own take on the Christian church's tambourines. These frame drums are often square, hexagonal, or octagonal with metal discs positioned within in the frame. Nigeria also has square frame drums of about 14 inches without metal discs known as a samba drum and a smaller clay frame drum called the sakara. Ghana's square drum, the tamalin, can be as big as 24 inches with a supporting beam across the back. The hands are used for tonal variety via muting.

The gome drum of West Africa is a frame drum of sorts. It bears a great resemblance to the Peruvian cajón, though while they are both constructed of a wooden box, the cajón features a wooden playing surface and the gome utilizes a goatskin stretched across the face. The player sits upon the box with his hands hanging down and plays with bare hands on the front surface while his feet are used across the drum face to muffle it for tonal variety. An internal wooden frame can be tightened via a screw, which pushes it into the skin from the inside to increase or decrease the tension.

Away from the mainland, the Mauritian ravann existed. This drum of around 20 inches in diameter is played on the lap with bare hands to accompany sega music. Of course there are many other versions of the frame drum, far too numerous for a comprehensive list in this book.

NORTH

The Sahara Desert's position between North and South Africa means that the two are culturally distinct. We find that the Arabic culture moved through North Africa and into Spain and Portugal with such people as the Moors.

Just as in Western Asia, ancient Egypt was highly civilized and enjoyed music for many different celebratory and ceremonial occasions, although evidence suggests that Egyptian membranophones were used widely much later than their Western Asian neighbors used them. Thanks to their excellent preservation of artwork, evidence of their drums can be seen on items such as one at the Metropolitan Museum of Art (Met) in New York, where a carved limestone relief shows women playing frame drums on a boat in 589 to 404 BCE. Older still, carvings from 1300 BCE showing women playing the frame drum for the deity Bes can be seen at the Louvre.

Other, bigger Egyptian drum types featured brace cords for drum-skin tensioning in 2000 BCE.[3] This is supported by a double-headed barrel drum around 28 inches long that uses leather and thongs for tension.[4] This drum, which was held at the Cairo Museum, is thought to be four thousand years old. Furthermore, another barrel drum about 18 inches high and 24 inches in diameter at the widest point, found at Thebes, also had cord running the length of the drum to secure the two membranes and featured catgut rings that could be pulled up or down the drum to tension the cords.[5] A similar although later drum from between 664 and 332 BCE is held at the Met. A barrel drum from the 4th century BCE rests at the Louvre, displaying cord tensioning between the two membranes.

Egyptian barrel drum, 4th century BCE, Louvre. Courtesy of the author.

The Egyptians also used a long, thin cylindrical drum over 24 inches tall, which was suspended from the player's shoulder via a strap. This double-headed drum featured cord tensioning and would be played with the hands. By the period known as the New Kingdom, other drums had permeated Egyptian culture from Western Asia, such as the doumbek and naqqāra, most of which were played by women. An example of the Moroccan doumbek or darbouka rests at the Royal Museum for Central Africa in Tervuren, Belgium (RMCA) as a good example of such a North African drum with a ceramic body, tensioned with plaited strings attached to a thicker string beneath the broadest part of the body. Such drums often used a fish skin for the membrane, which is less affected by high humidity than animal hides, and so the tone stays consistent. The taut fish skin upon a ceramic body produces a very high-pitched sound.

Other drums from Morocco include the long, thin conical drum known as the agoual, which is used to accompany the taskioune dancers, and a conical footed drum standing 4 feet tall. This is interesting, as the entire body is carved from the roots of the cactus. A goatskin is stretched over the opening at the base of the cactus and tensioned with a series of cords.

Sub-Saharan

Due to the aforementioned divide caused by the vast Sahara Desert, the south enjoys its own types of music, musical instruments, and festivities distinctly removed from Western Asia. Although the different regions have their own variations of drums and uses, many of the drumming styles and concepts are homogenous throughout the sub-Saharan lands. Some resonating chambers are formed from gourds, ivory, or clay, but a majority are hollowed tree trunks. The heads are often cow, antelope, goat, or sheep hides, but reptile skin and even elephant ear are also used. One of the rhythmic concepts that pervades much of Africa, especially in the west, is that of polyrhythm. Percussion ensembles are common, with each individual member holding a particular role within the group, creating their own individual rhythm that contrasts with other rhythms of that group but is still synchronized, resolving after a set number of beats before continuing on the cycle. The use of hemiola is very popular, imposing the duple feel over triple time, although Africans may well treat the triple time as the main rhythm while Westerners will see duple time as the main beat.

Away from their complex polyrhythms, the simple yet incessant pounding of the pestle in the large 2-foot-high mortar provides the female workers with the rhythmic backdrop to their work song. Rhythm and drumming are an integral part of everyday life.

Although the use of drums in sub-Saharan Africa is surely thousands of years old, written or archaeological evidence is scant.

Accounts from European travelers provide early evidence, although their lack of African cultural and musical understanding, as well as derogatory racial views, make this evidence less accurate than it could have otherwise been. According to John McCall, the Carthaginian explorer Hanno's report from 500 BCE is one of the earliest to mention drums.[6] Many more followed up to present day, but due to their varying reliability, the old village traditions that still exist today are possibly a better source. Although exact dates may not be recorded this way, the oral tradition through which rhythms, techniques, and uses are passed ensures that much of the historical information can be gathered from listening to such music in the rural communities.

CENTRAL

Drums are most commonly used in ensembles of other drums and idiophones in Central Africa, rarely appearing on their own. The drums are held in very high regard in many central regions such as Rwanda, where the royal drums are played for the Tutsi society king (Mwami) only by musicians deemed to be of suitably high social status and specially appointed as master musicians. Here the drums are performed in groups of between six and nine and are so important to the community that the capture of the royal drum during battle would signify loss of power and authority, and the victors would assume power of the defeated land. In a grotesque sign of victory, the drummer would sometimes attach the genitalia of the defeated enemy warrior to the royal drums.

Drums are also used in Rwanda to accompany dancers, as seen in the Intore dances, which feature the finest dancers of the community, who were highly trained to perform at dynastic functions. In some other regions of Africa, great ceremony occurs when a master drummer dies and a new one is appointed to this privileged post.

The Democratic Republic of the Congo (DRC, formerly Zaire) also enjoys a wide range of drums within its borders. Such a large country inhabited by a diverse range of ethnic groups has a full range of drums and uses for them too numerous to mention, as is the case with much of this continent. However, the RMCA has several different styles of drums from the DRC. One is from the Kasai-Occidental province and consists of a hollowed wood body with a single leather membrane attached with iron nails. The body has a concave base and another concave middle section, which features quite intricate carvings with geometric patterns beneath a large face resting above an arm and hand protruding from its chin.

One drum from the Kuba people displayed in the Utah Museum of Fine Arts (UMFA) is a single-headed wooden goblet drum with an elementary string tensioning system and evidence of resin on the drumhead to aid tuning. It is a fairly austere instrument, save for some simple triangular patterns of nails.

At the same museum is a *Lele* drum, which is different in basic design shape but displays greater ornamentation, with a handle that becomes an arm with a hand at one end and a face at the top.

Other DRC drums include one at the RMCA, which is biconical and carved from wood with a snakeskin nailed and glued to the upper opening. In the middle of the shell, where the two base-to-base cones meet, holes have been drilled to allow a leather carrying strap to pass through.

Two significant drum types that are worth mentioning are the sikulu and the makuta. These drums both have tall and narrow, slightly barrel-shaped shells, which were taken across the Atlantic Ocean before evolving into the internationally recognized conga drums of Cuba.

There is also a barrel-shaped wooden drum with a single membrane and a solid base. This drum features a small ball bearing inside the shell but most interestingly uses elephant skin for the membrane, which produces a low pitch and dull timbre. The skin is nailed on, and a carrying strap is passed through two holes that are housed in parts of the shell that jut out from the main body.

If the elephant skin was unusual, another drum called the fukula is surely stranger with its use of spider skin. The conical drum is turned upside down so the open end sits upon the floor and the smaller end becomes the playing head with an animal hide stretched across it. It features a hole on the side of the shell that is covered by the spider skin, producing a buzzing sound reminiscent of a kazoo. This hole is turned toward the player, and he uses it to manipulate the volume of the drum as he accompanies dancers. Like many such drums from Central Africa, this one displays geometric shapes upon its body but furthers this decoration with pictures of four-legged animals and lizards carved into the shell.

An interesting feature of one of the RMCA goblet drums is the use of small rubber balls upon the drumhead. These are believed to have helped tuning, although they have deteriorated drastically from their created state, and a larger circular area shows the signs of being covered with this material originally. It may conceivably have been a circular pad adding extra durability to the animal hide, but such rubber or resins were often used for tuning.

Many of the drums across Africa feature anthropomorphic and zoomorphic carvings. These can range from a small body part carved into the shell up to entire three-dimensional intricate human or animal statues with a drum set on the head making up just a small portion of the structure. The imagery used is carefully and purposefully selected to connote specific messages. Fertility is a popular subject, often implied by the inclusion of breasts that protrude from the shell, as seen on the Akan mother drum. In other examples, the entire drum may represent the male reproductive organ with a long, thin, conical drum acting as an obvious phallic symbol. Deities are often represented through carved faces, while hands might represent authority within the community and legs supporting the drum may suggest strength. The zoomorphic elements involved such strong and commanding animals as lions to embody the community leader.

Many of the drums from the Chokwe community feature faces carved into the shell, often with several faces representing particular figures such as Pwo, a female archetype that encourages fertility. These drums are usually owned by the chief, only to be used at secular dances or rituals of initiation. A drum of the Chokwe people, known as the mukupela, is held at the Utah Museum of Fine Arts, as well as another example at the National Museum of African Art (NMAfA) in Washington. Both drums have very similar dark wood hourglass-shaped bodies with integrated wooden handles carved in the thinner midsection. Decorative carvings cover

Various African drum-tensioning examples. Courtesy of the author and www.rhythmuseum.com.

the body with a face looking out, which may suggest ritualistic us-age. They are double-headed drums with the skins nailed or pegged onto the shell with a resin on the membrane to control the tone. Drums could be of such high status in the DRC that specially built structures were erected for their storage. These drums of super-natural importance sometimes only emerged for special occasions such as funerals, when the seven sacred drums of the Ikuma sect were played. In some cases the sanctity of drums was such that long apprenticeships were required to gain the right to play them. The adolescent Luba drummer studied with a master drummer to gain knowledge of the materials used and the rhythmic drum language before beginning trials to connect with the spiritual elements. One such initiation focused on the link with sexuality and required the drummer to perform on the drum while maintaining an erection.

EAST

As with other sub-Saharan areas, many communities of East Africa attach great spiritual meaning to their drums, which pervades the manufacture, player initiations, and performance aspects. To this end, Blades describes the storage place for the drums: "In East Africa, the drum-yard is considered holy. It becomes a sanctuary in which animals entering it become taboo and fugitives and fleeing slaves are afforded temporary immunity. If a condemned man succeeds in escaping to the drums, he is safe and becomes their perpetual servant."[7] In reference to the Wahinda people of East Africa Sachs says, "To see a drum is fatal; even the sultan must not look at a drum except at the time of a new moon. Men should carry them by night only, but they have the power to move themselves. Once a drum ran away."[8]

This can be seen in the drums of Uganda, which often form a link with the spiritual world when played at religious ceremonies. They are possessions owned by the king, and he controls large ensembles containing hundreds of drums. These mainly consist of conical wooden drums covered in animal hide with only the larger upper end being played as the drum rested on the ground. These drums, considered talking drums, were often used to relay messages to the king's people about his present situation. To this end the entenga ensemble drums were specifically tuned. Other drums such as the tall, thin baakisimba are used for social entertainment, while the ggwanga-mujje war drum called the men of the community to arms.

Ethiopia also has drums with spiritual connotations, although these examples are attached to Christianity. The koboro is a bowl-shaped drum with a lacing system to tension its single head. It is used for church ceremonies. Another church drum used in Central Ethiopia is the amhara, which is a double-headed conical drum made of silver, hung around the neck and played with bare hands. Sometimes the drums in these ceremonies are nearly 40 inches in diameter, played at religious ceremonies as the priests dance to the rhythm.

The world music specialist at Maryville University and adjunct associate professor of music at the University of Missouri–St. Louis and Webster University, Aurelia Hartenberger, possesses a wonderful world music collection of historical instruments. In it is a very unusual drum from Tanzania. This carved wooden sculpture of the Nyamwezi people consists of an entire female figure more than thirty inches in height, complete with a skirt made of reeds and cowrie shell necklace. Situated down the length of her belly is a stretched animal hide attached with metal studs. This unusual drum would have been played for rituals, ceremonies, or festivities.

Drums in Mozambique are held in high regard and play a significant role in ceremonies and rituals. Although they do have frame drums and bowl-shaped drums, it is the single-headed wooden cylindrical drum that prevails. These range from the small n'lapa, which is held between the knees and lowered in or out of a large, clay-pot resonating chamber to vary the pitch, to the large mussite, which has a diameter of 40 inches and requires the drummer to stand on a platform to play it. The drummers are well trained in the art of performance and instrument maintenance, while the drum makers themselves are subjected to a drawn-out ritual lasting for more than a month, which requires a period of celibacy as well as an application of a specially made paste to the forehead. A ceremony is then organized to bring the newly constructed drum into the community.

Another drum from East Africa is the ngoma, which differs from the South African drum of the same name. Although it is difficult to trace the exact origins these drums, legend accredits Queen Marimba, who was considered to be the mother of the Wakambi tribe, as the inventor of several instruments, the ngoma drum being one of them. According to Mutwa, "Marimba turned the old nut-grinding mortar into the first drum the world has ever seen, and for the first time since the dawn of creation the forests shook to the pulsing beat."[9] Stanley further supports the use of these drums in Tanzania, and his account when leaving the camp to go to battle indicates the numbers of drums and therefore the noise that would have been created: "As we filed out of the stronghold of Mfuto, with waving banners denoting the various commanders, with booming horns, and the roar of fifty bass drums, called Gomas (sic)."[10]

Although the word ngoma is used in different regions for different types of drums, and sometimes as a general word for drum, it is often seen as a tree-trunk drum in which a hollowed trunk is upturned into a vertical position and covered at one end with an animal hide. The base end is frequently carved with three or four feet so the bottom opening lets the sound out rather than being swallowed by the ground. The drum is then positioned between the player's feet and tilted slightly forward. Although the drum might be only around 13 or 14 inches in diameter, it is tall enough to rise above the player's waist.

The Buganda region of Uganda is widely known to have a strong connection with the drum. They also have ngoma drums, a term that relates to a group of drums. The people of Buganda attach great significance to their drums, which denote royal power and authority. To this end, upon coronation, each new king unveiled increasingly large numbers of drums until they had hundreds of them. The drums had to remain upright at all times, only upended in mourning of a king's death. It was considered a crime punishable by death to carry the drum upside down during a king's lifetime, due to the perceived intention or wish to kill the king.

These royal drums work in groups of different sizes and purposes. The large drum (embuutu/kafuba/baakisiimba) was used to articulate dance motifs in Buganda. These are played with bare hands as the drummer sits behind them. When sitting, the drum comes up well above the waist with a diameter of around 12 inches. The cow membrane is attached via strands of hide that attach at the other end to a cow-skin covering wrapped tightly around the whole of the wooden shell.

The central beat drum (empuunyi) is constructed in a similar way to the large drum and is nearly as tall but not quite as wide. The role of this drum is to keep a central beat while the other instruments play around it.

The small drum (namunjoloba/nankasa) is played with sticks made from enzo wood with the role of adding color to the rhythm while bridging the changes between sections of music.

Finally the long drum (ngalabi) has a long body with a small diameter. Monitor lizard skin is used for the membrane, and it is fastened with wooden pins to the long wooden shell. It is held between the legs while standing up, as if riding upon it, allowing the hands to strike the skin at around waist height. This drum bears greater resemblance to the initial ngoma description above.

WEST

West Africa has many musical and, specifically, drumming traditions. These are quite familiar to Europe and America because of its geographic position as the closest sub-Saharan African region to these continents and because of the slave trade between the 16th and 19th centuries that saw many West Africans traveling to the Americas and thus absorbing much of their culture.

In an unfortunate twist, many of these African drums would have been used onboard the slave ships to encourage the African slaves to dance as part of a compulsory exercise regime that kept them fit enough to be useful. Such a drum can be seen in the British Museum, which was brought from the Akan people of West Africa to Virginia around 1735. This cylindrical Ghanaian drum is supported by a small foot and features a skillfully carved wooden shell displaying a protruding ring around the top third of the drum with lines carved into it, as well as a series of vertical lines of protruding carved shapes in regular intervals around the shell. Patterns are carved into the shell below the ring of wood, while above it wooden pegs jut out, around which the ties are fixed to tension the animal-hide membrane. This tensioning method is common across many different African societies.

Ghana has a rich and interesting musical heritage, which is very reliant on rhythm and therefore drumming. They use many different types of drums, such as hourglass drums (donno or gungonga), gourd vessel drums (kora), frame drums, and cylindrical-shaped drums (gullu) carved from wood, which are quite familiar to the West through Africa's cultural insemination into the Americas and Europe as a result of the Atlantic slave trade. Some of these drums appear more sinister than others, as Aluede tells us: "In Ghana the sacrificial drums of the Ashanti are covered with the membrane of human skin and decorated with human skulls. Similarly, in East Africa, it is said that coronation drums were only played by sticks made from human tibias."[11]

In Ghana drums are often used to accompany another instrument or as part of a larger drum ensemble. As with many areas of Western Africa, polyrhythm has long been established, with two or more contrasting rhythms played within pieces simultaneously or as a call-and-response. These rhythms can appear chaotic to the untrained ear, but for those used to such musical devices, these rhythms can result in a trancelike state for the listener. The drums of such ensembles are categorized according to the complexity of their parts. The high-pitch drums often play a consistent pattern throughout the piece that acts as a framework for the other musicians. Over these often-simple parts, the intermediate drums play with slightly greater complexity, sometimes connecting with the higher-pitched drums and sometimes playing against that rhythm. And finally the master drum, which is usually the loudest and deepest, plays the most complex parts.

Every different society has its own variants on the common drum types, uses, and playing styles. For example, within the music of Ewe society, four or five drums are regularly used with rattles and gongs to accompany the vocal choruses as the dancers perform traditional dances; the adowa drumming of the Ashanti society, named after an antelope, is used to accompany court dances and often funerals; and the mpintin hourglass drum ensembles of the Akan society are used for processional duties.

The obrenton or apentema drum is a barrel drum carved from wood with a small cylindrical foot upon which it rests. The Ashanti tribes and Ga tribes are both users of this instrument, the former naming it obrenton while the latter call it apentema. It uses the same peg tuning method as seen on the Ghanaian slave drum. An example of a similar drum, which is over 40 inches tall and covered with colorfully painted carvings, rests at the NMAfA. Each image is symbolic, often referring to proverbs. The foot of the drum is a three-dimensional carving of a lion, which represents the support that these people give to their town. The cock and hen facing each other show that the hen allows the cock to announce dawn, which is symbolic of the male role of these Ntan people. The heart represents patience, but the meaning of the breasts below are less clear, possibly suggesting the gender of the drum. Drums are often considered female around the world due to the vessel connotations as noted by Sachs when describing East African drums: "Drum, round, domed enclosure, earth, night, moon, milk, which, in the primitive mind, are connotations of woman and female sex."[12]

Other Ghanaian drums feature similar designs and tuning methods such as the atumpan (see below); the barrel-shaped sogo and kponlogo, which are played with the hands as well as a curved stick; and the bottle-shaped aburukuwa from the Akan societies, which is played with curved sticks to imitate the song of the bird that shares its name with the drum.

Kete drums are the primary instruments of traditional Asante court music to accompany dances used for royal events. They are also used at other important gatherings such as funerals. Often included is a large, single-headed barrel bass drum with cords attaching the animal hide to wooden pegs, which is played with hooked sticks while it keeps time. Other cylindrical, goblet, and barrel drums accompany, using the same head tensioning and a combination of straight wooden sticks, bent sticks, and bare hands to create sound. These drums incorporate the master drummer who, as with other polyrhythmic regional styles, leads the group while the other drums either synchronize with the bass drum or follow the master drummer. These master drummers are highly skilled with a vast knowledge of different rhythms to react to the unfolding events. As Salm and Faolola state, "If a kete ensemble, for example, is playing a song and the paramount chief leaves his chair and starts walking, the master drummer should segue into a piece appropriate for the moment. One specialist suggests that the kete piece, "Apente," could be used because it expresses the message "the chief walks; he is not in a hurry" and advises him to walk carefully.[13]

Of course, it's not just Ghana that has drums in the west. With its northern regions in the Sahara desert, Niger has an interesting mix of sub-Saharan and Arabic drums. The western Asian ṭabl is very popular in various shapes and sizes, used to communicate orders and messages to neighboring villages. Other sub-Saharan drums are used for traditional tonal drum language and entertainment, such as the popular ganga drums, which are cylinder drums played with bent-ended sticks.

Bordering Ghana to its west is the Ivory Coast. Here the Adiukru society ascribes human attributes to tom-toms for use in ceremonies. One such example is the lohu, a male coming-of-age ceremony. During this rite of passage the tom-toms communicate with the men, who respond by speaking back. This dialogue demonstrates the importance of these drums, in which they are elevated to be equals of the human males. To this end the females are forbidden to strike them, just as it would be frowned upon to strike their male counterparts.

The Baule people play several small goblet drums strapped together, much like the modern tenor drums in a marching band. These are slung around the player's neck while he beats them with his hands.

An interesting drum, which is held at the NMAfA, is from the Dan society of the Ivory Coast. It is essentially a bowl with a membrane laced to the shell with metallic plates fixed onto the side, which rattle when it is struck. Although many African drums are footed, this one features a long, carved shaft between the foot and the shell. This displays a ring pattern, which is finished to a high standard.

Although drums are predominantly the property of males in Niger, the Tuareg people feature women as the primary instrumentalists. They use elementary fiddle, tambourines, hand clapping, and drums at festivities and events such as camel racing. One such drum is the tinde, which is an open vessel such as a gourd with a goatskin held taut across the opening by hand and sometimes tensioned with cord.

The same can be said about neighboring Mali, in which the men fulfill the professional musician needs but the women are permitted to drum for their own social events and pleasure. One of the drums they use is the bendere or calabash drum. This interesting drum is also known as the water drum, and in some regions it is played by women of high social standing. The water drum is found with the Senufo people of Burkina Faso, Ivory Coast, and Mali as well as the Malinke of Guinea, Mali, and Senegal. Known as the gi dunu, this drum consists of two hemispheric calabashes (gourds), which sit next to each other full of water. Two smaller partial calabashes float upside down upon the water with the upturned bowl-shaped bottom being struck by the drummer's spoon-shaped gourd sticks. The water in the gourds is carefully measured to create the correct sound. The larger vessel, which holds the water, may sometimes consist of a metal bucket with domestic spoons as the beating sticks, demonstrating the amateurish connection with women's domestic roles.

The Baga women of Guinea also had other drums, which were small barrel drums in essence, although beneath the drum were large carved female figures who often kneeled with the drum shell seemingly balanced upon their heads, just as the Baga women would have done in their daily routines. Weeklong initiation ceremonies were held annually to allow new members to join the association known as the A-Tekan. Generally only mothers were allowed to enter the A-Tekan. The drums themselves, known as a-ndef, featured symbolic imagery such as the example held at the NMAfA consisting of a drum with an animal hide held taut across the top via wooden pegs. Beneath this drum, a carved woman kneels holding a bowl in front of her as a sign of devotion. There is also a serpent connotation, which refers to fertility. On the whole, this drum signifies the importance of the woman's role within the Baga people. The a-ndef would also be used at funerals or marriage ceremonies of the members' daughters.

Furthermore, the Ba Lari women from the Congo play friction drums. These cylindrical wooden drums of about 18 to 24 inches in depth rest upon their side on the floor while the player sits with her legs stretched on either side of the drum. A wooden stick passes through the drum and attaches to the single nailed membrane via a hole in the center. The stick is moistened and rubbed against the head, altering the tension of the membrane and resulting in a sound that imitates the speaking of animals.

However, the men are usually the official drummers who will be seen at general ceremonial or ritualistic events. The people of the Dogon region, Mali, have one such interesting ritual following a death. The drums and bells provide the music for the dance of the Kanagas. The drummers wear bell-shaped hats while the dancers wear cross-shaped masks containing abstract connotations and masks depicting such native animals as antelopes, rabbits, lions, and other native creatures. Other dancers on stilts perform in a blaze of exuberance and startling color. The drummers beat their cylindrical double-headed rope-tensioned drums with bent-ended sticks as they rest at a 45-degree angle against a pile of stones or hang from their shoulders in mobile performance.

One of the most internationally famous African drums is the djembé. This goblet drum originated with the Malinke people in the northeast of Guinea before migrating to the Mali Empire in the 9th century and later Senegal and the Ivory Coast.[14] The djembé features a goatskin attached with a complex rope tensioning system and numerous rattles, metal rings, and sheets of tin affixed around the circumference of the shell for added sound effects. Using different muting, slapping, and cupping techniques, large tonal and dynamic variance can be achieved from this drum. This timbral palette makes it very popular with healers, dancers, storytellers, and signaling. Although it is mass produced today for global consumption, it would traditionally have been commissioned to be made by a skilled sculptor who would carve it from the lenke tree. The sacred wood would be obtained following the offering of cola nuts, sacrificing a chicken, and asking the tree's permission to be chopped down to build the drum. The cord tensioning system that is often used for these drums is known as the Mali weave, involving a series of vertical cords bound together with intricately woven horizontal cords. This most effective method hails from a culture where weaving in general has great importance. The Dogon people of Mali believe that Nommo, the son of God who was responsible for creating culture and humankind, invented the craft of weaving. As a result they associate the existence of speech within cloth and take great pride in their woven products. The threads weave together to form the fabric just as words weave together to create spoken language. This is consistent with the belief that the drum talks.

On the subject of drums talking, the use of drums for signaling is very common in Africa. One example is Cameroon and the Bulu dialect of the Bantu language, which was studied by Dr. Albert Irwin Good in the 1940s. Many of the languages are reliant on tones, the Bulu consisting of five distinct tones.

Every person in the tribe will have their own rhythmic name, a pattern that is unique to identify them. The drummer who is sending the message will begin by playing the recipient's name. They will then beat out their own name before giving the message. These messages can travel around 4 miles during the day but by night that extends up to 15 miles. The sound can travel farther, but the actual message may not be decipherable to the recipient.

As well as the Bantu people, the Yoruba people of Nigeria and Benin are especially skilled in this communication method with

Nigerian talking drum and performer, www.rhythmuseum.com.

the double-headed hourglass drum that features tension strings running vertically along the drum shell. When the drum is held under one arm, the underarm can be used to press against the vertical strings, which alters the tension of the drumhead while the other hand holds a stick and beats out the rhythmic pattern. Such variation of the drum-head tension alters the pitch, thus providing a rhythmic melody that mimics the cadences of spoken sounds. As a result, this instrument is also known as the talking drum. Within the groups that use this drum, tone languages are commonly spoken in which a single word can have several meanings depending on the tone used when saying it. This enables the drum to closely copy such language.

Other communication drums don't have the same tonal variation. The atumpan is a large Ghanaian wooden-barrel signal drum with an open foot and a single upper antelope membrane attached to wooden pegs. They sit tilted forward, away from the drummer, supported by wooden stakes as the drummer leans over them and hammers on the heads with hooked sticks. Two drums are generally used to obtain the tonal variety needed to communicate, although larger groups may also be used. The mother and father drum are quite large, but the children of this family are smaller drums, and between them they provide different tonal options when beaten with hook-ended sticks. The drum is hugely important in Ghana, which is evident in the logo of the Ghana Broadcasting Corporation depicting two talking drums beneath a transmitting pylon.

The royal sabar drum is exclusively Senegalese and began life as a message transmitter. It uses a stick-and-hand combination to create intense, manic rhythms through many different sound effects. These drums have since become more widely used accompanying births, weddings, ceremonies, and sporting contests, with different rhythms for different situations, often played in ensembles with seven drums.

Drum talk wasn't exclusive to West Africa, though. Drum language enabled some of the most remote areas of central Africa to communicate with great speed over long distances. Some regions relied on squeezing maximum articulation from individual drums. Muted notes were combined with openly played notes for two distinct tones. Each degree in between was also used for maximum expression. Expanding on this, dynamics and pitch are varied by hitting different areas of the drum are also transmit the tonal language rapidly.

Beyond the signaling drums, many drummers are highly trained in their art form. Just as Rwanda had specialist drummers with the Tutsi royal musicians, other types of dedicated professional musicians exist across Africa. One example is the West African griot, who can connect with the spiritual world via his music to request protection, healing, or a pardon. Although griots do not exclusively play drums, percussion is very popular with them, especially the hourglass talking drums. The griot may travel between villages and play for remuneration. However, despite his excellent musical ability, he is of low social standing and often feared due to his knowledge and ability to communicate with otherworldly forces. These griots and their counterparts of other rural African societies are especially important in protecting the heritage of traditional drumming and musicianship in light of the increasing exodus toward built-up areas where the village traditions can be overlooked in place of imported Western music.

Some other drummers are semiprofessional, such as the Bambara farmers of Burkina Faso, who tend to their agricultural assets during the farming season and then go on tour between villages as musicians during the dry season. In other communities drums are simply the everyday instrument to be played by anyone who wishes to.

African drums are often used in legal proceedings, as seen with the Bamun people of western Cameroon, who have very tall, thin cylindrical drums that may be used in such serious court situations as the execution of a criminal. An unchanging, monotonous rhythm sets the soundtrack for the dour scene, pounding out on this tall drum, accompanied by large metal bells that are grouped in twos by a U-shaped pipe and held against the player's body while a voice may explain the message of the music. The tall drum rests at its base between the drummer's feet with his thighs clamping it in a standing position and both hands playing the membrane.

Drumming can also hold a strong role within the administrative and legal proceedings of African communities such as the Igboland people of Nigeria. As seen in other areas of Africa, the death of a chief or the appointment of a new chief is heralded with drums. The judicial drums from all associated villages may be present, which further adds to the pomp of the ceremony. If a significant announcement is to be made, drums call the people of each village in to listen to the town crier's message. When a crime has been committed, drums accompany the authorities in procession to the criminal's home to arrest him. The drums used for these procedures are known as akpan. In this group they become more than just drums. Here they are considered as an actual institution whose command is set forth by human agents who play the drums to carry out each specific function.

Nigeria has many other drums, such as the large barreled drums that lie on their side as the drummer uses his hands to beat the skins on both ends, which are laced onto wooden pegs. Another interesting drum belongs to the Yungur people of northeastern Nigeria. Here they play the dimkedim, which consists of two large gourds fixed together, one atop the other, with a wooden cylinder creating a vertical tube above the gourds. The structure is smothered in dung to lower the tone, and an antelope skin is tensioned across the wooden cylinder. The instrument rises to the height of the drummer's face, so it is often tilted when played. These drums are regularly played at funerals.

Equally unusual in appearance is the udu, originally from the Igbo people of Nigeria. This vessel drum was traditionally a domestic clay jug with a second hole in the side. This drum is used in religious ceremonies, perceived to have a mystical quality, as the voices of the indigenous people's ancestors can be heard in the playing of the drum. The drum doesn't have a membrane but is played with the hands and fingers across the holes and all over the body to achieve different effects. This spiritual link with drums was popular across Nigeria.

The Yoruban people of southwest Nigeria have hugely sacred drums that form part of their everyday existence as well as important ceremonies. Just as with the djembé, many Yoruban drums are made from wood whose powerful spirits were calmed before it was felled through various rituals such as sacrificing a chicken. Most

Yoruban drums of importance are used as a means of communication by conveying certain messages and warnings. One of the most developed in this sense and also the most widespread Yoruban drum is the iya'lu dundun, known as the mother drum. It is played with a curved stick while it sits underneath the holding arm, which also squeezes the tension strings to vary the pitch of the drum. The cylindrical wooden shell is covered with animal hide and features brass bells, which hang from it to add to the distinctive sound.

The second most widespread Yoruban drum belongs to a spiritual drumming tradition more than five centuries old known as bàtá drumming. It began as a sacred spiritual drum, although as Christian and Muslim influence has spread, the traditional beliefs have diluted and the drumming has become more secular. The drums were originally constructed in honor of new kings as a matter of great prestige. Between three and seven drums are used with the mother drum, known as ìyáàlù, as the biggest while the girl omele (omele abo) and the boy omele (omele ako) are the smallest, although different regional names may be used. The gudgudu are common drums to add to the core three initially mentioned. These are small drums added individually in small numbers or as three drums bound together.

These bàtá drums are essentially double-headed goblet drums with one head much bigger than the other. They are generally played slung over the drummer's shoulder in a horizontal position so that both heads can be struck, although some of them sit vertically upon the floor so that only the larger head can be used. Some of the drumheads feature an applied paste that darkens the tone of the drum. The playing style differs between the drums and even between regions; either the bare hands are used or a combination of hand and a stick of animal hide called a bílálà. The ìyáàlù is the lead drum, which communicates with the dancers via its rhythms using hands on one skin and a bílálà on the other. The omele abo is a partial timekeeper, although it can speak with the mother drum when she speaks, while the omele aku is the main rhythm keeper and has no ability to talk with the other drums. As discussed later, this tradition made a great impact in the Americas following the Atlantic slave trade, with Cuba especially making great use of the style.

It is difficult to know how old these traditions are. In the ancient Yoruba city of Ife in Nigeria, terra-cotta plaques show carvings of drums that belonged to a group of footed cylindrical drums known as igbin. These carvings date the drums as early as the 10th century, which seems unlikely to have been their date of origin. Other terra-cotta evidence includes depictions of the dundun, which appear from around the 15th century in Benin to the west of Nigeria.

SOUTH

The communities of South Africa use music in much the same way as the rest of the continent. They traditionally attach deep and powerful spiritual meanings to their drums and use them in a number of rituals and ceremonies to connect with other worlds and their ancestors. Many of these drums also retain an ancient healing power in which the rhythm purges the sick of their evil spirits and entices new pure spirits to enter their body.

The records of musical usage are very old indeed. The nomadic San people from South Africa have left us thousands of painted images, many of which are still being discovered that date from around thirty thousand to a few hundred years ago. Levine says that these paintings introduce people playing instruments as early as twenty thousand years ago.[15] However, for nomads, the drum would have been cumbersome when in transit and may not have been used at this time. We do know that in later times they used a claypot drum that was covered with a taut hide and contained a small amount of water inside the vessel. The drummer would intermittently turn the drum to splash water on the underside of the animal hide, which allowed it to stretch as one hand held it tight over the rim of the vessel. The other hand then played on the taut skin with fingers, achieving tonal variety as the tension was adjusted accordingly. Another primitive drum in which the skin is held across the shell is the intambula of the Swazi tribe. This pot becomes a drum when another man holds a skin over it for the drummer to beat.

Many similar drums are found among different countries and regions, displaying little uniformity in shape and size because the owner produced his personal drum to his specifications.

One popular drum type found among the Venda of northern Transvaal in South Africa, and known as the ngoma drum (not to be confused with the Tanzanian ngoma), has a hemispherical shell, like a modern-day timpano, although the shell here is of solid wood. The cow membrane is fixed to the shell with pegs and struck with a wooden stick. Stones are often dropped into the shell before the moistened head is applied and dried out to contract around the body. A smaller version from the same area is the murumbu. These can be used in pairs of different pitches and as such create the required variation in sound for messaging. Ngoma are usually played with a single stick while the other hand supports it in a tilted position. The drum was initially a war drum but also acquired spiritual uses, such as inducing rain with its huge, cauldron-like body thundering across the land.

In fact ngoma is a generic word used for drums across many areas of South Africa and also has a wider meaning with ritualistic connotations. The drum is inherent in all rituals of sanctity or spirituality and therefore comes in various forms across the South. The Namibian Kwangali people are one example; their ngoma drum is a long, tall, conical hollowed tree trunk between 40 and 80 inches high. It dramatically tapers at the lower end up to a small pedestal to support the drum. A single head is pegged onto the upper opening. Unlike the ngoma of the Upper Venda, the Kwanali ngoma is played only by men, who hold it between their legs in a slanted position. The same drum type is also popular among other communities such as the Sambiu, Kxoe, Ambo, and Mbukushu. This drum type is also used by the Zulu people. The tall, conical drum features a single membrane tightened across the top with a series of hide ties that stretch vertically down the shell until it meets a ring of several strands of hide secured around the circumference. The vertical ties are attached to this to maintain tension. Wooden pegs are wedged between the ring of hide and the shell to prevent it from moving upward and slackening the tension. Carved feet were sometimes featured to allow the sound to escape. Such drums can be seen in collections at the Met dating from the 19th century.

Unlike the Kwanali ngoma, the moropa clay or wood drum from Botswana is played by women and used at women's coming-of-age initiations. This is a conical or cylindrical drum with a single goat-skin membrane often pegged to the shell.

The Zulu people also play a drum at the coming-of-age ceremony of adolescent girls (nubility rites). This friction drum, known as the ingungu, is a small, bowl-shaped friction drum with a membrane attached via cords, which are strung around the bottom of the bowl and fastened. A long stick stands up through the head so that the player may crouch down and rub it to create sound. The Namibian Ikwahani people play a friction drum around 20 inches tall with a single pegged membrane across the upper opening and a stick set vertically through the membrane. The drum is laid flat on the floor while the drummer places one hand in the open bottom end to rub the stick with some wet bast, which is bound around his hand. Unlike the Zulu friction drum, this one would have been used in celebratory circumstances.

However, Namibia did use drums for female initiation ceremonies, one example being the g!auru drums of the !Xu people. The Mbukushu gnoma drums of Botswana, mentioned above, are also involved in ceremonial usage. Played in groups of three by men, along with their friction drum, they are used for entertainment as well as such matters as exorcising the evil spirits that cause insanity. The drummer plays while female dancers encircle the patient, sometimes for several days until they feel that she is cured.

The Tsonga people of southern Mozambique also use a drum for exorcism. This drum, known as ncomane, is a frame drum with a single membrane pegged onto the shallow frame. The skin is tuned using heat from a fire, and pitch is varied by pressing the fingers of the holding hand into the back of the skin while a single stick is used in the other hand. The Tsonga also have a huge war drum called muntshintshi, which is shrouded in superstition; as such, it is forbidden to look inside the drum. It is a large, rounded drum on three legs with various different hides used, sometimes including elephant's ear. Junod states that "a bullet is introduced to it when it is made. In Shiluvane they asserted that the skull of the hostile chief, Sikororo, killed in the battle of Nov, 1901, had been put into the big drum!"[16]

Other initiation drums include the isigubhu. This belongs to the Ndebele people who straddle the border of South Africa, Zimbabwe, and Botswana. It is a tin drum covered in animal hide played at girls' initiations. The girls themselves then play another tin drum, which is used exclusively for this purpose, known as equde, at the first evening of their initiation.

Just as the Zulus have their initiation friction drum, the Pedi people have the moshupiane, a bowl-shaped wooden drum with a single goatskin membrane. This is played at girls' initiation rites by older initiated women who rub the cut, moistened end of bundled corn stalks together on the head in a circular motion to emit a powerful screaming noise.

Drums used for the opposite gender include the conical drums, which are played in groups in Zambia for circumcision rites. Men hold the drums between their legs at almost horizontal angles and beat the single membranes with their hands.

Africa's hugely rich and influential drumming tradition has been watered down in the last few centuries. The slave trade found European colonial authorities punishing natives for the use of drums in an effort to disconnect them from their heritage and their true identities. The drumming and the connected spiritual powers were viewed as a potential empowering catalyst for uprising. Even missionaries in early efforts to spread Christianity forbade the evil drums whose ability to connect with other worlds was seen as demonic and threatening to the cause. Luckily, in spite of such conflict, the music was stronger than these influences and has since become recognized internationally for all its virtues. It is now popular across the world with such drums being mass produced, played within all Western cultures, and taught in schools. The musical influences from Europe and America have entered Africa, especially in urban areas, and while traditional styles are sometimes only found in rural areas, the wider recognition of this music has grown considerably since the second half of the 20th century. Thankfully this rich musical heritage looks here to stay.

NOTES

1. Francis Bebey, *African music: A people's art* (London: George G. Harrap and Co. Ltd, 1975), 6.

2. Esther A. Dagan, *The heartbeat of Africa* (Montreal, Canada: Galerie Amrad African Art Publications, 1993), 202.

3. Francis W. Galpin, *A textbook of European musical instruments—Their origin, history and character.* (London: Williams & Norgate, 1937), 67.

4. John Garstang, *Burial customs of Egypt as illustrated by the tombs of the middle kingdom* (London: Archibald Constable & Co, 1907), 156.

5. Carl Engel, *The music of the most ancient nations* (London: J. Murray, 1864), 219.

6. Dagan, *The heartbeat of Africa*, 44.

7. James Blades, *Percussion instruments and their history* (London, UK: Faber & Faber, Ltd, 1970), 63.

8. Curt Sachs, *The history of musical instruments* (New York: Norton, 1940), 35.

9. Credo Uusa'mazulu Mutwa, *My people, my africa* (New York: John Day Co, 1969), 26.

10. Henry M Stanley, *How I found Livingstone in Central Africa* (London: Sampson, Low, Marston & Co., 1895), 207.

11. Charles O. Aluede, *The anthropomorphic attributes of African musical instruments: History and use in Esan, Nigeria* (Ekpoma, Nigeria: Department of Theatre and Media Arts, Ambrose Alli University, Ekpoma, Nigeria, 2006), 158.

12. Sachs, *The history of musical instruments* 36.

13. Toyin Falola and Steven J. Salm, *Culture and customs of ghana* (Westport, CT: Greenwood Press, 2002), 177.

14. Ashish Pandey, *Encylopaedic dictionary of music, Volume 1* (India: Isha Books, 2005), 210–211.

15. Laurie Levine, *The drumcafé's traditional music of South Africa.* (Johannesburg, South Africa: Jocana Media, 2005), 19.

16. Henri A. Junod, *Life of a South African tribe, social life, 1926, part 1* (New York: Macmillan, 1927), 430–431.

Chapter Five

─────────────────○─────────────────

Europe

As such a long-standing world force, Europe has been responsible for many significant musical-instrument and playing-method advances. It was here that the orchestra developed into the modern, sophisticated classification that we know today, it was here that drumming rudiments were established via the military marching bands, and it was here that leaps have been made in the world of popular music. But European musical success didn't just appear out of nowhere: "The musics of Asia and Europe constitute a single, historical continuum; that processes of development and evolution observable in one region are relevant elsewhere; that musical evolution in Europe is not to be understood in isolation from processes in Central or Western Asia, in the Ancient Middle East."[1]

As we have seen in just about every culture so far, the frame drum is a popular and often significant instrument. It had appeared in Europe by the 13th century, having traveled from Western Asia.[2] The date is contentious, as Redmond states that the frame drum, as one of the oldest ritual instruments, "first appears painted on a shrine room wall in ancient Anatolia (present-day Turkey) from the sixth millennium B.C."[3]

Baines may have considered Anatolia to be of Western Asian geography rather than European, but other evidence confirms an appearance earlier than the 13th century, and even a suggestion it was many thousands of years previous.

This evidence comes from Northern Europe and the Sami people, who were descendants of the first settlers that occupied parts of Norway, Finland, Sweden, and Russia more than ten thousand years ago. They possessed a very spiritual drum known as the runebomme. This ritualistic frame drum held great importance within the Sami culture as a means of communication between the shaman and the gods. The wooden-framed drums featured reindeer skin as the head, which was painted with a red-colored mixture of alder bark and saliva, and created a series of instructions, enabling the shaman to carry out any one of a number of specific tasks. The paintings would depict the ruling gods; the living Samis; their objects, homes, and animals; and the world of their dead. The sun was also important within their culture and was therefore worshipped, with animals sacrificed for it. Depending on which region they were from, many runebommes would feature a rhombus-shaped sun in the middle with rays stretching out of the four corners. Other popular designs separated the drum face into three sections, the upper section representing the world of the gods, the middle section representing life known on earth, and the lower section representing the underworld. When faced with a problem, the shaman would place a metal plumb or carved piece of reindeer antler known as an árpa upon the drumhead and then, using a hammer of reindeer bone or antler, strike the drum. As the drum vibrated the árpa would bounce, and where it rested indicated the answer to the problem according to which pictorial instruction was beneath it. It may have been used to seek guidance from the gods, foresee the future, or simply help with essential life tasks such as hunting. Nygaard (Berghaus) offers a slightly different method of use when comparing the painted figures with those found on a rock formation: "The Shaman's way of drumming, by moving the hammer in certain patterns over the drum and telling or singing the myths and rituals associated with the figures, provides a parallel to the arrangement of the figures at Storsteinen. It is therefore possible to regard Storsteinen as a stage and the figures as a script for the action."[4] He is suggesting that the figures instruct the movements over the drum to search for the answers to the problems. Nygaard tells us that the similar paintings found on Storsteinen in Alta,

Norway, were painted from 4200 BCE, although some may be as old as twelve thousand years. However, this does not prove that the actual drums are quite that old. Many of the drums that have been preserved until today only date back to the 17th and 18th centuries, when they were discovered. An earlier source is an account in the anonymously written *Historia Norvegiae* from 1170 to 1190 CE, which describes a Sami shaman's drum in ritualistic use. It is reasonable to assume that the drums and their spiritual use are much older than that, although quite how old is difficult to guess.

These ritualistic frame drums were generally oval shaped with a crossbar in the back, which both strengthened the structure and provided a handle. These were widespread and popular, but another design also became prevalent: a bowl drum made from a single piece of wood with a rounded body and often an egg-shaped face. This featured the same types of painted heads and shamanistic uses, just simply with an alternative body shape.

By the time Christianity reached the region, these items so strongly attached to paganism were considered a threat and were subsequently destroyed in large numbers. This brutal act of power also saw the users of such pagan items murdered by methods such as decapitation and burning, thus forcing many Samis to relinquish their polytheistic life or practice their beliefs in secret.

Finch suggests that "the single-headed frame drum had its origin in Siberia and was probably from the first a shaman's ritual object or instrument."[5] But firm early evidence from elsewhere in Europe includes a statue of a bird goddess playing a frame drum from Cyprus in 1000 BCE, which is held at the Louvre, as well as figures that were excavated from the site of Amathus, Cyprus, and now held at the Department of Antiquities, the Republic of Cyprus, that show women playing frame drums from the 8th century BCE.

A Greek vase from the 5th century BCE in the Athens National Museum shows a woman playing a frame drum in an effort to help the crops grow. Another item from Greece is the statue of a woman with a frame drum from 300 to 275 BCE that is held at the Fitzwilliam Museum in Cambridge, and yet another Greek statue of a seated girl with a tambourine from 325 BCE lies at the Museum of Fine Arts in Boston. In fact many items appear around this period

Greek statues with frame drums, 4th century BCE to 3rd century CE, Louvre. Courtesy of the author.

of time, such as a statue of a woman with a frame drum from 300 to 275 BCE in Southern Italy that is now held at the Art Museum, Princeton University, and a statue of a woman from Carthage 4th to 3rd century BCE clutching a frame drum, which is currently at the Museu D'Arqueologia de Catalunya in Spain.

Examples become very numerous after this period. But despite the advanced civilized might of the Greeks and the Romans, "the players of both Greek and Roman drums were almost exclusively women in the cults of Dionysos and Cybele. The drum had no place in any other form of music, including military music."[6] Montagu concurs, "They seem to have been used solely to accompany dancing and singing. Certainly there is no evidence whatsoever for the use of drums to give time to the march in the Roman army, nor for any other military purpose."[7]

These many frame drums appear across Europe in various forms. The adufe of Portugal and Spain is a double-headed square (sometime triangular) frame drum beaten with hands. In Ireland, the most famous drum is the bohdrán. This round frame drum of around 16 to 20 inches in diameter features a supporting crossbar similar to the Ghanian tamalin and may have developed out of a domestic tool used for sifting. A goatskin is nailed to the frame, although modern versions feature an internal ring that is screwed up into the head for tuning. The playing style varies between regions but generally requires a double-ended stick known as a tipper, which is held in the strong hand like a pencil and used with a very loose wrist action and a motion that could be likened to shaking out a wet cloth. The weaker hand rests behind the single membrane, acting as both a support and a tonal variant as pressure is applied to the rear of the skin. It is generally used as entertainment to accompany instruments such as the fiddle, accordion, or acoustic guitar for dances and other festivities, as heard in such places as backstreet watering holes in Dublin.

Beyond the humble frame drums are the jingle-bearing tambourines. The Ukranian tambourines are known as buben and are beaten with sticks. A cord is stretched across the back, onto which other metal jingles could be hung. The Uzbekistan tambourine, known as doyra, features many rings suspended around the circumference of the membrane on the inside of the frame. The fingers are used to slap and stroke the membrane, which may be goat, horse, fish, or cow. The Spanish pandeira is a tambourine played with the traditional grip. The jingles are staggered along the frame. While many frame drums are held stationary as the hands move across the drumhead to play them, the pandeira is often moved around the stationary playing hand to achieve variety in tone and rhythm.

The Southern Italian tamburello is a tambourine of around 10 to 14 inches. The deeper and larger tammorra can be as big as 18 inches. Regional variations of playing style exist with hand slaps, fingers snap, and thumb strokes.

Taking the Italian tambourine to new technological levels toward the end of the 20th century, Italian frame drummer Carlo Rizzi invented an interesting version. It involved a lever attached to the drum, which could vary the tension of the snares, the membrane, and the application of metal jingles to achieve a huge timbral range.

In the early 21st century, festivals specifically for frame drummers became popular. In 2005 the European Frame Drummers

Meeting festival was held by Gianluca Baldo, Paulo Cimmino, and Andrea Piccioni. Subsequently the Meeting Italiano del Tamburello was organized by Cimmino in 2007 and Frame Drums Italia by Piccioni in 2010. Also beginning in 2005 were the Caravansary English frame drum meetings instigated by Lennie Charles and the Spanish Fiesta de Pandeira organized by Juanjo Fernández. In 2006 the Turkish frame drummer Murat Coskun organized the Tamburi Mundi frame drum festival, followed by the Greek Frame Drums Meeting, which occurred in 2008 by virtue of Gerasimos Siasos.

The Italians have even taken the frame drum beyond a musical use and into the sporting arena with their game tamburello. The game bears similarity to many racquet sports such as tennis, although here there is an absence of a net or indeed a racquet. Instead the teams strike the ball with a simple frame drum; hence the name tamburello. The future of the frame drum in Europe appears strong, whether it will be for music or sport.

Beyond the frame drum, Europeans had clay goblet drums from areas such as Bohemia, which date back to 2000 BCE. Although these often appear exactly like domestic pots, protruding areas near to the top of the rim are evidence that a membrane might have been attached to the shell. Many of these drums were found in religious contexts; therefore, an assumption of religious drum usage is not unreasonable.

In fact goblet drums were very common throughout much of Europe in the late Neolithic and Early Bronze period, including Denmark, Poland, the Czech Republic, and most commonly Germany. The drums were used for entertainment, possibly with a ritualistic or shamanistic connection, while also serving as a means of communication, as seen in Africa. They were obviously considered important, as they were frequently buried in graves with the deceased. An example in the Museum of Prehistory and Early History in Berlin displays a well-restored drum of this type in the shape of a large egg cup with a clay body that is 10 inches tall and 7 inches wide at the upper opening. The shell features decorative circular shapes, parallel lines, and rows of arrows. A leather skin is stretched across the top and a string is passed through cuts in the leather and then fastened by means of seven eyelets, which are integrated into the clay shell. This drum is from the 4th millennium BCE and belonged to the Walternienburg-Bernburg culture in the Upper Neolithic period of Germany.

Interestingly, ceramic pots from the Funnel Beaker culture of Germany from approximately the same period display the exact same eyelets upon their main body, which may suggest that either the pots or the drums have been misidentified, or that the drums were likely to have developed from the pot design. An evolution is evident when looking at pots and drums in European prehistory. The closed bowl of the domestic pot that enabled it to be used as a container was eventually knocked through, leaving an open shell, which allowed the sound to resonate freely. In a study for the Department of Archaeology at the University of Exeter, England, Aiano reported that two identical replica drums of this period were constructed, one with a closed shell, one with an open shell.[8] The resulting sound difference was that the open shell produced two distinctive tones (much like the dum and bek of the Arabian doumbek), was louder and had a more pleasing timbre than the closed bowl. From this we can reasonably argue that the people of this period were evolving their domestic pots to create specialized drums with increasingly superior sound quality.

Much later in history, Germany was also significant in the development of the orchestra, and in particular the kettledrum. This development is discussed in greater detail in chapter 11. One object worth mentioning is the gruesome but fascinating depiction of drumming in the form of an elephant-ivory statue from the late 17th century. The figure is a naked skeletal male whose emaciated body holds a pair of drumsticks aloft. Such statues were often carved for wealthy collectors and represent death as a drummer. Equally gruesome is the folktale in which the 14th- and 15th-century Bohemian general Žižka, upon realizing that death was upon him, requested that his skin be made into a drum so that he could lead his men into battle after his passing.

But back to less gruesome subjects, we find that beyond those ancient Germanic ceramic pot drums other European goblet drums did exist, such as the Greek tarabuka and Yugoslavian darbuk, which are both closely linked to the doumbek of Western Asia.

The friction drum is also popular throughout Europe, although it may have only been present since the 16th century. The Pitt Rivers Museum in Oxford displays an Italian friction drum from Naples, which consists of a clay pot covered with a membrane featuring a reed stick passed through a hole in it. Sometimes a cane was also used with pellet bells attached to the top of it. Also in this museum is a Norwegian version that has a tiny, thimble-sized body with a long piece of horsehair passed through the small skin. A Russian friction drum also had horsehair through the membrane. This was fairly advanced, with a counter hoop and tension rods to tension the single membrane upon the cylindrical body. Such a drum appeared throughout Eastern Europe as the bukai. The Spanish version was known as the chicharra.

Known as the rommelpot, the friction drum was popular across the lowlands of Europe with the likes of the Flemish people of Belgium. It consisted of an animal bladder tied over the opening of a domestic pot with a stick plunged through a hole in the skin. The stick is rubbed between moistened fingers, which move rapidly up and down it, and as it spins, a loud percussive whirring or rumbling noise is created; hence the name, which derives from "rumble-pot." Children might have played these friction drums at Christmas and Martinmas. A similar drum is known in Spain and Portugal as the zambomba, and in England as the jackdaw.

Moving away from the friction drum, Turkey made a huge impact on European music. Although Turkey is considered Eurasian and not strictly a European country, and although only a small part of the country is on the European side of the Turkish Straits, it is close to being an official part of the European Union and so has been included here in the European chapter. To support this further, Istanbul was the European capital of culture in 2010. The area known today as Turkey is an interesting country due to its location between Asia and Europe as well as its history of being occupied by many different civilizations. It is perhaps best known for the music of one of the earliest military bands called the Mehteran, known better as Ottoman military or Janissary bands. These groups and the drums that they used made a huge impression on European military bands and ultimately the orchestras that we enjoy today.

Although this book is focused on drums, it seems right to mention Turkey's impact on the drumming world beyond the membranophone. After all, it was here that the modern cymbal was created and perfected, and although many major manufacturers are located elsewhere in the world today, it is the Turkish tradition and history on which many of them are built. Zildjian, one of the most famous cymbal makers, began with a strong Armenian connection but with its first workshop in Constantinople. Quickly becoming known for their superior sound, Zildjian cymbals were used by Sultan Osman II of the Ottoman Empire for daily rituals and ceremonies with the well-regarded Janissary bands. In fact, the cymbals were so well received that the Sultan in the early 17th century rewarded Avedis with gifts and a great honor. This honor was that the cymbal smith Avedis earned himself the name Zilciyan, literally meaning family or son of cymbal smiths or makers (Zil is "cymbal" or "bell," ci is "maker," yan is "family" or "son of"). The name, under Western influence, eventually altered to Zildjian."[9] Another big name in this market, Sabian, is also a descendant from the very same Zildjian family. Just as the name Zildjian was constructed from three parts, so too was Sabian, although the origins are less historically significant. Sabian's founder Robert Zildjian formed the name Sabian from the first two letters of his offspring's names (Sally, Billy, and Andy). These two cymbal giants enjoy a significant share of world cymbal sales.

Along with the metallic cymbals, bells, and trumpets, the military bands also employed the rhythms of the kus, nakkare, and davul. The modern nakkare in this setting comprises two small copper bowls with a skin stretched across them. They are used to add rhythmic color between the melodic lines and also to signal the beginning of the march.

The davul was a double-headed cylindrical drum and the forerunner to the European bass drum (as mentioned in chapter 11). It consisted of a narrow shell and wider heads, which hung in front of the player, allowing him to beat each head comfortably with a stick in each hand. Rope tensioning in a V formation was applied to the two membranes, which sat upon wooden shells with counter hoops made from animal skin. The two heads were from different animals

Painting of davul in *The Baptism of the Selenites*, 1507 CE. Painting by Vittore Carpaccio.

such as lamb and goat, to create a distinction in sound. This was further enhanced by the playing method involving a thick wooden stick in the right hand playing the accented beats while a thin rod created a snapping sound with the left hand on the unaccented beats. Such a drum is depicted by the Venetian painter Vittore Carpaccio in an Ottoman scene from the 1507 painting *The Baptism of the Selenites*.

With these core drums and sparse harmonic accompaniment, the Mehteran was clearly percussion heavy, and indeed, when trying to stir up enthusiasm on a noisy battlefield, loud rhythms will be more effective than intricate melodies. The music was often improvised but held together by a rhythmic ostinato known as a usul.

The Mehteran existed from around the early 13th century within the Ottoman Empire, but the band was "based on the tradition inherited from their predecessors the Seljuks. The Seljuk Caliph Keykubat III introduced the use of the drums and revels to announce the presentation of a beylic."[10] And indeed when the drums of these Janissary bands are considered, they show a great connection with the neighboring Arab world. The nakkare is a scaled-down version of the ancient lilissu, and the davul is a descendant of the Arabic ṭabl.

Janissary bands were not just ceremonial and were often used at strategic points in a battle to incite their men and fill the enemy with terror. Such instruments and band formations were passed on to the Europeans primarily through battle, such as when enemies fled in defeat and abandoned the instruments, allowing the conqueror to possess and use them. By the 18th century, the bass drum and small kettledrums firmly held a place throughout European military bands and had found their way into the orchestra, with the larger timpani emerging and the bass drum maintaining significance while also evolving into the long drum with smaller diameters and longer shell lengths.

Beyond the Mehteran, drums such as the kudum were played in religious ceremonies. These were simply smaller versions of the nakkare, with diameters of around 12 inches and a depth of 6.5 inches, although the copper-shelled kettledrums used different sizes to differentiate between the pitches. To aid this further, different thicknesses of camel skins and sometimes llama or cattle were used and could be tuned to fit each composition. Other drums used here that came from neighboring cultures included the tef (tambourine) and dumbelek (doumbek goblet drum of Arabia).

Despite its being occupied by various peoples, England doesn't boast a huge part in early drum development.

One definite example of drums, which demonstrates the importance that humans can place on them, is that of the famous 16th-century English sea captain Francis Drake and the side drum, which he took around the world. As he lay dying on his ship near Panama, Drake instructed that the 21-inch-tall walnut drum be brought back to Drake's home near Plymouth. Legend surrounds this drum; a poem was even written ("Drake's Drum," 1895) by Sir Henry Newbolt, and it is thought that if England is ever in peril, the drum should be beaten and Drake will return to save the country. This evolved into the belief that the drum would beat itself in times of need, and reports since have suggested that the drum was heard at such perilous moments as the onset of World War I and at Dunkirk in World War II. In fact, when the drum had been moved to a safer location during World War II, Plymouth was subsequently bombed and the drum was quickly returned to its home.

People remembered the legend that the city will fall if the drum is ever moved from its rightful home. The city wasn't hit again after the drum's return, and it has remained at Buckland Abbey to this very day.

As Europe was influenced and inspired by other cultures, it gradually adopted more variety in drums. Despite such powerful forces as the Greeks and Romans, comparatively little advancement in drumming occurred here. As seen with the Sami people and in Africa, Christianity was opposed to the drums and the spiritual power that they held, and this was no different in Rome. They were seen to evoke impure behavior.

But despite this Christian opposition, drums continued to pervade Europe. One example was the Greek dauli, which is simply a double-headed cylindrical drum with skins laced to each other reminiscent of the Turkish davul, sometimes played with a bent-ended stick while slung over the player's shoulder. As mentioned, the Moors of Spain brought many influences from the Arab world and created an instrument-manufacturing hub. Such drums as the adufe and balag were popular here.

But by the late Middle Ages Europe had woken up and was set to flourish as the leader in musical instrument advances for several hundred years (see chapter 11). Rather than copy the crowd, it began to develop and advance the technology and the music played on these instruments until it was the envy of other continents. The beat of Europe had arrived.

NOTES

1. Laurence Picken, *Musica Asiatica Volume 1* (Oxford: Oxford University Press, 1977), V.

2. Anthony Baines, *The Oxford companion to musical instruments* (New York: Oxford University Press, 1992), 329.

3. Layne Redmond, *When the drummers were women. A spiritual history of rhythm* (NewYork: Three Rivers Press, 1997), 10.

4. Günter Berghaus, ed. *New perspectives on prehistoric art* (Westport, CT: Praeger Publishers, 2004), 159–160.

5. Eva Jane Neumann Fridman and Mariko Namba Walter. *Shamanism: An encyclopedia of world beliefs, practices and culture* (Santa Barbara, CA: ABC-CLIO, Inc, 2004), 102.

6. Curt Sachs, *The history of musical instruments* (New York: Norton, 1940), 149.

7. Jeremy Montagu, *Timpani and percussion* (New Haven, CT: Yale University Press, 2002), 10.

8. http://www.google.ex.ac.uk/search?q=cache:1lbk5rcqve0J:www .exeter.ac.uk/cornwall/academic_departments/geography/Excapades/ PDFs/2006_v1_i2_aiano.pdf+Lynda+Aiano+&access=p&output=xml_ no_dtd&ie=UTF-8&client=redesign_frontend&site=default_collection& proxystylesheet=redesign_frontend&oe=UTF-8 (16 Sept. 2010).

9. Hugo Pinksterboer, *The cymbal book* (Milwaukee, WI: Hal Leonard, 1992), 139–140.

10. Rabah Saoud, *The Arab contribution to music in the Western world* (Manchester, UK: Foundation for Science, Technology and Civilisation (FSTC) Ltd, 2004), 15 http://www.muslimheritage.com/uploads/Music2. pdf (22 Sept. 2010).

Chapter Six

———————————O———————————

North America
and Canada

THE NATIVES OF AMERICA ARE OFTEN DESCRIBED as American Indians, and it is these people in their numerous and diverse subcommunities whose music was drenched with spiritual meaning; the drum was the most revered and respected. Their strong values and beliefs were portrayed in the music and often came through in their musical instruments as well. Their drums were considered living, breathing life forms with a heartbeat and could be looked upon as family members and named accordingly, such as Grandfather. The drums often accompanied dancing, which was sometimes purely for entertainment but often for spiritual ritual as well. Dreams are an important motivator for these cultures. A vision or dream will determine many of the Indians' actions, including when and with what design to make a drum.

The frame drums of North America were often called war drums, or chief drums, because they accompanied warriors due to their portability. When painted with certain symbolic designs, the frame drum was also found as a double-headed medicine drum. As well as the paintings, they often also sported small sticks hanging from a string that ran across the internal diameter and rattled against the skin as the drum was played. Small pebbles placed between the two heads had the same effect, although this version was used more as a rattle than a drum and appeared in smaller sizes between 2 and 8 inches in diameter. Further ornamentation was added to certain special drums, such as a ring of beaver fur, animal horns, or eagle feathers around the circumference of the drum.

It wasn't just the medicine drum that was painted, though. In fact many North American frame drums were decorated with symbolic patterns and figures, often totemic animals such as bears, fish, or birds or spiritual ideas such as moons. A frame drum of the Aleutian Islands is 13 inches in diameter with a cord-fastened membrane that is decorated with a colorful birdlike creature. Another frame drum from Oklahoma is double headed with the playing side decorated with the footprints of deer and a red circle in the center. It is held taut by strips of hide and rests on an X-shaped wooden frame. Instead of a single bent strip of wood, as is usual, the frame consists of four connected narrower strips of wood. A Sioux frame drum from the Etnografiska Museet shows a crudely cut and fastened wooden shell with two strips of wood bent and tied together with overlapping ends. A skin is then pinned to the top with metal nails as well as string, which is stitched around the edge and then fastened in the middle at the back of the drum. Another one at the Hartenberger World Music Collection of the Lakota Sioux, in contrast, displays a high level of craftsmanship. This drum features a highly tensioned animal hide with symbolic paintings across the face and a red cross on the back on the membrane. A blue cross dissects the drum into four sections and depicts the world of the spirit, while the red cross symbolizes the physical world. In each corner totem animals are shown, with the white buffalo, salamander, snake, and turtle all clearly visible. These animals would have passed through the drum maker's mind when he undertook a vision quest prior to making the drum. It also displays turkey feathers, which hang around the diameter of the drum.

An example housed at the Metropolitan Museum of Art in New York from an Indian tribe of the plains is 19 inches in diameter with a membrane attached with carved wooden pegs driven through the skin as well as strips of hide tied through slits in the skin. A buffalo is painted on the face of the skin as a sign of the importance of this animal in their daily lives. A padded beater was used to play this drum, as was often the case with the Indians.

One frame drum from the Northwest coastal region displays a hand painted on the drum face, which has the fingers open and an eagle feather sitting across it. More interesting perhaps than the decoration is the shape of this dodecagon as opposed to the usual rounded frame design. Another unrounded frame drum is an 11-inch square example from the plains of North America.

And so we see that the American continent is no different from any other. The use of the frame drum stretches from Alaska, through Canada, down America, and into South America, carrying with it spiritual and healing powers and the ability to alter the listener's, and drummer's, state of mind.

The frame drums were adorned with both single and double membranes; often depending on which tribe they belonged to, as they had their own preferences, such as the Northwest and Alaskan single heads or the Chippewa double heads. Drumheads were made from whatever animal was abundant in each particular tribe's locality and generally laced with thongs made from strips of the hide, although some tribes such as the Sioux did use pegs for tension. This meant that deer, moose, goats, buffalo, sheep, and caribou were popular, although the Eskimo people often used more unusual materials. The keylowtik was the large Eskimo frame drum of 24 inches diameter. The single membrane of fawn hide, whale liver, or walrus stomach was attached to the wooden hoop by sinew tied through the head to achieve tension. Generally men played these drums as accompaniment for dancing by striking the membrane and frame with a stick. The skin was dampened with water before playing. Varying playing positions were used in different regions.

Another Eskimo drum was the kaylukuk, a ritualistic box drum with four wooden sides forming an upturned rectangle with the two ends left open. Two of the top sides each displayed five triangular shapes carved into them while feathers, eagle claws, and paintings were also used to decorate the drum. This drum was most significantly used in the Messenger Feast ceremony and played by men.

Other less portable drums include the large dance drums, which were suspended between poles by the Chippewa Indians. These American Indians realized the importance of unimpeded resonance long before the modern drum-kit makers invented the

Modern powwow usage, www.rhythmuseum.com.

RIMS systems. The drum itself was shaped like a large tub featuring a decorative cloth skirt and two thick membranes. The upper membrane was played simultaneously by several drummers at social dances and spiritual rites. Each drummer only used a single stick, as was often the case in American Indian drumming. These were sometimes known as powwow drums due to their use at social, celebratory dancing and singing events known as powwows.

A similar drum that also featured a bell hung inside the shell is the dream dance drum used for the dream dance, similar to the older ghost dance that had connections with the deceased. This sacred instrument featured two heads that were painted with matching designs. The decoration involved colored stripes, which symbolize certain worldly attributes such as the path of the sun and require the drum to be positioned so that the stripes align with corresponding compass points. A cloth skirt hung from the side of the membrane ran the depth of the drum with additional beads, beaver fur, and tassels creating ornate decoration around the shell. These drums also utilized curved hanging poles, which rose above the drum decorated with beads and eagle feathers so as to hang the drum in rather more style than the usual powwow versions.

Although these drums are formed from bent cedarwood to form the tub shape, in the past a frame made from wooden poles hammered into the ground side by side in a large circle created the same effect as a sound chamber when a rawhide was fixed across the top.

Water drums were also common throughout North America, made from both clay and wood. They were primarily used as sacred or medicine drums by Minnesota's Anishnabe people, among others. These ranged in shape and size from shallow-bowl sound chambers to deeper domestic jug-shaped vessels and up to cauldronlike pots, always with a single membrane and a solid base to retain the liquid. These drums were often less ornate in decoration than other Indian drum types, although some coloration was sometimes used. A curved oak stick with a rounded knob, sometimes covered in hide, was used to beat these drums.

The Apaches possessed a large iron kettle with a buckskin, which was wrapped around the opening and held taut with the holding hand. The other hand beat the membrane with a thin stick around 12 inches long, which was bent to form a hoop. This provided a soft timbre when played at social dances.

In the west, Peyote church music has also made great use of the water drum since its inception in the 19th century. It is unusual because rather than the commonly used rawhide, this drum used tanned leather; thus, the usual padded stick, which is more delicate on the untreated rawhide, is unnecessary, so an unpadded stick is used. The drum is partially filled with water and often shaken at intervals so as to moisten the underside of the skin. This alters the tension of the skin, which is laced around the wooden, clay, or metal shell. The commonly used rawhide for other types of American Indian drums would be fixed onto the drum moistened and then left to shrink as it dried. This type of skin and wetting technique is a common attribute for all American water drums. It is these tanned skins that would have been stretched and hung vertically between a wooden rectangle frame near the wigwam dwellings to dry them and relieve them of their pungent smell after being cleaned and dehaired.

Another water drum made by the Iroquois people of the North consisted of a wooden keg wrapped in decorative cloth with a membrane held taut across the keg. A small amount of water in the vessel would have enabled tonal variation. At only 7.5 inches in diameter, it was held in one hand while the other hand beat it with a stick. The Seneca Indians also used a water drum, which was a taller and thinner cylinder drum at nearly 15 inches high. It had a simple hollowed wooden body, very similar in design to the Anishnabe drum, with a membrane attached at both ends via a tightly bound ring of material, just as the Anishnabe drum attached its head.

Throughout New Mexico and South America water drums could be found in the form of simple domestic pots acting as kettledrums. These become a drum when a membrane is held taut over the opening with a cord wound tightly around the rim as seen in examples at the Gothenburg Museum, Sweden, and the Museum of the American Indian, New York. The Pueblo Indians of the Southwest also make use of their domestic pots as temporary drums by tying a membrane across any suitable pot. A stick bent into a hoop, as mentioned with the Apaches previously, was used on this drum. A shallower version at the Linden Museum, Stuttgart, holds stones inside the shell, which rattled when played, as with the medicine frame drums mentioned previously.

The fourth main form of drum from Native Indians was the cylindrical log drum. Commonly found in the southwest regions of North America, they were often known as tombés, with two membranes fixed at either end with the usual N-shaped lacing system, although other systems were used among the tribes. Padded sticks were used to beat the drum, and again, to allow for optimum resonance the drum was either held by the hands or hung from a specially crafted wooden stick. Decoration was often more somber in color than was found on the previously mentioned war and medicine drums. Black was popular upon these membranes, although the shell itself did often display more vibrant coloring.

The Ute tribe of Colorado possessed such a drum, which was played for ceremonial use. The 16-inch-tall shell was cedarwood with an elk skin stretched across both ends and fastened with V-shaped strips of hide that ran between both membranes. A similar drum with padded beaters resides at the Metropolitan Museum of Art in New York from the native Hopi and Shosonean people of New Mexico.

Heading south, we find a fascinating and developed culture dating back hundreds of years. The Aztec civilization, which began around the 14th century in Mexico, was very well organized and kept extensive administration records, as well as artistic records such as poetry. This carried through to music, as they used a form of musical drum notation based on phrases of varying syllables. Set rhythms were recorded and used within ensemble compositions with phrases lasting up to twenty-two syllables. Over 750 of these were recorded in the 16th-century Nahuatl manuscript *Cantares en idioma mexicano.*

To play these rhythms they had an interesting drum called the ayotl, which consisted of a series of prongs stuck into the underside of a tortoiseshell that were struck by an antler to make a sound. These drums were often present at brutal sacrificial ceremonies.

But possibly the most common drum was the huéhuetl, a cylindrical drum with three feet cut into the base made from an oak, conifer (known as ahuehuete), or walnut tree trunk. It stood upright at a height of around 4 feet with a jaguar or deer membrane. These drums would be played with the fingers, using a range of sounds from the rim to the center of the drum, including rolls. In fact these drums were evenly and expertly tuned to the point that the center of the drum and the rim of the skin produced two tones that were a fifth apart. The Aztecs developed the tuning as seen on a later version called the tlalpanhuéhuetl, featuring rope tensioning with buffs. These drums were used singularly and in groups numbering as many as ten. Just like the ayotl, these were used at sacrificial ceremonies and sometimes included carvings on the shell that depicted such acts through symbolic figures. Often the humans waiting to be sacrificed, such as captured warriors, would be made to create the music themselves and dance to the beat of the drum prior to being clubbed to death, in a cruel and humiliating final act. Other popular instrument carvings included important ceremonial dates, artifacts, objects from daily life, and gods. The huéhuetl was also well used at celebratory events such as the fiestas or battle victories. A Malinalco version known as the panhuéhuetl with exquisite carvings featuring birds, cats, and date lines symbolic of war and sacrifice is on display at the Museum of Anthropology and History in Toluca, Mexico.

Besides the huéhuetl, singers and dancers would be present along with another drum. This was the popular teponaztli, a log slit drum with two distinct tones that were achieved by striking the tongues with rubber balls stuck on the end of a stick made from antlers. The body of this drum was often decorated with intricate symbolic carvings. Several examples lie at the British Museum, such as one from the 14th century at 29 inches long with a three-dimensional human head and arms carved at the front and various other carvings along the body. Another features battle scenes carved into the body. Similar instruments as these Aztec drums were also used in the earlier Maya civilizations.

Of course following the European colonies and then American independence, North America has seen great use of military drums (chapter 13), expanding on the rudimentary techniques and then subsequently enjoying a position at the forefront of the conception, invention, and evolution of the modern drum kit as seen in chapter 12 as well as the standardization of snare drum rudiments. It has remained at the helm ever since.

Chapter Seven

———○———

South and
Central America

As with previous continents, the frame drum is prevalent throughout Central and South America. In such Brazilian music as the
Amazonian boi folk style, the panderão and panderinho are heard.
The larger panderão of 20 inches is held facing the player while the
other hand beats it. The 12-inch panderinho is similar, although it
is held facing skyward as it is played. The Brazilians also possess a
small frame drum for samba music known as the tamborim. Tonal
variation can be achieved via hand damping while a stick of bound
wooden rods beats the highly tensioned skin as the drum is flipped to
achieve a distinctive rhythm. A Puerto Rican version of similar name
is the pandereta, which is used in traditional la plena music. It can
be found with or without metal jingles in any of three sizes through
10, 12, and 14 inches in diameter. The square Spanish adufe is
found in Guatemala as the prayer-accompanying tupe, while more
unusual shapes include the Chilean pandero tambourine, which is
hexagonal, and the Mexican version, which is octagonal.

The Quichua Indians from the Huanca tribe in Peru used a
double-headed wooden frame drum known as tinya, which had
strips of hide, llama wool, and stitching to tension the two heads
together. Across the exterior of one of the membranes were several
strands of string in two groups, which acted as a snare. This drum
was one of the few instruments in Peru that were traditionally
played by females.

Out in the Caribbean the Haitians possessed a single-headed frame drum of around 12 inches in diameter known as the bassé. Rope tensioning was used to hold the membrane taut and also for the performer to grip as he played with his bare hand to accompany vodou music.

How long drums have been used in Central America is unknown, although archaeological evidence shows us strong examples from the Mayan civilization. A clay goblet drum held at the Museum of Fine Arts in Boston is one example that dates from the 5th or 6th century CE Mayan lowlands of Belize. This drum was very portable, held under one arm and beaten with the free hand. It had a single membrane stretched across the 6-inch upper opening while the shell itself stood 14 inches tall and displayed red and black painted hoops around the circumference. Military drum use is confirmed from further north in the civilization as Mayan murals from between 600 and 1000 CE were found in archaeological sites at Chichen Itza, Chacmulten, Mulchic of Yucatan, and Ichmac of Campecehe in modern-day Mexico, which show that the Mayan armies communicated via trumpets and drums.

We also know that they used cylindrical drums such as the Mam example held at the National Museum of the American Indian (NMAI) in Washington and New York. This double-headed drum uses lacing to tension the membrane while a padded beater was used to play it. It also has an airhole in the side. Another cylindrical drum at the same museum is known as a tun. It features two heads, which are attached via Y-shaped tensioning and has counter hoops made of hide as well as a carrying strap. It was owned by the Q'eqchi Maya people and was played with two padded sticks.

The Maya Achi people of Guatemala had a penchant for pairing things together. They classified their musical instruments by the way sound was produced, which wasn't too dissimilar to the Sachs and Hornbostel classification, but with only two categories: instruments that were struck, q'ojom, and those that were blown, su. Within the q'ojom they had the aforementioned tupe as well as the tume slit drum, and the big drum, which is formed from a large single piece of hollowed log and cared for over many years, passed between generations. The significance that is placed on groups of two dictates that ensembles generally consisted of one instrument from each grouping, such as the violin and tupe, or flute and big drum. It was usually the men who played the drums, although the drum itself was considered female. These drums were used in both religious and secular situations, such as fiestas, dance dramas, and rituals, as well as to call people together for certain events and procedures.

Of Central and South America, as well as the Caribbean, the post-Columbian influence is an exciting mix of colonial Europe and Africa due to the slave trade. This has enabled many isolated music styles and traditions to form and flourish between the various countries and islands, creating some of the most rhythmically stimulating and interesting music in history.

Beyond the drums from the widely spread indigenous civilizations, many more localized instruments are found throughout the different regions. Traveling east to Belize, we find that European music arrived here courtesy of the British occupancy in the 16th century with polkas, waltzes, and church music, which was later mixed with the strong African rhythmic influence brought across by the slaves. The result was brukdown, a music style that used regular instruments such as the banjo, guitar, accordion, and drums integrated with a bell instrument known as the dingaling as well as a donkey's jawbone, which was played by using a stick on the teeth.

The Garifuna people also had their own style of music. Having traveled from Africa via St. Vincent, where they escaped slavery and bred with Caribbean natives, they arrived in Belize in the late 18th century, as well as Guatemala, Honduras, and Nicaragua. They used two main traditional drums made from mahogany, mayflower, and cedarwood. These drums were the small treble drum known as primero, which enjoyed a freer, improvisational role, while the larger bass drum known as segunda held a consistent rhythm.

As this style mixed with the cultures of southerly neighbors Nicaragua and Honduras, new styles emerged, such as the acoustic paranda music from the 19th century. This relied heavily on rhythms that had evolved from West African times and survived through St. Vincent to Belize. Guitar, drums, and percussion were also used in this usually secular music.

Another style born from this cultural mixture was known as punta rock when it was popularized in the 1970s. The primero and segunda drums were initially employed in this style but were sometimes later replaced by a drum kit or drum machines. With the creation of such media as MTV, this isolated musical culture suddenly became up-to-date, and an influx of North American and European influences took a much more immediate and significant role. Subsequently, some of the traditional styles are diminishing through each generation.

The southerly neighbors in El Salvador possessed three drums, which included a slit drum known as the tepunahuaste; the tortuga, which is made from the shell of a turtle and struck with padded sticks to achieve a high-pitched tone; and the huestete, a cylindrical single-headed drum that stands vertically upon three feet carved into the bottom of the wooden shell or molded into the design if made by clay. Pottery drums were common across Central America, dating back well into the pre-Columbian years. Archaeological evidence from across Costa Rican excavation sites show this to have been a popular medium from around four thousand years ago: "The early (2000–1000 cal BCE) and late (1000–500 cal BCE) facets of the Tronadora Phase represent the earliest dated ceramic producing culture in Costa Rica."[1] Many drums have been discovered among these sites.

Other surviving Costa Rican examples appear at the NMAI from the Talamanca people who possessed a long, thin conical drum with a single iguana membrane on the top, attached with a simple length of rope tied around the circumference. They also used similar cylindrical drums that featured a more intricate Y-shaped rope tuning system involving wooden pegs wedged between the ropes and the shell to increase tension.

These are common drum types, however, and are shared with other tribes such as the Chocó Indians of Panama, whose similar conical upright drums feature glass beads threaded onto a length of string, which is stretched across the membrane. They also use a double-headed barrel drum with an intricate lacing tensioning.

Lying east off the coast of Central America, the largest island in the Caribbean and one that definitely has a distinctive musical heritage is Cuba. It is a country whose musical, and particularly rhythmic, influence has stretched far and wide, spreading throughout North America and beyond. The island's history is a fascinating melting pot of incredibly strong African influence as a result of the heavy slave traffic that ran through Havana's large port along with Spanish colonies and iniquitous men seeking a lawless haven. Africa's rich polyrhythmic culture thrived here, bringing forth new

Peruvian cajón, www.rhythmuseum.com.

twists on African rhythms such as the blossoming rumba, mambo, and congo, as well as traditional African batá rhythms, and then Afro-European inspired music such as salsa. By the 17th century the distinctive Cuban sound had begun to take a strong hold, and it was rhythm that lay at the heart of it.

During these colonial times the slave drums were outlawed, but the rhythm was strong within these people. The shipyard inadvertently provided wooden crates upon which idle hands could strike up a rhythm without the fear of punishment. These drums were numerous and found themselves among various other percussion as well as the drums, which were eventually decriminalized and became interwoven in the daily Cuban life. The same type of drum became popular under the name cajón in Peru.

The core of Cuban music is the clave. It is the two-bar rhythm around which the music is built. The clave is always present in this music and if not played fully, it is always felt internally by the musicians. Its presence is influential, as it acts as a key to the music in a way that wasn't familiar to European musicians. The clave was traditionally played by two sticks of wood, which share the name. These would be used to accompany the singers and dancers along with a number of important drums.

One such drum is the tumbadora, or as they are also commonly known, conga drums. As mentioned earlier, these evolved from such Central African drums as the sikulu and makuta. Here the Cuban communities adapted them for their own use before they swept North America and beyond in the 1950s, introduced to other genres such as jazz. These tall wooden drums feature a staved barrel-shaped design, which tapers to a smaller size at the bottom. Originally used for rumba music and other religious occasions, the drums are widespread through many Latin American styles today. They can sit on the floor or upon a stand as the player uses his hands to perform. Intricate playing techniques are employed, involving several different strokes using the whole hand as well as fingers and various muting or pitch-bending effects. The conguero is the name of the person who plays the drums, and the groups of drums he plays can vary from one to six, ranging from around 14 inches to 9 inches in diameter with a length of around 30 inches.

The largest is known as the supertumba, descending in size through the tumba, the conga, the quinto, the requinto, and the smallest ricardo, although terminology varies between regions.

Another Cuban drum that often goes hand in hand with the tumbadora is the timbale, which also emerged in Cuba following the slave trade, although its origins lie in the European timpano. The traditional name is pailaitas cubanos or even bongo, although that name suggests an entirely different drum to many people. The name timbale may have been onomatopoeic as a result of two single strokes on each drum forming the sound of tim-bal. There is also a suggestion of the link from the Arabic ṭabl, which made its way to Cuba via the Moors of Spain with their atabal and is only a small leap to timbale. Midway into the 19th century these drums were experienced in Cuba, and hemispherical metallic shells were subsequently imitated in circuses and music groups. In time, these cumbersome drums became popular in music styles such as danzón and were reduced in size to meet the demands of transport and financial restraint. They were often made from wood, although steel and brass are common today. These drums are usually seen in pairs consisting of steel single-headed shells of around 12 to 16 inches in diameter, usually with a 1-inch difference between the two. The smaller drum is bestowed male characteristics and known as the macho while the larger drum is the female hembra. They are played with long thin sticks, devoid of any taper or bead, by the performer who is known as the timbalero. The heads are tightly tuned, which make them effective for rim shots, but many other sounds are achieved from the membrane, rim, and even side of the shell. The shell is known as cascara, a name that is also shared by one of the most popular rhythms to be played upon it. One of the most internationally famous timbaleros was actually from Puerto Rico. Tito Puente helped to bring the timbales and that style of music into North America and beyond with such hits as "Oye Como Va," which was subsequently made internationally famous by Carlos Santana.

The smaller relatives of the congas, which also evolved out of the Spanish aristocracy mixing with African slave influence, were the bongos. These small single-headed drums of around 8 to 10

Cuban congas, bongos, timbales. Courtesy of the author and Danny Cummings.

inches in diameter and similar in height come in a pair with one drum smaller than the other, much like the Western Asian naqqāra, and designated the names hembra and macho just as with the congas. The calfskin heads were initially tacked to the shell with heat from the fire used to tune them. Later, metal tension rods were employed to allow adjustable tuning. These early users were the lower-class Cubans who played son music, although they gradually gained acceptance and popularity in higher classes before reaching their worldwide status of current times. Sound was produced by striking them with bare hands. As with the congas, various techniques can be used, but finger slaps are especially effective on these higher-pitched, cutting drums.

One other Cuban drum type that made the journey across the Atlantic with the slaves is the Yoruban batá. These sacred Nigerian goblet drums retained their traditional spiritual meaning in Cuba initially with strict rules pertaining to who can touch the drums and how they are constructed. Gradually they became integrated into everyday Cuban life, and secular use took over until they were more often heard for pure entertainment.

As these music styles became more popular, artists gained more exposure in North America as styles such as mambo and cha-cha-chá took hold. Rock 'n' roll emerged with such overt influences from Cuba as the Bo Diddley rhythm, which was a rebranded son clave. Meanwhile these Cuban sounds began integrating with other genres such as jazz and then later fusion, with Return to Forever and Weather Report as two such examples.

At first this influence was heard through the traditional Cuban drums as discussed above, but gradually the appeal for this polyrhythm was realized upon the North American drum kit, where four limbs could be trained to create the sounds of several percussionists. Particularly enticing was the sound of the drum kit played with an incorporated clave performed by the left foot. Such pioneers as Walfredo Reyes senior and then Horacio Hernandez helped popularize this technique.

But there is far more to the Caribbean than Cuba, and although situated very close to Cuba's southern coast, Jamaica has managed to create its own highly distinctive musical heritage, the most famous genre being reggae, which is discussed in great detail in chapter 12.

Beyond reggae we find an art form of African descent. Nyahbingi has come to symbolize the struggle against oppression for radical Rastafarians and is often used as a music style and dance to accompany Rasta groundation ceremonies that can last for many hours and involve dancing, praying, smoking cannabis, and chanting. This drumming style utilizes three drum types with the large bass drum maintaining the repetitive solid rhythm of the music with open and muted notes. A drum that slightly resembles a requinto (small conga) supplies the heartbeat of the rhythm, often playing two consecutive notes at a time, and is known as the funde. The conical repeater drum completes the set and enjoys a more improvised role as it supplies the narrative to the music and weaves around the holding rhythms.

The nyahbingi concepts evolved out of kumina and burru beliefs, two styles that also make significant use of drumming. Kumina pays homage to ancestors and has developed from Congo origins in the 19th century. This spiritual event involves feasting, dancing, and the sacrificing of a goat. The rhythm to which people dance is created by the wooden bandu and playing kyas drums, which are laid flat on the ground so that the players can sit upon them and beat the membrane with the bare hands. Tonal variation is achieved by placing tension on the membrane with the foot. The bandu plays a holding roll while the playing kyas has more freedom to execute rolls and accentuate different beats.

The burru drumming utilized the three drums later seen in nyahbingi with the bass, funde, and repeater enjoying much the same roles in both styles. The African origins are possibly Ghanaian and may be from a Christmas dance or a derivative of the word aburukuwa, which was a high-pitched talking drum: "The culture of Jamaica is predominantly Ghanaian and Akan, so it would be reasonable to deduce that the word burru was extracted from its original and thus known to us today."[2]

These Jamaican cylinder drums may have found their way over from Africa, but other similar drums in the area have their roots in the Caribbean. East of Jamaica is the island of Haiti, and it is on the small island of Gonâve just off the Haitian west coast that a cylinder drum from 850–1000 CE was found. It is now held at the NMAI, and although the membrane has long since decomposed and the carved wooden shell has deteriorated significantly, a figure can still clearly be seen on the shell, carved with a large face and human features.

In fact, Haiti developed a very interesting musical culture based on the spiritual beliefs of vodou. Within vodou the drums hold a very important role as they accompany dancers and singers while leading followers into a possessed state. During this process a connection is made with the gods, who are given a voice through the drums via specific spiritual rites. These rites are divided into different groups or categories, the most well known being rada and petro. Each group, or nanchon, possesses their own drum batterie, and skilled drummers are required to play the correct rhythms for each individual rite. The batteries differ in numbers with the common rada batterie consisting of three drums: the mother drum manman, the second in rank segonn, and third in rank boula. The kongo set also has three drums in the mother, gronde, and katabou. Petro on the other hand contains only two drums, the ti baka and gwo baka.

One other, the assotó, is the most revered, sacred, and as such, largest drum in the community. At 2 meters tall it is constructed under strict conditions: "Only prescribed trees can be used, the trees must be cut at full moon, and the skin that covers the drum must be placed on it at exactly midday."[3] It is then baptized under ceremony. Other drums also undergo ceremony such as to replenish their energy, a process that involves animal sacrifice. There is a belief that they are weaker in the New World as compared to their African homeland and therefore need this energizing to maintain spiritual power.

The assotó is a carved cylindrical drum with a single upper membrane, which is pegged to the shell. Carvings at the foot allow the sound to escape while the shell is decorated with paintings and sometimes covered with flags and drapes. It is played only for certain solemn occasions, such as a high priest's funeral, as well as a celebration festival for the drum on the Tuesday following Easter. A sign of its importance is in the fact that many were destroyed in the 1940s by the Church in its antipaganism effort because it feared the drums' power as a threat.

The assotó is an exception, however, with most drums being much smaller. The rada manman stands around 1 meter tall while the boula is around half that. The petro drums are generally smaller. Although they share similarities, differences occur in tensioning and playing styles. Petro drums are rope tensioned while rada drums are pegged. Some batteries also use bare hands for playing, others use sticks, and some use a combination of both.

While Haiti sits in one part of the island, the other side of the island contains the Dominican Republic, and this eastern side gave forth some music that was quite different from the spiritual vodou traditions. In the 19th century the style that became known as merengue took hold before going on to become their national music. It was a fusion of the English aristocrats' country dance, which gradually found its way to colonial Saint-Domingue (Haiti) via King Louis XIV's France, whereupon it was subjected to an African-influenced evolution and took shape as a dance for couples across many Caribbean islands. Here the raucous, undignified nature of the dancing was expelled from the ballrooms and found its place in the country.

The music was initially played by flutes, violins, and mandolins, accompanied by panderetas and tamboras. It was later pushed into rural settings and developed the instrumentation of accordion, tambora, and güiro. The tambora was a double goat-skinned drum made from a hollowed tree or boards bound together like a barrel. Y-shaped rope tensioning was used to tighten the membranes, which were struck by a stick in each hand as the drum sat horizontally across the player's lap. Into the 20th century, merengue became popular and spread through the Caribbean, North America, and beyond with other instrumentation such as congas becoming popular; ultimately the rhythms were adapted for the drum kit, as with many Latin genres.

Leaving the Dominican Republic brings us to Puerto Rico, the home of bomba. Bomba has been a music and dance of festivities that emerged in the African communities of Puerto Rico's coastal towns possibly as early as the 17th century. Its origin in the African communities means that is centered on dance, song, and drums. It has a very interesting and exciting element in that the lead drummer mimics the dancer's movements with his beat, a task that becomes very competitive and challenging. But bomba dancing is accompanied by at least two drummers using two different drum types. The drums are barrel drums and offer different pitches. The lower-tuned buleador plays a consistent pattern while the higher-pitched subidor allows the lead drummer a level of improvisation in reaction to the dancer's movement. The single-headed drum is positioned between the knees of the seated drummer as he plays with bare hands.

Yet another completely separate and distinctive music that makes great use of drums lives at the bottom end of the Caribbean. Lying north of the Venezuelan coast is Trinidad and Tobago, the land of calypso music, famed for its carnivals. It is also the home of a 20th-century invention in the form of a drum of sorts, which creates some of the most upbeat and positive rhythms that the world has ever heard: that of the steel pan band.

After the traditional African membranophones were banned by the colonial British through fear of their spiritual power in the late 19th century, the African slaves created tamboo bamboo bands, which used cut, dried stems of bamboo struck on their sides or stomped on the ground to create sounds. Using different standardized lengths of bamboo enabled these musicians to have a boom stick providing the low frequencies, a foule for the middle-range sounds, and the cutter, which was the highest in pitch. These bamboo stems were accompanied by other percussive objects such as a part-filled glass bottle struck with a spoon or domestic tins.

By the late 1930s, metallic objects had grown in popularity and steel oil gallon drums had caught the eye of some keen percussion innovators. It wasn't long before they discovered that the end of these could be beaten to achieve specific tonal variation across the playing surface. Soon enough, the ends of these containers were hammered to form a concave well, and then small areas of that were selected and hammered back out, raising them slightly. After being fired over a bonfire and then having its raised areas subjected to a hammered tuning process, the drum was left with numerous areas that could produce specifically tuned notes. Over time, these became more sophisticated until each drum had between three and thirty-two individual notes. The instrument was now a very capable melodic drum, which could be beaten with short wooden sticks bound with padded ends to create a new sound.

Following a ban on the carnival during World War II, the following VE day allowed these drums to explode onto the streets and establish the sound so exciting that tamboo bamboo bands became obsolete. Strangely, these bands that created such majestic music were often run by fearless gang leaders who would fight with rival steel bands, causing violence and havoc. Despite this, the bands themselves were very organized and the drums had names within the group such as lead (or tenor), double second, double tenor, cello, guitar, quadrophonics, and bass.

Heading back to the mainland south of the border, the pre-Columbian drums of South America are found in several forms and materials. From the Esmeraldas province of Ecuador came a large clay drum from the early centuries CE, probably belonging to the people of La Tolita. It is molded into a conical shape with the larger end acting as the base. Small holes appear beneath the upper opening, which may have allowed a carrying strap or enabled the membrane to be tensioned. Four heads are molded into the side and painted red with two larger ones and two smaller ones.

Steel pan from Trinidad and Tobago. Courtesy of the author.

Another pottery drum comes from the Nasca Valley of Peru. This pot drum from 200–500 CE is at the NMAI, showing a rounded base that opens out to a bowl-shaped middle before finishing at the top with an upturned conical section.

Some Peruvian tribes used drums for signaling. One example is the Amahuaca people, who use a hollowed length of tree trunk covered with a howling-monkey skin. The Machinganga tribe of Peru possesses a similar double-headed drum of around 18 inches in length, which it uses to accompany dances for a variety of occasions. It features a type of snare made of beads strung on a cord across one of the membranes. It is played while carried by the lead dancer and tapped with the fingers.

Further south the Catuquinaru Indians of Brazil made use of the ancient log drum. Here they would place the hollow log of a palm tree over a hole dug into the earth, fill it with objects such as bone or rubber, and strike it.

Another drum type was the shallow kettledrum called the kultrung, which came from the Mapuche Indians of Chile. This wooden drum featured a horse rawhide tensioned across the opening via cords, which secured beneath the drum. An example of this drum is held at the NMAI, displaying red and blue symbolic artwork upon the membrane.

In post-Columbian Venezuela we see many other drum types that have enabled it to enjoy its own musical culture with a number of popular drums that display its historical connections with Africa and Spain.

One popular drum is the long, thin redondo. This drum displays a cylindrical exterior, although the interior is fashioned into an hourglass design with only a very small hole joining the upper and lower sections in the middle to create a more pleasing resonance. It usually appears in groups of three with the common female hembra and male macho distinctions plus the hermaphroditic el cruzado. A membrane of sloth skin is attached at either end and tensioned with ropes, which travel the 40-inch length of the body. The drum is held at an angle between the drummer's legs while he beats the top head with one hand and one stick. The female drum usually begins with a basic holding rhythm before being joined with an accompaniment from the cross-gender drum and then the male, which enjoys a freer, more improvised role. These may also be accompanied by maracas.

They also have the tambora, which is similar to the redondo although smaller. This double-headed drum is played with a single stick and fingers while held between the seated player's legs or strung around his shoulders for processional use. These are sometimes played solo or in groups up to five drums. The uses of these drums and the manner in which they are played resemble the redondo.

Other important drums include the big drums 80 inches long made from an avocado or guava tree trunk with a single head. These are known by various names in different regions, such as burro, camaco, mina, or tambor grande (large drum). Several drummers can play this drum simultaneously with the lead drummer straddling the end to beat the membrane with two sticks while others beat the shell at various points. The drum itself usually lies along the ground, although some regions set it upon a forked wooden frame. One such region is the Miranda state, and particularly Barlovento, where it is called mina. Here it is often played in an ensemble with another drum, which is essentially the same but less than 40 inches in length. This smaller size means that this curbata drum can stand upended when played with carved feet enabling the sound to escape beneath.

These drums are used for festivities such as celebrating St. John the Baptist. The Fiesta de San Juan is particularly significant, as it was a day in which the African slaves could hold their own celebrations. This was heightened by the date's very close proximity to the summer solstice.

Other drums found here include the bombo bass drum, which came from European influence, the redoblante, which is a side drum, and the furruco friction drum, which bears resemblance to the Spanish zambomba and those mentioned in Africa. It often makes festive appearances, especially at Christmas, and although the body can be found in different forms of wood or gourd, it is often a cylindrical shell with an upper membrane that features a waxed stick pushed through a hole and rubbed to achieve the sound.

The largest South American country is Brazil, and with such a physical stature, this nation has provided an appropriately significant heritage to world music culture. Although religious music styles such as candomblé are widespread throughout Brazil, it is the largely secular music styles that have become so well known internationally. One of the most well known is the fast and furious samba style, which grew to accompany the carnival celebrations prior to a period of abstinence for Lent. The samba dance is undoubtedly an African-inspired pursuit and does bear resemblance to such dances as the Angolan circle dance before it found its way to the impoverished favelas of Rio to evolve into samba in the early 20th century. Samba schools (escolas) were created, and hot competition became the norm in a blur of brightly colored, choreographed costumes, flags, and floats. All this is set to a rhythm provided by the batteria, a percussion section that can vary from a handful of people to a few hundred. Within this batteria, the audience will generally see a number of surdos, caixas, pandeiros, cuicas, repiniques, reco-recos, tamborims, caixeta, chocalos pratos, and ago-gos.

The surdo is the very important bass drum of samba, known as the zabumba in baiaó. Often seen in numbers of around thirty within each escola, it is a double-headed cylindrical drum of wood or metal that comes in three sizes, ranging from around 24 inches to 12 inches. The playing style involves one padded stick in the right hand, which plays closed and open tones, as well as striking the rim while the other hand uses the palm and fingers to strike notes as well as mute the membrane.

As the surdos lay down the foundation of the rhythm, the other percussive sections play syncopated rhythms. The tamborim and pandeiro are frame drums, the cuica is a friction drum, the ripinques are small double-headed drums tuned to a high pitch to cut through for solo cues when played with one stick and one hand, and the caixa is a snare drum. Beyond the drums are the wood block (caixeta), metallic bells (ago-gos), shakers (chocalo), scratchers (reco-recos), and cymbals (pratos). Other Brazilian drums include the atabaque, which are congalike in appearance and found in three sizes from the larger rum through rumpi to the smallest lê.

Brazilian repinique samba drum. Courtesy of the author.

In the north of Brazil other styles developed; for example, the African circle dance evolved in the 1940s with an accordion to create the style baiaó with a very specific bass drum pattern. These styles failed to have the same impact as samba outside of Brazil but were important to the development of the music of Brazil.

There was, however, another style that did achieve international fame. As samba spread to the higher classes, it gradually evolved through the 1930s, and by the 1950s bossa nova had been created. Imbued with sophistication and intellect, this was a slower, more laid-back rhythm with certain jazz sensibilities influencing the harmonic and melodic aspects. It then crossed back over to North America and began itself to influence the jazz scene, with many jazz groups incorporating bossa nova influences, and specific rhythms were adapted for the drum kit.

Beyond these styles, countless regional variations and sub-genres have appeared with varying popularity, and the fusion of African/European influences mixed with native South American sounds have gone on to pervade many musical genres around the world with instantly recognizable and enthralling rhythms that are unmistakably South American.

NOTES

1. Payson D. Sheets, *Archaeology, volcanism, and remote sensing in the Arenal region, Costa Rica* (Austin, TX: University of Texas Press, 1994), 161.

2. Colin Brock, *The Caribbean in Europe: Aspects of the West Indian experience in Britain, France and the Netherlands* (London: Frank Cass and Company, LTD, 1986), 197–198.

3. Martin Munro, *Different drummers: Rhythm and race in the Americas* (Berkeley, CA: University of California Press, 2010), 36.

Chapter Eight

---○---

Southern and Eastern Asia

EAST AND SOUTH ASIA HAVE BOTH INFLUENCED and been influenced by other parts of the world where drumming is concerned. With India's proximity to Western Asia and the rich drum history already discussed, it is logical that much of this drum usage has traveled east through India and combined with the indigenous customs before moving on through the likes of Thailand, Cambodia, and into Malaysia and Indonesia. Indo-Aryan migrants from the northwest influenced the east as seen in India with the Vedas, which provide some early musical evidence.

Drums that have been born or evolved in South Asia have made great impressions in the Western world with traditional Indian instruments like the tabla and sitar enchanting UK pop groups such as the Beatles or Kula Shaker and, more profoundly, Chinese drums leading to the tom-toms of Western drum kits.

Of course, they were not without their frame drums, which isn't surprising when a glance west reveals the numerous frame drums such as the adapu, tof, and timbrel. India has produced many varieties, too many to mention, which include the small duffle and the tape, dap, or dapu, which is around 15 inches in diameter, although this does vary. This drum is beaten with two sticks in such circumstances as karnataka funeral music. Other drums, the dambara and lambara, are mentioned in the ancient Vedic texts: "These drums are unknown, and there is no description of them in the text, but

from the names it is possible to connect these drums with the
Sumerian dapa, Egyptian tab, and, in the Semitic languages, Akka-
dian atapu, Hebrew tof, and Arabic duff, most of which have been
identified as frame drums."[1]

Nepal also possessed frame drums such as the single-headed
chepang shaman drum around 18.5 inches in diameter with iron amulets hanging from the base. Another Nepalese frame drum known
as dhyangro was a double-headed frame drum, which featured a very
ornately carved wooden handle enabling the drum to be held aloft
at head height while a curved S-shaped cane beater was held in the
other hand. A popular drum with shaman, as used in ritual, it often
displayed a ritualistic dagger (phurba) carved into the handle. An example at the National Music Museum in South Dakota of 14 inches
in diameter shows a handle that is carved to represent a ritual dagger
with the sea dragon Makara inlaid on it. Usually the membranes are
tied together with strips of hide, and sometimes wedges are forced
under the ties to create greater tuning possibilities. The Tibetan na
is a similar drum design with colorful paintings upon the shell. The
folkloric South Korean sogo was also very similar to the dhyangro. It
was beaten with a single stick to accompany dancers. The Japanese
uchiwa daiko also had a handle, although the frame was very thin,
consisting of just a ring, somewhat resembling a beach ball bat. They
are sometimes used in modern situations in groups with different-
pitched drums to enable a melodic quality.

One other interesting drum, which resembles a beach ball bat
of sorts, is held at the Metropolitan Museum of Art in New York
(Met). Known as a candrapirai, this 19th-century Indian example
consists of a thin iron frame that is slightly crescent moon shaped
with a membrane stretched taut across it, played while holding a
curving handle beneath. This temple drum comes with an accompanying drum in the shape of the sun known as suryapirai.

The Chinese made great use of the frame drum, as seen in a
double-headed example at the Ethnographic Museum in Stock-
holm, which is 26.4 inches in diameter and 8.8 inches high. The
shell is red with four blue dragons painted on it. Both membranes
are tacked on with two rows of nails, giving the drum the familiar
appearance that appeared on the early Western drum kits.

Tamang-type drum, www.rhythmuseum.com.

Another example from this museum is a convex double-headed Chinese frame drum using the same double row of nails for each head. The skin is attached low down the shell, with only a thin strip of wooden shell visible between the two skins. However, the actual resonating playing surface is a much smaller area in the center where a chasm is hollowed through the shell to create the sound chamber, producing a higher pitch than would otherwise be expected on a hollowed shell of the same size. In a similar way the people of Shanghai possess a drum called biqi gu (chestnut drum), which is used in their jiangnan sizhu music, also known as the diangu in kunqu music. Like the previous example, these drums consist of a solid piece of wood, with a small hollowed cylinder at the center. The shell is covered at both ends with hide, and only the central part above the small hole is the resonating area. It is played with thin sticks and struck either on the resonating area or the portion of membrane that covers solid wood with a much harder sound. The two areas can also be struck simultaneously for further timbral variation.

A single-headed example from China is found in the bangu, which also has a central opening much smaller than the membrane. The membrane is nailed onto the frame while the whole drum hangs from three posts that rise up to form a solid wooden stand connected to a fourth, central post beneath the drum. The frame itself is constructed from thick wedges of wood, which are glued together. It is played with two sticks in Chinese Peking opera known as jing xi. The tougu as seen in the South is very similar to the bangu except that it has an upper convex shape.

Away from the courts, the frame drum also found a home with the shamans of China. The Manchu shamans used frame drums with great symbolic importance. These drums are known as nimachin today, although traditionally the single-headed variety was known as wendun, which was beaten with a stick known as keshun. These drums are circular or oval with a diameter of around 20 inches. An iron loop was attached to the side so that the drum could be held, and attachments of rope enabled metal objects to clatter together as the drum was shaken. They also used a drum known as tongken, which means "big drum" despite having a slightly smaller diameter. It was a double-headed drum, which lay upon a stand as it was beaten with two sticks.

Moving further east away from mainland Asia, the small, single-headed Japanese frame drum known as paranku from Okinawa is found during the spiritual Ei-sa festival, which is rooted in Buddhism and respects deceased ancestors but has evolved into a huge, spectacular gathering of dancers and drummers that attracts tourists in masses. This drum is often played by youths in groups during the festival, who dance while beating the drum with a single stick. Another Japanese stick-beaten frame drum was the kacho, which came from the Northern Ainu tribe.

Tambourines also exist with the Indian kanjira, a small tambourine of around 7 inches in diameter with a single goat or reptile membrane but only one pair of metal jingles. A pitch-bending technique of applying pressure to the moistened membrane is used for general entertainment and the traditional classical music. The bajoiaogu of China also made use of a single reptile skin upon its octagonal frame, as did the Nepalese taamring, which saw it nailed onto a tapered wooden shell. Iron discs known as jhyaali fit into slits in the side and react when the drum is struck with the hand, shaken, or rubbed.

Another Indian tambourine was the duff, a single-headed Indian folk tambourine, which may employ a stick as well as hands to accompany light music and dances. In fact there were so many frame drums and various regional names throughout India and the rest of Asia that they cannot be mentioned here. They generally displayed great similarity to their counterparts from further west in the continent.

Drumming in India is a highly developed and respected art form, which has achieved a level of skill, dedication, and understanding that is difficult to rival elsewhere in the world. This is particularly evident with the tabla and mrdanga drums. Indian music on the whole, like much of its culture, is closely linked with religion, whether the traditions are from pre-Buddhism, Buddhism itself, Hinduism, Jainism, Sikhism, or Islamism. As a result of these religious groups documenting their lives, we have evidence that shows early drum examples, although their use in times before this evidence is of course uncertain.

Looking at the pre-Buddhist evidence, Sir Mortimer Wheeler's 1940s excavations at two of the earliest cities to have been discovered in the subcontinent of South Asia yield clues: "There is evidence that the seven-holed flute and various types of stringed instruments and drums were in use in these two cities. Indeed, these musical instruments must have been used and perfected hundreds of years before they came into the hands of the expert musicians and dancing girls of Mohenjo Daro and Harappa."[2] These Indus Valley civilization cities in modern-day Pakistan emerged around 2500–1900 BCE.

Furthermore, Indus Valley findings offer information: "An elongated drum with a skin at each end is seen on two of the amulets. Another form of drum, or tambourine, appears to hang from the neck of one of the pottery male figures."[3]

Beyond the archaeological finds is the literary evidence within the ancient Hindu literature known as the Vedic texts. The Vedic period emerged somewhere in the 2nd millennium BCE and lasted until around the first few centuries BCE, although exact dates are often contradictory between sources. Their texts describe Indian culture in that period. We know that it was during later Vedic times, possibly around 500 BCE, that the foundations of Indian classical music were laid down. As mentioned in chapter 2, the Vedic texts speak of a pit drum known as the bhumi dundubhi, which may have been a revival of an older usage. The texts also speak of dundubhi, a bowl-shaped drum or early kettledrum, which became very popular in later Indian periods, sharing its name with a devil in the form of a buffalo. This drum was beaten with a golden drumstick along with another kettledrum known as bheri.[4]

When Buddhism arrived in the 5th century BCE, religious songs were used to propagate their beliefs, making use of such drums as the dundubhi and a rather homemade instrument that involved a membrane stretched over a domestic pot to form a drum known as kumbhasthūm.

As musical art forms developed in Asia, musical theory was studied and ideas were published in early Indian music books such as the *Bharata Natya Sastra*. However, "The date and authorship of the *Bharata Natya Sastra* are both in dispute. The book has been variously dated from the 2nd century B.C. to the 3rd century A.D., but there is even less certainty about the author."[5] Here an emphasis on vocal music is demonstrated and melodic systems are outlined, although there is no mention of ragā, which developed later and became integral to Indian classical music.

Other early respected books on the subject of music, drama, and dance include *Abhinaya Darpan*, written by Acharya Nandikeswar, and *Sangita Ratnakara*, written by Sarangadeva in the 13th century CE. Other archaeological evidence of drums exists from the 2nd century CE in depictions found on the Indian reliefs from Bharhut, further supporting the importance of drumming in Indian cultures.

We also find from around the 10th century CE many images of the god Shiva as the lord of the dance, Nataraja, dancing with a drum. One such example is the 12th-century, bronze, four-armed figure at the Rijksmuseum in Amsterdam, which shows Shiva with an hourglass drum known as a damaru in one hand as he beats the rhythm of creation while another hand holds the fire that will ultimately destroy his worldly creation. An almost-identical item from the 11th century rests at the Met. Earlier depictions were often in stone, although exact dates of origin are still debated by scholars. The suggestion that the reverberations of this small damaru began the process of creation demonstrates the importance of drums in India.

Contact with Muslims saw a growing differentiation in musical styles between the north and south of India from around the 12th century CE. By the 16th century CE, Indian classical music had divided enough to recognize different styles, such as the highly improvisational Hindustānī music from the northern areas and Karnatak from the south.

But returning to the Vedic texts, some were considered too sacred for the general public domain and were subsequently encoded and passed down in chant form. These songlike verses evolved over time and converged with other influences, which may have been the forerunner to ragā. Ragās are the melodic systems that evolved around the 4th century CE and were used in such art forms as classical Hindustānī music; within this category there are hundreds of different ragās, each containing set criteria to define it. Running parallel to these melodic systems are the rhythmic counterparts known as tāla. These complex metric systems formed the basis for the timing and rhythmic stresses within the music. Just as Western musical bars contain a set number of beats, often measured by the number of crotchets or quavers, tālas work in this way too. There are hundreds of tālas, and they can range in number of beats, or matras, from just a couple to over one hundred. Just as crotchets can be divided into quavers, semiquavers, and so on, so too can matras be subdivided. They can also be added together to make a longer unit of time, just as with a Western minim. The main tempi used in traditional music are considered in relation to a man's natural pulse or resting heartbeat.

Having made the comparison with Western musical structure, there are some fundamental differences between the two. The number of beats within the tāla only tells part of the story. Particular strokes with the correct hand, and even part of the hand, are used with different areas of the drum to create varied timbres within the cycle in an order that is particular to that tāla. Beyond that, particular stresses on certain beats divide a tāla into smaller phrases. The rupak tāla, for example, contains seven notes but can be thought of as containing a three-note phrase and two phrases of two notes. In the southern regions of India hand clapping, knee slapping, and audience counting participation is often seen. A tāla ends on the first beat of the next cycle, which can be confusing to the Western ear that expects it to end on the last note of the previous cycle.

Beyond this there are other emotional and musical nuances as well as flexibility in the timing of notes, which helps to make the distinction with Western ideas. The rhythms are learned aurally using bols, which are traditional spoken syllables, each representing the different strokes that make up the tāla. Once the oral patterns are perfected, they can be translated on the drums.

Of the various Indian drums, the most internationally famous is the north Indian tabla, which is actually a term for a pair of drums. The two drums are known as bayan and dayan, meaning left and right. The dayan is also known as tabla individually, although the term is generally used to denote the pair of drums. These drums are sometimes viewed as having derived from the older double-headed mrdanga, discussed shortly, split into two separate drums. Each tabla drum has traits that are parallel to each head of the mrdanga. The higher-pitched dayan is wooden and tuned to a particular note corresponding to the rāga that it is accompanying. This drum sits on the floor at a slight angle, leaning in toward the bayan. The shell is biconical, with the lower portion much shorter than the top.

This shape is evidence that the drum was originally double headed as is the pakhāvaj, only discarding the second membrane when the drum became vertical.[6] It stands around 12 inches high and 7 inches in upper diameter, with a head that is surrounded by lacing, used to tension the membrane by way of wooden wedges that are forced between the lace and the shell. Although the drum would be considered single headed, as it only has a membrane across one opening of the drum, is actually consists of three membranes, often of different animals, although the upper head is a collar around the edge of the drum opening rather than a full membrane. Soot, iron dust, flour, and water are applied in the center of the top membrane to form a paste, which helps achieve the preferential tonal qualities. Modern drums may use a rubber substitute.

Alongside the dayan is the bayan, which provides the lower frequency, often tuned to the octave below the dayan. It is a copper, brass, or silver drum in a bowl shape as a type of kettledrum with a head diameter of around 10 inches and height similar to the dayan. This drum features two membranes, the top one being just a collar with a paste applied to the full head slightly off center to achieve the desired, slightly muted sound. A hammer can be used to gain even finer tuning of the head by striking around the rim. This is carried out on stage as part of the performance as the drummer settles himself and his instrument with the acoustics and atmosphere of the concert hall.

These two drums have developed into hugely complex and expressive tools, which allow the drummer to accompany instrumental and vocal music. Although instruments were traditionally used to accompany the vocalist, since the 18th century, some instruments have managed to break free from this restraint. One such instrument is the tabla, which today also enjoys a soloist's role with the ability to create exhilarating solos of great speed and virtuosity, only comprehensible to the members of the audience who are educated on such matters. Combinations of finger taps and palm strokes are exploited for wide tonal variety as well as pitch bending by compressing the membrane with one hand while the other strikes it. Beyond just using one tabla, a group can be played together, and when tuned to specific notes in the scale, they become a very melodic ensemble known as tabla tarang.

The exact origin of the tabla is unknown. As well as the connection with the mrdanga, it is also necessary to look at the etymology with regard to the Arabian ṭabl, which was a generic name for a drum. It is popular and reasonable to speculate that a form of ṭabl arrived from the west along with Islam and was integrated with the existing traditions and instruments to form the tabla. This development is supported by the northern location of this drum, which is where those from the west made their initial impact. Assuming this evolution through cultural amalgamation to be accurate, the tabla in current form may have existed since at least the 14th century.[7] The naqqāra of Western Asian origin is one such predecessor to the tabla, which was a bowl-shaped drum played in pairs. Another ancient drum that may have influenced the tabla is the puskara, a set of three drums, two of which are played horizontally and one in an angled position. These were seen as early as the 6th to 7th century on temple depictions at Bhuvanesvara.[8]

And from this naqqāra we can see that the bayan was not the earliest Indian example of a kettledrum. In fact pre-Muslim evidence exists in pictorial form, as seen on Javanese Borobudur as well as ancient Indian and Cambodian temples.[9] Possibly the earliest type was the ghata, a domestic clay pot, which was struck by

Indian tabla, www.rhythmuseum.com.

various parts of the hand and muted by placing the opening against the player's body. We also find the aforementioned dundubhi, a wooden bowl drum with bells inside the shell.

Later varieties include the ceremonial nagara, a shallow metallic bowl drum, and larger variations designed for temple use. Larger still was the extremely grand sahib-nahabat. These huge pairs of silver drums boasting diameters of 5 feet each were beaten with silver sticks while mounted upon elephants at state ceremonies. Other kettledrums of India include the nakkara used slung in pairs on horses and elephants for ceremonial and military events; the large, conical kettledrum known as karadsamilia; the wooden tudum; the dukkar, which hangs from the player's neck while he stands and is played with bare hands similarly to the tabla; and the metallic naghara, which is also played in pairs by a single drummer.

Beyond the frame and kettledrums were the double-headed cylindrical and barrel drums. The southern mrdanga is a biconical double-headed drum carved from a single piece of wood, although it may have originally been a clay drum and played horizontally across the lap or hanging by a rope around the player's neck. Just as the tabla are the most important and technically challenging drums to play in the north, the mrdanga holds that role in the south. The drummer uses various hand and finger techniques to play on both heads simultaneously.

It is seen with a variety of names such as mrudangam or mridangam and is very important in the karnatak musical form in the south. Myth has it that the Hindu god Brahma created this drum as accompaniment to the dance of Mahādeva, although today it accompanies instrumental and vocal music as well as being a solo instrument in both the northern and southern regions. Its true origin is difficult to assess, although Indian cylinder drums date back to the ancient Indus Valley civilizations, making it one of the oldest Indian drum types.

Just as the tabla, this drum is tuned to match the pitch of the melodic instruments, and the two ends maintain specific roles with different head thicknesses, which correlate to the tabla. Each head is attached to a ring of hide that is connected to the ring at the opposite end via a series of leather cords and works its way around

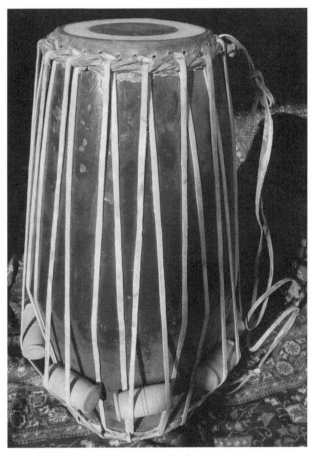

Indian mrdanga, www.rhythmuseum.com.

the drum shell. The hide rings are hammered to tune the drum, and wooden wedges are sometimes employed to further the tuning possibilities. The right head features three membranes, the top being a collar, and the same black paste as seen on the tabla. The left head features two membranes and a removable patch of black paste, applied to create a sound that is a specific pitched interval below the right head.

In the north, an almost-identical drum is used known as the pakhāvaj. This a double-headed barrel drum played with bare hands on both membranes. Very similar to the older mrdangam, it sits horizontally on the floor in front of the drummer, who uses two bare hands to play it. Lacing runs the full length of the shell with wooden wedges and paste. The upper membrane is around 9 inches, while it stands around 25 inches tall.

Apart from these drums are the many double-headed cylindrical and barrel-shaped variations throughout India. They generally follow the same approximate design with rope tensioning, although some modern versions display tension rods to tension the goatskin heads. They are played with bare hands, straight sticks, hooked sticks, or a combination, and there is great variation in names, sizes, and playing techniques across the country. Popular drums include the dhol, a double-headed barrel drum, often used as a generic name for this style of drum; it is therefore designated a regional suffix. A variation on this drum is the dhepā dhol, which features a small hole in the upper membrane through which water is poured to alter the tone while it is being beaten. Other common drums of this type include the thavil, khol, dhola, dholak, and chenda. Although many were made of clay or wood, some examples began to be produced in various metals. A beautiful 19th-century cylindrical brass drum featuring a figure of the mythological Hindu bull Nandi in the center rests at the Victoria and Albert Museum in London. It uses Y-shaped rope tensioning to secure the two heads, which are fixed to a circular board that projects outward beyond the circumference of the shell in the same manner as many Japanese drums.

Of the hourglass drums in India, the damaru may be the most sacred. This small hourglass drum is often formed from two skulls stuck head to head with membranes stretched over both openings. It is viewed as having spiritual powers and, as mentioned, is often pictured in the hands of the God Shiva as the drum of creation. It uses a leather thong attached to the narrow waist of the shell, which strikes the membranes as the drum is shaken with the right hand. A similarly shaped drum is the udduku. Other similar drum shapes included the budbudiki, hudduka, urmi, and huruk. The huruk and urmi had an extra quality that allowed pitch variation by applying pressure to the rope tensioning in much the same way as the talking drums of Africa.

Indian dhol, www.rhythmuseum.com.

Goblet drums are also used in India, often with a direct link to Western Asia such as the Persian tombak, which is now popular in India. A variation on this is the bottle drum, which features a membrane across the wide base of the sound chamber and a long thin, fluted section at the top of the bottle. One such drum is the tumbaknari of Kashmir and the ghutru, a 19th-century example of which is held at the Victoria and Albert Museum in London with

Indian damaru, www.
rhythmuseum.com.

painted silver leaf designs and ropes, which secure the head beneath the bowl sound chamber of the drum.

The island of Sri Lanka off the southern coast of India has a mixture of its own traditional drum history as well as sharing many design features with drums from India. Traditional Sri Lankan drums often feature a prefix accompanying the word bera, which is a generic term for a drum. Examples include the cylindrical yak bera and the barrel-shaped geta bera.

Other drums include the frame drum tamil as seen at the Museum of Fine Arts (MFA) in Boston along with an hourglass drum known as udakki, which bears a very similar design to its Indian counterparts. Once an object of the Sri Lankan upper classes, today it accompanies general dancing.

Back on the mainland and east of India is Tibet, which just like Sri Lanka enjoys a mixture of traditional and Indian influenced drumming. In pre-Buddhist Tibet, the Bön people existed as a spiritual and shamanistic community who enjoyed a lively music scene both for spiritual and secular activities. Such drums as the hourglass damaru were important in these spiritual customs.

Nepal is another country in South Asia that possesses similar drum designs, such as the dhimay double-headed cylindrical drum, the damaha kettledrum, the madal or larger khin barrel-shaped drum, and the damphu frame drum.

China is a vast country with many diverse localized traditions influenced by surrounding countries through affiliations and invaders.

Among these traditions are the revered theater and musical art forms that promote the values and beliefs of the Chinese people. Within the musical genres, the drum plays a pivotal role both in court and in the villages.

The drum is a very important symbolic item in northern Chinese shamanistic rituals. It sometimes represents a form of travel such as a horse or boat, which enables the shaman to journey to other worlds. These drums come in the form of frame drums, as previously discussed, with handles either attached to the back of the drumhead or to the bottom of the frame. They also have double-headed drums.

The very first drum may be traced back to a time before humans even existed if legend be believed. Manchu myth has it that the first drum and drumstick were made from the sky and a mountain by Abkai Hehe (sky mother). She also created the first shaman in Nisan Shamaness and her drumming created humankind.[10]

Much like the American Indians, the instruction on when and how to make a drum arrived at the shaman through dreams. Having sacrificed the appropriate animal and constructed the drum, decoration occurs, as explained in the dream, before the awakening ceremony takes place in which the drum is beaten throughout the night. The drum may then be used to make connections with the underworld and aid the souls of the deceased.

The drum was also popular in the courts, along with many other instruments that were categorized around the early 3rd millennium BCE during the Shun Dynasty and placed into eight groups (a number considered harmonious and lucky) based on their main material. The categories were known as the bayin classification and consisted of bamboo, metal, stone, wood, gourd, clay, skin, and silk. Each category was attached to one of the eight winds as a symbol of man's control of the weather. They were also assigned to different seasons of the calendar, the drum belonging to the winter, as well as compass directions, with the drum appointed to the north. This classification was likely to have evolved from an earlier similar system, possibly containing four categories.

Of course these other instrument categories were also important, such as the metal gong, which was widely used in China. However, the drums hold the greatest importance, as seen in the bangu. Here the performer holds a role similar to the Western conductor by directing the orchestra through the movements and dynamics of the piece in performances such as wu-chang martial arts.

The existence of the skin category in the 3rd millennium BCE is evidence that drums existed at this early stage. Indeed ten drums of granite reside at a temple in Peking, which possibly hail from 2,600 years ago, although the dates of origin are contested. These drums bear early inscriptions of Chinese writing and may have also been beaten in religious ceremonies.[11] Other early evidence of drums is found as inscriptions on bones and tortoiseshells from the Shang Dynasty 1562–1066 BCE, which mention drums with the word gu. A large percentage of all instruments were thought to be percussion at this time. One such example is a 7th-century BCE bronze goblet drum from northern China, which rests at the Brooklyn Museum in New York. Standing 9 inches tall and nearly 6 inches in diameter, this is a very plain drum with only three concentric rings displaying triangular carvings around the circumference below where the single membrane would have attached.

These drums and other instruments had an important role to play in Chinese society. Since Kong Fuzi (better known as Confucius) in the 5th century BCE, music was viewed as a powerful tool that should promote correct ethics and morals.

One artistic medium that could teach these stories, morals, and ideals was Chinese theater. It has been popular for many hundreds of years as a very important art form, and within it we often find drums used as accompaniment. We also know that court entertainers were popular by the time of the Han Dynasty in 202 BCE through which mythical stories were portrayed by actors, singers, wrestlers, clowns, acrobats, and musicians. Musical orchestras were also popular within the courts.

Evidence that drums and percussion were important within this musical society is found from the Tang Dynasty, around 618–907 CE, when Emperor Li Shimin in Jiangzhou possessed a percussion orchestra. Although not exclusively percussion, the National Gallery of Art in Washington has a beautifully crafted relief from the tomb of Wang Chuzhi, a high-ranking official in the later Liang Dynasty of the early 10th century CE. It portrays a female orchestra with one woman clearly beating a large barrel drum, which might be an early tanguu. The drum rests vertically upon a wooden stand as she strikes it with two sticks in accompaniment to the various lutes, flutes, harps, and zhengs. The group of thirteen musicians, including conductor, as well as two dancers shows the level of organization and formality given to music as well as the importance and respect of this art form to be included in the tomb.

Orchestras and drama flourished, with opera becoming very popular leading up to the 18th-century Peking opera, which involved extravagant and colorful displays of martial arts, dancing, singing, music, pantomime, and acrobatics, having drawn influence from its predecessors such as Kun-style opera.

Around the 17th to 18th century, northern China also witnessed the rise of the drum ballad. This rural art form that eventually found its way to the cities involved storytelling through song while the performer beat a frame drum upon a stand to enhance the performance.

Today many music schools exist, and it is considered a great honor for a child to be accepted into one. Here they will study regular classes before spending the afternoon perfecting their art, which is taken incredibly seriously.

The earliest drums of China were made from clay until later being replaced by wood and even bronze. Whereas Indians had a penchant for rope tensioning, the Chinese preferred nailing their heads. Thus there are very few drums in the country with the tuning options that Indian and other cultures enjoy. Of course, as discussed with previous cultures, such heads can be subjected to a certain amount of tuning with paste, heat, or even moisture, but the possibilities are severely limited in comparison to a drum with rope tuning or tension screws. To combat this problem the skins

Chinese drums, www.rhythmuseum.com.

are varnished to help maintain their tension. Their drums were often very striking with beautiful decoration, generally red painted shells and elaborate murals upon the membranes, often featuring dragons. In some areas another animal that is frequently found on traditional drums is the frog. Although it was foodstuff in parts of China, it was also symbolic of fertility, sometimes associated with the goddess Nuwa who created mankind, and also rain, therefore possibly used on drums to beat rain dances.

Chinese drums have been played for ceremonial use at temples, on the battlefield for troop organization and enemy intimidation, as well as for dramas and other entertainment. The playing is usually achieved with sticks, often two at a time, although bare hands are sometimes used. The complexity of Indian drumming is not evident here but instead displays of showmanship are clearly evident, with exaggerated arm movements and swaying of the body around the drums. Drama is an important aspect of Chinese drum performance.

The varied uses have necessitated variation in basic design and size, but by far the most common drum type in China is the barrel drum. The shell is often built up from strips of wood that are bound together, much like a beer keg, rather than a single solid piece of wood. The membranes, of which there are often two but not always, are nailed onto the shells and the drum is positioned in a vertical or horizontal position depending on the type and function in question. Sizes can range from very small to enormous, the large examples bearing a resemblance to the huge Sumerian drums such as the su-ala, which may be a result of a common origin. There are many religious instruments in China, and we find within the Chinese Buddhist monasteries that huge bells and drums are used as part of daily routines to announce the morning or evening, and to call the monks together for particular monastic duties. These instruments hang in specially built towers and hold great importance. The large barrel drum is known as da-gu, and it often has a diameter far larger than the height of the man who plays it with his wooden sticks. Chinese symbols are painted upon the membranes, which are nailed onto the wooden shell.

As well as the huge ceremonial drum, other Chinese temple drums include the ying-ku. This barrel drum is accompanied by the double-headed, midsize tou-ku and the smaller po-fu drum. The name of this small temple drum denotes the left and right membranes of the drum, which are beaten with bare hands in specific sequence purely for religious performance. Originally this drum contained grain inside the shell. These religious drums are beaten in answer to each other or as a response to other instruments and passages of verse during the ceremony.

Large drums used secularly within villages also existed, such as those in the purpose-built drum towers. These drums with diameters of 6 feet or more were beaten hourly as a timekeeping method or used as alarm systems. The vast barrel drums would lie horizontally on wooden frames and were beaten on one side with two wooden sticks. The resonant head was positioned so as to face outward from the tower to project the sound across the village. The period in which the Dong people introduced the drum towers depends on which scholar is being studied, as it ranges "from the Qin and Han dynasties (221 BC–AD 220) to the Tang and Song dynasties (618–1279) to the Ming dynasty (1368–1644),"[12] although the towers may have existed earlier in Dong culture with a different function devoid of any drums until the Han-inspired drum usage appeared.

The tanggu, or hall drum, is another large double-headed drum with a diameter of more than 40 inches. It is generally painted bright red with four iron rings around the circumference. From these it is suspended vertically or set in a wooden frame. It is beaten with two wooden sticks during celebrations and Buddhist rituals as well as in theater. Different tones can be achieved by striking different areas of the head as well as utilizing dynamics. A very elegant 19th-century example rests at the Met with a less-common black shell decorated with gold motifs. Smaller versions exist, such as the jing tanggu seen in Peking Opera.

An exciting large barrel drum is the lion drum used for the lion dance. This art form celebrates an animal that is highly symbolic, representing such traits as nobility, power, and virtue. The lion arrived in China from India with Buddhism often in iconographic form and sometimes in the flesh. In celebration of this creature a colorful dance emerged in which the dancers dress in elaborate lion costumes as they perform movements that could be likened to certain martial arts. Each lion consists of two men, the front one often leaping high into the air, supported by the rear dancer to make the lion move in dramatic and expressive ways to the frenzied accompaniment of cymbals and drums. The big lion drums are single-headed barrel drums, which sit on a frame at stomach height in front of the performer, who rapidly beats them with sticks. They follow the same design as previous barrel drums, although the northern version is usually painted red while the southern version is black.

Other smaller drums of similar design reside at the MFA, such as a jingo, which is more than 20 inches in diameter, a huagu with a diameter of 7 inches, and a bofu of similar size, which sits upon an ornately carved wooden stand.

Another similar drum categorized as a kou lives at the Met. Also at the museum is a 19th-century drum that follows the same design pattern and is labeled as gu. This is somewhat ambiguous, as gu is simply the generic word for a drum in China, in later times evolving into kou or ku as suffixes commonly found within this chapter. We also find a war drum called zhangu, which appears very similar to the dagu, and a small drum that hangs from the player's neck via a cord known as ya-kou. Therefore the same drum types are seen with different names, depending on age, region, and usage.

In the mid-20th century, following the yueqi gaige (revolution of instruments), a series of small barrel drums lined up in a row upon stands were created and given the name paigu. These are specifically tuned to fit the notes in the scale of a piece and as a result offer many possibilities in their groups of five or seven drums.

As well as the iconic barrel drums, China does have cylindrical examples as well. The smallest drums take on the form of frame drums such as the previously mentioned biqi gu and bangu. Another example is the pieng gu, which is more familiar in the West as the tom-tom that became commonplace on the trap kits in the early 20th century. These drums follow the common design of a red painted shell with a decorated, varnished membrane nailed onto the top and bottom.

In addition to these drums is a long, thin wooden tube over 26 inches in length and under 3 inches in diameter known as the yutong. A 19th-century example resides at the MFA that consists of wood and animal bladder. Another similar drum is the yugu fish drum, a tube of bamboo 3 feet long with a membrane covering one end.

The hourglass and goblet drums also exist in China, although they are vastly overshadowed by other drum types and may simply be an import from the west where the Arabs, and later the Southeast Asians made great use of such designs.

An example here that supports this is the Chinese zhanggu at the MFA. To begin with, the denomination zhanggu contradicts the commonly accepted drum design of this name, which is a barrel-shaped war drum. As well as that is the design of this drum, which has a bowl at the bottom, a horn at the top, and a thin waist in the center. A large head stretches out beyond the resonating chambers' diameters held taut with strands of string. This is uncommon in Chinese drum design and more likely Southeast Asian.

The Met also has a 19th-century goblet drum from China labeled as Thai-pang-kou. The design is very similar to the above zhanggu, and the use of Thai in the name also suggests a Southeast Asian origin. One other type is the jiegu, which again has its counterparts elsewhere with the Japanese kakko and Korean galgo.

Other evidence comes from Eberhard: "The Yao in Kuangsi have large hourglass drums of six foot length; the best come from Ch'ing-chiang (Kuangsi); they have a clay body and sheep-hide drum skin held by an iron ring."[13] However, the Yao resided in the southeast of China and mixed strongly with the Thai culture before the migration into present-day Thailand, further connecting this drum with Thailand rather than the Chinese as a whole.

Kettle or bowl-shaped drums also played their part within China, appearing in different forms throughout history. Large bronze kettledrums known as gong drums existed as early as the 4th century BCE. These sacred drums were usually suspended on ropes attached to handles on the side of the drum while the upper surface was beaten with a stick. This playing surface was a thin bronze sheet rather than leather, and the sound produced was accompanied by another sound achieved by beating the side of the shell with a lighter bamboo stick. This sound was believed to represent the spirits within the drum, a belief that was used as a deterrent to rival armies who would be terrified with the roar of such an empowered drum. An example of such a drum from 226 CE resides at the British Museum with a 20-inch diameter and 11-inch depth. The shell features four handles and inscriptions written within bands that also contain geometric shapes. Other kettledrums such as the Heger I examples are discussed later in Southeast Asia. There are other, less conventional drum shapes that defy these regular categories. The MFA holds a 19th-century box drum, which is a four-sided box that tapers at the base to create a wider upper opening. The main body rests inside a base, which has a small wooden carved fence. The shell itself is well crafted with flora painted upon the side. This drum had no membrane but was struck inside the body with a wooden stick.

Modern-day China has absorbed musical influences from around the world and particularly the West, just as most countries have. Fortunately they hold tradition dear to themselves, and many of the ancient arts are still performed or at least remembered. Efforts to spread this heritage worldwide have seen international touring groups taking the dramatic art form of Chinese drumming across the world as a pure entertainment show. Such troupes include Jigu!, a group of twenty-eight drummers from the Shanxi Province whose performances involve exciting drumming displays choreographed with dramatic movements and imbued with traditional stories of battles, mythology, and fable. The international profile was raised even further during the opening ceremony of the 2008 Beijing Olympic ceremony, when 2,008 square drums were played by as many people in an awe-inspiring choreographed performance in which the drums lit up to display certain messages to the thunderous sound of the rhythms. These drums, known as fou, were a modern interpretation of ancient Chinese drums, many of which were later auctioned off after intense interest in the instruments following the Olympic Games.

With Korea's only land link to the rest of the world being China, it is not surprising that huge influence has come from this northern neighbor and made great impact on Korea's music. Chinese influence can be found in such styles as T'ang music (t'angak), which derives from the Chinese T'ang dynasty. That said, Korea does possess a culture very much of its own, and within that are drumming traditions, which they can be proud of.

Just as Western classical music often utilizes flexible meter known as rubato, some genres of Korean music take this nonmetronomic rhythm to a greater extent. They also use metric systems known as changdan, each one distinguished by the accents, subdivisions, number of notes, and tempo. Here the rhythm is learned by singing a phrase and then using breathing, almost in a meditative fashion, to play the rhythmic pulse over the same time duration. Some musical forms can be heard played at very slow tempi but others such as kayagŭm sanjo often lasts for half an hour, in which time the tempo gradually increases, transitioning from one movement to another without any pause or warning except to the trained listener who can recognize the nuances.

Drums have been recorded in use since the Three Kingdoms Period, which ran from around 57 BCE to 668 CE, and today we find drums with membranes either nailed on or rope tensioned.[14]

Just as in China, barrel drums are important in Korea, with one of the most popular drums in Korea being the puk, also known as buk. This shallow, double-headed bass drum is hung around the neck in processions or set vertically on the floor when seated. It is beaten with the palm of the hand on one membrane and a stick on the other as the player also utilizes the timbres from the wooden rim to maintain a steady pulse to the music. It features a

Korean buk and sogo, www.rhythmuseum.com.

13- to 15-inch diameter head, which is usually nailed onto a shell of 7 to 9 inches in depth. It is used in such traditional music as p'ansori and p'ungmul with the older traditional versions appearing very plain and organic, whereas modern versions are often vibrant with a common multicolored design derived from the nationally important yin-yang symbolism painted upon the skin. A spectacular dance performed by women is the three-drum dance in which each dancer is enclosed on three sides by the face of a puk drum at chest height hanging in a wooden frame. Except for the outer two drums, each side-facing drum is played on either membrane as the dancers are positioned across the stage in a straight line. Using perfectly choreographed movements, which require great suppleness at times, the performers, who can number several, play the drums in perfect unison with each other through the medium of dance, thus creating their own rhythmic accompaniment.

Two large, double-headed barrel drums, most likely a result of Chinese influence, are the kon'go, which is set upon a decorated pedestal within a beautiful wooden pagoda decorated with carved dragons and birds; and the chin'go, which sits on a four-legged frame. The heads of these drums were often over 40 inches in diameter and could be 60 inches in length, although sometimes the diameter could also be less than 20 inches.

Single-headed barrel drums also existed, such as the kyobanggo used in the mugo drum dance; it sits horizontally on a wooden frame. An orchestral equivalent is found in the chwago, which also sits vertically on a wooden frame and is beaten with a padded stick. Pellet drums also existed in the smaller nodo and togo. The nodo consists of two small barrel drums positioned atop a pole at right angles to each other. As the pole is rotated, leather thongs strike the drumheads.

Among the other many variations found in Korea are the small frame drum known as sogo used in such music as p'ungmul along with the puk, changgo, gongs, and wind instruments; and the hourglass drum known as galgo, as derived from the Chinese jiego, and similar to the Japanese kakko found in gagaku music.

But possibly the most important drum in Korea since at least the Koryo Dynasty from 918 to 1392 CE is the changgo (also called janggo), a drum that most likely came to Korea from Western Asia via China. This double-headed hourglass drum with a beautifully crafted wooden shell stands around 25 inches tall with a head diameter of about 17 inches, although this can vary, with a heavier drum used in stationary orchestral settings and the lighter versions being portable for the farming community p'ungmul music and dance tradition. It is played in a horizontal position slung across the player's chest when in procession or upon the floor if seated. The two membranes are held together by V-shaped ropes and buffs, and depending upon its application is played with both the hands or with sticks, sometimes with two different thicknesses of membranes to aid tonal variation, while being treated to complex rhythms by the performer.

Leaving Korea and heading out to sea, we reach Japan. An island nation consisting of four main islands, which sit east from mainland Korea, Russia, and China, Japan has unsurprisingly been influenced by these countries. China has been a significant factor in the growth and development of Japanese music. Regarding this influence from Korea and China, "in the Soshun era (AD 588) the young men of Japan who were chosen for the musical profession, were sent to learn their art from the Koreans, and to study specially the kakko (Korean kol ko), the drum of southern China."[15] The instruments themselves were also impacted by their Chinese neighbors with basic drum designs and decoration bearing great similarity. As found in Korea, the Japanese have taken these art forms and developed them into their own, holding dear the great musical traditions of their past to this day.

Their musical genres include dance music, folksong, the ancient court music gagaku and Noh theater. Flutes, zithers, and lutes are integral to Japanese music, but drums also play a very important role.

Humans have populated the Japanese archipelago for around 100,000 years, but "until the introduction of agriculture and the use of iron tools and weapons around 300 B.C., people residing on that northeastern appendage to the Asian continent had made only slight progress towards civilisation."[16] This supports suggestions that music was present in Japan as early as the 3rd century BCE,[17] and enhanced further when "in the chronicles of the Wei dynasty of 3rd-century China, we find an account of a visit to the islands of Japan that includes a mention of music, dancing and singing as part of a funeral wake."[18]

As Japan began to progress in civilization and imperial rule was created, court music had already appeared, certainly existent in the 5th century CE.[19] Due to a lack of earlier Japanese written language, we turn to archaeology for evidence. Even here there is not an abundance of early evidence. Two haniwa figures at the Tokyo National Museum exist from the Kofun period, a time of increased contact with Korea and China. Although headless, these male figures are clearly playing drums, one depicting a barrel drum being beaten with a stick. This early archaeological evidence is from the 6th century CE, a period when Buddhism was only just starting to appear in Japan. In fact Buddhism has had a huge effect on music since the 6th century, where the drum is thought to represent the voice of Buddha. Drums also hold meaning in the indigenous Shinto beliefs whereby they contain a spirit that can communicate with animals. Drums were also used at weddings, funerals, in secular use to motivate warriors in battle, and festive celebrations.

As well as the religious music, folk music, and court styles such as gagaku orchestral music, Japan also saw the rise of drama and the music that accompanied it. One famous example is the Noh theater, which was established in the 14th century, having evolved from previous theatrical forms. The musical ensemble in Noh theater is known as hayashi, and within it are three drum types. The ō-tsuzumi is an hourglass hip drum played with the hands, the smaller ko-tsuzumi is a hand drum, which is held on the shoulder, and the taiko stick drum is set upon a small stand and beaten with two thick sticks.

The use of these drums varies dramatically to those, for example, of Africa or South America, where maximum tonal variety is sought from each drum with multiple techniques and sound-producing areas of the drum being exploited, or India's intricate drumming systems. Here the drums are used for just a single tone, and sometimes that tone is even used sparingly. In this way maximum drama and effect is achieved from minimal notes, and

Japanese taiko performance, www.rhythmuseum.com.

we find that improvisation is rare in many Japanese musical forms. Although minimal notes may be played, the way in which they are played is very important, with incredibly exaggerated and dramatic movements employed. Playing styles may contrast with Western ideas about good technique, as we find stiff forearms as opposed to loose Western wrists, and digging into the membrane rather than Westerners seeking immediate rebound. This helps achieve staccato notes, which are desired in some circumstances.

Much of the traditional music is passed down aurally, maintaining an element of secrecy so that only those taught by the relevant teachers can understand.

In the 16th-century Momoyama period drum making was
considered a high art form from which drums came with beautiful lacquered black shells, bright with golden floral decoration and
geometric shapes. At this time, playing drums was considered a
gentlemanly pursuit, and many aristocrats and high-ranking military
officials can be seen in paintings from this period playing drums
and dancing at parties. A 17th-century example at the Tokyo National Museum is called *Merry Making under Aronia-Blossoms* by
Kano Naganobu, which shows a taiko in the left hand and a stick
in the right hand of a well-dressed dancer at a party of samurais and
other aristocracy.

The drums that became common in Japan were varied as a
result of their mixed origins, and we find both rope tensioned and
nailed membranes across several different forms of drum. Here
the rope-tensioned drums often consist of a membrane attached to
a metal ring that has a larger diameter than the drum shell itself,
causing the membrane to stick out further than the drum. Rope
then connects both membranes along the length of the shell via
Y- or W-shaped systems. More ropes are then tied around the waist
of the drum, pulling on these vertical ropes, which in turn applies
pressure to the membrane.

Probably the most internationally recognizable drum is the
taiko, which is a generic word for drum, or fat drum, in Japan, although when used with a prefix the T becomes a D to form daiko.
Taiko has become recognized, however, as the barrel drums that
are numerous throughout Japan. This drum has been used in court
music, theater, religious processions, and battlefield signaling, although it became so respected that only specially permitted holy
men could play the drums during special occasions at the temples
and shrines. Despite this, by the mid-20th century, taiko ensembles
began to appear, allowing amateurs and professionals alike to play
the drums, which have since become very popular. In reference to
the war drum usage, we also find numerous works of art depicting
a cockerel resting atop a taiko. This signified peace, as the cock
would never rest on a war drum that was in action. One example
is the 1826 painting by Totoya Hokkei titled *The Cock and the Admonishing Drum.*

The Cock and the Admonishing Drum by Totoya Hokkei, 1826 CE, Japanese war drum during peaceful times. Painting by Totoya Hokkei.

As a general term, there are different categories of taiko that encompass the barrel and hourglass drums. The first major category is byou-daiko, which consists of drums with tacked membranes. These cannot be tuned but are very popular and contain the sub-category nagado taiko, which is the common barrel-shaped drum seen in a majority of modern ensemble applications. The other major category is the shim-daiko drums, which have rope-tensioned membranes and therefore can be tuned.

Of the rope-tensioned barrel drums we find the kakko, which is a small, double-headed barrel drum that acts as the lead drum in the tōgaku form of gagaki accompanied by a hanging barrel drum with a tacked membrane known as tsuridaiko, and a gong known as shōko. It rests on a wooden frame in a horizontal position allowing both heads to be beaten. These heads are stretched taut across a metal frame and then positioned across the drum shell, tied with ropes along the length of the body. This drum leads the tempo of the pieces with several different strokes, including double-handed rolls.

Another very striking gagaku instrument is the enormous da-daiko, which sits in an ornate frame with the drum skin at about head height while the frame towers up over the player, who beats it with lacquered beaters. Its two heads stretch out on metal rings beyond the circumference of the shell and are laced together along the length of the shell while another lacing system encircles those laces around the circumference, applying pressure to the vertical laces and, in turn, the membranes. Due to its large size, it lacks tonal quality but makes up with its sheer presence and psychological dominance. The drum is incredibly beautiful in the frame, which is bursting with color and shapes while set upon a painted wooden platform. These drums are generally used in pairs, the left-sided drum having a red painted body, two dragons carved into the body, and a sun ornament at the top while the right-sided drum has a green body, two phoenix carved into the body, and a moon ornament above.

Similar to the da-daiko is the ni-daiko, which is a smaller version, carried on poles by two men. This portability allows it to be played in procession

The taiko of Noh theater (known as geza-daiko or uta-daiko) is often quite small, such as an example at the MFA, which is around 3.5 inches high and nearly 8 inches in diameter. This small 19th-century taiko with Y-shaped lacing is a very austere example. A second lacing system is bound horizontally around the vertical ropes, which allows the low wooden stand to support the drum on these ropes without impeding the resonance of the shell. While the shell is often made of zelkova wood, the skins are usually cow or horse with the top thicker than the bottom. A circle of deerskin is sometimes placed at the point of contact on the upper skin. The performer kneels to play the top membrane with sticks known as bachi as he performs the set rhythms, which are prescribed to accompany particular dances. Although these patterns, and those of the other Noh instruments, can be notated for learning, they are numerous and often vary between the musical instrument guilds who teach their students by rote over a lengthy period in order to fully master the repertoire and nuances involved. A level of secrecy may be maintained within each guild so that the specifics of their playing become esoteric.

When considering the nailed heads found on barrel drums, we come across the o-daiko. This is a huge, barrel-shaped Shinto temple drum that is set upon a wooden frame with a diameter of up to 40 inches and similar in length. However, this can exceed these dimensions in special circumstances, such as the drum made for the Festival Forest Art Museum in Takayama City, which has a head diameter of more than 80 inches and 100 inches at the widest part of the barrel. It sets upon a wooden stand with wheels that have disc brakes to cope with the colossal 4-ton drum. Here they boast to have the world's largest drum. As well as being a temple drum and museum piece, this drum occasionally makes appearances in orchestral pieces.

The ko-daiko is a smaller processional and orchestral variation of its larger sibling. Another smaller barrel drum with nailed heads is the tsuri-daiko, a gagaki drum that uses only one head for playing while it is beaten with two leather-covered sticks. The highly decorated skin is tacked onto the lacquered body, which rests on a stand or hangs from a frame. A second drummer simultaneously beats the shell with sticks. Techniques comparable to Western rudiments are used on this drum, such as the flam.

Of these ancient instruments, one of the most respected taiko manufacturers is Asano Taiko, which has been in business since 1609 CE.

Hourglass drums are also common throughout Japan. Just as with taiko, tsuzumi is a generic word for drum, although it usually denotes an hourglass drum, whereas taiko is used for barrel and cylinder drums. Tsuzumi is a family of hourglass drums that most likely derived from the Korean changgo. These small hourglass drums are used in Noh drama with cherry or zelkana wood shells, which are lacquered on the outside and skillfully carved on the inside. They are double headed, with the two heads stretched around iron rings that are wider than the shell of the drum. Rope systems tension the two heads together. They are played with the hands, held in position with one head facing toward the player's face and the other head toward the floor. One hand plays the drum while the other clenches the ropes to vary the pitch of the drum. The shell slots between the heads and is dismantled between performances, reassembled for each new performance in a ritualistic manner. The Japanese drum kit manufacturer Pearl replicated this concept in their 20th-century free-floating snare drums. Here the heads are attached by tension rods that connect to each other, leaving the shell free from any hardware contact and therefore avoiding resonance impedance.

Returning to traditional drums, the ko-tsuzumi was very popular in Noh theater and the Momoyama period in which drum making was at a very high standard. Although deriving from Korean-inspired drums, these have evolved into their own recognized and distinguished Japanese form. Unlike some other Japanese drums, the internal carving of these drums was considered very important to the tone of the final product. These hourglass drums were around 10 inches in length and 8 inches in diameter, although the resonating chamber was less wide with the membrane stretched across metal rings protruding beyond the circumference of the shell. The two membranes were rope tensioned, bound together along the length of the shell. It is hung across the shoulder and beaten by the bare hand on one head. The ō-tsuzumi was similar in design, although slightly larger and held against the left hip while the right hand beat it using finger techniques. These heads are actually heated prior to performance to achieve a brighter, drier tone, and papier maché thimbles are sometimes worn on the performer's fingertips to further enhance this.

Within Noh they generally play set patterns containing eight beats, but not always, with specifically placed accents and vocal shouts between the beats. The two tsuzumi drums may play exactly the same rhythm or two different but related rhythms.

Another drum from this category is the san no tsuzumi, which is used in the komagaku form of gagaku where we also find a tsuri-daiko and a shōko. Here the san no tsuzumi is the lead instrument, playing a similar role to that of the kakko in tōgaku, as discussed, although it is larger than that drum and only one head is played. The ikko is also an hourglass drum used in gagaku. This drum hangs around the player's neck and is played while dancing.

Not only do the Japanese maintain these old traditions with pride, they actively promote them across the world, ensuring that international recognition of their art forms is greater now than ever before. This is achieved through the numerous touring groups throughout Japan and now based in many Western countries, the

Tsuzumi family, www.rhythmuseum.com.

most famous being the Kodo drummers taiko ensemble, which was founded in 1981. Beyond their own traditional drumming art forms, the Japanese have made great impact on the Western drum kit. Since the mid-20th century, Japanese companies dominated the market for drum kits, overtaking competition from England to America with success stories such as Pearl, Yamaha, and Mapex, as discussed in chapter 12.

NOTES

1. Eva Jane Neumann Fridman and Mariko Namba Walter, *Shamanism: An encyclopedia of world beliefs, practices, and culture*. (Santa Barbara, CA: ABC-CLIO, inc, 2004), 102.

2. Reginald Massey and Jamila, *The music of India* (New Delhi, India: Abhinav Publications, 1996), 11.

3. R. K. Pruthi, *Indus civilization* (New Delhi, India: Discovery Publishing House, 2004), 75.

4. Ananda W. W. Guruge, *The society of the Rāmāyana* (New Delhi, India: Shakti Malik Abhinav Publications, 1991), 179.

5. Massey et al., *The music of India*, 19.

6. Curt Sachs, *The history of musical instruments* (New York: Norton, 1940), 230.

7. James Blades, *Percussion instruments and their history* (London, UK: Faber & Faber, Ltd, 1970), 138.

8. Robert S. Gottlieb, *Solo tabla drumming of North India: Its repertoire, styles, and performance practices* (Delhi, India: Motilal Banarsidass Publishers Private Limited, 1993), 2.

9. Blades, *Percussion instruments and their history*, 136.

10. Christina Pratt, *An encyclopedia of shamanism, Volume 1* (New York: The Rosen Publishing Group, Inc., 2007), 282.

11. Blades, *Percussion instruments and their history*, 113.

12. Xing Ruan, *Allegorical architecture: Living myth and architectonics in southern China* (Honolulu, Hawai'i: University of Hawai'i Press, 2006), 102.

13. Wolfram Eberhard, *The local cultures of south and east China* (Leiden, The Netherlands: E. J. Brill, 1968), 363.

14. Keith Pratt and Richard Rutt, *Korea: A historical and cultural dictionary* (Richmond, Surrey, UK: Curzon Press, 1999), 107–108.

15. Blades, *Percussion instruments and their history*, 122.

16. Donald H. Shively and William H. McCullough, eds., *The Cambridge history of Japan, Volume 2* (Cambridge, UK: Cambridge University Press, 1993), xv.

17. Elizabeth May, ed., *Musics of many cultures: An introduction* (Berkeley and Los Angeles, CA: University of Californian Press, 1980), 48.

18. William P. Malm, *Traditional Japanese music and musical instruments, Volume 1* (Tokyo: Kodansha International Ltd, 2000), 31.

19. May, *Musics of many cultures: An introduction*, 48.

Chapter Nine

Southeast Asia

SOUTHEAST ASIAN MUSIC AND THE PERCUSSION within it appear exciting and exotic to the West, while at the same time confusing. The names and terminologies often vary from one region to another, while the same word may be used for two different instruments in different regions. Therefore, this chapter offers examples of the relevant drums to attempt to describe the drumming cultures and how they arrived. It is far from comprehensive in giving every permutation of each drum's name, nor could it possibly describe every single variation of each drum type.

Southeast Asian culture has allowed an interesting syncretic musical landscape to develop with instruments from China adding to the Hindu-Buddhist culture, which also absorbed Indian cultural influences in early CE before Islam significantly settled around the 13th century and then European influences from the 16th century. Although early Western travelers to the region belittled the area as an accessory to India and China, offering names such as Indo-China or the East Indies, Southeast Asia does in fact have a very interesting culture of its own with very distinctive musical elements. However, and possibly unsurprisingly, Southeast Asian drumming owes much to Chinese influence, and the nailed heads seen on many of the drums are testament to this, although many are also laced, as seen in India.

But we do find that Southeast Asia already had the ability to forge iron and bronze instruments to use in their musical and theatrical art forms for many years in their significantly advanced autonomous societies, occurring separately from Indian or Chinese influence. They were later very successful at adopting outside influences and integrating them with these indigenous activities, resulting in an evolution of those influences until they were very much unique and distinctive to Southeast Asia again.

Often the drumming is dictated by rhythmic cycles, in a similar way to Indian music with percussion marking the beginning of each new cycle, such as the cymbals in Cambodia or Burma, and slit drums in Vietnam. However, the cycles are generally duple or quadruple, thus avoiding the complex and diverse cycles of Indian music.

But despite these Indian and Chinese influences, they may not have been the original designers: "The frame drum originated in the Middle East, where it was also used to accompany Islamic religious chanting."[1] This is supported further with the Malaysian rebana, described as "a pair of tambourine like instruments of foreign Muslim origin."[2] It is true that a great deal of influence arrived in this area along with Islam as well as Christians, Hindus, and Buddhists, all of whom contributed to the syncretic art forms that evolved in much of Southeast Asia.

The drums in Southeast Asia are often played alongside gongs, and this is seen with frame drums, which are found in mobile ensembles such as in Java, where pot-shaped gongs are beaten with a stick upon the central boss while frame drums are played with the hand.

Of these frame drums, the Indonesians possess a tambourine known as the terbang, which was used in traditional Javanese Muslim–influenced music known as terbangan. It is played with the hands in the traditional grip by men, achieving tonal variety with different parts of the hand playing the drum as well as using muting techniques while the players accompany themselves with Arabic song. It features a single membrane tacked onto the slightly bowl-shaped wooden shell, which is highly decorated with such designs as floral paintings. The diameter is around 10 to 12 inches, and several metal jingles are set into the frame. The same drum is known as the rebana kercing in Malaysia. In fact rebana is a general term for certain drums in Malaysia, many of which are frame drums, and the kercing suffix specifically denotes the use of jingles.

The rebana penganak, and the almost-identical rebana pening-kah, are smaller frame drums, which are played with the fingers in pairs. They are used in such groups as the mekmulung ensembles, which create folk song entertainment through their dance and drama–oriented displays in Kedah, Malaysia. These drums combine with a pair of larger frame drums (rebana ibu), singers, gongs, and clappers. They are instruments of a single goat membrane laced and secured beneath the jackfruit wooden drum. Wooden wedges are also utilized to increase tension. The smaller examples have a diameter of 12 inches, while the rebana ibu has a 24-inch diameter.

Another example, the rebana ubi, is not a frame drum but rather a large conical drum approximately 20 inches tall and 28 inches in diameter. It can sit on the floor or hang suspended vertically from a frame. These are often played in ensembles, the different drums playing in unison. Wooden tuning arms appearing like wheel spokes numbering around fifteen and about 16 inches long fan out around the circumference of the shell at the base, while a water buffalo membrane is secured to the upper opening with thick lacing sewn through it and attached to the wooden base. The shell and edge of the membrane are highly decorated with painted floral patterns. This drum is often played at celebrations and social events or used in competition with ensembles from neighboring villages following the rice harvest. It is usually used in groups of more than six drums with a pair of drummers striking each drum alternately. It is played outdoors with bare hands and a padded beater, with each pair playing a set ostinato while one drum has slightly more freedom, playing a syncopated pattern.

There exists another rebana, known as rebana besar, of even larger proportions, which is heard within the Islamic praise and festive celebration music known as zikir, found in numerous forms and utilizing various ensembles. One form of zikir is the vocal tradition of Kelantan, which sees the singers accompanying themselves with the rebana besar. Similar to the rebana ubi, the rebana besar is a very large conical drum of more than 40 inches in height and around 40 inches in diameter. Its single water-buffalo membrane connects via ropes to a wooden brace at the base of the drum with wooden wedges forced between the shell and the brace, as seen on many other drums in this chapter. The drum is suspended from a rope in a vertical position so that the player is face on to the membrane, which he beats with bare hands. Like the rebana ubi, this drum features wooden arms around the base, which jut outward.

But returning to the frame drum, it is known in some regions of Sumatra as the rapa'i. Here the rapa'i holds huge importance as connected with religion and the shaman. These might be used to accompany religious songs or beaten for hours in praise of God during times of trouble. They can range from 40 inches in diameter down to just 20 inches.

The classical music of Thailand and Cambodia makes use of the rammana, a frame drum that bears similarity to the Indonesian terbang. It can be played alone or with the accompaniment of the thon, which is a goblet drum played by the same player or a separate one. High-pitched rim sounds and low-pitched slaps are some of the techniques that suggest an Arabic influence, as does the thon itself, which resembles the darabukka. This drum is either ceramic (mahori) or wooden (chatri), with the thon chatri displaying a ring below the bowl-shaped round chamber to which lacing is tied from the membrane to achieve tension. It is played with a single bare hand while the other hand manipulates the tone by covering the open end. The rammana itself is wooden, with a single membrane that is nailed onto the head as seen in Chinese drums. In this pair the thon is considered the wife and the ramana the husband. Another drum that is used in Cambodia is the skor yike, a frame drum with a single crocodile or ox membrane. It is played within the yike ensemble, which features seven skor yike drums and a single skor chey, a conical drum that is played by the ensemble lead drummer. One other Cambodian frame drum is the rumanea, which is played with the thaun as mentioned below.

The Malay kompang is a similar drum to the Indonesian terbang or rapa'i, being a slightly bowl-shaped frame drum with a single head tacked onto the wooden shell. It arrived in Malay territory having traveled with Arabic traditions, which began to appear in the 13th century BCE. The drum was initially used for secular activities but was later employed to accompany Islamic poetry and readings. The playing technique is also reminiscent of the Arabic world, with dum and tak sounds achieved with the fingers and palm. Today such frame drums are very important in these countries, and in Malaysia many kompang ensembles exist, which feature right through school and beyond, involving groups of drummers. Some of the drum ensembles began in an agricultural form, arising from the repetitive rhythmic motions that manual labor can produce. Today these ensembles also appear at events such as weddings and other celebrations, where they play powerful rhythms in unison with each other. Four different drum sections make up this ensemble, each with different roles and interwoven rhythmic patterns.

Away from these secular uses, the rebana besar, as mentioned previously, also appears in a small ensemble for the religious singing of zikir.

Similar ensembles to the kompang exist in Brunei, where they use a small frame drum called the tar in their hadrah ensembles as well as a gendang peningkah, which is without jingles. They accompany religious songs at such events as circumcision rites and weddings with rhythms that are interwoven around each other. In Singapore there exists the Hadrah and Kompang Association. The hadrah grew from religious songs and thus has only existed in this form since the inception of Islam.

But heading into Myanmar (formerly Burma), it becomes clear that Southeast Asia offers much more beyond the frame drum. As a country that shares borders with India and China, two great nations that have impacted much of Southeast Asia's culture, Burma's music traditions show comparatively little sign of such insemination. Siamese (modern Thai) influences are perceptible, but Burma remains distinct in its evolution of any external influence.

Burma has faced a varied and complex history with a string of different inhabitants from around Southeast Asia. Early sources demonstrate the use of Burmese music from 800 CE with Chinese Tang Dynasty documents describing a group of musicians sent to a Chinese court with fourteen different groups of instruments.

With their various groups of instruments, percussion features prominently and takes a strong role within their various ensembles. This is seen in the lively, raucous outdoor ensembles but less so in the quiet, elegant indoor chamber music. The outdoor types often feature drums and gongs such as the hsain ensemble, which accompanies religious events as well as theatrical performance. Two important features of this are the gong circle and drum circle. The drum circle may be Indian in origin and takes the head position in the group, with the drummer as the ensemble leader. Known as the pa'wain, it traditionally consisted of nineteen cylindrical drums (although modern versions might have twenty-one) hung on cords within a wooden circular frame, which stands 40 inches tall with the player inside the circle. The double-headed drums, varying between 5 and 17 inches tall, are positioned vertically and tuned to specific notes by way of a paste made from rice and ash so that a degree of melody may be achieved on the range of around three octaves as the upper membranes are beaten with bare hands.

Beyond the drum and gong circle, the ensemble also presents the large, highly decorated, double-headed barrel drum known as pa'ma, which hangs horizontally from a wooden support. This is accompanied by the sakhun, which rests horizontally upon a rack. Other similar drums complete this set as they stand vertically on one membrane with the remaining membrane beaten with the hands. Although the heads are secured with strips of hide, these drums are tuned to fit with the mode of the piece using the same paste as previously mentioned. A large range of usage is achieved between these drums, with the larger ones playing fewer notes but holding the rhythm down while the smaller, higher-pitched drums play more notes and contribute to melody as much as rhythm.

The largest Burmese drum is the important sito, which at 50 inches long and 20 inches in diameter enjoys connections with royalty as it performs at court ceremonies; it has done so since at least as far back as the early 12th century. Despite having two membranes, only one side is struck with a stick.

Another stick-beaten drum is the double-headed byo, which is seen in pairs at religious ceremonies accompanied by other drums, oboes, and cymbals. The doupa is similar to the byo, although smaller at around 30 inches long. The two membranes are slightly different in size, with the larger one tuned to the fundamental pitch and the smaller one tuned slightly higher by way of paste. These hang from the neck across the chest in a horizontal position at village festivities and are often accompanied by improvised vocal parts, cymbals, and oboes. The larger bounci drums of around 40 inches long also hang across the chest when played at festivities in pairs.

A common drum that resembles those of Arabic origin is the ozi. The National Music Museum (NMM) in Vermillion, South Dakota, and the Museum of Fine Arts in Boston (MFA) both possess beautiful examples of the ozi, which was a tall, elegant goblet drum of around 30 inches in height and 9 inches in diameter. The single head was attached via numerous strips of hide that entirely covered the resonating chamber of the drum, connecting to a ring beneath the bulbous shell with the curving, elongated base stretching out below. A tuning paste was also applied to this drum to achieve a desirable tone when it was played at the player's chest, hung from a cord around his or her neck at processions. Several drums might be adorned simultaneously by the performer, who may dress in bright colors and decorate the drum with colored skirts hanging from around the membrane's diameter as they dance, sing, and play.

Heading southeast to Thailand, we find a music culture that was largely derived from China, where these people most likely emigrated from. The Cambodian Khmer people in the southeast also brought influence with possible Indian origins. Written evidence of Thai music only dates back to the 14th century, and earlier depictions on tombs and temples are sadly few. Similarly aged depictions include a rubbing of a stone carving from the Sukhothai period (13th to 15th centuries) that features drums.[3]

The four regions that have emerged to create modern-day Thailand enjoy distinct musical cultures, which make use of human theater, shadow puppet theater, classical court music, dances, and lighthearted rural courting songs. Music is generally ensemble and contrasts with the individual complexities or improvisation found in Indian music. Within these ensembles, beyond the lutes, zithers,

flutes, and melodic percussion instruments of metallophones, xylophones, and gong chimes, drums were used extensively with barrel
and goblet drums dominating.

In general the drums that came to Thailand from the Khmer
people are wooden barrel drums that use lacing to tension the
heads, whereas drums of Chinese origin often use pegs or nails.

Used in pī phāt ensembles and having slight sacred connotations, the taphon is a popular double-headed barrel drum of possible Indian origin and closely linked to the Cambodian sampho.
Similar drums also appear in reliefs at Angkor Wat. The membranes
are sewn to a ring of twisted cane at each end of the shell with
leather thongs connecting them so numerously that they cover
the entire shell. The drum is played horizontally, either hung from
the player's neck or upon a stand. Tuning paste and sap are used
for tuning, with one head larger than the other, the larger 10-inch
membrane on the left and the smaller 9-inch membrane on the
right. While the taphon is around 19 inches long, a larger version
of around 30 inches long and with diameters of 20 inches and 15
inches is known as taphon mawn.

The klōng that is a double-headed barrel drum from classical
music with identically sized heads of around 18 inches in diameter
that are nailed onto the wooden shell. The drum is positioned with
one head against the ground tilted at an angle and supported on
a frame of crossed poles. The drum is beaten with two padded
bamboo sticks in such instances as the pī phāt ensemble. It often
appeared singularly within the ensemble until more recent times,
when it would come as a pair sometimes with paste applied to the
batter head for tuning options, the higher-pitched drum being male
and the lower one female.

The klōng khaek is a type of barrel drum with an off-center
bulge in the body, which is very similar to the Indian mridangam
and Malaysian gendang mentioned below, but often comes in
pairs in Thailand to accompany boxing matches as well as the
classical mahori music. The higher-pitched drum is considered
male while the deeper one is female, and it takes two performers
to fully exploit the sounds of the four available membranes. A
smaller klōng with the suffix chātrī is found in the traveling theatrical art form lakhōn chātrī.

As well as these barrel drums, we find the boeng mang, a double-headed cylindrical drum 21.5 inches long and around 7 inches in diameter, which was used in processions. It is also seen in pī phāt mawn, often heard at funerals, in a set of seven drums hung vertically in a semicircular frame. Paste is applied to the heads to achieve specific notes from the Thai tuning system in a similar way to the Burmese pa'wain. When used in this set, the instrument is known as boeng mang kawk.

One other processional drum worth mentioning is the klawng yao, a long, single-headed goblet drum. It is generally played with the bare hands, although skilled players may use other body parts as the drum hangs from their neck on a strap. A short fabric skirt hangs from the bottom of the membrane, which is lace tensioned to the drum, and a paste is applied for tuning. As the ensemble may feature several such drums as well as other percussion, the tuning of each drum must relate to one another. One of the other drums seen here is a large rammana that is suspended within a wooden frame, held by two men who move around as the drummer follows them beating it with a stick, and even athletically hurls his body parts into it.

As mentioned, the goblet drum known as thon is popular in Thailand and is often accompanied by the rammana. These goblet drums bear great resemblance to Western Asian goblet drums, possibly arriving in Southeast Asia with Islam. These are seen in such contexts as the khlui (flute), krajappī (lute), and sō sām sāi (bowed string instrument) ensemble, which also uses a rammana. These goblet drums were often highly decorated with glass and jewels upon the shell and a snakeskin upon the upper opening. Exclusively female ensembles of this kind exist in which the performers dress in beautifully elaborate costumes with jeweled headwear with matching neck, wrist, and arm pieces and silk dresses. The playing styles seen today are consistent with those already mentioned in earlier depictions from the Sukhothai period, which demonstrates the retention of ancient traditions.

Arriving in Cambodia, the largest ethnic majority is the Khmer people, but once again, the musical cultures of the Khmer and other people of Cambodia's population don't always pay strict attention to the political boundaries of a country. Within the Khmer people we find court music, folk music, dance, theater, and ceremonial music, which has grown from Indian and then later Chinese and other influences, being absorbed and altered to meet their needs. Indian culture pervaded Cambodia in early CE, and musical evidence from before that time is scarce. This is partly due to the fact that music has always been passed from master to student by rote without the need of documentation. It is also in part due to events such as the ransacking of major dwellings such as Angkor several hundred years ago and the oppression of arts and culture in the 20th century. However, the 12th-century temple of Angkor is a survivor of the Khmer civilization's pinnacle. Here we see depictions of harps, oboes, gongs, cymbals, and barrel drums upon a huge bas relief in the western gallery of Angkor Wat, which displays the Battle of Kurukshetra, suggesting a military musical usage. The battle in question took place somewhere between a wildly large and inaccurate period of nearly six thousand years BCE depending on which author is believed, but the 12th-century CE Angkor Wat depiction is of course no evidence that these drums were really used in this way back then.

What we do know is that Cambodian drums fall into the struck instruments category known as kroeung damm and the term for the drum is skor, which appears as a prefix to most drums. The Khmer people of modern-day Cambodia possessed various drums, which they used for musical accompaniment, devoid of any spiritual power.

Barrel drums were popular as mentioned on the temple reliefs, and the skor yol, also known as skor klang khek, is possibly the double-headed barrel drum as seen at Angkor Wat hanging from the player's neck and being beaten with bare hands. Other than the suggested military use, another use for it is as a funeral drum in an ensemble with oboes. The greater the social standing of the deceased, the more drums are used in the ensemble. These double-headed conical drums utilize lacing for tension.

The skor thomm was the largest drum type, consisting of a large, barrel-shaped shell with an ox or buffalo membrane nailed on each end, generally played in pairs. As well as festive and general entertainment use, these also played a role within society to make announcements or call people together, and similarly in the military as signal drums. Consisting of a shell 20 inches long with 16-inch head diameters, the membranes are pegged or nailed to the shell with different tension so that one produces a higher sound than the other. They hang from a metal ring attached to the shell.

Another barrel drum is the sampho, which just like the Thai taphon, has one head slightly larger than the other to achieve a high and low tone, both tightened with rattan strips and tuned with an applied paste. This enables four distinct sounds, with each drum allowing two muted and unmuted sounds. Although small at less than 20 inches long and around 11 and 10 inches in head diameters, it is the most important drum in Khmer music as the leader of the pinn peat ensemble and the only one that has spiritual importance. It is played with bare hands in a horizontal position on a wooden stand.

As well as barrel drums, we find that wooden or clay goblet drums with a single reptile or calfskin were common for spiritual ceremony as well as functional ceremonies such as weddings. These drums were known as skor arakk. Another goblet-type drum was the skor chhaiyaim, although it featured a smooth, curving shell more vaselike than goblet. A decorative skirt sometimes hung from just below the single membrane, which featured a paste of rice, ash, and water in the center. It was played at events such as religious festivities, usually by men, and hung around the player's shoulder while they wore humorous clown masks on their faces as they danced and played. The drums are usually seen in groups of four, with two projecting a higher-pitched tone and two providing the lower pitch.

Just as with the Thai thon and rammana combination, the Khmer possessed the thaun, which was a smaller version of the skor arakk used in the mahori along with the previously mentioned rumanea frame drum. The thaun lies horizontally on the drummer's lap as he uses his right-hand fingers while the rumanea sits upon the left leg and is played with the fingers of the left hand.

A great deal of Vietnam's musical instruments also arrived from China, some originating in Central Asia and many modern examples from European colonization. However, prehistoric art forms, particularly music and dance from Vietnam's Dong Son period, are clearly evident.

Vocal music is significant in most performances, but drums are numerous, with many variations in name, shape, and size between different regions. The generic name for a drum is trong, and this is usually a prefix on all drum names.

The trong com is a cylindrical drum that is similar to the Indian mridangam in appearance, with two membranes laced together along the length of the drum. A rice paste is applied to the heads, which tunes the drums a fifth apart.

Buddhist monks use drums such as the trong bat nah at ceremonies or the trong bung, which the monk carries through an attached strap in one hand while the other hand beats the two heads with a stick. The trong dao is also used by monks to accompany chants.

Other drums are used for entertainment such as the trong chien, a theatrical war drum, or the trong nhac and trong ban, which pair together in ensembles to provide a high and low pitch between them.

One drum that omits the trong prefix is the single-headed ensemble drum known as bong. Its snake membrane is tensioned with cord to the small, pottery, hourglass-shaped shell.

Another drum that does feature the designation trong but is from a different classification in the Sachs-Hornbostel system is the idiophone trong dong or bronze drum. Although not membranophones, these prehistoric instruments are thought of as drums and are worthy of a mention due to their ancient history and association with Vietnam.

Bronze metallurgy in mainland Southeast Asia dates back to the 3rd millennium BCE and the Dong Son bronze drums date to at least early BCE and possibly much earlier.[4] The drums may have originated in Northern Vietnam where a large concentration of such items have been found in the Bac Bo region, although they have also been found in China, Burma, Thailand, Malaysia, Laos, and Indonesia. Due to the unconfirmed origin of the drums, agreed dating of the drums is also often in dispute as the Vietnamese and Chinese vie for the claim of originators. Since 1902 these drums have been classified in four categories known as Heger I to IV, based on size, weight, shape, design, production methods, and chemical composition. The general characteristics include being cast in bronze using the lost wax casting method with a flat top sitting upon vertical sides, which formed a circular body, although sometimes splayed at the top and the base. The shell was hollow with an exterior highly decorated in symbolism and iconography. The top and sides often displayed concentric circles, geometric shapes, and always a star in the top center. Anthropomorphic and zoomorphic designs were also popular as well as battle scenes, domestic duties, and rituals. This information makes the drums a great source of how life was in that time, as depictions such as weapons and warfare suggest large militaristic activity. One Burmese example is that known as the Pazi frog drum at the Victoria and Albert Museum in London, dating from the 19th century and standing 20 inches tall. It is decorated with animals such as elephants, birds, fish, and also geometric shapes. It also boasts three frogs, one upon another, positioned equidistantly at four points (totaling twelve) around the upper circumference of the drum. This could suggest a use connected with rainmaking rituals.

The Dian culture of Chinese Yunnan, which was very close to the Don Song culture, possessed very similar bronze drums, which have thrown up evidence regarding the usage: "Chinese archaeologists have studied scraping marks on the inside of Dian drums and believe that they are the result of tuning. All this suggests that individual drums were manufactured to conform to a specific pitch and that several drums could be, and were, combined into ensembles."[5]

Each drum used an enormous amount of raw materials to produce, and therefore great skill and cost would have been required to manufacture such a drum. It is reasonable then to assume that they were created for men of power, although whether they were individually owned or community owned is disputable. The drums have been depicted in ensemble usage in such scenes as with warriors on their way into battle and during instances of human sacrifice. In these scenes people are sitting on the floor and beating the drums with sticks while dancers circle around. The drums were sometimes positioned slightly off the ground and over a hole to increase resonance. The drums are found at least in sizes up to 27 inches tall and 36 inches in diameter.

Thai bronze drum, www.rhythmuseum.com.

Away from the mainland we find the Southeast Asian islands, which display diverse and interesting music influenced by many different religions and cultures blended with their traditional art forms.

The indigenous Filipinos enjoyed the sounds of drums, gongs, zithers, clappers, and flutes long before European colonization began, although since the 16th century significant Spanish attributes have pervaded much of the Philippines' own art forms. They used music for festivities and religious ceremony, and although they possessed drums, it was the bronze gong that took precedent and dominated their music. Of the drums used, the Sulu people of the southern Philippines enjoyed a sturdy wooden goblet drum of around 20 inches in height and around 12 inches in diameter.

Some floral carving existed on the shell below where the single membrane was tied through material counter hoops and secured with metal nails. A huge example from the 20th century exists at the NMM. This wooden goblet drum with intricate Islamic carvings across much of the shell stands 8 feet tall with a single membrane attached via two rings holding it tight.

As the southernmost point of mainland Southeast Asia, peninsular Malaysia has seen many different people arrive with their various cultural contributions, as has East Malaysia, which is part of Borneo, with neighbors Indonesia and Brunei. Invaders and traders alike have marched or sailed through, many staying and bringing with them their beliefs, customs, and musical traditions so that the indigenous Orang asli population absorbed Hinduism and Buddhism from Indians; Islam from Arabia; Christianity from Europe; and then the Chinese and others to create a truly syncretic land.

Music has many purposes here such as for theater, dance, healing, accompanying storytelling, accompanying martial arts, festivities, court ceremony, and religious events. Of the theater, puppet shadow plays are popular, employing melodic instruments such as the lute, Thai fiddles, and oboes, along with a narrator of the play and then percussion instruments to provide rhythm. Cymbals and gongs are ubiquitous, as with much of Southeast Asia, but the drum is also very popular. The two main drum types here are the barrel or cylindrical drum known as gendang and the frame drum, already discussed, known as rebana.

The gendang is a large, rope-tensioned, double-headed, barrel-shaped drum that is similar to other Malay barrel drums with the membranes secured by ropes. The ropes are positioned in Y shapes running the length of the drum to connect both skins via a section of bound cord around the circumference of the shell to hold it in place. It is likely of Indian descent, with similarities to the pakhavaj. A Thai version has also evolved, known as klawang khaek, which appears with exactly the same design and technique. Two drummers play each drum with their hands, creating syncopated rhythms, although a curved stick is sometimes used on one of the membranes. These are used in such contexts as the southern state caklempong ensembles, which are primarily gong chime groups

used for entertainment and state ceremony, accompanying dancing, processions, and martial artists. In the northern states, the
gendang silat ensemble exists to serve a similar function, consisting
of an oboe, a hanging knobbed gong, and two gendang.

Drums appear in many other gong ensembles. A double-headed
drum called the sidabat accompanies the bidayuh gong ensemble
in which the drummer uses small sticks or bare hands to produce a
rhythm while a second drummer plays a counter rhythm on another
sidabat.

The katoa is another drum that accompanies gong ensembles.
This cylindrical, single-headed drum uses the rope tensioning system that fixes to a ring positioned further down the shell. Wooden
wedges are then forced in between the fixing ring and drum shell
to achieve sufficient tension, as seen across many drums from this
part of the world. It is played with bare hands and sticks, mimicking
the rhythms of the hanging gongs.

A further example of a single-headed drum used with such
groups is found in the hanging gong ensembles of Sabah, who employ the use of the cylindrical karatung, which is not too dissimilar
to the katoa. The marwas is also a cylindrical drum, although this
shallow version is double headed with the two membranes rope tensioned together with Y-shaped systems. The membrane diameter is
as small as 6 inches with a shell depth of around 5 inches, which
makes them very portable. They are used in rural orchestras, often
alongside a conical, single-headed drum known as dok.

Barrel drums also exist, such as the geduk, a short drum that
has two membranes attached with glue and pegs while two lengths
of bamboo are fixed to one end to prop it at an appropriate angle for
performance. It is struck with a single stick in dramatic and warfar-
ing scenes of theater. Another barrel drum is the small tipung.

We also find drums from possible Arabic origin, such as the
gedumbak, which is a goblet drum similar to the Western Asian
darabukka. Its single membrane is attached with lacing and wooden
wedges for tuning while it is played with a single bare hand. The
remaining hand alters the tone by covering the open lower end of
the drum to varying degrees. This allows great expression, although
it is often used as a timekeeper in certain theater settings. In Malay
Borneo there also exists the ketubong hourglass drum.

At the southern tip of Asia, dripping down from the Malay Peninsula, we find Indonesia, which exists in the form of many islands spreading from Sumatra below peninsular Malaysia across the Java, Flores, and Banda seas to the eastern reaches of New Guinea. Just as with Malaysia, much of Indonesia has developed a syncretic culture with influences from Hinduism, Islam, Buddhism, Christianity from Europe, and secular migrants mixing with the indigenous traditions, but we also find very distinctive musical styles coming from individual islands and regions.

Therefore music is often seen within religious events, as well as shamanistic rituals. One extreme performance style is the Muslim-influenced dabus dance, which can also involve a shaman with the accompaniment of a rebana drum playing along with Arabic songs to take the performers to a state of spirituality so strong that they can endure incredibly painful acts such as cuts or burns with apparent ease.

Beyond spiritual and religious uses are the celebratory, seasonal, mourning, processional, healing, protective, theater, and general entertainment music. Within these many uses are found a diverse array of instruments, which includes a very significant drumming contingent.

Evidence of drums exists with Dong Son bronze drums as old as 1600 BCE found here.[6] Similar such evidence is seen on Sangeang Island, where a bronze drum was discovered that may have been from the 3rd century BCE. We do know that by around 250 BCE the Javanese had added a central knob to the gong, which began to be used in the gamelan as discussed below.

Certain aspects of music only appeared in Indonesia after contact with other religious groups. Religious temples and statues help give us clues as to how certain beliefs were adopted and the way in which they honored their Gods. Of the many reliefs adorning the 9th-century Buddhist monument known as Borobudur in Java, depictions of musicians are clearly evident. Within these pictures we can see musicians with bamboo flutes, gongs, lutes, and drums, such as rope-tensioned cylindrical examples. Of the drums, "They include barrel-shaped, truncated conical and cylindrical drums. The drums were often carried in a selendang (shoulder scarf)."[7] Similar evidence also exists at the 9th-century

temple Prambanan, 13th-century Singosari, and 14th-century
Panataran in Java.

Of the many situations in which Indonesian drums are found,
one of the most widely recognized is that of their most famous ensemble. As mentioned, Indonesia had developed an early craft in
metalworking in which the bronze drums and a fantastic array of
gongs were produced. Out of this craft was born the gamelan of Indonesia, which is now known internationally as the ornate percussive ensemble, sometimes of nearly one hundred instruments, that
accompanies ceremonies, puppet theater, and rituals with its mix of
gongs, xylophones, and metallophones. Variations of gamelan have
grown and evolved over time, but generally the instruments of each
gamelan are carefully tuned together and cannot be used with any
other gamelan whose tuning will differ. The majority of instruments
in gamelan ensembles are made of bronze and are tuned to specific
pitch. Furthermore, different formations and instruments are used
between different gamelan genres. Several drums, however, do exist, and they play a very important role.

Sometimes the drummer is the ensemble leader, and he commands from behind several drums, giving cues for tempo changes
and endings. In gamelan sekaton it is the bedhug that gives these
cues and instructions. This drum is a barrel-shaped instrument
with two water buffalo membranes of equal size held taut with
wooden pegs, which are driven through it and into the shell. It is
beautifully decorated with gold leaf around the shell and hangs
from a frame that is equally well decorated with carvings such as
floral designs and dragons. It is played with a padded beater. Huge
bedhugs are also found in the majority Muslim areas of Indonesia,
where they may be used to call people to prayer.

Often though, back in the gamelan, the bedhug plays more
of a supporting role to the large kendhang ageng, which leads
the gamelan. This hand drum achieves tonal variety via different
strokes, but the general sound is that of deep tones. It is a barrel-
shaped drum, which is similar to the Malaysian gendang. It has two
water buffalo membranes with one larger than the other, held taut
over the jackfruit wooden shell by way of Y-shaped rope tensioning.
The ornamentation of the drum is often a stained wooden shell with

Indonesian gamelan drums, Kendhang. Bate Collection, Oxford. Courtesy of the author.

gold leaf floral designs painted around the circumference at the top and bottom. It sits horizontally on a small wooden frame.

Other kendhang exist, such as the kendhang ketipung. This is the smallest drum found in the gamelan and is either played by the same player that used the kendhang ageng or played by a separate performer. It is played with the hands in a reserved, timekeeping manner just as the kendhang ageng is. On the other hand, the kendhang ciblon exists to allow more variety and flamboyancy in rhythm than the kandhang ageng or kendhang ketipung. In design, this is simply a smaller version of the kendhang ageng. Another medium-size kendhang is the wayang variety. This also appears as a smaller kendhang ageng and enjoys an exciting role with ornamental rhythms that mimic the puppet's movements in puppet theater. This drum classification is found with different spellings such as kendang, kendhang, and even gendang. The kendang is found across several countries such as Java, Lombok, and Bali, each with their own traditions and variations on the drum. Sometimes, such as the Balinese kendang, the outward appearance of a very basic cylinder drum belies the interior, which boasts carvings that create an hourglass shape.

Beyond the gamelan other ensembles do exist as found on Sumatra, one of the largest islands of Indonesia. Buddhist music is very popular here, and the ancient drum and tuned gong ensembles are widely seen, even today. However, also popular is the royal nobat, an ensemble of Muslim origin that features two double-headed drums and an oboe. It is likely to have arrived in this area from India in the 15th century. Such an ensemble accompanies large events such as royal weddings, funerals, or religious ceremonies. Another example is the talempong ensemble of the highland Minangkabau people. This Sumatran ceremonial and entertainment bronze orchestra uses knobbed gongs and kendhang.

The drums of Indonesia are numerous, however, and extend beyond the kendhang and bedhug with conical, kettle, and hourglass designs evident.

Vertical conical drums of around 34 inches long with a fluted base exist in Sumatra with the Batak people. These drums featured a single reptile skin, which had numerous drops of resin applied for tuning purposes. The membrane was attached via rattan laces, which connected to a rattan ring positioned a distance below the top of the drum featuring wooden wedges like many of the African drums mentioned previously to further enable tuning. A 19th-century example at the NMM is said to represent the Dutch and Portuguese colonial brass cannons in design, which were common in that period. This example displays an austere shell with some carving around the splayed foot.

Another Batak drum was found in the taganing drum chime, which consisted of five barrel drums tuned to specific pitches to play melodic rhythms in accompaniment to rituals that communicated with spirits. The drum is slightly similar to the kendhang, although an example at the Metropolitan Museum of Art in New York displays very unusual tensioning that sees wooden pegs passed through the side of the skin around the circumference horizontally with lacing attached that runs the length of the drum and connects to the base. The base itself is a wooden ring that is disconnected from the shell with wooden wedges forced between the base and the shell to apply added tension to the lacing and the membrane.

The Javanese people also possess a conical drum known as the tifa. This single-headed Javanese drum involves a membrane stretched over a tube of bamboo. It is held under one arm as the player dances and beats the membrane with his bare hand. An Asmat example also exists in Melanesia.

An example of Islamic origin is the small kettledrum is found in Indonesian islands such as Lombok. Known as a duduk, it uses wooden wedges beneath the drum to hold the membrane at the top taut. Another small kettledrum from Indonesian Borneo (Kalimantan) is held at the MFA. This 19th-century example is a small wooden instrument of less than 4 inches tall and 11 inches in diameter with the membrane fastened by a rope system that attaches at the base of the drum.

Bronze casting was well established by at least two thousand years ago in Java and Bali, who were producing weapons, domestic items, and instruments of music. Just as found in Southern China and Vietnam, the bronze drums that became popular in Indonesia and Bali became associated with such a drum type that defined its own category, separate from the Heger classifications. These large hourglass drums are known as the Pejeng-style bronze drums, which were cast in molds creating the largest examples of such a drum. The most famous example of such a bronze drum is the Moon of Pejeng, which at almost 80 inches wide currently resides in a temple east of Ubud as a popular tourist attraction. It is surrounded by legend, with myths claiming that the drum was a wheel from the chariot that pulled the moon. As it was passing over Pejeng, the wheel fell off and landed in a tree.

Smaller but similar drums existed, known as the mokko as seen on the Indonesian Sunda Islands. Standing around 20 inches, the shell is cast in bronze with some decorative patterns engraved on the side and several integral handles on the upper resonating chamber.

NOTES

1. Keat Gin Ooi, ed., *Southeast Asia: A historical encyclopedia, from Angkor Wat to East Timor* (Santa Barbara, CA: ABC-CLIO, Inc, 2004), 924.

2. Elizabeth May, ed., *Musics of many cultures: An introduction* (Berkeley and Los Angeles: University of Californian Press, 1980), 114.

3. David Morton, *The traditional music of Thailand* (Berkeley, CA: University of California Press, 1979), 103.

4. Terry E. Miller and Sean Williams, eds., *The Garland encyclopedia of world music: Southeast Asian.* (New York: Garland Publishing, Inc, 1998), 596.

5. Miller, *The Garland encyclopedia of world music: Southeast Asian,* 45.

6. Miller, *The Garland encyclopedia of world music: Southeast Asian,* 598–599.

7. Truman Simanjuntak, M. Hisyam, Bagyo Prasetyo, and Titi Surti Nastiti, eds., *Archaeology: Indonesian perspective* (Jakarta, Java: Lipi Press, 2006), 353–354.

Chapter Ten

─────────○─────────

Oceania

OCEANIA IS AN AREA OFTEN DIVIDED INTO three areas to encompass many of the islands in the Pacific Ocean. Over such a large area, these islands collectively have many different cultures and influences from which to draw for their musical art forms. To discuss them all in detail would be far too big an undertaking for this chapter and possibly not necessary or wholly interesting to the reader of this book. Therefore this chapter attempts to give an overview of drum development and discusses some of the more popularly or well-known aspects of Oceanic drumming. The first area discussed here is Polynesia.

Up in the northeasterly reaches of this chapter we find the Hawaiian Islands, which today make up a state of the United States. With around two thousand miles of sea between the islands and the American mainland, the drumming traditions are far removed from that of the Native Indians; so too is it from the rest of Oceania. It exists in this respect as a separate entity. Drumming was hugely important here as an accompaniment to ritualistic dancing and chanting. One such sacred ceremony was hula, in which men would dance, recite poetry, and play drums. The instruments involved in these ceremonies were generally made from plants, trees, and fish, and therefore early examples are rare as a result of decomposition. We do know, however, that they possessed three main drums. The pahu hula is a footed cylindrical drum of coconut tree wood with a single sharkskin membrane fastened with cords that run down and tie beneath the decoratively carved base. This drum would have been played at the hula rituals with a single bare hand using finger, palm, and fist techniques while the drummer also performed with the other hand on another smaller drum.

A fine example of a pahu hula drum from over three hundred years ago resides at the British Museum. Several male figures are ornately carved into the foot, showing their knees slightly bent as they bear the weight of the drum on their arms above. The rest of the drum is quite plain, with the membrane fastened in place with strands of plaited coconut fiber. This example is quite small, standing 11 inches tall and 6.5 inches in diameter, although larger versions also existed for use in the temple.

The drum that was played along with the pahu hula was the puniu, or coconut knee drum. This kettledrum was formed from the shell of a coconut with the head cut off to form the bowl shape. A ring was created from plant material such as coconut fibers plaited together (known as sennit) and placed beneath the coconut to form a soft base. A membrane from a fish with small scales was then added to the open top and fixed to the base ring via sennit to provide tension. Two braided lengths of sennit were then attached to this base, enabling the drummer to tie this drum around his thigh in order to play at the same time as the paha hula. More sennit with a knot tied at the end was used as the beater to provide the high-pitched staccato notes that blended with the deeper paha hula.

Another interesting drum was the ipu hula gourd drum, which involved two gourds hollowed out and stuck together with tree sap so that their openings met in the middle. A hole was then made on the top of this structure for increased resonance. It was played to accompany chants, song, and dances by either gender using the fingers to slap the body of the drum. Tonal variation was achieved by using different groupings of fingers while the drum was held in the air and then another timbre was created by dropping the drum onto the ground. A 19th-century example of 30 inches in height is held at the Metropolitan Museum of Art in New York (Met).

Speaking more generally about Polynesia, the rhythms played on the drums are often an accompaniment to poetry or song, and to this end they lack the consistency that Western music relies on in many genres. Instead the rhythms fluctuate as they follow the lyrics of the song. Regarding the drums themselves, European influences from exploring sailors and missionaries have seen Western music styles and subsequently double-headed snare drums and kettledrums adopted by the indigenous people in some modern cases, but many traditional drums are still evident across the islands and in museums around the world. Similarly to the pahu hula of Hawaii, the single-headed, cylindrical, footed drum was common across many islands in Eastern Polynesia. Carved from a single piece of wood with one shark membrane across the upper opening, they were employed for entertainment and ceremonial occasions. This usually utilized cord tensioning that fastened inside the lower end of the drum shell. Although there was this common basic design, sizes varied. Smaller drums were suited to kneeling, sitting, or squatted playing positions; others were suited to being played while standing upon the ground; and some over 40 inches tall would be played on a raised platform. In fact, the sacred Tahitian pahu ra drum was of such large proportions that it could sometimes exceed 80 inches in height, as it was beaten at special occasions and pre-battle rouses with sticks while accompanied by similar drums of smaller dimensions played with the bare hands.

A painting by John Webber in 1777 from Captain Cook's third voyage depicts a human sacrifice in Tahiti as accompanied by two drums. The first is a thinner, slightly conical drum rising to the player's chest with a membrane diameter that appears to be a similar size to his hand. It sits upon an integrated, vented wooden foot, which is around two-thirds as long as the resonating chamber itself. The usual lace tensioning system affixed beneath the drum shell is evident. The second drum is similar in all respects except that it is larger in diameter, around 14 inches, to achieve a deeper tone. This observation of drum types supports what we know from surviving drum examples.

The common drum types that have come to be known in the Tahitian percussion ensembles include several items. The pahu is a general term for a membranophone in Tahiti but is often associated with the double-headed, cylindrical drum that is played horizontally

A *Human Sacrifice at Otaheit*, 1777 CE. Painting by John Webber.

in a sitting position using beaters. It is most closely related to the European bass drum, and as such it provides the low frequencies to the music.

The pahu tūpa'i rima is a standard cylindrical drum with a single rope-tensioned membrane as previously mentioned in reference to the Hawaiian pahu hula. It is played in a standing position with the bare hands to create a rich and low tone.

The fa'atete is a more modern, European-influenced Tahitian drum, which has become common throughout the island with its high-pitched tone that is created when beaten by two sticks. It consists of a footed cylindrical, sometimes slightly conical, wooden frame with a single membrane attached to the top via cords that attach inside the bottom of the drum.

Slit drums are also common in Oceania. Tahiti possessed the tō'ere slit drum, which was made from such woods as milo or coconut and played with a tapered wooden stick.

These names have become slightly ambiguous as the European-influenced drums have borrowed existing names. The result in some cases is that suffixes have been added to distinguish them. This can be seen with the pahu tūpa'i rima, which was previously called pahu.

These percussion ensembles exist to accompany the drum dances, which are a fusion of traditional and European influences. The rhythms are made up of preestablished patterns called pehe, which last for varying lengths and involve set parts for each instrument. Different pehe are joined together to create larger pieces.

Within these ensembles the double-ended cylindrical drums that had adopted the name pahu assume a holding role, beaten by a single stick. The fa'ahete play patterns around the pahu, and the tō'ere accentuates the pehe rhythms. The lead drummer uses his tō'ere to cue the dancers and lead the ensemble into new pehe while other tō'ere players enjoy a freer improvised role.

A similar heritage exists in other Polynesian Islands, such as the Cook Islands and their drum dance known as ura pa'u. Within the ensemble that accompanies these dances is the pa'u, which is similar to the Tahitian pahu except that a panel of wood is left intact inside the drum to act as a partition in the bottom third and the bare hands are used to play it rather than sticks as with the pahu. Alongside this drum was heard the barrel-shaped pa'u mangō and the slit drums, which are known as pātē. Tall, narrow carved cylinder drums are also found here, as in Tahiti.

Heading west to Melanesia we find large emphasis on slit drums, many of which are believed to represent spirits of the dead.

In fact, myth and legend surround drums in Oceania just as they do in other parts of the world, and this doesn't only apply to the slit drum. Although part of New Guinea is Indonesian, it is being discussed here as it seems logical to examine the island in one place. The Asmat people of New Guinea believe that at the dawn of humanity a being known as Fumeripits created the first Asmat men's ceremonial home in which he became lonely, and so he carved wooden figures. These speechless, inanimate wooden people didn't alleviate the boredom, so he carved the first drum. As he played the drum, the rhythms brought the wooden figures to life, and the beginning of the Asmat civilization had begun.

In these areas further east than Polynesia, where the cylindrical drum was prevalent, we find the hourglass drum to appear more frequently, and the Asmat people support this conclusion. One example at the Utah Museum of Fine Arts (UMFA) displays a beautifully carved handle, which runs right from the base along the 64 inches of carved wooden shell and stops just beneath the single lizard membrane at the other end. The entire shell also features a busy carved design, which is the work of a skilled craftsman. In fact many of the long drums from New Guinea feature a handle carved from the same piece of wood as the body with intricate carvings of animals, geometric shapes, and patterns. Such instruments are often present at important ceremonies or celebrations, generally played by men, although women may occasionally do so.

Another Asmat example over 22 inches tall lies at the Met, which features an ornately carved handle of an entire human figure, believed to be the owner's father. Further Asmat examples include a drum of 23.5 inches in height and around 10 inches in diameter known as tifa, which rests at the UMFA, featuring a single lizard membrane on the upper opening held taut with a rattan ring. The most striking feature, however, is the ring of carved figures that stand around the circumference of the shell holding one another's limbs.

Other hourglass drums existed for a slightly different use. One example is the water drum, which was an instrument used solely by the men at initiation ceremonies away from the eyes of the women and children. Unlike previously mentioned water drums that contain water within them, this example is driven vertically into the water, making a thud as the drum hits the surface. An example at the Met stands over 53 inches tall and features a crocodile-carved handle, which is held by the drummer to strike the water. The inclusion of the crocodile is symbolic, as the drum hitting the water is thought to mimic the sound of the crocodile eating the initiates and then spitting them out. The initiates are cut during the ceremony, and these cuts are thought to be the scars left by the crocodile's teeth.

The independent state Papua New Guinea is also part of New Guinea. This geographic connection with Papua and West Papua has resulted in a similarity of drums. The hourglass design is prevalent, as is the use of crocodiles upon these drums often known as apa or kundu.

An interesting example is displayed at the Met, which features the standard hourglass drum with a single reptile membrane on the upper opening and a central handle carved from the same body of wood. At the bottom end an opening resembling a crocodile's mouth is carved into a sharp design, complete with teeth.

The crocodile features on another beautifully decorated example, which displays painted motifs and faces around the shell.

Oceanic hourglass drums, www.rhythmuseum.com.

This time the crocodile is a three-dimensionally-carved figure of the whole animal straddling the drum, as if climbing up the outside.

Other animals also feature on drums, such as one standing 18.5 inches tall with a single reptile membrane. This is fastened by way of a rattan band that is squeezed tight upon the upper end of the shell with the membrane securely pulled between them. Geometric carvings adorn the shell, while an integrated wooden handle stretches nearly the whole length of the drum in the shape of a bird. Similar to the open crocodile's jaw at the end, some examples feature a snake's head. Another one is very plain in drum design except for the ornate handle, which features scrollwork with a human figure at each end, one of which is possibly petting another animal.

Despite the widespread use of drums in Polynesia and Melanesia, drums were not common with the indigenous people of Micronesia, found only in a few places, such as the Caroline Islands and the Marshall Islands. One such drum is the aje of the Marshall Islands. This was a carved wooden hourglass drum with smooth, curving sides that gracefully drew in at the center to create a thin shaft and then smoothly curved outward again to form the upper resonating chamber that housed the single membrane. Around 26 inches high and 9 inches in diameter, this drum, devoid of decoration, was played by women as opposed to the usual Oceanic custom of men. The aje was used in groups along with female singers to accompany male dances, as location communicators when groups of boats were sailing at night and to rouse courage when going to war.

Chapter Eleven

---○---

The European
Orchestra

THE MIDDLE AGES (500–1400 CE)

IN THE EARLY MIDDLE AGES, Christianity's power enabled its preferential vocal music to excel and caused instrumental advances to grind to a halt in Europe. The collapse of the Roman Empire left the continent in a state of poor literacy and lacking in advances on every level, and so the church had the greatest influence. Persia and Arabia, on the other hand, were major forces, with huge advancements in the arts and sciences.

From the perspective of Europe and classical music, the most significant drums of this time were the early versions of the modern kettledrum. The Latin origin of the word kettle (catillus) translates as "bowl," and such a utensil has existed as one of the earliest cooking pots. Evidence suggests that early kettledrums originated with a flat bottom, so an obvious evolution can be assumed from the primitive domestic pot drums. These could conceivably have originated in natural vegetative form such as a piece of gourd. By the early Middle Ages, many different regions among Persia and Arabia held their kettledrums dear.

Another drum that was also popular in Persia was the dohol. It was a large, double-headed barrel drum used to accompany the Persian oboe sorna and is a possible early version of the European

161

military bass drum. The Turkish people possessed a similar, although wider and shallower, frame drum called tabl turki or davul.

Europe became much more involved in the development of the drum during the later Middle Ages thanks to the influence of Asia, whose exotic and wonderful percussion instruments had traveled to Europe through Byzantium (which became Constantinople and later, Istanbul), North Africa, and general increased contact with Muslim cultures. The Crusades had a huge impact on this cultural diversification in Europe during the 13th century, bridging the gap between primitive drums and advanced modern classical instruments.

An example of such significant drums was the nakers, pronounced to rhyme with "crackers." The name was derived from the Arabic naqqāra from the verb *naqr,* meaning "to strike, beat." These were very similar to the Persian and Arabic kettledrums except that in Europe a pair was worn suspended from the player's belt, hanging in front of his upper thigh. The appearance and location of these drums led to a slang reference applied to male testicles, still in use today. The two drums in each pair were identical diameters (around 4 to 12 inches), and both often utilized a snare running across the top of the batter head. Depictions of these drums often show them being beaten with the matched grip.

Their exact use is unclear to us, but there is evidence of a strong military use and reports of use in aristocracy for entertainment. Although Germany is considered the European home of these drums, they became popular in England by the 14th century.

Another important European drum of this period was the tabor. It was also used for military as well as entertainment purposes. The tabor was slung under one arm and played with one stick in the other hand. The hand holding the drum also held a pipe, which was played simultaneously. Carvings of the pipe and tabor in Carlisle Cathedral, 1400–1419 CE; the 13th-century font at Northleach Church; Exeter Cathedral, 1240 CE; and Beverley Minster, 1330 CE, all show what we call matched grip today. The tabor often had a single string of gut across the batter head as a snare. The resonant head sometimes had one as well. Rope tensioning was employed with a skin tucked onto a hoop and the rope taken through the skin just above the hoop. The rope traveled in a V shape between each

English pipe and tabor at Beverley Minster (left, 1); nakers at Northleach Church (center, 2); and nakers at Beverley Minster (right, 3). Courtesy of David Barton (1), Stephen Ashby (2), and Mervyn King (3).

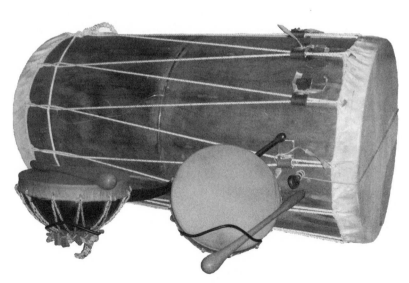

Deep tabor, 1965 replica of Provençal tabor by Jeremy Montagu, and 1975 copper nakers replication by Paul Williamson. Courtesy of the author.

head, all around the drum's circumference. Leather or rope buffs at the apex could be pulled down to increase the tension of the skin by pulling the ropes tighter. These were then slackened off between playings to preserve the skin as it fluctuated according to weather conditions.

The use of a rope for tensioning was not a new invention, or even a European one: "The use of chords or 'braces,' attached to the heads, to tighten the parchment when required, is very ancient, being found in Egypt in the second millennium BC."[1]

A third drum worth mentioning is the timbre, known today as the tambourine, a frame drum with metal jingles. The jingles were larger in diameter and thicker than today's version and were sometimes accompanied by pellet bells and a snare running across the head. They had one or two membranes and may have come in square or rectangle variations, but invariably would have been too shallow to allow any means of tuning, other than by applying heat, and therefore were of a fixed tension.

There is also pictorial evidence of large, double-headed drums strapped upon the chest much like the military bass drum that we see later. These may well have been European versions of the Arabic ṭabl or Persian dohol, especially when considering that records were made of the ferocity of such drums beating terror into the Christian armies by the Saracens, so it is not inconceivable that Europeans adopted such a drum at this stage.

During the 12th and 13th centuries, professional musicians came in the form of minstrels and waits and, as a result of these professions, surnames pertaining to their specialized instrument were formed. Many of these names survive today, such as Harper, Piper, Horner, or the drum-related French name Tabor, whose English variants include Taberner, Tabernor, Tabberner, Tabbernor, Tabiner, and Tabner.

Waits were affiliated with a specific town and started as the town watchmen, whose occasional playing of the drum proved they were awake and alert at night, as well as playing beneath windows on dark, cold mornings to coax people out of bed. Later, they took on an extra role as the town band musicians, playing at ceremonies and festivities and given their own livery and salary. As is common practice today, these musicians were also hired for private functions such as weddings. Across Europe, waits were common with the German stadtpfeifers, Dutch stadspijpers, and Italian piffari.

Minstrels, on the other hand, were often employed by a prince or court and considered to be highly skilled. They too were paid a salary and became members of musicians' guilds, which were the forerunners to our musicians' unions, enabling a standard to be upheld and, in turn, preventing less able musicians to work, thus protecting the trade and livelihood of the members. Some minstrels opted for nomadic life, constantly traveling, playing in exchange for meals and accommodation in each town or village. In the famous Swiss drumming town Basel, the Association of Drum and Fife existed in 1332 as evidence that they too enjoyed a well-organized and serious view on musicianship.

RENAISSANCE (1400–1600 CE)

Labeling musical periods in history is by no means an exact science. One period does not cease overnight as a new, clearly defined one comes to life. People's attitudes and inspirations evolve over time as a result of social, economic, political, and technological changes. Also, a period of musical history doesn't always match exactly with the dates of the same period in literature, art, or architecture. For the purpose of this book, the commonly recognized musical periods with their approximate dates have been used.

The renaissance that began around the 15th century brought an industrial revolution, greater literacy, and a shift from vocal music to instrumental. Orchestration was being considered by composers with specific parts written for specific instruments and the number of players in each section also being dictated. This heightened appreciation of musical color and timbre filtered through to instrument manufacture and design, and the drums were certainly not eschewed from this impetus.

By the late 15th century Swiss soldiers were serving in Europe as dogged, loyal mercenary troops; the last surviving of these is the Papal Swiss Guard, still serving the Vatican in Rome. As they marched, they were accompanied by their musicians, who brought new instruments. The transverse flute, or "fife," became very popular, and its two-handed technique necessitated a dedicated player, thus making the pipe and tabor player obsolete. This freed up the drummer, allowing him to focus purely on drumming, enabling a bigger drum and more intricate playing techniques. Although the tabor was still used in folk situations and for aristocratic entertainment, the new larger drum dominated military usage within the infantry such as the German Lansquenets.

This bigger, heavier drum of around 20 to 40 inches deep and 20 inches in diameter had to be worn hanging at the drummer's side, and so the side drum was born, also known as long or field drum. Often hung at a 45-degree angle, it was played using what we call today the traditional grip. This allowed the left hand to play over the elevated rim of the drum, which pointed away, toward the player's right-hand side. Such a drum can be seen in Rembrandt's 1642 (commonly known title) *The Night Watch*.

We also find the terminology for a drum changing from tabor, bedon, and tabrett to the likes of drome, trumme, and tromme. This is significant, as drum terms are generally created to mimic their sounds (onomatopoeia). The singular strokes of ta-bor have been replaced by the roll of the tongue to pronounce dr-ome or tr-omme.

This is indicative that drummers were using such techniques as flams, ruffs, and drags, which all serve to produce that multistroke sound that would inspire such names. And so it is in the late 15th century that we first see the rolling techniques that are so commonplace today.

Concerning the drum itself, ropes or cords were still in use, and the adjustment of tension was via buffs as in the Middle Ages, but the skin was now lapped onto a flesh hoop and the cords attached to a separate counter hoop, which was pulled down onto the flesh hoop, as we see on a modern bass drum. This enabled higher tension to be applied to the skin with more consistency in tone around the drum.

The snares had moved from the top skin on the tabor to the bottom skin, as seen on a modern snare drum, and these were often in the form of two strands of gut. We also have pictorial evidence of airholes in the shell to allow the compressed air to escape upon striking the batter head, enabling the skins to resonate more freely. These may also have been introduced originally as a vent to prevent condensation from forming on the calf heads, causing adverse effects. But it is likely that it was simply that a drum without vents will suffer from a choked sound, and indeed a drum with a thin shell could even sustain damage if the air had no means of escape.

The size of side drums appeared to vary dramatically, but they came as big as 2.5 feet in diameter and equal in depth, which probably necessitated thick skins and heavy sticks.

Much of what was played was committed to memory, learned by rote, but records of some military rhythms have survived to help us understand what was played. From this we know that a common marching beat involved playing five minims (tans) and then three silent minims. These rests enabled the soldier to clearly hear beat one in each phrase and therefore start his march on the correct beat. His left foot stepped on beat one and the right foot followed on the flammed beat five.

Kettledrums in the large form that we see in today's orchestras advanced in Germany by the early 16th century and spread throughout Europe. These were as large as 28 inches in diameter and usually made of copper. The old method of lacing had, by now, largely been replaced by square-topped metal screws fitted around the head and screwed through rings attached to the counter hoop. A separate drum key fitted onto the square heads to screw the rod. These went into lugs, raising or lowering the iron counter hoop, which in turn stretched the skin. It is not thought that separate counter or flesh hoops were used; instead the skin was lapped directly onto the counter hoop with slits cut in the skin to allow the rings to pass through for the screws to penetrate.

The drums were considered incredibly stately and nearly always grouped with trumpets, which were held in high regard among aristocratic circles. At this time they were viewed as instruments of ceremony and function, such as signaling in battle, rather than of musical or great artistic possibilities. They were even shunned as devil's instruments by some critics. Where side drums represented the infantry, trumpets and kettledrums were the quintessential instruments of the cavalry.

Only certain people were allowed to play a kettledrum, and the troops who were permitted to use kettledrums were closely controlled. It was a disgrace to relinquish a kettledrum on the battlefield, and if this occurred, that troop was banned from using the kettledrums until they had retrieved the lost ones.

The players were expected to display a high element of showmanship when playing, by such extravagant moves as throwing the sticks up and catching them between notes. The cavalry players used sticks with cord attached to the end, through which their hand was passed to avoid dropping the sticks when performing spins on horseback.

The kettledrums were still carried on horseback in the military but usually stationary in royal courts, although they have been noted as carried on the back of a man in procession while the player walked behind him, and even mounted on a carriage in the late 1600s.

Despite their regard as inventions of the devil, some composers were starting to recognize their musical qualities, and so their use was set to increase.

BAROQUE (1600–1760 CE)

The baroque period brought to Europe a musical revolution. The early 17th century was a time when composers and performers were reestablishing the value of expressing human emotion and passion. The emphasis was now on musical drama, and the Renaissance tendency to place equal significance on each part had been replaced by a monadic style where one single melody stood out, relying strongly on dynamics to create excitement. With a wide dynamic range and the ability to excite with huge effect, drum usage continued to increase in this period.

Kettledrums, or timpani, maintained their strong military importance in the cavalry and ceremonial use, but they also became widely absorbed into the orchestra by the 17th century. Jean-Baptiste Lully is often regarded as one of the first composers to score for timpani, which he included in the ballet that he wrote for

Francesco Canalli's *Serse: Comédie en Musique* first performed in 1660. It is impossible to be sure of the first usage, and many state that it was in Lully's 1675 opera *Thésée*, although there is suggestion of their use in even earlier musical ensembles. Later, Johann Sebastian Bach used them with both the brass and full choir as well as George Frideric Handel, who wrote very elaborate timpani parts. Their use was restricted somewhat by the key of the piece, with trumpets and timpani only available in C or D major and the general feeling that they had much greater dramatic effect when used sporadically.

In Europe, the drums were of copper or bronze, often with goat membranes, which were tuned with tension rods screwing into lugs with the use of a loose key. The diameter could range dramatically from around 16 inches to 24 inches, the upper limit of which was limited by the size of available animal skins. These often had a depth of just over half that of the diameter. Some of these drums had begun to introduce a flared horn that protruded internally from the airhole in the drum shell. This varied in shape and size and was most likely introduced to improve and amplify the sound as well as increase the tonal range. Wood sticks of about 8 inches were fitted with a rosette at the end to produce a more pleasing sound, although pictorial evidence suggests that sticks with material wrapped around the end were in use. Hard sticks with an uncovered end were preferred in the military.

The two drums were generally of different diameter, although there was often only around 1 inch in difference. This sizing helped to achieve the tuning that had become standard, with one drum tuned to the tonic and the other to the dominant key of the piece. They were often treated as transposing instruments in baroque music with the notes written as C and G and the actual pitches indicated at the top of the score. When a pitch change was necessary, due to the laborious tuning method of attaching a drum key to each tension rod and tuning it independently, the process was lengthy, and an adequate period of time had to be allowed. The complication was compounded further when tuning midperformance during a tacet section. It was then executed in silence so as not to distract from the rest of the performance. Since the introduction of screw tuning, the number of screws had increased, sometimes exceeding ten per drum. Although this allowed more accurate tuning, the difficulty of tuning quickly was increased dramatically, and they were soon reduced to eight screws per drum.

Side drums were also increasing in use during the baroque period, and the instrument was evolving to adapt to the new demands. In the military, the initiative was to decrease the depth of the shell for practicalities while retaining the volume. These shells had come down as small as 16 inches in diameter and similar in depth by the mid-18th century.

This smaller version of the field drum is nowadays called the Basel or parade drum. The shells were often of oak, chestnut, or walnut, but brass could also be used. Calf or sheepskins were used for the drumheads, which were tensioned very tightly by crisscrossing cords. Leather buffs were used to tension the ropes, which attached to the counter hoops.

The skin was lapped onto a flesh hoop with the counter hoop securing it in place. The snare wires were either held between the counter and flesh hoop or fitted snugly with a carved snare bed to allow them to sit flat against the drumhead with greater resonance. Along with this carved bed, the use of screws was developed to hold the snares tightly in place, producing a brighter sound than a looser snare could manage. The snares themselves consisted or either two strands of gut or one strand doubled with a diameter of more than 2 millimeters.

Although still very important in the military, the side drum had finally followed the timpani into the orchestra, albeit on a lesser scale. George Frideric Handel used the side drum under the name of tambour in his *Fireworks Music* in 1749, and it was used increasingly toward the end of the century, often to create a military atmosphere due to its wartime connotations.

The tabor was still in use, especially in folk circles, and the tambourine became popular in French opera. It was about 28 inches deep, made of light wood, and with only a batter head.

The quality of a musician's life in this period of history could vary dramatically. Trumpet guilds, of which timpanists were also members, were still in existence in Germany, with strict rules as to when and by whom trumpeters and timpanists could be used. These were facing incurable dissolution during the baroque period, but they did still offer job security and upheld high musical standards. The restrictions imposed on these instruments because of their social significance meant that composers could only write for trumpet and timpani when permitted. In other countries such as England and France, composers enjoyed the freedom to write for any instrument they chose, although financial restrictions sometimes limited this.

In contrast to the members of the guild, a military side drummer or timpanist was faced with special duties. Not only did they march into battle alongside the soldiers, they also accompanied any negotiation parties with their music so as to warn the enemy that they came to talk and not fight. This negotiation could be met with great hostility, and the severed heads of the party were sometimes all that returned to their army.

CLASSICAL (1730–1820 CE)

The classical period was an interesting one for the drummer and orchestras as a whole. European society embraced formality and structure. Art, literature, architecture, and music moved toward clean, well-defined styles with bright colors and maximum contrast.

In music, this came in the form of simplified structures, where a single main melody was the main focus with harmonic accompaniment known as homophony. This highlighted tonal structure and clear division between parts. The desired contrast was aided by increased use of dynamics, and as a result forced the drums to become much more musical rather than just for special effect.

The size and instrumentation of the orchestra was advancing, and composers were taking more interest in stretching what could be done by an individual instrument to the limit.

Other percussion instruments started to make an appearance in the orchestra but as always, it was a slow integration process. Theater orchestras were quite comfortable with embracing new sounds; in fact they were proactive in looking for new ideas to sound fresh and exciting in an effort to keep ticket sales high. The classical orchestra, on the other hand, was much more wary of anything untested and generally only tried instruments that had passed a length of time in the theater and built up a level of propriety. As a result the common route for a drum was from the military band to the theater and then to the orchestra.

Another significant change was the specific instruction of the composers. Where musicians in the baroque period, especially of the guilds, were free to interpret parts and embellish at will, composers had now become much more specific and expected parts to be played exactly as written. Composers took much more interest in the techniques of the timpani and as a result, wrote very specific parts, essential to the music.

By the late 1700s, the dissolution of the trumpet guilds and the increasingly audacious compositions led to less-frequent pairing of trumpets and timpani. Timpani arrangements had now progressed from exclusively using the tonic and dominant to other intervals such as diminished fifths. By this time, pieces were sometimes scored involving up to ten kettledrums, still involving flamboyant performances with the performers racing between the drums and flinging the sticks into the air in some cases.

Some composers such as Mozart were still writing their timpani parts in C and G and giving the key of the piece for transposition, while others such as Haydn and Beethoven were writing in the actual key of the piece. In fact, in this field, it was the composers who were pushing the musical boundaries, which in turn forced the technological advances. The players were, to an extent, just following instructions, but it was these instructions that motivated their constant search for better ways to cope with composers' demands. Beethoven was instrumental in this area, using unprecedented tunings between the drums, stunning rolls, and dramatic dynamics to great effect.

Coping with these midconcert retunings was a dilemma for the drummers. The problem of noisily shifting the tuning key between the twelve or so screws on the drums was partly remedied with the introduction of a fixed T-shaped key atop every screw around 1790. It made life much easier in the opera pit when limited time between arias often called for hasty retuning and eliminated the audible "clunk" of attaching the loose key. Furthermore, it enabled two screws to be tuned simultaneously. Despite this, some English players were still reluctant to adopt it at first because of the obstruction caused by this fixed key when moving between drums. Either way, obtaining the vital even tension across the whole vellum to achieve a pure tone was difficult and, as previously mentioned, the process was lengthy.

Motivated by these advances in timpani composition, it was a player who is credited with starting the next timpani revolution. The royal court timpanist in the Munich court orchestra was a man

18th-century timpani, double drums, and (inset) T handle for c. 1900 George Potter timpani; Bate Collection, Oxford. Courtesy of the author.

named Gerhard Cramer. In 1812 he designed the first mechanically tuned kettledrum. Living in an area of great mechanical advances at the time, he made full use of the resources available and created a drum with the ability to tune all screws simultaneously by turning just one key. The rim of the drum featured screws, which screwed down into another independent rim running parallel below. This was fixed to framework that followed the contours of the drum and led to a single screw below the base of the drum. Through a horizontal axle and a gear, the attached vertical lever could be pulled to raise or lower the rims, which stretched the head evenly across the shell. Perfect tone could be achieved instantly and, although desperately heavy and impractical, the blueprint for the future had been formed.

The sticks used at this time varied depending on the situation, piece, venue, and volume needed. To cope with these demands both hard ends and covered ends were demonstrated.

The side drum was increasing in use and had now adopted the modern name of snare drum in English-speaking countries. Elsewhere names such as militärtrommel in Germany and tamburo militare in Italy were used.

The drum had continued to shrink in size and was now often found to display a diameter equal to its depth at around 16 inches. Two strands of gut were now doubled up beneath the snare head, giving four strands in total, stretched between either wooden or newly adopted brass shells.

With increasingly noisy artillery on the battlefield, drums as signal instruments were less commonly used, but still the bands were issued signaling manuals and had to maintain the ability to pass on coded messages if needed. Tutors of the 18th century were passing on the rudiments that we use today, such as long rolls, short rolls (5-, 6-, 7-, 8-, 9-, 10-, 11-, 13-, and 15-stroke rolls), flams, ruffs, drags, and paradiddles.

Along with these changes to the drum and increased technical ability came acceptance from the orchestra a whole century later than the timpani. It was still mostly used to demonstrate a military atmosphere, as this was the origin of the drum, but Gioacchino

Rossini actually used it as a solo instrument in his opera *The Thieving Magpie* in 1817.

In the classical period the Western Asian davul (bass drum) was brought over to Poland, Austria, and then the rest of Europe with the Turkish Janissary bands and was soon adapted for the armies of Western Europe.

From there it became popular in the courts to create an exotic oriental atmosphere and then inevitably became more common in the orchestra.

As it was adapted, its proportions changed, and owing to the length of the shell exceeding the head's diameter, it became known in England as the long drum. Larger versions that retained the original wide diameter and short shell were known as Turkish drums. The Turkish playing method was initially adopted involving a large unpadded stick in the right hand playing the accented beats while a thin rod created a snapping sound with the left hand on the unaccented beats.

The bass drummer was primarily a timekeeper, helping to keep the whole band synchronized in time and therefore the army marching as well. He could alter the speed of the march or facilitate a complete stop with a double tap at the end of a phrase.

In military settings, the sticks were attached to the wrists of the player by a cord similar to the early kettledrummers to enable stick-twirling showmanship, and the player also adorned an impressive uniform with the full dress, including a leopard-skin apron.

In the early 19th century, the bass drum made its debut in the orchestra. Played with a padded beater, it was instantly stripped of its oriental flavor and provided the recognized Western bass drum thud that is heard today.

Another drum to grow popular in Western circles during the classical period was the tenor drum. It first appeared in the form of a small kettledrum late in the 18th century before evolving into a wooden cylindrical drum akin to a large side drum. In fact, it sat somewhere in between the side drum and bass drum in both size and pitch with a diameter of about 16 inches and depth of 12 to 20 inches.

English 18th-century tenor, early 19th-century side drum, and 1841 military bass drum; Bate Collection, Oxford. Courtesy of the author.

It was played with felt-headed sticks, which also attached to the player's wrist with a looped cord. Although similar to the side drum, a notable difference was the lack of snares, thus providing a much softer tone. The tenor drum player was a showman; therefore, as much emphasis was put on the stick twirling and flourishes as was on the decorative drumming.

Because it was played with soft-headed mallets, in the orchestra it created very somber rolls as opposed to the sharp crack of the side drum. In some countries, gut snares were attached on the tenor drum, making the side drum, tenor drum, and field drum often quite ambiguous names. This is made worse by the fact that orchestral scores don't always specify whether a tenor or side drum is required, so this makes it difficult to be sure which drum was actually intended for a piece.

It is worth mentioning here that the tambourine was also admitted into the orchestra at this time despite usually being thought of as a folk instrument. Having accompanied the fascinating exoticism of sounds evoked by Janissary music, it found its way into the orchestra along with triangles and cymbals.

The tambourine may be an ancient and a simple instrument, but its array of possible sounds are impressive. The skin can be struck with the fingers, knuckles, palm, or any other available body part; it can be shaken in rhythm to create a notated tremolo or out of tempo for a trill with the jingles; it can be struck on the rim with the fingers; hit with a soft or hard stick; it can be rolled by pressing a moistened thumb along the head for a quiet tremolo; placed on another drum to be struck; or any one of a number of creative ideas that a composer may have.

ROMANTIC (1815–1910 CE)

This was an exciting time in Europe. Following the Enlightenment, industrial revolution, political changes, and economic ideologies, it is hardly surprising that the change filtered through to the arts.

The strict structure and order of the classical period was replaced by a spirit of adventure and imagination. Emotion and self-expression were foremost in composers' minds.

Great technical virtuosity flourished within performers, orchestras expanded to unprecedented sizes, and dramatic contrasts in dynamics were displayed to the full. The development of valves in brass instruments meant that whole brass sections were formed, and this necessitated larger string sections and enabled a vast range of pitch and volume.

The percussion section was also set to expand and diversify with drums being pushed beyond just special effects and increasingly used in musical ways to add color. Added to the timpani, bass, side, and tenor drum were xylophones, cymbals, gongs, triangles, chimes, keyboard glockenspiels, and celestas.

The romantic period was a very important period for the kettledrum, and some of its technological advances shaped what was possible in the orchestra and also paved the way for other future drums outside of orchestral music.

Picking up from where Gerhard Cramer had left off earlier in the century, many new ideas and innovations came to fruition.

One of these came from a Dutch musician named Johann Stumpff when he conceived a rotary tuning machine drum and patented it in 1821. When this was screwed, it lifted the drum shell onto or off of a metal hoop attached inside the drum beneath the drumhead. This altered the pressure placed on the head and, therefore, the pitch of the drum. This was a great innovation, but it generally occupied both hands when turning the drum for tuning and in doing so, moved the ideal playing spot of the drumhead further from the player.

The next concept in this evolution was to use a handle for tuning to avoid rotating the drum at all. This occurred in Frankfurt in 1836 thanks to Johann Kaspar Einbigler. The upper part of his drum shells were attached to a frame, the base of which also supported a horizontal wheel-like plate. Attached to this wheel were rods, which traveled up to a counter hoop sitting above the flesh hoop with the drum skin lapped to it. A lever could be turned to activate a rocking arm lowering the rods and therefore the drum-skin hoop. This pulled it down for more tension or up for less tension, and simultaneous even tuning around the head was achieved. The shell shape of these drums was considered to be superior for tone, and the fact that the mechanism wasn't attached to the shell enabled it to resonate freely and achieve a fuller tone as well. Although the tuning was even all around the drum, the rods attached to the hoop also doubled up as individual tension rods to allow specific inconsistencies in the skin to be alleviated.

A year later in 1837, a Londoner named Cornelius Ward filed a patent. This patent was for a kettledrum that had two threaded T-bars inside its shell. These were threaded with an endless piece of cable that passed in and out of the shell via a series of pulleys. It also passed through the flesh hoop in several places as well as attaching to a threaded metal rod in the center of the drum. The thread moved in opposite directions at either end of the rod so that when it was turned, the attached T-bars at either end both moved toward each other or further away. This pulled the cable tighter or looser and therefore moved the flesh hoop up or down, thus tightening the skin. However, the wooden handle used to turn the rod became difficult to use under high tension and made the method inefficient.

Not one to be easily deterred, Ward designed a second, improved model with a rack and pinion system inside the drum, which

Timpani from 1837 by MacConnell Woolwich, Bate Collection, Oxford. Courtesy of the author.

via a series of cams and levers, pushed an internal ring up against the drum skin to increase or decrease tension. This also relied purely on a single handle being turned, and so both models shared the same major disadvantage; without individual tuning rods, the inconsistencies of animal skin were untreatable. Nonetheless, Ward's designs were made well into the 19th century by drum makers such as George Potter in Aldershot, England.

A gunsmith named August Knocke from Munich made an important development around 1840. His system did include a vertical lever, if needed, for fine-tuning, but the important aspect was the system of gears that led down to a wheel at the base. With this wheel, the performer could use his feet to rotate it and engage the gears, which in turn raised a series of rods attached to the counter hoop and therefore altered the tension of the drum skin. For the first time, tuning could be achieved with the feet, allowing

Timpani by Kohler & Son, post-1880, with internal tuning and individual tuning rods; Bate Collection, Oxford. Courtesy of the author.

the hands to stay free to play. Knocke also included one of the first tuning gauges, although the inconsistency of animal skin meant that the accuracy of such a gauge is doubtful. It was reported that this mechanism was clumsy and inefficient to use, but foot tuning and tuning gauges were a major breakthrough for the kettledrum's future. Many other designs never made it past the prototype stage or even the design page.

Among this race for the perfect mechanized kettledrum, a Belgian instrument maker named Adolphe Sax was dabbling in another area of timpani evolution leading up to 1859. Hailing from a musical instrument–making family, he is best known for developing the saxophone in 1846 but had turned his attention to a shell-less kettledrum. The skin was held in place by a counter hoop that was screwed to lugs attached to a thin metal rim less than 6 inches deep. The advantages were that multiple drums could be overlapped on stage and required less space, as well as being stacked in storage. The main issue was regarding tone, a subject open to debate.

Ernst Gotthold Pfundt and Carl Hoffman, both of Leipzig, had made the next important machine kettledrum step. Pfundt was a virtuoso timpanist in Germany and had been playing Einbigler timpani for some time. His natural inventive nature led him to talk with Glanert, the maker of the time, and together they made improvements on this successful model. Another German timpanist named Freidrich Hentschel added his own ideas to further this design before drum maker Hoffman made his impact. As a result of their combined input, the Einbigler drums incorporated a larger kettle but with a thinner shell. This was made possible by using stronger, forked braces to support the shell and a heavier iron armature with reinforcing crossbeams. The added strength caused far less inertia on the screwing mechanism and made fine-tuning much easier. The thinner shell was attached to the forked braces by the rim, minimizing contact, allowing it to be almost completely free from tension to ensure maximum resonance and therefore, greater tone. The drums were hailed in the early 1870s, and it seemed that their extremely heavy impracticalities were far outweighed by their superior tone and efficient tuning mechanism.

Dresden in Germany was a major economic center in the 19th century, and industrialization meant that all industries were facing major changes. The German Steel Federation was established in 1874, and many businesses took advantage of this newly available high-quality metal that was stronger and yet lighter than iron.

Musical instruments were not exempt, and so it was Carl Pit-trich of Dresden who invented the Dresden model, which has gone on to be used until this day. The system was patented in 1881 and started life as a tuning device that could be bought separately and attached to existing drums such as Pfundt/Hoffman models, although it was later sold as a complete drum. It made use of a foot pedal, ratchet, and mechanical couplings to convert the semicircular movement of the pedal into a vertical movement via a rocking arm that moved the counter hoop onto or off of the rim of the shell, and therefore altered the tension of the skin; a similar concept to that of connecting rods on steam engines. Next to the pedal was a clutch that was pushed back by the performer's heel to release it and allow the pedal to operate. When the clutch was reengaged, the mechanism stayed put and the tuning was secure. The early design did take considerable foot strength to operate, so a heavy counterweight was added later to ease the pressure needed.

A tuning gauge was also included on the design, which proved to be very useful, although it only tells the player where the note is in relation to its starting note. Therefore, it is necessary to tune the drum to the desired starting note before each performance. A fine-tuning master key was also added to alleviate problems caused by temperature, humidity, and skin imperfections. The timpanist could now change pitch incredibly quickly and still use his hands for playing.

This enabled composers to write far more challenging parts involving changes that were instantaneous in some cases and included glissandos and fast chromatic passages that were only possible with pedal drums.

Into the romantic period the side or snare drum was still primarily a military drum, although use in the orchestra did continue. The big changes came in its design. The enterprising Cornelius Ward applied rod tensioning in 1837, enabling greater tuning control and accuracy, although regimental bands still used the traditional rope tensioning.

This new tuning method meant that a longer shell was no longer necessary to allow for ropes and buffs and consequently, the shell size reduced to about 8 inches, although sometimes as little as 4 inches. The diameter was also reduced, although later in the period, this grew to be larger than depth and was often made to the familiar 14 inches. The shells were also made stronger with the use of brass instead of wood, which gives a much brighter tone.

The increased tension of the skin that was now possible paved the way for faster playing and greater complexity. By this time the American rudiments were being documented in educational material as discussed in chapter 14. The military side drummer also had to know a series of calls such as instructions to commence fire, cease fire, and a call to arms.

The Turkish-style bass drum or the long drum was still very common, but a demand was growing for something else, something bigger. In the orchestra it became well established and was mounted on a wooden frame set at an almost horizontal angle. However, some composers were opposed to its overuse with excessive accentuation for effect rather than musicality. It also experienced a change in materials and became available in wood, brass, or aluminum, with a calf or horse skin attached with tension rods rather than ropes.

A single-headed version became very popular due to its increased resonance, although this did cause problems when it produced a definite pitch, a quality that wasn't intended for the bass drum. This became known as the gong drum.

Henry Distin took these bigger sizes to the limit when he built the single-headed monster bass drum in 1857. With a skin of over 7 feet, it wasn't the most practical instrument but certainly symbolized what could be achieved with the bass drum.

The bass drum was also still popular in the military bands, which were increasing in size and becoming more regimented, but it generally came in smaller sizes than in the orchestra for logistical reasons.

TWENTIETH CENTURY

During the 20th century the world became much smaller. Different cultures mixed more freely, and the general public were all exposed to sounds, smells, tastes, and sights from every corner of the globe whether through traveling, television, radio, or Internet. Their hunger for these various experiences grew, and this desire didn't pass the orchestra by.

Composers became incredibly adventurous and pushed the boundaries to the limit to see what they could get away with. Sounds, ideas, and instruments from all over the world were introduced into the orchestra, including those of Latin America, India, and Africa. Often the percussionist was called upon to accommodate these. A big focus was put on timbre and the blending of each sound to form the perfect overall sound. Composers became very specific in their scores, demanding exact sticks or beaters and methods for producing the relevant sound.

As ever, to keep up with this, technology and ingenuity ensured that the instruments evolved accordingly, and the 20th century certainly saw huge and rapid changes.

The orchestra grew in size, and with it the percussion section grew to accommodate these many new sounds that were being brought into the orchestra. An example of this is the huge orchestra for *Arcana*, which the innovative composer Edgard Varèse wrote in 1926. This included thirty-nine tuned and untuned percussion instruments. Many composers built on these ideas, such as Carlos Chávez, John Cage, and Lou Harrison, focusing on complex rhythms, color, and texture.

Inspiration was taken from everyday life. The increase in sounds from machines, factories, and traffic influenced composition. This environmental noise was best expressed through percussion and various sound effects that were administered by the percussionist.

Orchestra work became even more varied and diverse, with recordings for television and radio being added to the usual concert hall performances. This diversity in location, repertoire, drum designs, and materials that were on offer yielded many choices for the percussionist.

A frenzied search for sonorous variety took hold, and the vast percussion section that had grown within this monstrous orchestra found itself facing ever more challenging parts. The instruments had to be choreographed and positioned accordingly to make the changes physically possible. Specific instruction was often given by the composer regarding the type of stick or beater and the method of producing the sound.

Later in the century, financial restraints took their toll as two world wars absorbed all the major nations and their resources. Small group compositions became common, string or woodwind quartets saw popularity, and even solo work was produced where just one player would perform on a range of instruments, pushing them to the limit. This was also the case for the solo percussionist, and many parts were written involving only percussion, so that a player may have to perform on numerous instruments in one piece.

Whereas in the past, a percussionist would specialize on a single instrument, they may now be expected to be able to perform on multiple percussion instruments, both tuned and untuned, although they would usually have a specialist instrument within this. As the core of the percussion section, timpanists often stay more exclusively on these drums but do possess the ability to play other instruments when needed.

One factor that aided this diversity in percussion players was the available formal education that came as percussion was accepted into conservatory with specialized percussion courses.

There was also an emergence of specific percussion ensembles. These had existed in various forms throughout drum history, but the first concert hall composition solely for percussionists is considered to be *Ionisation* by the aforementioned Edgard Varèse, which was unveiled in 1933. It consisted of bass drums, snare drums, side drums, a tarole, bongos, a tambourine, a tambour militaire, tam tams, triangles, chimes, sleigh bells, a celesta, a piano, Chinese blocks, maracas, claves, castanets, a guiro, a whip, a crash cymbal, suspended cymbals, a gong, anvils, high and low sirens, and a lion's roar. The piano and celesta involve the striking of strings or metal plates and are therefore sometimes included as percussion. Other effects to note are the sirens; a membranophone known as a "lion's roar," which uses a chord to create friction on the membrane to imitate the roar sound; and the musical instrument called the whip, which utilizes two planks coming together to imitate a whip crack.

As well as inspiring classical composers, the rock guitarist Frank Zappa has given praise to the influence of this piece on his own work.

We now have many excellent conservatoire and professional percussion ensembles such as the Tokyo Percussion Ensemble, the Percussion Ensemble of London, the London Pro Arte Percussion Ensemble, Les Percussions de Strasbourg, Dick Schory's New Percussion Ensemble, the Singapore Wind Symphony's Percussion Ensemble, and Nexus. Countless others are playing to excellent standards through the many musical colleges, universities, and conservatories around the world.

Emerging from the military traditions with the fife and drums, marching bands were evolving into drum and bugle corps. This really took off in America after World War I and became very popular as a form of entertainment at public events and in specialist competitions, as discussed in chapter 14.

By the 20th century composers continued pushing the timpanist and his instrument, demanding a wide variety of specific techniques and effects, along with changes in pitch necessitating instant and accurate retuning. Examples of these effects include felt or leather mutes placed on the drums for dampening effects; maracas, hands, fingers, or coins used to strike the skins instead of sticks; the copper shells being struck rather than the membrane; moistened thumbs being slid across the skin to replicate whale sounds; and metallic objects placed on the membranes while they were struck. Pedal glissandos and up-tempo bass lines were also required of the drums.

The drums became larger and the interval between them greater. To adequately deal with all challenges, a modern timpanist would often use four or five drums. Today a standard set often ranges from 31 to 22 inches in diameter with a combination of pedal timpani and hand-tuned models, bearing in mind that a human has only two feet with which to tune via a pedal at any one time.

The most significant changes were in the evolution of the tuning mechanisms, pushed forward by the demands of composers.

Early in the 20th century the timpanist from the Vienna Philharmonic, Hans Schnellar, developed drums known as the Vienna timpani, which utilized a very simple but effective design whereby a handle attached to the base was used to push the drum shell up into the drumhead. Tuning was very easily achieved, and the tone was considered of high enough quality that these drums are still used today. Schnellar also experimented with wooden-shelled timpani.

A name that was to become synonymous with the development of timpani and drums in general was Pittsburgh Symphony Orchestra timpanist William F. Ludwig. In 1911 he presented the hydraulic pedal system, which used pressurized fluid to control an expandable tension ring to tune the drums. This design allowed the drum shell to be separated from the pedal and stand for easy transportation but proved very expensive and ran the risk of the ring bursting and fluid leaking onto the stage.

Ludwig, who was working with brother-in-law Robert Danly, then unveiled the cable system in 1917, which built on the positives of the hydraulic system but replaced the fluid system with cables that attached the pedal to the tuning handles. Then in 1920 they went a step further with the balanced action timpani system. A powerful spring was used to balance the tension of the drumhead and keep it in place. This used a rocker pedal so that the toes pressed down to raise the pitch and the heel pushed down to lower the pitch, doing away with the need for a clutch and allowing greater precision when tuning.

In 1923 Cecil Strupe designed a system under the Leedy manufacturer, which also dismantled into three parts for easy transportation. This used a ratchet and clutch system that connected to rods on the outside of the drum traveling up to the tension rods. This system was sold in Britain under license by Premier. Leedy was later sold and combined with Ludwig.

In 1924 a system was developed by the German Hans Anheier involving a cable that ran around the diameter of the drum and wound around reels fixed at each tuning handle. When one handle was tuned, all the other handles were tuned simultaneously. Although it was a clever idea, the smooth cable was prone to slip and also didn't allow for individual fine-tuning. In 1952 an American named Saul Goodman modified this, replacing the cable with a

Pedal timpani by Leedy, Indianapolis, 1920, Cecil Strupe design; Bate
Collection, Oxford. Courtesy of the author.

miniature chain and sprocket, like that of a bicycle. He also allowed
for disconnection of the chain so that individual tuning was possible. Although the designs were cumbersome and could obstruct
the playing space, they did offer an alternative for the outer timpani
when both the player's feet were concentrated on the inner timpani.

The Ludwig drum company then produced a Dresden model in the 1960s with a deep shell and an external mechanism that didn't interfere with the internal sound waves of the drum. These factors were said to help produce a superior tone as opposed to the shallow shells of the earlier Ludwig and Leedy models. Premier unveiled a similar-style drum in England, and the two dominate the market to this day.

In contrast to these deep shells, Marcus de Mowbray designed tour timps based on Sax's shell-less timpani. They are lightweight and therefore very portable, and although it is a likely conclusion to think that they lack resonance and tone, they do in fact resonate greatly and indeed have a tone that is considerably deeper than standard timpani. This may lead one to ask if the shell of a drum may actually inhibit the sound of the instrument by restricting the vibrating air from resonating and projecting to the full.

But returning to conventional drums, there are now three main types of timpani: pedal operated, rotating bowls, and drums with a master screw. Within the pedal versions available there are also three main types: the ratchet and pawl system, which needs a clutch to disengage the pawl in order to tune the drum, but due to the pawl, doesn't always allow very accurate tuning; the balanced action system, which uses a powerful spring or hydraulic cylinder to balance the tension and therefore doesn't need a clutch; and the friction clutch system, which allows the clutch to move along a post and engage at any point for accurate tuning.

Kettledrums are tuned to a very specific note, which if even slightly inaccurate will cause dissonance. Therefore, the need for manufacturing perfection is possibly more important than in any other type of drum. Any difference of thickness in the drumhead, tuning inadequacy, or imperfection in the circle of the drum will cause adverse effects.

The search for the perfect timpani continues as timpanists battle with compromise. A deeper shell presents a better tone and the diameter must relate to the depth, but then the lower-pitch drums, which inherently require a larger diameter, become so large that they are impossible to play due to their height. The Dresden model offers a pedal mechanism to the side of the drum, which allows it to sit lower, but then it is harder to move from pedal to pedal than with a drum that houses all the pedals beneath the shell of the drum.

It is generally accepted today that a timpani shell should consist of a depth that is half its diameter, but the shapes and materials vary dramatically. We have hemispherical, parabolic, and sloping shells of copper, brass, silver, fiberglass, wood, and even aluminum. The mallets used vary dramatically and are often subject to intensely personal taste, with most professionals making their own or having them made to strict specifications. They will take many variations to a concert, often changing frequently to meet the pieces' needs and the acoustics of each different venue.

The most common grips for timpani mallets are generally grouped into two main categories, although individual players adapt their own permutations to suit style, mallet type, drumhead type, drum type, and tonal preferences. With both grips, the mallet is held near to the end of the shaft and at a parallel angle with the drum upon striking.

The matched or German grip is similar to the matched grip of a drum kit player. The palms face the ground with the thumb on the side of the stick, and the entire wrist performs a vertical motion to play a note. With the weight of the hand bearing down on the stick, this grip produces a darker tone. The thumbs-up, or French grip, positions the thumb on the top of the stick with the fingers held around the underside of the stick and permits a finger motion to play the note, thus creating a lighter tone.

The 20th century also gave the drumming world the synthetic skin. For the first time in the history of the drum, the laborious task of cleaning and treating an animal hide by hand and then fitting it to the flesh hoop was no longer needed, and these factory-produced plastic heads were available much more cheaply (see chapter 12).

Many players to this day prefer calf heads due to their tonal superiority in certain situations, but few can ignore their durability and resistance to weather and atmospheric changes. Even timpanists who prefer calfskin often use synthetic heads for outdoor concerts and tours when constantly moving the drums. Some plastic skins have been specifically created to replicate that of the calfskin, an example of this being the Renaissance head by Remo. However, some players feel that plastic heads have their own quality, which should be celebrated rather than trying to copy the sound of animal hide.

Whether using calf or synthetic timpani heads, each one has an optimum playing spot, which is approximately one-quarter of the distance between the rim and the center of the drum. Some effects are employed by playing the middle of the head for a resonant sound without definition or exact pitch and also at the very edge of the head, which lacks resonance of a single pitch and creates several harmonics with a much thinner sound.

Thanks to this variety and constant improvement of the instrument, timpani concertos continue to be written. After a lull in the romantic period and early 20th century, composers began to explore timpani possibilities, such as Werner Thärichen, who composed his *Concerto for Timpani and Orchestra* in 1954 followed by William Kraft's *Concerto for Timpani and Orchestra* in 1983. Then came a *Concerto for Timpani and Wind band* from Gordon Jacob in 1984, and in 1985 John Beck composed a *Concerto for Timpani and Percussion Ensemble*. Rolf Wallin composed his *Concerto for Timpani and Orchestra* in 1988 at the request of the Oslo Philharmonic Orchestra, and in 2000 the American Philip Glass composed *Concerto Fantasy for Two Timpanists and Orchestra*. In 2004 William Kraft wrote his *Concerto No. 2 for Timpani; The Grand Encounter*, involving a soloist encircled in a cockpit of fifteen timpani, six large timpani at ground level and nine tenor timpani in the upper row, hanging from a frame. These and other examples demonstrated timpani as a powerful lead instrument, both sonically and visually.

With these concertos focused on timpani we find timpani soloists, although they are rare, in such performers as Jonathan Haas, principal timpanist of the Aspen Chamber Orchestra; David Herbert, principal timpanist of the San Francisco Symphony Orchestra; and Stuart Chafetz, principal timpanist of the Honolulu Symphony Orchestra.

Timpani also crossed over into the pop, rock, and jazz genres as bands began exploring new timbres to push their sounds beyond expectation. Examples include the Beatles' "Every Little Thing," John

Bonham of Led Zeppelin in his live act and especially during his famous drum solo "Moby Dick," the Beach Boys throughout their classic album *Pet Sounds*, Queen's Roger Taylor in his live solos, Emerson Lake and Palmer's Carl Palmer on "Toccata," Mike Old-field's "Tubular Bells," the Pet Shop Boys' "Paninaro," Bjork's "Human Behaviour," Keith Moon on Jeff Beck's "Ol' Man River" and the Who's "Love Reign O'er Me," Phil Collins on his 1982 album *Hello, I Must Be Going*, the Dave Brubeck Quartet's Joe Morello in "Countdown," Elvin Jones in John Coltrane's "Love Supreme," and in Sun Ra's "El Victor," courtesy of Jim Herndon.

The bass drum saw little change into the 20th century except for the use of alternative materials. The shell is usually made of one of several types of wood and has retained a thick wooden counter hoop while other drums have seen metal become the norm. Sometimes other materials are used in different genres, including brass, aluminum, acrylic, or fiberglass. The introduction of metal tension rods and synthetic heads was also welcomed, especially for outdoor use.

In the orchestra it is either set upon a stand at an almost vertical angle or allowed to swing freely from a frame, adjustable to any required angle. It is used to accent particular strong beats within the piece or for a variety of other sound effects. Often one hand plays the drum while the other is used to muffle it, and sometimes a double-ended beater is used for a tremolo effect with one hand. It comes in sizes ranging from around 28 inches to 40 inches in diameter with a depth of between 14 inches and 22 inches.

Military bass drums have continued to come in smaller sizes for portability. These are usually 14 inches to 30 inches in diameter with a depth of 10 inches to 18 inches and carried on the player's chest with straps supporting the drum over the shoulders. Its function as the metronome of the military band has seen no change. They have a more varied use in the marching bands outside the military where several drums of different pitches are used to support melodic phrasing.

Back in the cities, the jobbing drummer around town was facing the age-old problem of getting the drum set to the gig, except in the early 20th century, the luxury of a personal car was restricted to the wealthy. Interesting designs emerged to aid this tiresome task.

William A. Barry of Philadelphia was granted a patent in 1917 for a collapsible bass drum. The 28-inch by 14-inch sheet-aluminum shell was held by three metal pins. When these were disconnected, it folded into four parts and packed neatly into an elliptical case. The single tensioned head was permanently fixed to the single hoop and simply needed the tension rods to be loosened off, and that too folded into quarters, with a specially treated skin for durability. The case even had room for a snare drum or some auxiliary percussion, and weighing only 12.5 pounds could be carried in one hand, ready to hop on the bus.

Other companies were also moving in the same direction, such as Charles Boyle's drum company in 1927 or the English drum manufacturer John E. Dallas and Sons Ltd., also in the 1920s, with their collapsible bass drums. George B. Stone and Son designed a bass drum with a trap door in the drum shell to allow for storage of snare drums, cymbals, and traps, as did a Walberg and Auge creation involving a two-part cylindrical shell that connected via a latch and hinge. Lights and heaters were also placed inside some bass drums in the 1920s with the growing use of electricity. These highlighted graphic designs on the resonant skin and helped save the skin from moisture in the air.

The side drum was increasingly attracting the name of snare drum, although in the orchestra to this day "side drum" is very common. Orchestral composers explored the tonal possibilities and timbres, moving away from just the traditional timekeeping role. Rim shot accents, cross sticks, and wire brush effects were used. The best-known orchestral piece in which the snare drum plays a vital role is Maurice Ravel's 1928 Boléro.

The drum itself was witnessing very important changes. The actual snares could now be made of gut, wire, or wire-covered silk, and later an open-coil, spring-style strand was invented, giving more of a buzz than a snap.

The counter hoops were built from metal, giving greater strength, and rope tensioning was replaced by single metal tension rods, which enabled more precise tuning and didn't suffer from humidity changes like the ropes did. This involved one screw for each tension rod to tighten the upper and lower head simultaneously.

Next came double tensioning, giving a separate tension rod for the upper and lower heads. Now each head could be tuned individually, opening up the possibility for different tensions of the two heads and therefore, increased sonic options.

In 1898 the percussionist Ulysses Grant Leedy made the first adjustable stands for the snare drum, but this was about to be moved on to greater levels. Robert Danly is commonly credited as having designed the first snare throw-off for Ludwig and Ludwig in 1914, which by means of a lever, moved the snares down and out of contact with the resonant head. This enabled a tom-tom effect to be played on the snare and also abolished the aggravating buzz caused in quiet passages when another instrument's frequency reacted with the snares.

However, it is often forgotten that Harry A. Bower of Boston applied for a patent in 1903 for his snare throw-off. Not only was this fifteen years prior to Danly's invention, but it also went a step further and enabled the pressure of the snares upon the head to be adjusted independently of the tension of the snares.

The previously mentioned invention of plastic heads was embraced on the snare drum. The greater tension achieved with these heads enabled greater ease for fast rolls, military drummers in all manner of varying weather no longer worried about their tuning, and the tonal compromise wasn't as apparent as with timpani.

As the century progressed, snare shells were made of numerous wood types, steel, brass, acrylic, fiberglass, and also of nothing. Marcus de Mowbray, who was responsible for the tour timps, also designed a snare drum known as the spacer drum, devoid of a shell. These drums consisted of two drumheads connected only by tubes or "spacers" to house the tuning rods. Without enclosing the sound as a shell would, Mowbray markets these as having huge dynamic range. They also offer more diverse microphone positions, as they can use a standard top and bottom position along with a side or even inside position.

These drums are surprisingly loud and full toned, the snare below the lower head resonating well. Although the effect of the shell is obvious when comparing a wooden snare with a brass snare, for example, the Mowbray designs show how much of the sound comes from the heads and how they are tuned.

He also invented busker drums, which are designed for small, quieter settings. This unusual kit uses rectangular drumheads stretched across a frame with no shell, which utilizes linear tension along the membranes and thus produces a quieter sound. The bass drum, snare drum, and three toms are fixed to a wooden base, along with a small cymbal set, and the whole thing can be folded and pulled along on the wheels, making it ideal for buskers on the street or a drummer playing in a pub who doesn't want a big, heavy, loud setup. This design has been taken even further and fitted with an engine allowing it to work as a motorized vehicle. Now those nightmarish traffic jams can be used productively for an impromptu concert.

Regarding the tenor drum, physical changes had not been dramatic since the 18th century, although it had undergone the same treatment as the snare drum in terms of synthetic heads and rod tensioning. It has also evolved from the shallower depth of the field drum to be roughly of equal size.

In the 20th-century orchestra it continued to be used in works such as Edgard Varèse's *Ionisation* in 1933, Aaron Copland's *3rd Symphony* in 1946, and Benjamin Britten's *The Prince of the Pagodas* in 1957 to add color and a rolling quality to certain beats.

Tenor drums have really progressed most in the world of marching percussion. In this environment, they are fixed on a frame that hangs from the players' shoulders, encircling the waist with between three and six drums. They are single headed, fitted with tension rods, and tuned to a specific pitch so that melodic phrases can be performed. The style of play is incredibly visual, with frequent crossovers and spinning. The tenor parts often support the snare phrases, adding further color and flamboyancy.

TWENTY-FIRST CENTURY

As we plow deeper into the 21st century, music is evolving rapidly. As vinyl gave way to tape and then to CD, all of these hard copies have now made way for digital downloads. People no longer need huge devoted spaces of their homes for recorded music collections, as it all fits onto devices whose size is ever decreasing.

The audience has many more options now, and much of these traditional forms of music that have been charted in this chapter are required to adapt to stay relevant. Tan Dun wrote a *Paper Concerto* in 2003 involving huge hanging sheets of paper, boxes, paper bags, tubes, and abrupt page-turning noises in a novel approach to composition.

In 2008 the live and totally improvised British drum and bass group the Bays teamed up with the Heritage Orchestra to create a concert in which the score was being written as the music was played, responding to the live band. These scores were then sent to the orchestral performers' LCD screens, and they instantly responded by sight reading.

In 2009 a concert took place at Carnegie Hall, New York, by an orchestra recruited via the Internet. The online phenomenon YouTube invited classical musicians from around the globe to submit an audition video, performing a specially written Tan Dun piece, which was judged by members of some of the world's greatest orchestras to pick the finalists, and then the general public picked from those remaining. The selected members then gathered for rehearsals before performing the *YouTube Symphony*, a first of its kind.

Where the future will take us is impossible to guess, but the incredible evolution of drums will continue to support and inspire whatever the composers' minds are capable of.

NOTE

1. Francis W Galpin, *A Textbook of European Musical Instruments: Their Origin, History and Character* (London: Williams & Norgate, 1937), 67.

Chapter Twelve

---○---

The Modern Drum Kit

THE MODERN DRUM KIT IS GENERALLY CONSIDERED a product of Western civilization, an invention that emerged from America or Europe, allowing a percussion section to be condensed into a single-man operation. However, as we now know, the snare drum came from European battlefields, the tom-toms from China, the bass drum from Western Asia, and the cymbals from Turkey. It has truly global parentage.

The modern drum kit is an integral part of most popular music genres today and one whose prevalence is rivaled by no other single instrument. It forms the backbone of a majority of bands, whether it's a jazz trio, a thrash-metal quintet, or a seventeen-piece big band. Ever-increasing technological advances and boundary-pushing musician requirements mean that it is a fast-evolving area of the music business.

Buying a drum kit can take some serious consideration. Once the brand, number of drums, and shell sizes have been selected, the choice of shell materials yields many options, such as fiberglass, metal, acrylic, birch, maple, mahogany, ash, or beech, among others. If wood has been chosen, the number of plies must then be decided and whether they are all of the same wood or mixed varieties. Now all that remains is to pick the type of bearing edges of the shells, the tuning rods, the lugs, the color and finish of the shells, the hardware, the drumheads, and the countless cymbal options.

Thankfully, most manufacturers offer kit packages, thus removing the need to be a drum-manufacturing expert before the product has even been bought.

These high-tech instruments seem to have been around forever, but their fast-paced history starts around the early 20th century, where we left off in chapter 11.

IN THE PIT

As with many advances throughout human history, it was necessity that gave rise to the drum kit. The popular theater bands often employed several percussionists to cope with the snare, bass, cymbals, and various sound effects. Each percussionist required payment and space in the limited theater pit. The first breakthrough was known as double drumming. This involved positioning the bass drum close enough to the snare so that a single percussionist could play both parts simultaneously. Two jobs could now be carried out by one musician, but this didn't constitute a drum kit yet.

The major breakthrough was the ability to use the feet for playing rather than just standing. This came courtesy of the bass drum pedal. Experimentation was under way in the 1890s with pedals that required laborious toe-heel motions to strike the drum and then pull it back to the start position. Some were in the recognized form, attached to the bottom rim of the bass drum, and others hung from the top rim of the bass drum with a cord attached between the bottom of the upside-down beater and the foot pedal on the floor. Some of these were even without a foot pedal; the cord was attached directly to the drummer's foot, which may help to explain the term kick drum, still in use today. Many of these were large, cumbersome models, not practical for easy transportation. It took a German emigrant to devise a version with a spring to return the beater after striking the drum and suitable for widespread production. German-born William F. Ludwig of timpani-manufacturing fame moved to America at the age of eight in 1887. By 1908 he was drumming in the Auditorium Theatre, Chicago, getting increasingly frustrated with his poor-quality wood bass pedal, while playing emerging up-tempo jazz and ragtime styles. He decided to build his own pedal, which turned out to be so successful that by 1910 he and his brother were mass-producing metal pedals under the company name of Ludwig and Ludwig. The drummer was now a seated musician and had every limb at his playing disposal.

The popular kit at this time was known as a trap kit, shortened from contraption, and was a far cry from the kits we use today. A metal frame on wheels known as a console or trap-tree curved around and over the huge, marching-style bass drums, providing a frame from which everything else hung, similar in concept to the modern-day rack systems. The small cymbals available at this time (mostly what we would call splashes today) were hung from curved (gooseneck) arms attached to the console. Chinese tom-toms with painted heads crudely tacked on hung alongside the contraptions tray from which the kit took its name. Upon the tray rested all manner of percussion items needed for the orchestral music of the time, including klaxons, temple blocks, hooters, triangles, and whistles. There were also mounted temple blocks and cowbells, as well as a cradle for the snare, all attached to the large bass drum.

The hi-hat didn't exist yet, but its development was under way. Ludwig and Ludwig's early bass drum pedals featured an extension arm on the bass drum beater, which allowed for simultaneous playing of the bass drum and a small cymbal clanger mounted on the bass drum rim. This wasn't an entirely new concept, as similar patents had been registered before the turn of the century, such as Albin Foerster's in 1888. The main problem with most of these designs was that both instruments played simultaneously without the option of playing one of them alone, although Ludwig did introduce an alternating feature that allowed the cymbal to disengage with the kick of a lever. As drummers' desires grew beyond this unrefined clanging noise, many turned their attention to the snowshoe. This advance, also called a Charleston pedal after a popular dance of the time, positioned two cymbals at the end of two snowshoe-shaped wooden boards with a hinge at the other end. It enabled drummers to place their left foot in a loop on a wooden foot plate and press down, causing the small cymbals to crash together in a similar fashion to the modern hi-hat. Four-limb drumming had arrived.

The next step was the lowboy, which often had 8-inch cymbals with large bell areas, vertically mounted 9 inches from the floor. The foot pedal enabled them to be pulled together, but the lack of height meant that it was still purely a foot-operated voice on the kit. By the mid-1920s, the simple step to the recognized hi-hat occurred. Metal tubing was added, bringing the cymbals up above the height of the snare, enabling the cymbals to be played with feet and hands. The drastically tilted snare drum positioned the left hand in

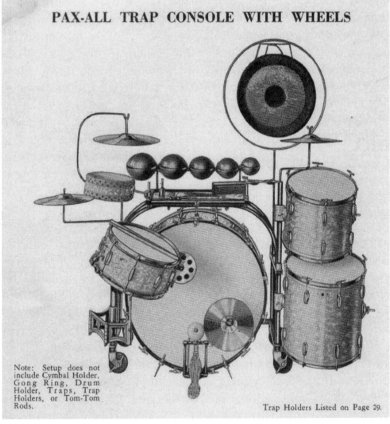

Slingerland Pax-All trap console with wheels, displaying Chinese tom, traps, and clanger bass drum beater, www.coopersvintagedrums.com.

such a way that the stronger, leading right hand crossed over the top of the left and became the hand to play the hi-hat. The cymbal size was enlarged to 11 or 12 inches and the bell size reduced for greater playing-surface area, allowing the hi-hat to become a time-keeping element of the kit for the first time. Walberg and Auge were pioneers of this design, which was also marketed by Leedy, Slingerland, and Ludwig in the same decade.

There was one more development to come, and it came in the 1930s courtesy of the now-household name Gene Krupa. Krupa chose to endorse the lesser-known Slingerland drum manufacturers and stripped away all the contraptions, opting for a streamlined kit. His standard four-piece Radio King setup included, for the first time, tom-toms with tunable heads on the top and bottom. Having done away with the rattles, bells, whistles, and other sound effects, his setup of snare, bass, 13 × 9-inch mounted tom, and 16 × 16-inch floor tom is still favored by many drummers today. At first the floor tom sat in a three-legged cradle, but soon the legs were attached to the shell as recognized in today's drums. The modern drum kit had been born.

SWING/JAZZ

Jazz and ragtime evolved out of the marching funeral bands of the southern states of the United States, and especially New Orleans in the early 20th century. These soon diversified from outdoor marching bands to play concerts indoors or on the river steamboats. With a newly desired accent on the weaker beats of two and four in the bar, this new style drew from blues, ragtime, and African influences.

Drummers such as Warren "Baby" Dodds and Zutty Singleton were at the forefront of this evolution, as they supported the rhythm of the band but also reacted and improvised according to what they heard rather than just playing a consistent ostinato. Dodds was used as a guinea pig for Ludwig's idea of two cymbals positioned on a stand that could be controlled by the left foot. Dodds didn't like the forerunner to the hi-hat, but we now know how integral it became to the modern drum kit. Throughout the 1920s Dodds opted for a 28 × 24-inch Ludwig and Ludwig bass drum, a 14 × 6.5-inch Ludwig snare drum, a 10-inch tacked Chinese tom-tom, two cymbals, four cowbells, and a woodblock. Singleton used a very similar setup to Dodds's, only upgrading in the 1930s when he became a Leedy endorser, at which point he added the single-headed tunable toms and an 8-inch-deep snare drum.

With the 1920s came the illicit speakeasies, pushed underground by Prohibition in the United States. These clubs, with their free-flowing alcohol, gave rise to lively jazzy dance bands, which were scorned upon by the older generations as a major factor in the Roaring Twenties and the downfall of a moral society. With the development of the hi-hat as a timekeeping device, lively swing drumming developed.

The 1930s brought a rising popularity in the big band jazz orchestras, which were louder and faster. They also gave more opportunity for individual soloing and improvisation. Krupa's development of the modern four-piece drum kit and elevated status of tom-toms had a massive effect on drumming. Helped by his Radio King, he and others such as Chic Webb, Dave Tough, Buddy Rich, Louie Bellson, and Papa Jo Jones helped to drive these powerful orchestras. In fact, at this stage Chick Webb deserves a mention. Webb suffered from a short stature and a hunchback as a result of childhood tuberculosis, which meant his physical presence was far from imposing. And yet he led the band that dominated the Savoy Ballroom in Harlem throughout the 1930s. Many great drummers battled with him for the moniker of "King of the Savoy," and these battles came to be billed as spectacular events. One such event occurred in 1937, when four thousand audience members crowded in to watch the Benny Goodman Orchestra fight it out with Webb's band. Webb won. His driving and exciting playing inspired the likes of Krupa and Rich, setting the way for the drummer-led groups. He did this on his Gretsch Gladstone kit, over which his head peeked when playing. The 28-inch bass drum, 14 × 6.5-inch snare, 13 × 9-inch rack tom, and 16 × 14-inch floor tom were customized to add to the visual effect. He had green sparkle pictures of chicks wandering around the white oriental pearl shells and a gold sparkle finish on his wooden counter hoops. As was the norm at this time, he had a rolling console, which housed his cymbals, woodblocks, cowbells, and temple blocks.

The legendary Buddy Rich was inspired by Webb and came to fame before he was four years old in vaudeville shows in America. By the late 1930s he had entered the jazz world and was soon making waves in Tommy Dorsey's band. Rich took over from Webb and then Krupa as the star of the show, filling concert halls with his intense solos and seemingly impossible speed. Just like Krupa, he was a fan of the Slingerland Radio Kings but knew he would find it difficult to be number one at a company with the superstar Krupa as the main man. With that in mind he jumped ship to WFL and then continued moving around for the rest of his career, finding temporary homes with Ludwig, Vox, Rogers, and Fibes. In the late 1980s, before his death, he had returned to the Radio King in white marine pearl with a single rack tom and two floor toms set around his 26-inch bass drum and standard 14 × 5.5-inch snare. Just as with Krupa, the outdated woodblocks and cowbells had disappeared, along with the console, making way for the modern drum kit, which we still use today.

Another important development in this decade came courtesy of a child. In 1938 while at school, Louie Bellson drew a sketch of a double bass drum kit, thus pioneering a setup that was to become hugely popular several decades later. He went on to play with many popular leaders of the time, such as Count Basie, Duke Ellington, and Benny Goodman, making good use of his Gretsch 20-inch double bass drum kit.

By the 1940s, orchestras had become less fashionable, partly due to economics, and some musicians were turning to a new groundbreaking, improvisational subgenre of jazz, which had started to emerge in the form of be-bop. This improvisational style focused on audience listening rather than dancing, allowing greater tempo flexibility and intellectual playing concepts. Specific cymbals were created and termed ride cymbals as drummers began to ride on them, using them as the main timekeeper instead of the hi-hat. The size of these cymbals grew at the demand of the drummers. The role of the bass drum also changed from a timekeeper playing

steady crotchets to an interactive element punctuating certain accents along with the snare drum in reaction to the lead instrument.
This technique became known as comping. The biggest change
for the actual drums was the bass drum size reduction. Jazz drummers required compact kits for getting in and out of the basement
jazz clubs and into a car. Bass drums decreased from the usual 28
inch to 20 inch and even 18 inch later on with Fred Gretsch, a
manufacturer in New York, showing great innovation both with the
downsized drums and lighter hardware.

A drummer who was instrumental in the be-bop era was Max
Roach. He afforded a musicality and intelligence of a rare magni-
tude, creating lyrical phrases within the rhythms and lighting the
path for other drummers to follow with regard to improvisation and
soloing. His silver sparkle Gretsch kit was typical of the time with a
20-inch bass drum, 14 × 5.5-inch snare, a 12 × 8-inch rack tom,
and a 14 × 14-inch floor tom. These drums were accompanied by
two Zildjian ride cymbals, a crash, and hi-hats. Other great drummers at the forefront of this progressive genre included Art Blakey,
Tony Williams, Elvin Jones, Kenny Clarke, and Philly Jo Jones,
all of which played Gretsch drums throughout this period. These
drummers loved the Gretsch drums so much that they received no
compensation for their endorsements other than the drum kit itself.
These were not commercial partnerships from the drummers' perspectives; these were based on passion for the instrument.

It's worth noting that in the same decade, Gretsch implemented another huge change that influenced the future of the
drum. Drums were initially one solid, steam-bent sheet of wood.
This evolved, and manufacturers used several sheets of plywood
held together by a glue ring. Gretsch's groundbreaking concept
involved staggering the sheets of wood so that the join was in
several places, removing the need for a glue ring. The number of
plies has varied over the years, but the concept has been successful, and many believe it to offer superior strength and truer resonance. Many drummers, from the be-bop legend Max Roach to the
modern jazz drummer Vinnie Colaiuta, endorsed this prestigious
brand. As well as conquering the lion's share of the jazz market
in the 1940s to 1950s era, Gretsch were also the only importer of

K. Zildjian cymbals, which were developing a huge, loyal following. Where Slingerland had reigned supreme in the swing era, Gretsch were certainly the rulers of be-bop.

As with everything else, music felt the tremors of World War II. With it came a shortage of materials and most significantly a restriction that forced nonessential products to contain only 10 percent of their weight in metal. Kits such as the Slingerland Rolling Bombers showed great resourcefulness in being made almost entirely out of wood. The shells, hoops, tom legs, cymbal stands, shell fixtures, lug casings, and strainer were all wooden. To save on metal tuning rods, the drums had fewer lug options with the snare only having six. Although ingenious, these kits were not popular beyond the war years.

A more significant development was that of a synthetic polyester film called Mylar, which was used and tested throughout World War II by DuPont. Up until this point, all drumheads had been real animal hide with drum manufacturers competing to buy the best skins for their products. Suddenly this modern alternative was available, and Chick Evans and Remo Belli were both quick on the uptake to seize this business opportunity. The first synthetic drumhead was made in 1953 for Sonny Greer by Jim Irwin, but it was Remo and Evans who built the successful businesses that still supply drummers to this day. The drumheads weren't widely accepted when first unveiled in 1957, and there were teething problems, preventing the heads from slipping out of their hoops. The products improved by the early 1960s, and drummers couldn't ignore their durable, weather-resistant, and consistent properties.

Adolphe Sax conceived the idea of coating drum skins in a mixture containing India rubber to help protect against the effect of weather and atmospheric changes. Other patents were granted for similar specially prepared heads into the 20th century in the push for the ultimate all-weather head. Even though today many drummers with their synthetic drumheads barely consider such inconveniences as this, we can still see evidence of Remo Belli's first line of Remo Weather King drumheads, as it is clearly stamped under the Remo logo.

With the reduced sizes of the be-bop era and the demand for smaller, more portable kits, some people were looking for innovative ways to satisfy this need, giving rise to an unusual kit that took the compact, small combo ethos to an extreme. This was to become known as the cocktail kit. It was actually the British company Carlton who started this concept, to enable the West End pit drummer to better cope with the cramped conditions, and it came in the form of the Carlton King Combination.

Produced from 1948, it featured a 20-inch floor tom with a bass pedal set beneath it utilizing an upward motion that enabled the beater to strike the bottom head. It also had a hollow, cast-aluminum base with a cable connected to another pedal. This allowed for pedal tuning in much the same way as timpani demonstrated. A cradle was attached to the side of the tom that allowed a snare drum to be mounted and there were various clamps for cymbals, cowbells, and any other percussion. Although the kit did save on space, it was still of considerable weight and laborious to set up with the tuning cable system.

It took until the mid-1950s for this concept to become more practical, and it was the big names in America that did it. Gretsch, Slingerland, Rogers, and Ludwig produced kits that became known as combo or jobber kits and were similar in appearance to the Carlton model, except for the abolition of the tuning pedal system. With a tom of 18 x 20 inches and a fairly shallow snare with a 13- or 14-inch diameter, it worked very well with regard to tone and volume for the small jazz combos. The large tom often had a metal rim at the top and a wooden rim at the bottom so it could be turned on its side to be used like a conventional bass drum.

Another version that took the compact ideal to the limit involved only one drum. The long, upright tom had a bass drum pedal beneath it, as previously mentioned, but the top head had snare wires set beneath it so instead of a tom, it was now the snare. Now the drummer had the ultimate portable drum kit, although the sound was compromised with the buzzing that occurred from the snares even when the bass drum end was played. Baffles were later used in an attempt to reduce this. The kits required the player to stand up, which is not an easy task when one foot is playing the

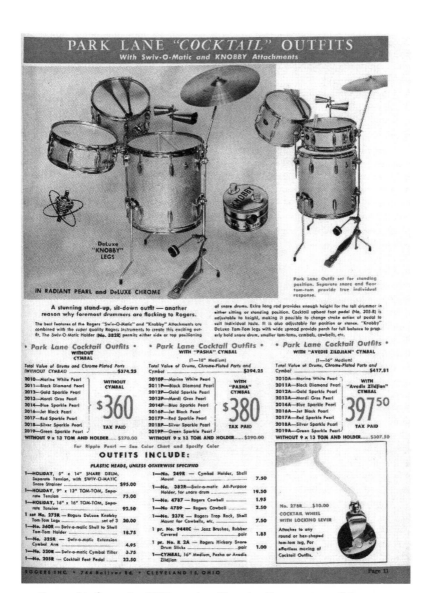

Rogers kit from the 1951 catalog, Yamaha Corporation of America.

bass drum pedal. Although they are still manufactured by the likes of Yamaha and other smaller companies, the kits are not a common sight today.

With the sizes, materials, and techniques that were available by the 1950s, little has changed to this day. Many jazz drummers avidly seek the old traditional sounds from these eras, and vintage drums such as the Radio King are as popular as ever.

ROCK 'N' ROLL

Rock 'n' roll was an exciting new take on rhythm and blues (R&B) that emerged in the late 1940s, also incorporating influences from country, folk, and gospel. The band lineup generally consisted of drums, bass, piano, or sax with the latter two replaced by the electric guitar in the mid-1950s.

This musical style was very influential on young people's lifestyles and attitudes, but it was equally influential on the development of drumming.

The drummers drafted in to play on these records were often jazz musicians with a strong swing in their playing and used to keeping time with the ride and hi-hat. A new, energetic musical direction and the growing popularity in electric, amplified instruments necessitated louder, more solid drumming. Although it may seem hard to believe, previous to this rock 'n' roll revolution, the two and four *backbeat* was very rare and usually only existed for "take it home" sections in jazz. The backbeat wasn't a totally new concept and could be found in the hand clapping and tambourine banging of gospel music. It was also prevalent in the late 1930s, produced by slapping the upright bass on beats two and four to drive the up-tempo rhythms of rockabilly music, and then later it can clearly be heard on the drum kit with the recognized backbeat played on the snare for Harry James's 1939 release "Backbeat Boogie." However, it wasn't really used as a driving force upon the drum kit before rock 'n' roll came along. An early pioneer of the two and four backbeat was the session legend Earl Palmer on the West Coast of America with rock 'n' roll artists such as Little Richard and Ritchie Valens.

One of the first R&B songs to feature this style of drumming by Earl Palmer was Fats Domino's "The Fat Man" in 1949. This driving backbeat in the R&B setting soon became commonplace throughout the entire song, and the rock beat was born, giving rise to the music that would be coined rock 'n' roll.

The other huge development was straight quavers, which are notes with even spacing between them, as opposed to the swung, triplet-based rhythms of jazz played on the ride to keep time. These jazz-based drummers tried their hardest to keep swinging, but in the end the relentless up-tempo, straight-eighth feel that dominated on other instruments, such as Little Richard's piano in "Lucille" (1957), was too strong, and they submitted to straight quavers. During this transitional phase, an interesting juxtaposition of straight notes on piano and the still slightly swung notes on the ride sometimes occurred. This partially swung drum feel can be heard on Little Richard's "Tutti Frutti" (1955). Palmer was instrumental in these hugely important rhythmic developments, and he favored a little Gretsch Broadkaster with a 26-inch bass drum, a 14 × 6.5-inch snare drum, a 13 × 9-inch rack tom, a 16 × 16-inch floor tom, Zildjian hi-hats, a crash, and a ride. His contribution to drumming could be easily underestimated, but without these changes, most of what we listen to today on commercial radio stations wouldn't exist. The beat that became the foundation for a majority of rock and pop songs wouldn't have been available, and things might have sounded very different today.

Rock 'n' roll didn't completely do away with shuffles as heard on tracks such as Elvis Presley's 1956 single "Heartbreak Hotel" and Buddy Holly's 1957 hit "That'll Be the Day," among many others, but the realization of the possible grooves when playing straight eighths on a drum kit had a profound effect on the development of music.

As rock 'n' roll had been born out of the coming together of African Americans and white Americans, the fusing of different musical heritages gave many new possibilities that were exciting to the mass audience hearing it for the first time. Many of the straight quaver songs had an African rhythm origin, which in its clearest form can be seen in Bo Diddley's 1955 "Bo Diddley," which is based on a rhythm we now know as the *son clave*. It was an innovative concept, relying on this strong rhythm accented in unison by guitar, drums, and maracas rather than intricate melodic or harmonic changes.

Although the actual drum kit itself hadn't changed significantly from that inspired by the previous jazz drummers, the style had changed so dramatically that manufacturing advances were inevitable to accommodate the growing volume and intensity that the drums were being subjected to. The development of synthetic heads was to become crucial, as well as the actual kit sizes and designs.

Skiffle/Beat

In the mid-1950s UK musicians were waking up and looking beyond their traditional jazz scene left over from a bygone era. A new style that started in New Orleans in the early 1900s called skiffle took hold. This folkloric mix of jazz, blues, and country was usually played on basic instruments such as the washboard, tea chest bass, comb and paper, cigar box fiddle, kazoo, and musical saw, as well as the acoustic guitar or banjo.

Drum kits in Britain had slipped behind the glitz and glamour of America, still often exhibiting old-fashioned console kits. This was compounded furthermore by tighter importation restrictions following World War II, which made it nearly impossible to bring back American kits. Skiffle was unaffected by this lack of fancy drum kit, as the major rhythmic force came courtesy of the humble washboard. Major UK players such as Lonnie Donegan, the Vipers skiffle group, and Chas McDevitt and Nancy Whiskey notched up some unprecedented record sales with their up-tempo, raucous releases.

In the grand scheme of musical history, skiffle in Britain only had a small direct impact on music, but it was a crucial one on the evolution of commercial music and rock/pop as a whole. It bridged the gap between the post–World War II aging traditional jazz scene and the explosive British rock scene of the 1960s. It made people realize there was commercial worth in popular music and encouraged some of the most influential musicians of history to pick up their instruments and start playing.

Many of the big names of the '60s began in a skiffle group, including Jimmy Page, Van Morrison, Mick Jagger, and the famous Quarrymen that later gave us the Beatles. Skiffle encouraged these men to pick up an instrument in the first place, and the result of that definitely had a direct impact on musical history.

With the electric guitar as the new lead instrument, British rock 'n' roll started to become popular with Tommy Steele, then Marty Wilde, and Cliff Richard and the Drifters (later renamed the Shadows), and this was the forerunner to *beat* groups.

In America the Ventures were doing a similar thing, and their drummer, Howie Johnson, was playing a sparkle finish drum kit, which drummers in the United Kingdom, who were deprived of such luxuries, looked upon with envy.

From the Shadows and the Ventures, Britain pioneered a huge musical movement led by beat groups. These were usually categorized depending on their location. Birmingham gave us Brum beat and Liverpool gave us Mersey beat. Perhaps the most famous now, Mersey beat was only a localized movement until the likes of the Beatles and Gerry and the Pacemakers broke into the big time.

Britain was also starting to wake up in the drum-making race, with Premier sitting at the top of the pile, followed by Ajax and Carlton. These each supplied a budget version of their kits under the names Olympic, Edgware, and Gigster respectively.

These manufacturers were trying to emulate the glamour and sex appeal of their American counterparts, and this was accelerated with the arrival of the German Trixon drums. Trixon's popularity in Britain and America rose quickly, with endorsements from drumming giants such as Phil Seaman, Buddy Rich, Gene Krupa, Bobby Elliott, Clem Clattini, and Lionel Hampton. The great innovation of Trixon founder Karl-Heinz Weimer was probably ahead of its time, and the fast-paced, wacky nature of the designs may have led to Trixon falling out of favor, but it certainly showed the drummers, especially in the dreary British market, what was possible. The most famous innovations included the Speedfire kits, which boasted an

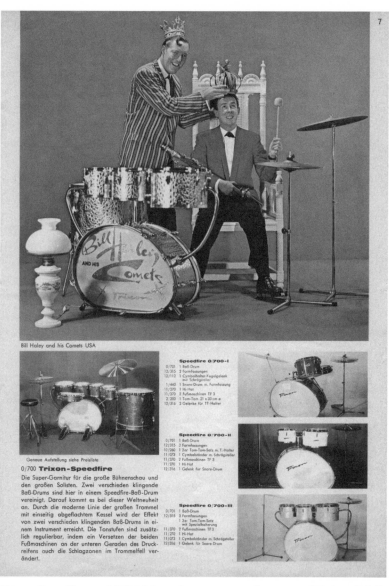

Trixon Speedfire and Bill Haley advertisement. Courtesy of Robert Pfaff.

ellipsoidal bass drum, flattened on one side with a partition inside dividing it into two sections. Two bass pedals could then be used to achieve two different pitches. Across the top were up to five concert toms (single headed) in reverse order attached with a single metal frame through them all and connected to the bass drum on either side so that the whole unit could be lifted as one, similar to the modern drum racks. The other famous innovation was the Telstar. This used conical-shaped shells, which tapered to a narrow end but retained a larger batter head.

Trixon innovations, of which some were later copied by other manufactures, also included fiberglass drum kits, ball joints for holding drums or cymbals, and a double hi-hat stand that allowed two sets of cymbals to be operated by one pedal.

With this new desire for exciting drums and the growth of electric instruments necessitating more volume, drums became very prominent in bands. Great emphasis was placed on the snare and bass drum, which wasn't clearly heard until now. Bass drums of 20 and 22 inches became standard along with a 12- or 13-inch mounted tom and a 14- or 16-inch floor tom. Snare drums as shallow as 3 inches were used, but the most popular size was 14 × 5 inches, although drummers did experiment with 6-, 7-, or even 8-inch-deep snares for a bigger sound.

American drums in the United Kingdom were still scarce due to high import duty and purchase tax, but with a little help from our friend Ringo, this was about to change. An entrepreneurial man named Ivor Arbiter opened Drum City in central London, supplying the British with Gretsch, Slingerland, Ludwig, Trixon, and all the UK brands. After a visit from the Beatles' manager, Brian Epstein, Ringo Starr had discarded his Premier drum kit with mahogany Duroplastic wrap and became the owner of a Ludwig kit based largely on his liking of the black oyster pattern. The bass drum skin was suitably painted with a Beatles logo, sitting just below the Ludwig logo. After great exposure on TV, not least the first American appearance on *The Ed Sullivan Show* in February 1964 to 74 million viewers, the Beatles' Ringo Starr quickly inspired many future drummers to pick up drumsticks, and they all wanted Ludwig kits to match. Following Slingerland and then Gretsch's success in the recent past, it was now Ludwig's time to take over. The Ludwig Oyster Black Pearl kits that Starr made famous are incredibly valuable to collectors to this day and are sought after in either of the two shell size options that Starr used. One configuration consisted of a 20-inch bass drum, 12-inch rack tom, and 14-inch floor tom, while the other option had a 22-inch bass drum, 13-inch rack tom, and 16-inch floor tom. If these configurations are mixed up, the value is decreased significantly. The drums' shells were three ply with a poplar layer between mahogany outer plies and a maple reinforcing hoop, finished off with a white Resa-Cote interior paint. He used the popular Speedking bass drum pedal and the legendary Rogers Swiv-o-matic tom holders. The cymbal setup was similarly simple with 14-inch Zildjian hi-hats, an 18-inch crash, and a 20-inch cymbal, which often included rivets. Regardless of the kit that he was using, Starr opted for the 14 x 5-inch wooden Jazz Festival Ludwig snare rather than the Supraphonic 400 steel drum that was so popular at the time.

Suddenly Ludwig kits were flying out of the shops, and the manufacturer had trouble keeping up with demand. This American drum kit dominance in Britain consumed some of the smaller UK brands, although Premier managed to struggle through and even gained great popularity with some big American jazz drummers. A new age of popular music was upon us, and the rule books had been thrown out of the window.

Rock

The 1960s had a staggering effect on popular music, evolving incredibly quickly from the structured, polite beat scene to an energetic, chaotic world swamped in distortion, feedback, and improvisation. In a time when positioning a separate microphone on each individual drum (close miking) wasn't usual practice, drummers looked for more natural volume to compete with the louder guitar amps and effects that were under experimentation.

American drums were deemed louder and brighter in tone, with Ludwig, Rogers, Slingerland, and Gretsch all proving very popular.

American drum maker Rogers became very popular on home soil as well as the United Kingdom and began to place more emphasis on hardware. Their first big advance was the Swiv-O-Matic stands, pedals, and tom holders, which boasted more flexibility and the much-needed increased strength. Rogers utilized a hexagonal rod to eradicate the circular movement the round rods created and then added a ball-and-socket joint at the end, which gave unlimited movement options. This was such a successful concept that manufacturers' designs today still incorporate this ball-and-socket-type joint, as seen in early Pearl kits and post-1970s Yamaha kits.

Along with this louder, stronger build quality, the size and configuration of the drums was changing. Two floor toms or two mounted toms on the bass drum became popular, giving us the five-piece drum kit. At first the two mounted toms used identical dimensions, but soon the standard rock sizes were developed, consisting of a 22-inch bass and 12-inch, 13-inch, and 16-inch toms with a 5 × 14-inch snare. This has continued as the standard until the present day.

By the end of the 1960s, Earl Palmer's straight-eighth-note beat dominated, and what became known as the eight beat was the staple of any rock drummer's skill set.

In Britain a style of loud music emerged, born out of American R&B. They injected their own flair, energy, and volume, repackaged it, and ultimately took it back to America as part of the British Invasion that the Beatles had started.

One key figure in this movement was the legendary British blues musician John Mayall. Through his Blues Breakers came many of the musicians who went on to play in some of rock music's biggest groups. Alumni include Eric Clapton and Jack Bruce, who teamed up with the drummer Ginger Baker to form Cream; Peter Green, John McVie, and drummer Mick Fleetwood, who left to form Fleetwood Mac; Mick Taylor, who left to join the Rolling Stones with Charlie Watts on drums; drummer Aynsley Dunbar, who also played with the likes of Jeff Beck, Frank Zappa, David Bowie, and Whitesnake; Andy Fraser, who left to join Free with Simon Kirke on drums; and drummer Jon Hiseman with Dick Heckstall-Smith on sax, who left to form Colosseum.

Another influential figure of the blues boom was Graham Bond and his Organization, through which Ginger Baker came before teaming up with Jack Bruce and Eric Clapton to form Cream. Together for only three years, Cream left a monumental mark on rock music history with their blues- and psychedelic-fused music that demonstrated heavy use of improvisation, with Baker and Bruce displaying the perfect rhythm section for Clapton to let loose with his solos. Baker brought a flamboyant style rooted in jazz to this blues/rock scene and is regarded as the instigator of the double bass drum kit in rock. Although Louis Bellson had already used this in the jazz world, Baker's double bass drum (one 20 inch and one 22 inch), four-tom Ludwig kit kick started a trend in rock music for increasingly big drum kits. He also helped popularize the drum solo in this genre. His solos often revealed his interest in African rhythm, which he utilized with hypnotic tom-tom ostinatos building up into a frenzy and lasting up to fifteen minutes in some live performances. His most famous effort, *Toad* from 1966, displayed many different rhythmic themes that are explored and developed with great use of dynamics.

Another influential rock drummer taken from the world of jazz was Charlie Watts, the cool-natured drummer who powered the Rolling Stones. Despite the fact that he was drumming with one of the world's biggest rock bands in huge stadium venues, he chose to use his beloved 1957 round badge Gretsch kit in natural maple finish. After using a mismatch of different brands, Watts had longed for a Gretsch through the embargo restrictions of the early 1960s that prevented American brands from being imported in large numbers so as to protect British manufacturers. Some high-profile drummers, such as Tony Meehan of the Shadows with his Champagne sparkle Gretsch kit, obtained imports, and Watts eventually followed. His 20-inch bass drum, 14-inch snare, 13-inch rack tom, and 16-inch floor tom would be more suited to a compact be-bop group, but Watts stayed loyal to it through his long tenure with the Stones.

In 1966 another band formation occurred that was to propel a drummer by the name of Mitch Mitchell into the rock history books. He joined Noel Redding to form the rhythm section of

the Jimi Hendrix Experience, a trio that bore many similarities to
Cream in its exploration of improvisation in a rock setting. Employed after being sacked from Georgie Fame and the Blue Flames,
Mitchell's playing displayed a strong jazz influence with no formal
training. As a result his style was wild, imaginative, and highly
creative. His slightly swung semiquaver fills are a strong part of his
playing and became very popular in this era. Although he wasn't as
proficient at soloing as Ginger Baker, he played the drums like a
lead instrument, supporting, complementing, and inspiring Hendrix's ideas on the guitar. The style of drumming was not unusual
in jazz, but to bring it into the rock setting and mix it with high
volume and incredible guitar effects such as fuzz and wah-wah was
groundbreaking. In many cases the elongated instrumental sections
of improvised noise, rolling drum fills, and mind-blowing effects
were overshadowing any form of melody or song structure. Gone
were the days of the family-friendly, two-minute pop melody; the
start of what was later to be called fusion had arrived. Throughout
this period of his career, Mitchell used a variety of the typical rock
drum sizes of that era, beginning by playing the British Premier kits
before later using Ludwig and Gretsch kits with extra toms and two
24-inch bass drums.

Another influential band of the time was the Who and their
seventeen-year-old drummer, Keith Moon. Known as Moon the
Loon, his style was energetic, erratic, and legendary. Having risen
out of the Mod culture rather than the blues boom, the Who
quickly achieved commercial success and drew crowds to live
performances with their raw energy on stage and the infamous de-
struction of equipment. Pete Townshend is said to have started the
trend by smashing his guitar at a London pub in 1964. Keith Moon
wasn't one to be outshone, and his drum kit became the victim at
the next gig. Moon soon built a reputation for blowing up hotel
toilets, driving cars into swimming pools, and playing drums full of
water and goldfish. He created the stereotype that is still held today
that drummers are the loose cannons of the band. Drummers are
the liability in the band with an uncontrolled primal instinct, ready
to explode at any minute. This is embodied in *The Muppets'* lunatic
drumming character, Animal. It has been a long, hard struggle for

drummers to shake off this stereotype and find consideration as equal, intellectual musicians in the band.

Moon rarely used his hi-hat, preferring instead to crash on cymbals and shift rhythm regularly, interspersed with overblown drum fills at every opportunity. His style was wild with a desire to experiment and improvise that was new to rock music. As a Premier endorser, Moon's drum kits grew in size, often displaying twelve toms around his double bass drum kit as well as other items, including a large gong, timpani, and timbales. The most famous kit of his was the Pictures of Lily kit from 1968, designed around the images from the Who's single of the same name. Several drums from this kit can be seen in London's Victoria and Albert Museum. Moon was another, along with Ringo Starr, Brian Bennett, and Ginger Baker, who used Swiv-O-Matic tom holders on other branded drum kits in the same decade, demonstrating Rogers' reputation for quality hardware.

Another important work in the development of rock and pop music was the Beatles' 1967 album *Sgt. Pepper's Lonely Hearts Club Band*, which was groundbreaking in many ways. As well as promoting the close microphone recording technique that became commonplace on drum kits, it also set the way for concept albums and lengthy studio sessions. Reported to have cost US$41,000 (£25,000) and over seven hundred hours to record, it was a far cry from the session players who were producing several songs in one day.

While half of the rock world was getting louder, faster, and crazier, some musicians were adopting a more restrained, considered approach. A group of London architecture students formed Pink Floyd and proved instrumental in what was coined as psychedelic art rock or space rock, leading the way to progressive rock. Bands had become more than just singles artists; they were capable of producing entire cohesive albums rooted firmly in subjects of sexual freedom and rebellion. Now with progressive rock, an intellectual element became strong. Lyrics were much more poetic, fantastical, and philosophical, and musicians with jazz or classical backgrounds were drawn to the style, bringing a much deeper technical and compositional ability. The main concept was to abolish limitations. Suddenly chords and melodies borrowed from jazz and classical music were common; time signatures stretched far beyond 4/4 and often changed within a composition; timbre was stretched to the limit using traditional folk instruments and sounds from other cultures, as well as cutting-edge synthesizers and effects.

This meant that the drum set had even greater need to increase. Pink Floyd's Nick Mason adopted a double bass drum kit and four toms, which he later had personalized with customized artwork, in keeping with the Floyd's emphasis on visual arts as well as aural. This movement was largely British to begin with but soon swept into Europe and America. Other prog rock bands to appear in the 1960s included Yes with drummer Bill Bruford; King Crimson with drummer Michael Giles; Soft Machine with Robert Wyatt on drums; Genesis with Chris Stewart, John Silver, and ultimately Phil Collins on drums; Jethro Tull with drummer Clive Bunker; and Rush with drummer Neil Peart.

Peart has enjoyed a long career and developed a great reputation as a talented lyricist, excellent drummer, and gifted soloist, who is confident in odd time signatures and advanced conceptual ideas. His kit was big from the start in the 1970s, but with the evolution and growth of the band, the drum kit expanded accordingly. By the 1980s Peart had incorporated a great deal of electronic percussion into his acoustic setup. By the mid-1990s his Ludwig kit was actually two entire kits with augmented percussion that formed a 360-degree circle encasing him in the middle. It featured thirteen drums, numerous trigger pads, four Akai S900 samplers, various percussion such as cowbells and agogo bells, as well as a MIDI mallet controller. Upon Rush's thirtieth-anniversary tour in 2004, Peart designed a kit in collaboration with Drum Workshop (DW) made from maple with inner plies of curly maple, holographic Rush album cover imagery, and 24 karat gold–plated hardware helping to finish the eye-catching exterior. Inspired by Keith Moon's Pictures of Lily drum kit, which was Peart's childhood dream drum kit, thirty versions of the kit were built to enable the public to enjoy the design, each consisting of eight toms, one 22 × 16-inch bass drum, and three snares, as well as a full set of his signature Sabian Paragon cymbals. His familiar configuration with the toms hanging above the hi-hats, dropping down in staggered heights, has stayed consistent for many years. They were a Rush fan's dream and at the market price of US$36,000 (£22,000), they remained a dream for most.

To keep the R30 anniversary kit special, in 2006 DW built a new kit for Peart called the Snakes and Arrows kit, designed for the album and subsequent tour. It was very similar in configuration to the R30 kit, which effectively consisted of an acoustic kit integrated with an electronic kit behind him with custom-built DW shells housing the Roland electronic mesh heads and triggers to control a Roland XV5080 sampler. It also contained a custom-built 23-inch bass drum that combined the power of the 24 inch with the punch of the 22 inch. The finish consisted of gold leaf and metallic gray satin over Aztec red shells. In 2009 Peart recorded an ice hockey theme song for TSN Networks, and for this DW built him a new drum kit finished in Blue Frost with National Hockey League team

Neil Peart on the 2010/2011 *Time Machine* tour. Courtesy of Matthew Becker, Melodic Rock Concerts. www.melodicrockconcerst.com

logos displayed around the shells. Even more recently for the 2010 tour, a Victorian-styled kit complete with copper pipe–styled hardware and a time machine theme made an appearance, although the alterations were largely aesthetic, as the configuration didn't display any significant changes from past kits.

It is interesting to see how drummers such as Peart have evolved since the beginnings of these overblown drum kits in the late 1960s and into the 1970s. In those early years, drum manufacturers' catalogs reflected this rock trend and often featured these enormous kits. Twin bass drums and extra toms had been shown for some years as big band setups, but the shift was now toward the rock market.

The 1966 Duet Outfit was displayed by Slingerland, featuring two bass drums and three toms, and the Premier catalog in 1968 showed the 505 Outfit with a double 20-inch bass, 12- and 14-inch mounted toms, and 14- and 16-inch floor toms. Another feature that is evident on these Premier kits is that of the slot-headed tension rod. This European-style tension rod was the norm with Premier until they experimented with the American square-head tension rods in the mid-1970s on the Model 35 snare drum. The square-head rods are ubiquitous across all manufacturers' products today and require the specialized drum key to operate, in contrast to the slot-head rods that could utilize a small coin or screwdriver.

In 1970 Rogers displayed the Ultra Power kit with twin 24-inch bass drums, 13-, 14-, 16-, and 18-inch toms, and a Dyna-Sonic metal snare. This was pictured with the hi-hat stand legs in a closed position and the upright post clamped to the bass drum. This had become a popular solution to the problem of positioning the hi-hat legs among the left-hand bass drum and pedal.

By 1971 the Ludwig Blue Note Outfit nine-piece kit with double 22-inch bass drum, three toms, and bongos from the 1959 catalog had been renewed to include mounted toms of different sizes, an extra 18-inch floor tom, and the legendary Supra-Phonic 400 snare drum. They also offered the Rock Duo kit, which included the standard rock sizes of 12-, 13-, and 16-inch toms, two

Premier 505 Outfit

This is the BIG one—the Premier twin-bass set-up that has set the world's top drummers alight! This is the outfit selected and played by Sam Woodyard, Rufus Jones, Eric Delaney, Keith Moon and many more leading drum men. Need we say more . . . Available in all of the superb Premier finishes—see page 8.

OUTFIT '505' with 20" Bass Drum. 'B505' with 22" Bass Drum.

With Standard Zyn cymbals at price reduction. Any other changes may be made to suit the individual.

Two bass drums 20 x 17" (14" shell) with disappearing spurs	130
Snare drum 14 x 5½"	2000
Tom-tom 12 x 8"	442
Tom-tom 14 x 8"	444
Tom-tom 14 x 14", 3 legs	435
Tom-tom 16 x 16", 3 legs	446
Snare drum stand, new	313
Two bass drum pedals	250S
Two disappearing tom-tom holders, new	389
Two disappearing cymbal holders, new	470

Cymbal stand, new model	314
Hi-hat, new model	315
Stool (de luxe model)	246
Sticks	545
Brushes	555
RECOMMENDED CYMBALS	
Two 5-Star 15" Super-Zyn matched Hi-hat cymbals	355
5-Star 16" Super-Zyn Crash cymbal	356
5-Star 18" Super-Zyn Crash/Ride cymbal	358
5-Star 20" Super-Zyn Ride cymbal	360

Premier 505 outfit double bass kit from the 1968 catalog, Premier Music International Limited.

20-inch bass drums, and the same Supra-Phonic snare. All of these kits came with an optional cymbal package.

Also in the early 1970s came a seemingly backward step thanks to American session legend Hal Blaine. Double-headed tunable toms had only been in existence since Gene Krupa introduced them in the 1930s, but abruptly they returned to single heads labeled as concert toms.

Blaine also accelerated the move toward bigger drum kits with the help of drum tech Rick Faucher and a local drum shop. Using an innovative rack system, they managed to suspend eight concert toms above the bass drum to create a monstrous drum kit. Blaine appeared on *The Ed Sullivan Show* with his creation of eight single-headed toms, and they were an instant hit. Subsequently his endorser Ludwig produced the drums and marketed them as Octoplus before every other manufacturer quickly jumped on the bandwagon. Blaine had been doing a lot of session work with the Carpenters at that stage in his career, and Karen Carpenter asked to have an Octoplus set specially made for touring, while George Harrison was so impressed that he bought a set for Ringo. The Ludwig Octoplus set boasted 6-, 8-, 10-, 12-, 13-, 14-, 15-, and 16-inch toms, and suddenly what had been the sign of a budget kit became the mark of the professional's setup. The single-headed toms enabled enhanced projection of the sound and caused fewer overtones when close-miking each drum. The extensive range of toms allowed the long tom-tom fills that became commonplace.

Suddenly every catalog was displaying concert toms with a vast arrangement of drums in descending size encircling the drummer. Unfortunately for Blaine, he had never patented the idea.

Another huge step in this innovative period was experimentation with alternative shell materials. Wood and different metals had been used for many years, but with the growing use of synthetic materials people were striving for a superior shell material. Plexiglas had come along way during World War II. Just as synthetic drumheads benefited from wartime technological advances, acrylic plastics were no different.

Bill Zickos is often regarded as the first man to make use of this material for drums. In 1959 he built his first Plexiglas drum set in Kansas City, and a decade later they began official production for some big-name bands of the time, such as the Who and Jefferson Airplane. As the kits went on tour with the bands, their popularity grew, and a manufacturing plant was developed to produce the Zickos 400. Although Zickos secured a patent for the drums, it proved very expensive to defend that patent, and subsequently other manufacturers soon joined the market.

Ginger Baker of Cream is also known to have produced a kit in 1961 from sheets of fiberglass that were bent into shape over a gas stove. He gigged with this kit for several years until he converted to Ludwig.

In 1966 John Morena and Bob Grauso of the Fibes drum company unveiled a product that they deemed to be stronger than steel and yet lighter than wood. The tonal response of each shell was reputably identical and the internal vibratory response was superior, thus achieving a far greater sound than traditional materials. With a brand name conceived of the words *vibes* and *fiberglass*, this product was embraced by such drummers as Buddy Rich, Billy Cobham, Alan Dawson, Lloyd Morales, and Jack Sperling, helping Fibes become a popular competitor in this market.

Other manufacturers jumped on board, the most notable being Ludwig with their Vistalite range. In the early 1970s they were introduced in clear Perspex, amber, green, red, yellow, and blue but soon added a multicolored swirls-and-rainbow design, which carried on the prominent psychedelia of the 1960s. Their 1978 Trivoli set pushed the concept further with lights built into it, but the most iconic kit had to be that of John Bonham, consisting of an amber-colored 26-inch bass drum and a 14-inch rack tom with 16- and 18-inch floor toms, although he generally prized his Ludwig Supra-Phonic 402 snare drum.

For some innovators, cylindrical fiberglass shells were not enough. An American structural engineering graduate and professional drummer by the name of Roger North felt that his drums were unable to project the sound toward the audience and consequently, the subtleties that the player heard were not being communicated to the listeners. His solution was to curve the bottom of the shell toward the audience, resulting in a horn-shaped drum shell. He began work in the late 1960s, and by 1972 he started selling the drums, with high-profile users such as Billy Cobham enjoying their cutting-edge design. These radical fiberglass horns not only looked unique, but the sound was even louder and more focused, allowing clearer separation between voices, and produced a sound lower than the shell diameter suggested. As a result the tom sizes ranged from 6 inches through 8, 10, 12, and 14 inches. The 6-inch tom had a bell diameter of 10 inches.

The drums were initially handmade fiberglass drums, but as demand increased, North allowed Music Technology Incorporated to produce them in Italy in the late 1970s by means of an injection-molded resin process, which created greater consistency.

A man named Pat Townsend was also thinking along the same lines in the United Kingdom, and by 1977 he unveiled Staccato drums. These were similar in design to North's, although the toms had a slight lip at the bell end and the bass drum split into two openings to face the audience. The drums were soon attracting the interest of drummers such as Mitch Mitchell, John Bonham, Simon Phillips, and Nicko McBrain, while Keith Moon was also possibly about to sign a deal with Staccato just before his death. Today a new carbon version is offered as an alternative, and the shells have been modified to enable them to fit inside each other, easing the problem of transporting such bulky drums.

The speedy rise of acrylic kits was followed by an equally speedy decline. Aided by oil prices quadrupling after the Yom Kippur War, the kits were just too expensive, and the world reverted to wood shells, leaving Zickos to cease trading, Fibes to be sold off, and Ludwig to concentrate on their other lines. North drums had also petered out in the early 1980s, although they enjoy a healthy used market among enthusiastic collectors. Such kits, now considered vintage, have grown in popularity again, inspiring Zickos to restart their business in 1993 and Fibes a year later. In 2001 Ludwig reintroduced a Vistalite line, and the Bonham setup is a highly sought after and collectible item.

Another quirky example of the fiberglass craze came courtesy of Ivor Arbiter, the man who first imported Trixon and then Ludwig into the United Kingdom before working with the Rogers UK division and setting up Hayman drums. In the early 1970s he invented a concept that should please any drummer: the Autotune. This system used a rim that connected to a ratchet. When the single lug was activated, the whole rim revolved on a toothed rack and the skin was pulled down onto the shell in a similar way to the Gerhard Cramer timpani, which was designed in 1812. Here, though, the skin wasn't pulled directly down but twisted onto the shell like the lid of a jar. The drums had an unusual appearance without the series of lugs around the shell and with a shell that was wider than the head itself. Although a very clever design, it did have its pitfalls and proved unsuccessful.

In 1997 Arbiter had another go at the single-lug tuning method, which he named the Advanced Tuning (AT) kit. It was offered in maple or basswood, and the rims sat over the shells in a conventional manner unlike the Autotune. This design was like any other drum at a glance, except that it showed no lugs set around the circumference. A flanged rim is embedded in the shell and a steel counter hoop is set above the drumhead, which via a V-clamp is tightened against the lower rim, thus achieving an even tuning. This was met with rave reviews but went out of production in 2001. The design does live on, however, in the *Flats* discussed in chapter 17.

Arbiter certainly wasn't the first to try adapting single tuning for the drum kit market. In the early 1950s, a music shop owner in Manchester, England, named Jimmy Reno developed a system that involved riveting the drumhead to a frame and then using an intricate metal frame inside the drum to push a rim up into the underside of the head to alter the tension in a similar manner to a Cornelius Ward timpani design in the 19th century. A single tuning key was needed to operate this gear system. The drums came in a range of sizes, including those for bass drums, snare drums, and tom-toms. Reno made great use of surplus wood left over from World War II, but ultimately these drums were just too heavy and cumbersome

On this subject, the American electronic instrument company Peavey also attempted a radical drum design in 1994 that relieved the shell of the resonance-impeding lugs. The Radial Bridge drums incorporated a heavy wooden bridge that protruded from either end of the shell and onto which the mounting hardware and drumhead could be attached. This enabled a very thin tom shell with only three plies of 0.1-inch maple wood, although the bass drum consisted of five plies. Unfortunately the drum wasn't a huge commercial success and was discontinued in 2002. This design was actually very similar in appearance to the 1930s Duplex Spirit of St. Louis snare drum in which the tension rods screw into aluminum rings atop the metal shell or tone chamber, as the company described it.

Other materials to be experimented with in the 1970s included the weighty and boomingly loud stainless steel. John Bonham had a Ludwig stainless steel kit with his usual rack tom and two floor toms. Ludwig produced a 100th-anniversary kit in 2009 with help from Ronn Dunnett, owner of Dunnett Classic Drums. Many brands offered the same steel look with a chrome finish over the more practical wood shells. Slingerland, Gretsch, and Pearl took advantage of this, as well as a Premier version made for Keith Moon in 1968, which sold at Christie's for US$20,000 (£12,000) in 2004.

But the most incredible example was Carl Palmer's early 1970s kit, which weighed in at two and a half tons with the nine toms, all of the cymbals, and microphones supported by two consoles, in a nod back to the early-20th-century consoles. The single-headed toms and 28-inch bass drum had animal scenes engraved on the shell by jeweler Paul Raven with a dentist's drill, inspired by a hunting rifle decoration. The drums were fixed in exact positions to enable precisely the same setup each time. Around the mid-1970s, Rogers had also worked on this idea and invented the MemriLoc, which allowed a metal clamp on the tom holder arms to be positioned and tightened with a drum key so that it sat at the same position each time. This ingenious but simple idea is now ubiquitous across all brands of drums.

In his continued hunt for groundbreaking concepts, Carl Palmer became the owner of a drum kit in 2002 made entirely of recycled Paiste cymbals, which he claims to be the clearest, heaviest, and loudest drums he's ever played. Weighing in at 400 pounds with a suggested retail price of over US$35,000 (£21,500), this isn't a kit for the fainthearted.

Going back to the 1970s, the industry was facing a shock with the rise of electronics, but acoustic drums fought on with pioneering designs.

A man named Gary Gauger noticed that his drums resonated much better and with a fuller tone when they were held by the counter hoop with his fingers rather than attached to his drum kit mounting hardware. The remedy was his RIMS system, which he brought out through Gauger Percussion Incorporated. The system used a half hoop externally around the shell to connect to the tension rods to support the drum and avoid drilling the shell. Using rubber connecting parts, he made sure that there were no metal-on-metal issues to transfer any sound from the drum. This concept is now a standard feature on a majority of professional and semiprofessional kits, but it took ten years for the market to catch on after it was demonstrated at the 1980 National Association of Music Merchants (NAMM) show.

In the 1980s everything seemed to be getting bigger and more overblown. Drum sizes weren't left out, and power sizes were introduced on tom-toms, giving them an extra couple of inches' depth. Into the new millennium, tom sizes could be seen shrinking back from power sizes, beyond the standard depths down to even shallower sizes than those of the 1960s. These shallower sizes could be seen in such products as the Tama Superstar range in the latter half of the first decade. The Superstar was marketed by Tama as Hyperdrive sizes, available in 10 × 6.5 inch, 12 × 7-inch rack toms, and then 14 × 12- or 16 × 14-inch floor toms. As well as giving more freedom of positioning, Tama describes them as having enhanced attack, a quick response, and a punchy sound. Interestingly, though, they are keeping with the trend of longer bass drums by selling the 22-inch-diameter drum with a 20-inch depth alongside the shallow toms. Pearl offer a similar design with their short-stack toms, boasting sizes such as 10 × 7, 12 × 8, and 14 × 12 inches. This was not a new concept. Long before the era of the power tom, Keith Moon was playing his 1967 Pictures of Lily kit, which comprised three 14 × 8-inch rack toms.

With the interest in drum sizes came an increasing obsession with drum materials. In the 1960s, drummers were rarely aware of the drum materials used. The insides of the shells were painted to hide any imperfections in the wood, and they often made do with whatever they were given. As close microphone techniques were adopted and drummers' sounds were placed under close scrutiny, they were forced to pay greater attention to their instruments. Unfortunately the lack of knowledge during the 1970s meant that extreme use of gaffer tape and other muffling methods were employed to control excessive overtones from drums. During the 1980s shells were lacquered both on the interior and exterior, creating more resonance and revealing the wood to the owner, enabling the shell to have a greater impact on the sound. By the new millennium great importance had been placed on the shells' composition, and many drummers had become experts in the many different woods so that the drum companies were manufacturing products with all manner of different wood combinations to satisfy every demand. Most top-end companies offer a custom design option, such as Pearl's Masterworks series, in which every aspect is selected by the customer prior to building.

As well as power tom sizes, the 1980s also saw the popularization of the remote hi-hat. This involved a second hi-hat stand, often positioned on the right side of the kit, connected via a cable to a second hi-hat pedal next to the regular one. As with many new ideas in drumming, they are not really new at all but simply regurgitated ideas from the past. In 1939 Gretsch had featured such a hi-hat concept in its catalog, as designed by Billy Gladstone, but it was only in the 1980s that the idea really took off.

Another lasting invention was inspired by the increasing demand for two bass drums. The obvious inconvenience and expense of two great bass drums saw the amateur player delving into the life savings and swapping the family car for a freight truck. This got Australian drummer Don Sleishman thinking, and in 1968 the solution came with the idea of playing one bass drum using two pedals. By 1971, this double bass pedal was on the shelf in music stores across the world with its central design and a pedal set equidistant on each side of the bass drum.

But the idea can be seen in drawings even earlier, such as the German drum maker Sonor, who had a design in 1927 called the Duplex pedal, consisting of two flimsy-looking pedals next to each other mounted on a single central vertical rod that sat between them with a beater attached for each pedal. However, the beaters have two differing heads, which suggests that the pedal was designed to be used by only the right foot to enable two different sounds to be achieved rather than lightning-fast heavy-metal semiquaver patterns.

The American drum company DW, who had profited from Camco's demise by buying their tooling and manufacturing equipment in 1979, brought out the 5002 double pedal in 1983 utilizing the recognizable design with the right pedal in front of the bass drum, as with a conventional single pedal, and the left pedal next to the hi-hat pedal. The concept went mainstream, with every other manufacturer following suit.

The double pedal concept has been pushed even further in recent years with the brainchild of Scottish drummer Kevin Mackie. His single pedal called the Dualist houses two beaters. One strikes the bass drum when the pedal is pushed down and the other when the pedal comes up. It has a speed switch for easy change between conventional single beater use and double use with a quick press of the heel. To develop this idea further, a second pedal has been added to this design for the left foot to operate a third beater, giving the drummer an option that has never before been available.

Again, this idea is not totally new, and a patent was granted in 1930 to John Pignocco for a similar design. It seems that sometimes ideas are ahead of their time or lie dormant until someone else can refine them to meet the consumer's needs.

Some drummers have taken full advantage of these extra pedals to forge their own sound or approach to drumming. One of these is the Austrian drummer Thomas Lang, who strives to play equally with every limb and has subsequently developed astonishing coordination with his feet, utilizing several pedals for each foot to play a range of instruments. Another is Terry Bozzio, who has made a great impression with foot ostinatos and creating orchestral-based compositions using complex polyrhythms with his huge drum kit, including chromatically tuned tom-toms and eighteen pedals for his numerous bass drums, hi-hats, toms, and other effects.

The Def Leppard drummer Rick Allen is an example of great determination and dedication due to a car accident in 1984 in which he lost his left arm and had to relearn to drum with one arm and many pedals. His left foot operates a closed hi-hat sound, a snare, a tom, and a bass drum, while a mixture of acoustic and electronic drums are positioned for his right arm to play.

Terry Bozzio and his chromatically tuned drum kit, Geoff Cooper.

Although Allen survived his accident, among all the excess of rock music, there have been some dramatic deaths, and drummers were not infallible. Three great drummers to pass away far too early included Keith Moon, who overdosed on prescription pills in 1978; John Bonham, who choked on vomit in 1980; and Jeff Porcaro, who tragically suffered a fatal heart attack in 1992 after suffering an allergic reaction to pesticide in his garden.

The 1984 rock documentary spoof *This Is Spinal Täp* boasted a list of drummers who faced miserable endings such as spontaneous combustion, choking on someone else's vomit, bizarre gardening accidents, and being packed away with the band's equipment and never seen again.

Dramatic deaths aside, rock is healthier than ever, and new subgenres are increasingly appearing. To pigeonhole something as rock in modern times is fairly vague. Dictionary definitions of rock are fairly pointless but exist nonetheless in an attempt to categorize this music. It is generally accepted that rock music has a strong beat; often the definition implies use of certain instruments such as drum kit, electric guitars, keyboards, and singing, and loud volume is also often listed in the criteria.

As always, things move in cycles, and the rock drum kit, having built up to monumental sizes, soon came back down to the minimalist four-piece kit that it started out as. Throughout the various subgenres that appear, it will change depending on musical necessity, technical ability, and band philosophy.

POP

Pop music has become recognized as a specific genre of music, and not as just any type of music that is popular within a particular group. It can be defined, although not confined, by certain factors.

It is designed to appeal to the mass market, and many modern hits may be primarily recorded by the producer using various technologies, as opposed to live musicians, with the song written by a third party before being matched with the artist who will sing it. The importance placed on commercial success means that popular trends are often copied rather than risking any great musical innovation, although technological and studio production advances are embraced and often explored more readily than in other genres.

The pop industry as we know it really started in the late 19th century, when many music publishers had set up shop in a street in New York that became known as Tin Pan Alley. From here they would sell the sheet music for the popular tunes of the day to professional musicians and then, as parlor pianos became obtainable, to the homes of the American people. This began to generate a massive income, and a tracking system was created to keep track of the most popular music. This was the forerunner to the music charts we have today. Over in London's West End, Denmark Street had built up a similar reputation and became known as England's Tin Pan Alley. At this time music was passed via the written sheet music, and so the musicians had to be able to read music to play these tunes.

With the phonograph or gramophone and maybe more importantly, the radio receiver, music could now be digested aurally across the whole country, and it was not necessary to read music to hear these tunes.

The immense popularity of rock 'n' roll ensured that recorded music played on the gramophone became the primary method for

American people to hear music, so that it finally took the lead in its long struggle with sheet music. The commercial strategy was to focus on high numbers of short-term sales, and therefore the proven-successful musical-song formulas were required from the artists rather than taking risks with abstract or groundbreaking music. These important sales numbers were recorded in various, and sometimes conflicting, singles charts in various music magazines. That was until the American Billboard Top 100 was created in 1955, which is still in existence today.

Much of the first significant pop music has been discussed earlier in this chapter. After World War II, the rise of the teenager took hold, and they fell in love with the raucous rock 'n' roll. Up until that point there hadn't been such a clear divide between the older generation's listening options and their children's. Suddenly the teenagers had their own music, and this set the path for the future of pop music.

The American rock 'n' roll was largely imitated until the British Invasion and the development of rock music. It was at this point that pop music can be viewed as something different from rock music. Although rock music was commercially successful and record sales were very much at the forefront of record company executives' minds, the artists themselves were pushing boundaries, exploring new structures, sounds, time signatures, and ideologies that were changing music. This section will focus on the commercially oriented pop music that we recognize today, a genre in which the drummer rarely enjoys the freedom to express individual virtuosity as was employed by Ginger Baker or Keith Moon.

As this distinction between rock and pop became more pronounced, many rock artists wished to distance themselves from the niceties of pop and the artistically shallow music that the highbrow critics abhorred. Although other bands had used instrumentation outside of the standard rock band setup, such as the string quartet used by the Beatles in their 1965 song "Yesterday," some British rock bands took this to the extreme, attempting to attach greater status and meaning to their music by using terminology and formats from the classical world. Pete Townshend's *Tommy* was the first well-known rock opera in 1969. A year later Deep Purple recorded

Concerto for Group and Orchestra with the Royal Philharmonic Orchestra, and similar projects have been undertaken since, such as Metallica's *S&M* recorded with the San Francisco Symphony Orchestra in 1999. Such projects were at times criticized as pretentious and out of touch with rock sensibilities. However, it did open the way for bands such as Emerson Lake and Palmer, Yes, Genesis, and Jethro Tull to expand the exploration of concept albums without the classical connection and structures, while instead focusing on the rock band instrumentation and concepts.

These albums were popular with the record-buying public, but they would not readily be considered as pop music in today's terms. These areas of music allowed for great expression and displays of individual proficiency for every band member, the drummer included, with extensive solos on their large setups of drums, cymbals, and orchestral percussion in some cases. The pop drummer, however, was and usually still is required to demonstrate other, very different skills, two significant examples being discipline and restraint.

Pop music generally focuses on a front person or persons and elevates them to superstardom, while the band members are often left in the shadows and largely unnoticed. It is likely that many of the greatest session pop drummers in history, whose beats are enjoyed daily by people of all ages, would not be known by name to the general public.

A prime example of this lies in the early soul records of 1960s America, which grew out of the R&B of black America and gospel music from the church. As rock music was becoming experimental and virtuosic, a movement was developing on which countless other acts would base themselves. At the helm of this movement were two famous record labels that were creating a sound that was to be known as soul music.

Founded in Memphis, Tennessee, in 1957 with an old movie theater converted on a shoestring into a recording facility, Stax records went on to produce some of the most memorable records of the 20th century with artists like Otis Redding, Isaac Hayes, and Eddie Floyd. But at the heart of this vast catalog of hits were the Stax house band, a group of musicians whose creativity, musicality, and feel has endeared these tunes to several generations and will surely continue into the future. The core members of this house band were Steve Cropper on guitar, Donald "Duck" Dunn (who replaced Lewis Steinberg) on bass guitar, Booker T. Jones on keyboards, and Al Jackson Jr. on drum kit. Together they were known as Booker T and the MGs, the MG being the initials of Memphis Group.

Although they went on to release a number of instrumental hits under their own name such as "Green Onions," "Time Is Tight," and "Hang 'Em High," they recorded in excess of six hundred tracks for artists signed to or affiliated with Stax records. The sound that they created was raw, it was funky, it was energetic, and it was uncluttered. The rhythmic playing from Cropper and Jones mixed with the driving, syncopated bass lines from Duck Dunn were complemented perfectly by the sympathetically crafted and highly economical grooves from Al Jackson.

Al Jackson also played on numerous hits at other studios such as Hi Studio (which was also in Memphis and was where he had been working before Stax poached him), where he was called in specially to play for artists like Al Green when the producer thought the song would be a hit and therefore necessitated that special drum player.

In the music produced during this era, the rhythms themselves were often binary, although the ternary swung rhythms that were popular before rock 'n' roll, and the likes of Earl Palmer, were still used in some cases. When confronted by a swung track, Al Jackson tended to play straight crotchets on the ride or hi-hat, using the snare, or more likely, the bass drum to emphasize the shuffle. The overall sound of Stax with its supertight house band and the Memphis Horns was very funky, before funk was a recognized genre, and Jackson's sound helped hugely in this. Although it is reported that he had great technical ability, he always played for the song, choosing to create a drum part with so much feel and groove that the whole track was instantly lovable. He used fills sparingly, opting for a strong, consistent rhythm to drive the entire song.

The simplicity of Jackson's playing is mirrored in the equipment he used. He had a drum kit set up at the Stax recording

studio (known as Soulsville USA) that would stay set up every day
of every year during the peak recording era. His kit was a mix of
American-manufactured drums consisting of a 20-inch Rogers bass
drum, a 12-inch rack tom, and a 16-inch floor tom, and then a 14-
inch Ludwig Acrolite aluminum snare drum. His Zildjian cymbal
setup was simply a 14-inch hi-hat, a 16-inch crash, and an 18-inch
ride, and the whole setup was picked up by two microphones. It is
widely reported that he rarely changed the drumheads, unless they
broke, and used a leather wallet on top of the snare as a means of
muffling. This dead snare sound, highly tuned toms, and minimal
cymbal noise is now synonymous with the warm, smooth sound of
soul music from this era.

Tragically, Al Jackson Jr. was fatally shot at his home in 1975,
but his legacy lives on through the many timeless classics that are
driven by his sound, and also by the many drummers of each new
generation who are influenced by his playing.

However, it wasn't only Jackson who was creating this blueprint
for great pop drumming. A little over six hundred miles northeast
of Memphis, in Detroit, another record company was breaking new
ground in the soul scene.

Detroit was known as the home of the automobile, and in
1960 that motor town was about to achieve recognition for a very
different reason. Motown was created by Berry Gordy, and it was
to run with many parallels to its Memphis competitor Stax. Where
Stax had humble beginnings, cheaply converting an old theater into
the studio, Gordy started his studio, Hitsville USA, in a two-story
house, converting the basement into a recording room, which was
to become affectionately known as the Snakepit.

Motown was able to produce a sweeter, smoother sound in
the Snakepit, which developed the formulaic pop song to another
level. Just like Stax's Booker T and the MGs, the Motown machine
was driven by an efficient hit-making band of musicians who went
largely unknown to the public. This group is said to have astonish-
ingly played on more number-one records than the Beach Boys, the
Beatles, the Rolling Stones, and Elvis Presley combined. And yet
no one knew who they were. In the early days they weren't even
credited on the records that were released, which was in contrast

to the Stax house band, who were pushed into the frame with their own single releases.

The group became known as the Funk Brothers, but unlike the four core Stax house band members, the Funk Brothers group is generally considered to have had thirteen members, three of whom were drummers and two who were percussionists. The drummers were William "Benny" Benjamin, Richard "Pistol" Allen, and Uriel Jones, while Eddie "Bongo" Brown played congas, bongos, and other various percussion instruments, and Jack Ashford played vibes, shakers, and the tambourine, a vital ingredient of the Motown sound.

Benny Benjamin was considered to be the main Motown drummer, and he was often specially requested for sessions along with bass player James Jamerson. Berry Gordy talked of Benjamin as a man with incredible feel and better timing than any metronome. These are the two main skills necessary for any studio session player, and it was in these intense pop-hit-making machines that sessions were recorded around the clock, and where each band member was called upon to play efficiently and with flawless execution, before the days of Protools technology fixing the mistakes. What was played is what you hear. A new mold for drummers was setting, and one that is still strong today.

Benjamin was famous within the group for outrageous excuses as to why he was always late, once telling them that a circus train had been crossing his path when he was driving to the studio and he had to wait for the long line of animals and circus entertainers to pass, despite the fact that he didn't actually drive. But his timing on the kit was impeccable, and his big band background allowed him to bring a swing to his R&B grooves along with some interesting Latin influences that helped define the Motown sound. The other Motown drummers were expected to replicate Benjamin's style when they were in a session, and sometimes they recorded a track with two drummers playing simultaneously. He recorded on the Hitsville studio kit, which was permanently kept in the Snakepit. It was a kit formed from various Slingerland, Gretsch, Rogers, and Ludwig parts, and various other unbranded parts. There was also a similarly mixed-component second kit for double drummer sessions. In much the same way as Al Jackson in Memphis, the Motown drummers had little concern about the type of drumheads on the kit. They rarely changed them and only produced a tuning key to give it a half-turn tweak if a drum went noticeably out of tune. They didn't mind that the kit was battered and covered in food stains, just as long as it sounded great on the record. Uriel Jones has stated in the past that Benny Benjamin would be known to pawn the instruments given half a chance, so it was wise to avoid expensive drum equipment anyway. They used a very similar setup to that of Stax with one rack tom, a floor tom, hi-hats, and one or two cymbals all picked up with one or two microphones in the early years. The sound was also similar, with a high tuning and a crisp sound. The tight snare sound was obtained by taping either side of the snare strainer to the bottom head to keep the snares closer to the skin for quick response. They also employed the common technique of taping tissue to the top head to restrict resonance.

Although each Motown drummer had his own style, they all fit perfectly into the Motown mold to create a vast collection of unforgettable tracks. Each one had a common pickup fill that they would regularly use.

The drummers of Motown all came from a jazz background and had a strong swing in their playing. At night they would frequent the Detroit jazz clubs and let loose with their much-loved swing and Latin rhythms. This influence often came through in their studio sessions and gave the playing a depth and color that wouldn't otherwise have been present. However, Benny Benjamin often amassed such a bar bill that it exceeded the band's fee from the night's playing, and they ended up owing money. It was in these clubs that they also began working with Lottie the Body, who was an exotic dancer of the day. Her dancing required heavily Latin-infused rhythms, which then made their way into the Snakepit in subsequent recording sessions and can be heard on such tracks as "Heard It through the Grapevine" by Gladys Knight and the Pips.

The producers of Motown lived by the KISS principle, an acronym for Keep It Simple, Stupid, to create that famous Motown sound. The drum parts, as with the other instruments, had to be simple so as not to get in the way of the complex arrangements of horns, vocals, guitars, keys, and percussion. There was no room for Keith Moon heroics, which would have been severely detrimental to the song. A new breed of drummer was being cultivated. The emphasis was on groove and *playing for the song*, a phrase that is well used among the pop musicians of today.

Over at Stax, they were using songwriters such as Isaac Hayes and David Porter to churn out the hits. This is where pop differs greatly from the credible rock band. Someone writes for the artist, and a group of session players play for the artist. In a rock band, the band play their music and the band collectively write the music, except when playing a cover. The Motown pop machine was no different with its team of writers, the most famous of which were the trio of Brian and Eddie Holland and Lamont Dozier. The written parts were then supplied to the Funk Brothers, and necessary arrangements were made. Often, though, the drummers were responsible for finding the perfect groove with the perfect feel to make that song a danceable hit.

Sadly Benny Benjamin died in 1969 aged forty-three after struggling with drug and alcohol addictions, Richard "Pistol" Allen died in 2002 aged sixty-nine, and Uriel Jones died aged seventy-four in 2009. Their legacy will inspire drummers for generations to come, and their achievements in pop drumming have changed pop music forever.

By now the formulaic three-minute pop song with the verse, chorus, verse, chorus, middle eight, chorus structure was well established. The race for the greatest pop star was in full flow, with a plethora of different groups battling it out for the top spot. This ultimate pop package was embodied in the girl groups, small groups of attractive female singers offering simple, catchy, and highly danceable tunes filled with teenage lyrical emotions and angst. Motown had been quick to fill this demand with the Four Tops, the Supremes, and Martha and the Vandellas, but they weren't the only group fueling this craze.

One of the best-known producers of the 1960s and the pop genre as a whole was Phil Spector. While still in his early twenties, Spector gave the world hit records for such groups as the Crystals and the Ronettes, and in doing so, earned himself a reputation as a highly skilled and creative producer. He realized the importance of a great song but equally valued the sound of the recording. Where Motown and Stax created an incredible live sound and simply recorded it, Spector was instrumental in the philosophy of making a record. He strove to make a recording that was as much of an artwork as the song itself, and to achieve this he paid great attention to the drum sound. The distinction between a live performance and a highly produced studio recording had been made, and in doing so he had created the famous wall of sound.

Spector also believed in using the best men for the job, and as a result, he regularly employed the group of seasoned Hollywood session players who had earned the name the Wrecking Crew, a title that the old, well-dressed, behaved traditional session players had given these denim jeans–wearing youngsters who played rock 'n' roll and were looked upon with disdain. That was until they saw how many hits these next-generation players could churn out; then many of the old school tried to get in on the act as well.

The Hollywood-based Wrecking Crew differed from the Stax and Motown groups, who were soul specialists. The Los Angeles studio players were called upon to play vastly different styles every day, and they needed the ability to quickly read the charts and then competently create the correct part to fit the song in the required genre. And as time really was money, they had to be able to work incredibly efficiently to craft that perfect part. Often playing between three and seven dates a day, these musicians needed to imbue the song with an energy and impeccable feel even when they were exhausted and short tempered. Ability to keep the spirits high through a fun-loving personality is a trait often found in successful session men. Motown's percussionist, Eddie "Bongo" Brown, was well known for this, and so too was another man named Hal Blaine, who was one of Spector's favorites down in Hollywood.

The two main drummers that Spector would use for his sessions were Earl Palmer, the inventor of the backbeat, and the legendary Hal Blaine, who is sometimes regarded as the world's most recorded musician. In fact, these men shared many of the same skills as Al Jackson at Stax and Motown's Funk Brothers drummers.

They had great feel, perfect timing, and always played for the benefit of the song rather than personal glory.

One of the finest examples of the wall of sound is the 1963 track "Be My Baby" by the Ronettes. This is a great example of some of Blaine's commonly used techniques. The drum part consists of just bass and snare drum with plenty of reverb for a huge sound. The lack of hi-hats or cymbals can be attributed to the need to cut through the wall of sound and so as not to conflict with the numerous percussion parts. The chorus also displays the use of tom-tom doubled up with the snare for added impact.

But the best-known Blaine drum lick to come out of the Phil Spector sessions might be the crotchet triplet fill. Spector would often call upon Blaine to play his big crotchet triplets across the track, regardless of whether the track was composed in binary or ternary subdivisions. This would often occur in the latter stages of the piece, such as the final chorus. This is a much-loved and much-copied trademark of Blaine's and can be heard on the Crystals' "Da Doo Ron Ron" or the Ronettes' "Be My Baby," as well as the Beatles' "Day Tripper" and ELO's "All Over the World."

But Blaine didn't restrict himself to just the drum kit. The studio was a place to be creative and play whatever it was that created the best sound to suit that particular piece. Under the guidance of Brian Wilson, many different sounds were used on the Beach Boys' 1966 album *Pet Sounds,* which was a complex soundscape in the same vein as Spector's wall of sound, and it similarly utilized many different and diverse percussive elements. Furthermore, on Simon and Garfunkel's *Bridge over Troubled Water* Blaine used snow-tire chains by dragging them along the floor on beats one and three and then hitting them on beats two and four. But back before the huge Octoplus kit and the studio experimentations, Blaine was playing a four-piece Ludwig drum set before experimenting with Rogers, and then the Japanese manufacturer Pearl.

Due to his great demand in the LA recording studios, playing several dates a day, he found it was impossible to set up and take down his kit for each recording session and still have the energy and time to actually play the drums. It became necessary to hire someone to arrive at the studio before him and set the kit up so he could just walk in fresh and play to his most creative potential. This caught on, and eventually the musician's unions made sure that the recording companies would pay a set cartage fee for drummers, percussionist, harpists, and a range of other burdensome instruments.

While on the subject of the blossoming LA studio pop scene, it seems relevant to mention the Monkees. Whereas many pop groups, such as the Beach Boys and the Carpenters, had their own drummers, they also used session men such as Hal Blaine, Earl Palmer, or Jimmy Gordon in the studio in an effort to achieve the best possible performance for the immortal record that would be enjoyed for many years to come. They were open about this, and it was readily accepted as common practice in the pop music industry.

But the Monkees took this to a whole new level. Often cited as the first totally manufactured boy band, the Monkees were created in response to the Beatles' film *A Hard Day's Night* and subsequently had their own television series. Whether it was due to their intense schedule or lack of ability in the recording studio, many of their recordings were courtesy of the Wrecking Crew with Hal Blaine or Earl Palmer on drums. There was a scandal in 1967 when this recording process was exposed. The Monkees reacted with a session at RCA studios in Hollywood, inviting the press to watch for themselves. They convinced the media and restored their reputation, while Hal Blaine and the Wrecking Crew were in another part of the building secretly recording more tracks for the Monkees. Regardless of this, the Monkees were hugely popular and really paved the way for the future of manufactured pop. Rather than signing an already-formed band, a group was conceived and hundreds of hopefuls were auditioned to fill the allocated spaces for this band; their songs were often written by someone else (such as Neil Diamond's "I'm a Believer"), they often didn't play on their own records, and image was at the forefront of their popularity. This concept would be repeated time and time again.

The role and the inner workings of the pop session drummer today are very much influenced by the likes of Hal Blaine, Earl Palmer, Benny Benjamin, Uriel Jones, Richard Allen, and Al Jackson during the 1960s, and such a staggering number of the enduring hits that still keep dance floors packed to this day were driven by these men. The tragedy is that many of them ended up with very little money to show for it, despite the fortunes that were made through the tracks that they played on, but even sadder was the lack of recognition. This has been put right to some extent with the insight offered by films made about the Stax record company and Motown's Funk Brothers, and through various other materials that have brought these men to the attention of the public. But one of the greatest acts of recognition might be the inclusion of a number of these drummers in the Rock and Roll Hall of Fame under the sidemen category. Hal Blaine and Earl Palmer, introduced in 2000, were the first to make the list in the first year of the sidemen category, followed by Benny Benjamin in 2003, and then DJ Fontana in 2009. At last these performers are being recognized by the general music-listening public, but unfortunately for some, the award is posthumous.

FUNK

Although the elements of pop are very different from funk, as funk is definitely a genre that is created by outstanding and innovative musicianship for the love of the music rather than for commercial success, it is included in this section because in many ways it bridged a gap between the soul and pop before it and much of the music that was to come after it.

The backbeat on two and four was still in its relative infancy when the genre of funk started to materialize out of the soul, jazz, R&B, and gospel of America. The drummers that powered the new funk style brought a new manic, dynamic, and displaced approach to the drum kit that has affected many other genres since.

Where the pop-oriented soul music of Stax and particularly Motown relied on sweet, commercial melodies, funk took the raw energy and the undeniable grooves of the rhythm section and allowed this focus on instrumental feel to dominate. Also borrowing from jazz-styled extended chords, it ignored the changes between chords, preferring to vamp on a single chord while relying on very rhythmic parts from the drums, electric bass, and guitar as well as such instruments as the Hammond organ and various brass instruments, all interlocking with each other and usually involving great levels of syncopation. This energy and cohesiveness was, in part, due to the common writing process. A funk song is nothing without its groove, and therefore the writing was a very collaborative effort. The drummer may start playing a rhythm to which the bass player finds a suitable part, and then the guitarist comes in, and so the track is layered up by each musician in contrast to the pop writing where a songwriter will write the chords, melody, and lyrics before an arranger arranges the parts for the band to play by reading.

The now-accepted two and four backbeat that came from rock 'n' roll and kick-started rock music was used as the basis for funk drumming, but some very important things happened to define funk drumming. A key element of the style is the great use of the semiquavers that fall between the quavers that are so dominant in rock drumming. These notes are used extensively on the bass drum, hi-hat, and snare drum to create a flowing, less rigid feel to the rhythm. Immediately this doubles the number of notes that can be used beyond the regular quaver-dominated rhythms, and therefore the different permutations reach their thousands. To further develop the sound, these semiquavers are often executed with a suggestion of swing, either fully swung or played in the cracks somewhere between the straight and swung semiquavers.

Another defining attribute of the funk sound was the displacement of the backbeat. This can be and has been applied in many different ways, but a common example can be heard in Clyde Stubblefield's drumming on the 1967 track "Cold Sweat," performed by James Brown and written by his band leader Alfred "Pee Wee" Ellis, in which the backbeat remains on beat two but the second accent is played a quaver later on the four + instead of on the recognized beat four. This occurs every other bar to form a two-bar phrase and became a staple technique in funk drumming.

Further still, these many options of semiquaver patterns involving the snare drum gave rise to the use of dynamics enabling multiple snare notes to be played in a bar but still keeping the driving backbeat via accents. The notes between these accented notes became known as ghost or grace notes and are played from a very low height with minimal force to add color and depth to the rhythm. This may have originated in New Orleans with drummers such as Smokey Johnson or Charles "Hungry" Williams, but soon the ghost notes permeated the rhythms of James Brown and came to help define funk drumming. The drummer now had incredibly busy and unusual beats, which were difficult for many musicians to play with at first due to their reliance on the two and four backbeat to keep their place within the bar.

Drummers who were instrumental in these developments included the members of the Brown band, such as Clyde Stubblefield, John "Jabo" Starks, Melvin Parker, and Clayton Fillyau. Brown had a very clear idea of where he wanted the rhythmic emphasis to be placed, and he was insistent that "the one" was felt strongly. This meant that beat one of each bar was very important to the groove, and knowing where the beat was allowed the band to successfully play with advanced syncopation without ending up in different places.

The first drummer who played with such syncopation for Brown was Clayton Fillyau, who took over from the straight-playing Nat Kendrick on the live shows before he had a huge national impact when the 1962 album *Live at the Apollo* was released. Fillyau was instrumental in developing the sound of Brown's rhythm section, with whom he shared the philosophy that the notes could be placed anywhere within the bar, as long as you always know where beat one is so that you can stay in time with the band. This enabled him much more freedom of expression instead of restriction as the metronome of the band.

The effect this had on the band was to make sure that every musician was keeping time in his head. It was no longer possible to rely on the drummer for that steady accent, because he was now capable of placing accents anywhere within the bar, and if the other musicians were not keeping their own time, they would suddenly be thrown out and lost, making it very difficult to find their way back in time again.

On those early live recordings such as *Live at the Apollo* and *Pure Dynamite* from 1963, Fillyau was playing a Slingerland kit

with a wooden snare, which was set up with wide snare strainers at a certain tension so as to obtain a tight crisp sound, vital to
cut through with punchy accents in unison with the horn section
and other band members. He then played a Rogers kit and was so
impressed that he bought one and added a metal snare, including
experimenting with a piccolo snare (a shallow snare of around 3
inches in depth).

Anyone who was fortunate enough to have seen James Brown
perform live will have witnessed one of the tightest bands in history.
An important feature of the live show was the kicks and punches
with which the band was able to accent in order to emphasize certain body movements that Brown performed. He was a disciplinar-
ian, and if one of the musicians were to miss a beat somewhere,
they would be fined. If they made too many mistakes they could
potentially owe Brown money rather than being paid by him. This
fostered a very close, tight band unit in which all eyes and ears were
constantly open and vigilant, waiting for the subtle signals to which
they must react. To help create an air of impossibility, Brown would
often count the band in without making an audible sound. This was
achieved by turning his back on the crowd and walking toward the
band. The speed at which he walked was the tempo for the next
song, and as soon as he spun back to the audience, the first note
of the track burst into life. This was not a gig for the fainthearted
drummer.

Brown was an artist who developed a live band that used multiple drummers. At any time there could be one, two, three, four,
or even five drummers. Sometimes a drummer might double up
and take on stage-managing responsibilities but he was ready to
play if another drummer was sick. Brown was known for drafting
a drummer in on the basis that he could play an original-sounding
rhythm. Sometimes these musicians would only stay for several
months until James realized that their playing was limited to that
one rhythm that had originally excited him. This caused a quick
turnaround of musicians and frequent arrangement alterations,
so that every band member had to be adept at changing the
rhythms and feel of each track depending on who was playing
each night.

By the second half of the 1960s, the James Brown band had found its two most well-known drummers in Clyde Stubblefield and John "Jabo" Starks, and the number of drum kits on stage was reduced to just the two. These men often played together and can be heard on the *Live at the Apollo Volume 2* album from 1967. Often, one of them would play the main groove of the song while the other augmented certain accents to reinforce the beat.

Starks was Brown's first drummer for five years from 1970 and recorded many well-loved tracks such as "Get Up (I Feel like Being a Sex Machine)" in 1970 and numerous hits that reached number one on the R&B chart. Clyde Stubblefield was responsible for some of the funkiest drum tracks recorded for James Brown, with such offerings as the 1967 "Cold Sweat," "I Got the Feeling" in 1968, and "Funky Drummer" in 1970.

James Brown liked to control everything in the band, and so he paid for the stage outfits for each member and also secured an endorsement from the Vox instrument company in the 1960s, which meant his band members played with Vox guitars, amplifiers, and drums regardless of the musician's preference. Despite this, Clyde Stubblefield was not impressed with the drums and usually opted for a Ludwig or Slingerland snare drum. Once he was free from the Vox contract, he returned to Ludwig and then later Remo drums.

Later in the decade and through the 1970s came the rise of the San Francisco band Tower of Power and their innovative drummer David Garibaldi. Although predominantly playing a black style of music, Garibaldi and his fellow bass player Francis "Rocco" Prestia were white musicians who brought a fresh approach to the funk grooves. Where the snare and bass patterns were being explored beneath a fairly consistent hi-hat pattern, Garibaldi began using Latin-influenced patterns on the hi-hat or ride cymbal. At the same time interesting hi-hat patterns can also be heard on tracks such as the Meters' 1969 offering "Cissy Strut" with Joseph "Zigaboo" Modeliste on drums. But Garibaldi really excelled in this area and pioneered a new complexity of funk drumming. By playing these complex patterns with the right hand using ghost notes alongside accents, he then played complex left-hand snare rhythms, which also relied on accents and ghost notes before adding yet more complex patterns on the bass drum. To execute such a rhythm demands a great deal of limb independence and coordination. Garibaldi's beats are almost compositions in themselves, with many grooves so identifiable when heard on their own without a band that they are instantly recognizable to fans by name, such as the Oakland Stroke, Soul Vaccination groove, and the King Kong groove. In fact the King Kong rhythm, which became famous through David Garibaldi, was actually played by Pete DePoe in the band Redbone and bears a startling resemblance to the Puerto Rican rhythm used in bomba music to which dancers move frantically in time with the drums. This clearly shows how such a rhythm created for dancing can also be infectious when adapted for the drum kit and applied in a funk context.

These pioneering rhythms were first performed on Garibaldi's white satin flame pearl 1963 Slingerland kit with a 20 × 14-inch bass drum, 12 × 8 and 14 × 14 single-headed toms, and a 14 × 6.5-inch Ludwig Super Sensitive snare drum. After this he moved through Ludwig, Rogers, and then finally Yamaha when he signed up as an endorser in 1982. Regarding cymbals, Garibaldi started with Paiste before being coaxed to Sabian, where he designed his own signature products. His recognized Yamaha setup revolves around a standard five-piece kit with 10-, 13-, and 16-inch toms and his own signature 14-inch piccolo brass snare drum. He also uses a 10- or 12-inch auxiliary snare to the left of his hi-hat. Along with his signature ride cymbal and four crashes, he often uses a second signature 12-inch hi-hat above the floor tom. Along with a cowbell clamped onto the bass drum, he has many different sonic options for utilizing the Latin influences with his right hand as well as snare options to vary the dynamic and timbre of his left-handed ghost note patterns.

These and the many other funk drummers of that era have created highly infectious rhythms that have influenced many styles and countless drummers since, and it was their grooves that have become some of the most sampled beats in history to drive a new breed of composition.

Although funk is hugely popular today and has enjoyed successful revivals through time, the essence of the music that was born in the 1960s was set to change, as with all movements, and it was again at the hands of technology that this was brought about.

DISCO

As the funk groups' popularity grew, so did their stages. Suddenly the emphasis was changing for the drummer. All of those subtleties and majestic ghosted notes were being replaced by a louder, more driving rhythm that could fight through the noise and fill these larger halls to keep the crowds dancing. Funk was also filling the floors at nightclubs with its extended instrumental tracks on 12-inch vinyl singles. This popularity helped artists and producers to take a step further in that direction and write music specifically for the dance floor. They wanted a sound that would keep people dancing all night long.

Where Memphis and Detroit had been instrumental in soul music, Philadelphia was instrumental in disco. Writers such as Leon Huff and Kenneth Gamble were arranging grandiose orchestral soul backing tracks and achieving greater success than the Motown label as this soul sound evolved. The dance floors were enjoying the complex grooves of the funk drummers and the driving, syncopated electric bass guitar lines, and as discothèques in Philadelphia and New York required more dancing music to satisfy the paying members of public, this funky soul veered off to fulfill this demand for dance floor hits.

The result was coined as disco, and it primarily incorporated soul and funk but also borrowed heavily from Latin rhythms, which were played on various percussion instruments alongside the drum kit. The luscious string arrangements were often mixed with layers of synthesized pads while funky horn lines and rhythmic, palm-muted, wah-wah–infused guitar sounds were prominent. One of the most defining aspects of disco, however, is the drumbeat. It consists of a four-on-the-floor bass drum pattern that involves a consistent note on every crotchet. The snare reinforces the back-beat on beats two and four, while the hi-hat involves semiquavers with an accent on every third semiquaver in each beat. This is often achieved with a slight opening of the hi-hat and is now recognized as the generic disco beat.

The New York session drummer Alan Schwartzberg is often cited as originator of the disco beat due to his heavy involvement in the recording scene at studios such as New York's Power Station during the early 1970s. One of his defining recordings in this era was the Gloria Gaynor classic "Never Can Say Goodbye" in 1975, which incorporated that generic disco beat and was the one of the first disco-styled tracks to reach the Billboard top ten as well as helping to start a trend of taking an original song and giving it a disco makeover. Many other tracks were rerecorded or remixed in the disco style throughout this period.

However, despite Alan Schwartzberg's efforts, he was not the first to play such a rhythm. The Harold Melvin and the Blue Notes track "The Love I Lost" from 1973 incorporated the disco hi-hat sound that accented every second quaver note and had a definite disco-rhythm feel. Earlier than that in 1971, the great session drummer Bernard Purdie can be heard executing the semiquaver disco hi-hat pattern in Aretha Franklin's song "Rock Steady," but even earlier than that was the 1969 hit "Only the Strong Will Survive" by Jerry Butler, which included many disco elements in the chorus such as the string arrangement and the driving drum pattern with offbeat hi-hat accents from Earl Young.

But trying to narrow the inventor of a whole movement or even just the creator of the quintessential drum rhythm for that musical style is unfeasible and quite possibly pointless. As with all changes, it takes a number of social, technological, and personnel factors for a gradual shift to occur before a genre can be defined.

What is certain is that by the mid-1970s the genre was readily accepted and the charts were rife with disco hits as well as dedicated radio sessions and ever-increasing discothèques at which people could enjoy the music and the hedonistic social scene that accompanied it.

At the fore of this movement were two writers (previously mentioned) in Philadelphia named Kenneth Gamble and Leon Huff, who formed Philadelphia International Records (PIR) in the early 1970s. They were significant in the move away from the simple orchestrations of soul toward the expansive, layered sound that evolved into disco, and they produced over seventy number-one hits from numerous artists such as The O'Jays, Patti LaBelle, and Harold Melvin and the Blue Notes.

Just as Stax and Motown had their house band, PIR relied on a pool of musicians to record their tracks. The musicians formed a group in 1971 to play as the resident studio group for PIR at Sigma Sound Studios and became known as Mother Father Sister Brother (MFSB). At the heart of the group was Ronnie Baker on bass, Norman Harris on guitar, and Earl Young on drums, but there were several other drummers, including Carl Chambers, Charles Collins, Keith Benson, and Quinton Joseph.

These solid musicians were able to take advantage of the recording technology, which had moved on from the 1960s. In the 1970s, the recording studio producers and engineers had access to twenty-four-track recording and as a result were able to record the drums with individual microphones on each voice of the kit. Despite this, certain techniques from bygone eras were still favored. One of these was the use of a wallet on the snare drum batter head, and indeed in the case of Sigma Sound and its engineer/owner Joe Tarsia, the toms were sometimes subjected to the same treatment. In fact, due to the close microphone techniques, the drum sound was placed under the proverbial microscope, and so Tarsia became well known for his attention to detail and constant search for the perfect sound. To this end one of his favorite subjects was the drumming of Earl Young and in particular, his hi-hat work. With him and other drummers, Tarsia experimented with various drum kits, tunings, placement of microphones, and even the type of bass drum beaters. Often the MFSB drum sound consisted of highly tuned, single-headed toms, and the bass drum was recorded with the front head removed, allowing a pillow to be pushed up against the inside of the batter head and a microphone placed inside. An improvised tunnel was also constructed and attached to the bass drum to elongate the shell for a more ambient sound without unnecessary bleed from the other voices of the drum kit.

As Sigma Sound Studios were one of the first studios to own a fully functional automated recording console and with the aforementioned advent of twenty-four-track recording, they were able to deal with such huge orchestrations with greater ease than in the previous decade by recording the rhythm track first and then adding the string or horn sections later. This helped to achieve the prominent bass drum sound, which Earl Young often played in unison with the phrasing of the bass player, resulting in a tight rhythm sound in the lower frequencies, another feature of the disco sound.

As with so many eras of pop music, the singer is the face of the songs, but the producer is significantly responsible for creating the sound. The producers and songwriters have a great impact to make the genre what it is and explore the newly available technology to create something fresh sounding. Of course the musicians have a large part in this, as do the vocalists, but the producer is often bringing in the new sounds that ultimately help to define a genre.

Disco was one of these eras. When a record is full of lush string orchestrations and a full band, recording sessions can be expensive. If suddenly a synthesizer can be programmed or played by one person to create the same effect in a small control room, then that technology becomes very appealing to the producers. This was the beginning of the battle with technology for the drummer as well. When a drummer is forced to record a robotic rhythm with little variation and execute that pattern with such precision that it sounds like a machine, it is easy to see why a machine that could play the pattern more precisely than any human, without spending hours setting up microphones on a drum kit and with a perfect quality of sound, would also be appealing to a producer. As a result, this became increasing popular throughout the 1970s and helped to shape the evolution of dance-oriented music.

By the end of the 1970s, the term disco and all that it stood for had fallen out of vogue, possibly hastened by the disco demolition riot in 1979, but the pathway had been cleared. People now demanded specific dance music to be created for nightclubs and all-night dancing.

Many new dance music fashions have come and gone since, but in most of them the four-on-the-floor bass drum rhythm and the incessant hi-hat pattern with an offbeat accent is central. That moronic, robotic beat is what drives the masses to dance. Its simplicity is its brilliance. No knowledge of music is needed to be drawn into the trancelike rhythms and become lost in a state of euphoria. Many acts took this idea and embraced it wholeheartedly, an extreme example being the German group Kraftwerk and their 1974 album *Autobahn,* which relied heavily on electronic instruments to obtain the machinelike, monotonous sound.

One of the other products that began with the mighty Motown label and also experimented with disco ideals was that of the Jackson Five, the most famous member of which was Michael Jackson, who went on to enjoy a hugely successful adult solo career and became known as the King of Pop. Michael's career was long, beginning at the age of six, and was only cut short due to his tragic death in 2009. During that time he moved with every change in the pop industry, often leading the way with groundbreaking concerts, videos, dance moves, songs, and recording styles.

Of the many drumming greats who contributed to Jackson's recorded catalog, one of the early players in his solo career was John J.R. Robinson who had built a reputation with the band Rufus and Chaka Khan before working on the 1979 *Off the Wall* album. Producer Quincy Jones brought him in to create the parts to tracks such as "Rock with You" and "Don't Stop 'til You Get Enough" with such iconic fills as the "Rock with You" intro and imbued with crisp and precise hi-hat work. For this album he used an old Gretsch kit with a 22 × 14-inch bass drum, 12- and 13-inch rack toms, and a 16-inch floor tom, as well as well-worn Zildjian cymbals. All of this equipment had been acquired while studying at Boston's Berklee College of Music in 1975. As well as this he performed on wine bottles with Jackson for "Working Day and Night." Robinson also came back for the 1987 *Bad* album with Quincy Jones still at the helm.

Between Robinson's two albums was the record-breaking 1982 *Thriller* album, which saw Jeff Porcaro and Leon "Ndugu" Chancler supply the drumbeats. Although Porcaro played on four album tracks, Chancler finished the rest of the album with hits such as "Billie Jean" and "Thriller." Playing on a Yamaha Custom kit and Paiste cymbals, Chancler's drum parts were mirrored exactly with programmed drums, much the same as Robinson's drum parts would be for *Bad* five years later. To achieve such an excellent drum sound, engineer Bruce Swedien also employed such techniques as isolating the snare drum microphone with a screen to cut out other kit voices as well as using a bag over the front of the bass drum, which zipped up with the microphone inside.

Another player in the Jackson sound was session ace and Yellowjackets member Ricky Lawson, who joined Jackson for the 1987 *Bad* tour and the *Dangerous* tour of 1992, although he had initially played for the Jackson Five's 1978 *Destiny* album. By the late 1980s and into the 1990s, many of Jackson's tracks included programmed drums, and so although Lawson relied on his Remo kit for much of the playing (which had a custom-designed wrap for the *Dangerous* tour with album cover artwork), he also had a custom-made rack of Akai samplers that he triggered with pads and acoustic triggers to replicate the studio sounds.

Despite all the highly professional drummers that have kept the hallowed drum seat warm, it was Jonathan "Sugarfoot" Moffett that Jackson repeatedly returned to when available, and it was his knowledge of the necessary visual prowess as well as his impeccable timing and perfect feel that earned him this respect. Having begun playing with the Jackson Five in 1979, Moffett was the man chosen for the ill-fated *This Is It* tour, which was in rehearsal thirty years later when Jackson died.

Moffett had a great interest in the visual aspects of his stage appearance, and part of his visualization is an enormous drum setup with futuristic-looking frameworks or racks to support the drums. This has important practical reasons when setting up a large drum kit, as all the drums, cymbals, and microphones can be supported on the same framework instead of having legs from individual stands competing for floor space. However, by the 1984 Jackson Five *Victory* tour Moffett had created a customized rack design costing in the region of US$13,000, which was as much a visual showpiece on stage as it was practical. Moffett went on to forge a successful pop career playing with Madonna, Elton John, George Michael, Janet Jackson, and many others, and throughout this time he was constantly searching for new rack designs. He teamed up with the hardware specialists Gibraltar in the early 1990s and they enabled him to realize his visions of metal sculptures, which gave an impression of the drummer trapped inside a huge cage, reinforcing the image of the drummer as a wild animal, which had been popularized by drummers such as Keith Moon, John Bonham, and *The Muppet Show*'s Animal.

For the intended 2009 *This Is It* tour Moffett chose to position the front support bar behind the rack toms so that the toms would appear to be floating, as the audience could see no visible means of support. He used several extended poles to raise the cymbal stands above his head and then position them to hang down to the correct playing level. These highly elaborate rack systems require consultations and several days to design with a Gibraltar representative. Among his many drums and cymbals suspended from this framework were three bass drums in 22-, 24-, and 26-inch diameters. He would swap between the three sizes to achieve greater dynamics and a sense of melody. The overblown, excessively big drum kit with two bass drums, several toms, and numerous cymbals all framed by a gigantic gong has become synonymous with the stadium rock or heavy metal drummers. Thanks to Neil Peart of Rush, Peter Criss of Kiss, Nicko McBrain of Iron Maiden, Tommy Lee of Mötley Crüe, Joey Jordison of Slipknot, Carl Palmer of ELP, Mike Portnoy of Dream Theatre, and many others, audiences have come to expect such vast drum sets upon the stage of these types of bands. But it is because of drummers like Jonathan Moffett that we also commonly see this in the pop setting as well.

Although such pop drum setups may look as big as the heavy metal counterparts at a casual glance, the content of the kit will differ vastly between the different styles. The drum kits of hard rock and metal acts are focused on thunderous volume and aggression, and these will be discussed later in this chapter. In contrast the pop drummer requires a tighter, more focused sound that provides the driving, often dance-oriented beats that are common in the pop style. Pop music by nature is of the moment. It is often short lived and based on feelings, sounds, and opinions of the time. As a result, it is prone to change and adapt constantly, unlike more traditional styles such as jazz or classical, in which innovation has to be accepted over time and often at the disgust of purists. This means that pop readily embraces new technologies, a point that can clearly be observed on the drum kit.

As the 1970s disco disappeared and the robotic sounds of Kraftwerk permeated the music industry, many artists felt drawn to these new sounds from every genre, although a majority of the more musically proficient performers returned to their acoustic instruments after this temporary deviation. Pop, however, had no intention of returning to those archaic acoustic sounds, and so it continued to experiment with the sounds on offer. The term disco became very unfashionable, but the relentless four-on-the-floor bass drum pattern and offbeat hi-hat were irresistible, and as a result, the counterculture club scene was thriving as different dance genres such as house music emerged and evolved into the rave scene along with its accompanying drug culture of cocaine and MDMA.

Pop was becoming increasingly manufactured, and where the likes of Berry Gordy or Gamble and Huff had created a factory line for hit records, other production teams were taking this to new levels, such as Stock, Aitken, and Waterman (SAW) in England, who were instrumental in creating the highly synthesized pop record sound that dominated the 1980s charts. But Gordy had the Funk Brothers just as Gamble and Huff had MFSB to create their music. SAW relied on their engineers, producers, and plastic boxes full of circuit boards. The Yamaha DX7 was used for many of the bass lines, and the Linn 9000 drum machine was famously called upon to supply the drumbeats. This left the tracks devoid of any musical artistic expression, interaction, and human feel, but then that was irrelevant. The output of SAW was created with the single goal of commercial success without any consideration for artistic value.

Another producer who was pushing the use of technology was Trevor Horn, who has enjoyed a long career working with artists such as Grace Jones, Cher, Frankie Goes to Hollywood, the Pet Shop Boys, and Robbie Williams. He was using a Roland TR808, Simmons modules, and also the Linn machines. This popularity of drum machines was the worst possible news for session drummers across the world. They feared they would become obsolete. A cheaper, easier, more efficient, and more precise version of them had been built. This was compounded by the fact that much of the session players' bread-and-butter work is with advertising jingles. Advertising has always followed the popular trends, and so when pop music was using heavily synthesized sounds, jingles were also doing the same, and so the session industry shrank instantly.

With producers such as Trevor Horn, pop was taken to a new height of commercialism. Image, attitude, and sound were considered to be of equal importance, and the creation of the pop package as a whole was paramount. The relentless four-on-the-floor bass drum, which was popularized in the 1970s disco era, although dull and predictable, gave the listeners the perfect pattern to dance to, and it could be argued that this simplistic drum rhythm allowed the producer to successfully syncopate other instruments around it, just as James Brown's band had done with the emphasis on beat one. Either way, the drummer was not needed anymore, as the producer was perfectly capable of programming in and layering up these different sampled drum and percussion sounds.

Interestingly, even some of the progressive rock bands underwent significant changes in their musical output and entered new arenas, which have been described by many fans as selling out. These bands that originated as progressive, boundary breaking, innovative, and virtuoso turned their attentions to simplistic, catchy pop. Two such bands are Yes and Genesis. The 1983 Yes album titled 90125, which gave us the single "Owner of a Lonely Heart" and reached number one in the U.S. Billboard Hot 100, is a good example of this change. It may be significant that Trevor Horn, the producer, is mentioned on the credits, but the drummer, Alan White, is not. Many elements of this track are very much more a pop sound than progressive rock, and not least the drum part. The sound is very tight and produced, and the playing of a basic eight beat is rigidly maintained throughout the track with very little variation. The sound and mindset was achieved with the guidance of Horn, who stripped back White's kit piece by piece until he was left with only the snare and bass drum. This eliminated any distractions from other kit voices and focused White's playing on the essence of the basic pattern. The hi-hats and cymbals were then overdubbed afterward before the rest of the track was built up as individual parts. Small sections of drum loops can also be heard at the beginning of the track and midway through it. These were recordings of James Brown songs that had been sampled on the Fairlight CMI and then added to the track. The album inspired comments from Bill Bruford, the former Yes drummer who was adored for his innovation, when he declared that the band was a very good pop group.

Even earlier than *90125* was the 1980 Genesis album titled *Duke,* which produced very mainstream pop-oriented songs relying heavily on drum machines and synthesizers. The single "Duchess" taken from that album actually displays the Roland CompuRhythm CR-78 in the opening scene of the video, highlighting the fact that despite containing a very able drummer within the band, they were still proudly using a machine to create their rhythm track. This album is considered a turning point for Genesis as they moved toward more commercial synthesized music.

As the 1990s came along, the manufactured-pop market intensified, and records were increasingly made in small studios by one or two humans and lots of machines. By the turn of the century reality television became the medium through which many of the singers that were to perform these songs were found, but the drum patterns hadn't changed all that much. As with most eras of pop music, influences were brought in from other genres and applied to the pop format. The popularity of hip-hop and modern R&B also increased dramatically, although this will be discussed later in the chapter, but generally pop drumming is still based around the simple eight beat, often inciting people to dance with it. It focuses more on simplicity than virtuoso playing, criteria that are achievable by a programmed beat. And so with the studio drummer becoming unemployed or otherwise adapting and evolving to fit in with the technological shifts, much of the work remaining was for live playing. Although the machine was preferred to make the records in the studio, the human was still more entertaining to watch on a stage.

With all the newest studio techniques in use by the producers, the drummer was left with the demanding task of replicating these sounds in a live setting. This meant that it was necessary to embrace all that technology had to offer and move with these trends rather than against them.

Furthermore, the personnel of live pop bands in general had decreased over the years as a result of technology. The drummer now often had an increased responsibility with regard to reproducing the sounds from the studio recordings with total accuracy. The drummer often had to find the right balance between playing some of the parts live and triggering samples for other parts. He would also have choices to make at times when approaching a track that had made use of multiple rhythmic overdubs in the studio as to which parts should be played and which could be left out. A pop drummer was now also required to have a good working knowledge of samples, programming, and triggering as well as all of the technical and musical skills that any musician should have. As a result of much of the music using samples or even backing tracks, the drummer was increasingly required to have a very comfortable relationship with a click track or metronome. Although the whole band may have had a metronome in their ear monitors, often it was just the drummer, and he would have to stay locked in with that even if other band members might be pulling the tempo in other directions.

The drum machine is constantly advancing, allowing nondrummers to create rhythm tracks that the drummer has to replicate live. The rhythms may feel very unnatural and demand that the drummer plays in a way that a human wouldn't necessarily choose to play. Whoever has recorded or programmed those studio-recorded drum parts, it is usually one drummer alone who has to play all the parts convincingly and authentically in the live arena.

One example of this type of player and the equipment that he needs is the UK-based pop session player Steve Barney, who has played with many artists, such as Annie Lennox, Jeff Beck, Anastacia, the Sugababes, and James Morrison. His typical pop setup around 2010 was based around a Premier Artist Series black sparkle kit with 22-inch bass drum, 12-, 14-, and 16-inch toms, a 14-inch brass snare, and a 10-inch birch snare to cater to other sounds. The snare drum is such a core part of the drum kit that even when drummers use less toms and cymbals, they often utilize a second snare drum to give greater flexibility in their expression and to make available more timbres for the main rhythm parts of tracks. This is a typical set for many different genres, but there are also some extra items that really help define this as a pop set. To replicate the album sounds for each artist with which he works, and with total accuracy, Barney carries an Akai *MPC1000* sampler, Koby mesh pads, a Roland TD10 electronic drum module, and his own mixer to achieve the perfect balance between these varied sounds.

It is the same story in the United States with drummers such as Mark Schulman, who has played with Billy Idol, Foreigner, Simple Minds, and Pink. Although he began with a smaller drum set, he felt the necessity to increase this kit to deal with Pink's material, and by the 2010 tours he was using a Gretsch USA Custom kit comprising 24- and 20-inch bass drums, 10-, 12-, 14-, 16-, and 18-inch toms, and a 14-inch brass snare accompanied by a 12-inch bubinga wood snare. Along with an array of thirteen cymbals, he also uses the Roland PD125 12-inch mesh heads and a TD20 module. His dedicated drum technician, Mark Bennett, has also helped design a custom Gibraltar rack, in a similar vein to Moffett's cages that are as much a visual aspect as a practical one. With his stick-twirling antics, Schulman embodies the audio/visual stadium-pop showman drummer that is required in this area of the music industry.

As programming has been around for over three decades now, some drummers have turned the tables. Rather than programmers striving for real drum patterns, some real human drummers are choosing to achieve the ability to replicate some of the most unorthodox and challenging programmed beats in a live setting. An example of this work can be seen in Jojo Mayer's project called Nerve in which he plays drum and bass rhythms on acoustic drums at astounding speeds and with metronomic precision.

With every technological advance, pop music advances in some way through the timbres, effects, and various sounds that are applied. Harmonically, rhythmically, and melodically it might be slow moving, but it is certainly the music of the people and most directly responds to the social and political attitudes of the consumers that buy it.

Wherever pop music goes in the future, it is sure to require a drummer who can adapt to the cutting-edge technology and find the perfect drum part to work for the song with minimal fuss and maximum efficiency, just as the likes of Blaine, Jackson, Benjamin, and Moffett have done in the past. Regardless of which period of time we examine, the main traits of the working professional pop drummer remain the same. They can play what is required with perfect timing, they can adapt to work with every style and technological advance, they demonstrate musical discipline and restraint to avoid playing unnecessary notes, and they do all of this with an amiable personality and good nature so that others want to be around them in the heated studio session or long and arduous tour.

HEAVY METAL

The influence of the British rock bands of the 1960s was huge and spread through many styles of modern music as musicians drew from various aspects of these groups. The increased amplification and dominance of electric guitars had become very popular, and greater emphasis was being placed on these elements to take them to new levels. The earliest roots of heavy metal (HM) have been argued about enthusiastically for decades, with various influences cited as the catalyst for the genre. Regardless of where it actually began, the first bands to really focus on the aspects that are considered core in HM were British groups such as Black Sabbath, Deep Purple, and Led Zeppelin.

The necessary and fundamental elements that define HM include loud, distorted guitars, which are now regularly down tuned for a darker, more menacing sound since Tony Iommi from Black Sabbath did so to compensate for his missing fingertips from an earlier accident; screaming vocals often in the higher register (although in modern HM they are often incredibly low); and fast, athletic, and powerful drumming on monstrous drum kits, which together helped create this vast onslaught of sound and gave the fans a new identity. They became heavy metalers.

Although by today's HM standards they are definitely placed in the hard rock category, Led Zeppelin did display many traits that helped inspire the HM genre, and John Bonham on drums outwardly displayed the type of ferocious, primal drumming that demonstrated absolute power. Beyond the animalistic outward appearance, a closer examination reveals much more than just volume and big drums. Bonham, who hailed from England's Midlands just south of Birmingham, displayed great soul and groove in his playing, despite being responsible for the largest-sounding beats of the time. He was, and still is, largely imitated, having recorded many iconic grooves such as the huge drum sound in Zeppelin's 1971 version of "When the Levee Breaks" and their 1979 offering "Fool in the Rain," which demonstrates a well-executed half-time shuffle inflected with ghost notes on the snare in a similar manner to the Purdie shuffle, made famous by American session drummer Bernard Purdie. As well as honoring the shuffle of Purdie, Bonham paid homage to Charles Connor's drum pattern on Little Richard's 1957 hit "Keep on Knocking" with his intro and main rhythm in Zeppelin's 1971 track "Rock and Roll," which bears a startling resemblance to Connor's part.

But although there were many skillful and soulful elements to Bonham's playing, his sheer force and presence continues to inspire people to pick up sticks and strike drums. He only used a single bass drum with a Ludwig Speedking pedal and is noted for a very fast and powerful right foot to play such trademark rhythms as the bass drum triplet. This involved playing the second two notes of a semiquaver triplet with the foot while the right hand played the first note. This can be heard to great effect on the 1969 track "Good Times, Bad Times." Although Ginger Baker had created an entire piece of music based around a drum solo with "Toad" and Gene Krupa to an extent even earlier with "Sing, Sing, Sing," Bonham also helped popularize the extended rock drum solo, which has become a big feature in many HM bands' live set. Bonham actually recorded his famous solo called "Moby Dick" for their 1969 album *Led Zeppelin II*, although his live reproductions of the track varied dramatically and could last anywhere up to thirty minutes, including sections where he played with his hands, often resulting in bleeding and blistering. His reputation for power, speed, and bringing the drummer to the fore with solos became staple elements of the HM drummer.

Just as Ringo Starr had done with the Beatles, Bonham flew the flag for Ludwig drums and helped to make their drum kits synonymous with rock drumming. His most iconic kit was the amber Ludwig Vistalite used from 1973, but he was also known for his green sparkle Ludwig and later the stainless steel Ludwig. Although the sizes varied and changed over the years, he is most known for using a 26 × 14-inch bass drum, either 15 × 12-inch or 14 × 10-inch rack toms, a 16 × 16- and an 18 × 16-inch floor tom, and the 14 × 6.5-inch chrome Supra-phonic 402 snare. His big drum sizes were complemented with big Paiste cymbals such as the 15-inch Sound Edge hi-hats, an occasional 24-inch Giant Beat ride cymbal, and the almighty 36-inch gong behind him. He also added two Natal congas, which were followed by Ludwig Universal Model Timpani from 1972 as well as the chin-a-ring tambourine above the hi-hat and a cowbell clamped to the bass drum for his Latin-infused rhythms. His drumheads of choice were either the Remo CS "black dot" or the Ludwig "silver dot" heads, which used a laminated dot in the center for extra durability and a focused tone. But much of the huge sound came from the treatment of these massive drums. Rather than dampen them as many drummers of the era were fond of doing, Bonham tuned the resonant heads high and the batter heads slightly slacker and didn't dampen anything, which allowed the drum to resonate and boom freely.

Despite those tough heads, Bonham did break equipment, and his roadie, Mick Hinton, was known to keep an identically tuned spare bass drum with rack tom attached in case one broke. At times Bonham would play the bass drum so hard that the pedal beater would fly off and the remaining metal rod would split the bass drumhead. He'd also keep a spare snare tuned and ready on a stand, a spare set of cymbals, and plenty of Ludwig 2A hickory sticks ready for quick replacements. In fact, he had a whole separate box, which was 6 feet long, just filled with spare parts for when the heavy rock drummer broke the next part of the insufficiently strong drum kit.

It was drummers such as Bonham who placed such great demands on the equipment that they had exceeded the capabilities of

manufacturers who couldn't react quickly enough. Bass drum pedals would crack, cymbal stand joints would routinely suffer damaged threads, and increased amplification for guitars meant that
the minimal drum microphones couldn't prevent the drummer's
being drowned out altogether during live performances. Add to this
the trend in drum size and quantity expansion and it was clear that
things needed to evolve.

Throughout the 1970s and into the 1980s kits were getting pro-
gressively sturdier, and this durability was often the focus of drum
manufacturers' marketing strategies. It was this change of focus
that was seized by the Asian competitors who took full benefit from
the West's complacency.

Japan did possess drum companies already, but they offered me-
diocre kits, often with someone else's badge on the shell. They saw
an opportunity to raise their game and give the drumming community what it wanted. The acrylic phase had died out and wood shells
had returned, but they needed an overhaul to meet rigorous touring.
Drum shells had evolved from the thin three plies to six or more,
and double-ply drumheads had given greater strength in that department. The hardware, however, had been somewhat overlooked.

Three companies were set to make an impact, and they have
continued to do so until today as three of the biggest names in
modern drum kits. Tama began dealing in drums in 1955, Pearl in
1946, and Yamaha created a drum department in 1966. Many of
the changes they made in the 1970s and 1980s have shaped the
modern drum kit.

Yamaha introduced the ball-joint tom mount, which allowed
360 degrees of rotation; floor tom stands as requested by session
legend Steve Gadd (add to this the 10-inch- and 12-inch-diameter
rack toms and the fusion kit sizes were born); the first hideaway
boom cymbal arm; the locking hi-hat clutch to maintain top hi-hat
cymbal positioning; and the subkick, which helps capture the full
range of bass drum frequencies and especially the low end. Yamaha
also gave us the 9000 recording custom drum kit, which proved to
be hugely popular through the 1980s.

Tama introduced cymbal boom arms in 1974 with wide,
double-braced legs and great strength, allowing cymbals to be

conveniently positioned around the expanding mammoth kits; the multiclamp; nylon restriction bushings in the joints of cymbal stands to prevent the common problem of threading; and the X-hat, which allowed a permanently closed second hi-hat. They also gave the world some new drums with the gong bass drum, a single-headed, 20-inch drum with an oversized 22-inch head hung on a frame; and the Octobans, a collection of melodically tuned 6-inch-diameter drums whose tone is differed by varying depths. These have been favored by Stewart Copeland, Mike Portnoy, and Simon Phillips among others.

Pearl went searching for original products and gave us wood-fiberglass drums (wood shells with a fiberglass interior lining) and then in 1978 the Vari-Pitch range, which combined the wood-fiberglass shell with rototoms on top so that the heads could be tuned by rotating them. With regard to hardware they developed the hinged-tube tom arm, which has been copied by many other manufacturers, and were also the first to introduce the rack system in 1983 at the request of Toto's Jeff Porcaro. This sturdy framework enabled every drum, cymbal, and microphone to be attached via a clamp, thereby doing away with countless legs awkwardly slotted among each other.

They also boast a unique shell-construction technique, which combines hydraulic pressure, precision-cut scarf joints, and intense heat to melt the glue through every fiber of the wood. The SST (Super Strength Technology) is demonstrated in their advertising by a Hummer H1 vehicle of nearly 4 tons with one wheel perched atop a Reference Series tom. Suffice to say that the drum survived unscathed.

Then in 1984 Pearl used its trump card. While other companies focused on high-end kits, Pearl introduced its Export Series as a budget kit, which went on to be the biggest-selling kit of all time and, over its twenty-five-year span, managed to improve, incorporating many elements of the professional series.

It was the HM drummers that were placing the most demand on these kits and forcing the Japanese manufacturers, and then the rest of the world, to adapt to these demands. And these demands were only going to increase as the heaviest of all genres evolved.

One of these bands was Deep Purple. Just like Zeppelin, Deep Purple are not strictly heavy metal but were part of the movement that added more power and volume to the rock genre. Their drummer Ian Paice played with a great intensity, but just like Bonham, he displayed great control of dynamics and subtleties that elude, or are of little interest to, many heavy metal drummers. Despite his power, his first influences were obtained by watching the likes of Gene Krupa in Hollywood movies before being inspired by English drummers such as Ringo Starr and Ginger Baker. In fact, after admiring Ringo Starr's black oyster pearl Ludwig kit, Paice got one for himself in 1964 for US$740 (£450), although he had to reposition the setup to fit with his left-handed playing. Deep Purple formed and went on to be one of the biggest-selling rock bands during the 1970s, and Paice carved out a strong following who were drawn to his power and individuality.

He now endorses the Japanese company Pearl and plays a Masters kit with a single bass drum, seven toms, and numerous cymbals. He also has his own signature snare with Pearl, which is a 14 × 6.5-inch, chrome-plated SensiTone shell with locking nuts for the tension rods to prevent the drum from detuning itself when played as powerfully as Paice likes to play and the strange addition of an internal dampener, which has generally fallen out of favor due to the damage that it can, and often does, cause when overtightened.

For most of his career, however, Paice stayed loyal to Ludwig until he felt that they had allowed quality to slip, and so he jumped ship to Pearl. Just like Bonham, Paice favored the single bass drum (which he changed from a 22-inch to a 26-inch in the early 1970s for more power), one rack tom, and two floor toms.

During his Ludwig heyday, Paice recorded numerous influential drum tracks that inspired many future HM drummers, such as Lars Ulrich of Metallica. Despite never really being a double bass drum user, such a technique can be heard on the 1971 track "Fireball" from the album of the same name. It was initially attempted with a single bass drum pedal, but to achieve the consistency and power a second bass drum was utilized. In fact, it was one of Keith Moon's bass drums, still in the studio from a previous recording session, that Paice borrowed for this recording. Also from the *Fireball* album was a track titled "The Mule," which although absent on the studio recording, became known in live performances for the drum solo. Just as with Zeppelin's "Moby Dick," Deep Purple's "The Mule" began with the whole band playing before they left the stage to leave Ian Paice remaining for a freeform, improvised solo until the band returned to finish the song. Paice had very good command of rudiments and based much of the solo on the snare drum, utilizing great dynamics and speed to bring the solo up to crescendos and then back down to near silence in places. He also used the triplet roll that was popular during that era and much used by Bonham too. This involved a right hand on the floor tom or snare, followed by a left hand on the rack tom, and then a bass drum note. Of course this would have involved a reversed sticking pattern for the left-handed Paice. Played at speed, this technique created an impressive wall of drum sound. Interestingly, the 1972 release "Smoke on the Water" features a semiquaver hi-hat pattern that is reminiscent of a disco beat placed into a heavy rock context, before the drum part breaks into a standard rock beat for the verse. Paice utilized different techniques, dynamics, and musicality with his early jazz and rock influences, but he helped light the pathway for the future heavy metal drummers.

It was really in 1968 when the band Earth changed their name and modeled themselves on the dark and harrowing elements of horror movies that the first true HM band was born: Black Sabbath. The original members were Ozzy Osbourne, Tony Iommi, Terry "Geezer" Butler, and Bill Ward, all of whom hailed from postwar, working-class Birmingham in the United Kingdom, surrounded by metal factories and small, run-down terraced housing. It was a depressing setting but one that could inspire exciting and powerful music imbued with strong emotions; particularly aggression. Bill (William Thomas) Ward, who grew up in the Aston district of Birmingham, was the drummer who had to compete with the intensity and volume of Osbourne on vocals, Butler on bass, and Iommi on electric guitar. Interestingly, and in the same manner as Paice, his early influences included the swing drummers Gene Krupa, Buddy Rich, and Louie Bellson. He was also inspired by the 1960s British drummers such as Keith Moon, Ginger Baker, and Mitch Mitchell. Due to the Krupa influence and the fact that the British rock players were all from a jazz background, Ward maintained an element of jazz and a desire to add swing to his playing.

This jazz foundation was not the main element of his playing, though. His style was very heavy, making great use of the cymbals to build huge washes of sound, which he used extensively in his long drum solos. As well as his power, Ward was a band member and listened to the other musicians. His parts were often created to work closely with the guitar lines, an example of which is the track "Iron Man" from the 1970 *Paranoid* album. He also demonstrates consecutive semiquaver bass drums for more than a bar at a time throughout this song with only a single bass drum.

What really set this band apart at the time was their loyalty to playing music as dark and heavy as was physically possible. This is especially evident in the demonic intro to the 1970 title track from the album *Black Sabbath,* which is a strong example of Ward's ability to play at very slow tempos yet still fill the rhythm with an utterly heavy quality to perfectly complement the menacing guitar riffs and vocals. Where HM came to be often thought of as incredibly fast and manic, Ward practically epitomizes HM here on a small drum kit and at a slow speed.

In the early 1970s he often used a simple four-piece Ludwig kit in gray ripple finish with a 22 × 14-inch bass drum, a 10 × 9-inch rack tom, and an 18 × 16-inch floor tom. The three Zyn cymbals were 14-inch hi-hats, a 20-inch crash/ride, and an 18-inch crash ride. However, in the live concert footage from Paris in 1970, he can be seen on a white marine pearl Slingerland with a shallow bass drum, one rack tom, and two floor toms. Many of his most famous drum parts were performed on these small configurations, and yet he achieved the heavy sound that has embodied heavy metal ever since.

However, it wasn't long before Ward felt that this configuration was not sufficient for a drummer who was laying the foundations for a genre of excess and extremity. He soon felt it necessary to play with two bass drums, just as many of his predecessors had several years before, and this addition to the kit can be heard on the track "Children of the Grave" from the 1971 *Masters of Reality* album. By then Ward was also using a timbale and explored other percussion on the album.

By 1978 and the *Never Say Die* tour, Ward had an enormous Ludwig kit with in excess of ten toms (some single, some double headed), two bass drums, timbales, and numerous cymbals. The toms were stacked up above each other and encircling him, setting the tone for future HM drum sets. This didn't change dramatically from that point forward, as he kept the double bass drums and extra-effects drums, although the number of toms reverted back to his earlier configuration. Even in 2004 he was using a Tama kit with two 26-inch bass drums, a 15 × 13-inch rack tom, a 16 × 16-inch and an 18 × 16-inch floor tom, a 22-inch gong drum, a 14 × 8-inch Sonor snare and a 14 × 5-inch snare, four Octobans, and a 14-inch timbale.

Unfortunately, like many musicians in the period, the level of excess was not confined to volume and drum kit configurations. Ward suffered from alcohol and drug abuse and left the band numerous times throughout their history. During these periods of absence, other drummers filled in, such as Bev Bevan, Eric Singer, Vinnie Appice, Terry Chimes, Cozy Powell, Bobby Rondinelli, Mike Bordin, and Shannon Larkin. However, Ward has always been considered the true Black Sabbath drummer and was the one who, in the early days, helped carve out the foundations for HM drumming.

Despite a lack of critical acclaim, this new style of music was selling records, and following up behind Sabbath was another British Midlands band called Judas Priest. They embraced the aggression and heavy qualities of Sabbath and took it to the next level, gladly adopting the HM label and truly defining it as a separate genre from rock. They used an array of notable drummers such as Alan Moore, Simon Phillips, Les Binks, Dave Holland, and Scott Travis, and with front man Rob Halford, Judas Priest popularized the outfits of black leather and studs now seen in many HM bands when they bought them from a fetish shop in London's Soho. Rob Halford was homosexual, but this was unknown to the fans at the time, and before long this look that had been adopted by a seemingly macho and aggressive band became very popular with the fans, who didn't dwell for too long on the possible sexual connotations of these outfits.

But although Judas Priest had shaped the style of HM, it was another British band that really took HM to the masses. Iron Maiden were part of the new wave of British heavy metal or NWOBHM as it became known. Such groups as Saxon, Motörhead, Diamond Head, and Blitzkreig are also often included in this category. This saw the bands consciously move away from their blues-based predecessors and instead focus more on the hard-edged and speed-oriented sound that helped truly define HM as a separate genre, thus furthering the work of Judas Priest.

At the helm of the movement were Iron Maiden and their drummer Clive Burr. Like many heavy players before him, Burr began his career on the American Ludwig kits and then, following the trend of the time, he switched to the tougher Japanese market and created the white Tama kit for the *Beast on the Road* tour in 1982, which he is best remembered with. Although this involved only a single 22-inch bass drum, it was still a big kit with four Octobans; 8, 10, 12, 13, 16, and 18 toms; a 14 × 6.5-inch Black Beauty snare; a 20-inch gong drum; and numerous Paiste crashes, china crashes, and a 38-inch gong. Iron Maiden with the addition of Bruce Dickinson brought a very theatrical element to the genre with his larger-than-life charisma and huge vocals soaring above the screaming guitars and high-tempo, powerful drumming of Burr. Just as Ward had demonstrated with Black Sabbath, Burr played many figures in unison with the guitar lines, creating a very tight, structured, and powerful sound. Unfortunately, just like Ward, Clive Burr left the band as a result of alcohol abuse and struggling with grueling touring schedules. By 1982 Iron Maiden had become huge on a global basis, and they needed a new drummer. It was at this point that Nicko McBrain began his long tenure on the drum seat. McBrain didn't follow the American Ludwig trend or the Japanese kits but instead favored the longstanding German drum maker Sonor for much of his career. It was with them that he crafted his ideal setup, which is instantly recognizable for the huge array of toms set at impossibly steep angles so that the batter head sits almost vertically before him. With those toms and the eight crashes, 22-inch ride, 15-inch hi-hats, 7-inch heavy bell, and three china crashes (all of which are Paiste), it can be difficult to see any part of his body from most angles. In 1975 he used the Sonor *XK* series, which involved the single-headed concert toms that were popular in that era. Despite the Sonor endorsement, he used a Ludwig Super Sensitive snare up until the 1990 album *No Prayer for Dying*, and then he changed to a bell brass snare. But after 1994 he switched companies and became an endorser of the British company Premier. However, the setup hasn't changed much to this day with square-dimensioned toms ranging from 6 inches through 8, 10, 12, 13, 14, 15, 16, and finally an 18 x 19-inch floor tom. He also uses a single 24 × 18-inch bass drum, which is notably longer than the 14-inch lengths that Bonham and Ward had favored just over a decade before.

It was drummers such as McBrain who were coming through with such a powerful playing style and a desire to suspend up to 16-inch toms from stands that necessitated stronger hardware. As previously stated, the Japanese were capitalizing on this where the Americans were not. However, McBrain's 1994 move to the English Premier occurred the year after the end of a period in which the Japanese Yamaha company had been funding and controlling Premier to save it from liquidation. They had enabled Premier to develop the tooling and skills to build top-quality kits and, equally importantly, top-quality hardware. Although it took some time for them to get the hardware issues right, it was ultimately the Japanese influence that enabled Premier to progress and achieve the later success that it did.

Regarding tuning, McBrain achieved his sound by tuning the batter head slightly higher than the resonant head. With so many toms, he begins with the 18-inch floor tom and works up along the kit to the smallest tom, being careful to achieve the correct sound for each individual drum but also the drum kit as a whole. With shell diameter increments of 1 and 2 inches, this process could easily go wrong. To maintain the tightly tuned snare drum that he prefers throughout his powerful playing style, a new snare head is used every night while on tour, with the toms changed every three or four performances.

McBrain has also stayed strong to his preference of only using a single bass drum, and his speed and agility with the right foot is one of his strongest attributes. One track that demonstrates this to great effect is "Where Eagles Dare" from the 1983 *Piece of Mind* album, in which he plays three-note quaver groupings at high speed.

As the 1980s hurtled on, HM's focus shifted to America's West Coast, where two things were happening. The first was erupting in Hollywood's Sunset Strip, which became the birthplace of glam metal. Los Angeles witnessed this boom with bands such as Mötley Crüe, Wasps, Hanoi Rocks, and Poison, who injected a theatrical and highly feminine element to their brand of heavy metal. Their image was based on huge feminine hair styles and tight spandex trousers, which led to the term hair metal. Their albums of this period reflected massive sales and a mainstream audience. Mötley Crüe were at the fore with the drummer Tommy Lee. The music was often equal or even second to the off-stage antics, leading many HM purists to view these bands with disdain.

The bands didn't necessarily have a great impact on drumming or drum development, but they did offer some entertaining viewing. The outrageous Tommy Lee made a great spectacle in the late 1980s with his drum solo at live concerts. The solo itself wasn't overly spectacular, but the fact that a huge cage in which he and his kit were attached slowly rose, flipped forward, and rotated full circle while he played was a spectacle. Others had done it before, such as Carl Palmer with ELP and his stainless steel drum kit on a revolving platform in the first half of the 1970s. Palmer credited the English swing drummer Eric Delaney as his inspiration. Although just as he had been there first with the double bass drum, the big band drummer Louie Bellson had already used a revolving drum riser even earlier when playing with Tommy Dorsey's band. However, Buddy Rich had taken it even further with his white Slingerland kit bolted to a riser that appeared to float unaided into the air before spinning Rich and his drum kit upside down while he continued to play a blazing drum solo. But although Tommy Lee wasn't the first to do this, doing it with the flamboyance and pyrotechnics that he used was typical of the excessive, overblown spectacle of these bands.

Another more musical offering from this subgenre was the impressive footwork from the group known as Van Halen and their drummer Alex Van Halen, who wowed audiences with their 1984 release "Hot for Teacher" from the album named after the year of its release and written in Roman numerals as *MCMLXXXIV*. The intro involved a shuffled double bass drum pattern reminiscent of Billy Cobham's "Quadrant Four" from his 1973 *Spectrum* album, and then Simon Phillip's drum pattern on Jeff Beck's 1980 "Space Boogie" track from the *There and Back* album, although Van Halen added an intricate tom-tom pattern over the top to give it its own personal touch.

But while the hairsprayed air at rock venues was at its most pungent and men around the world were reassessing if they really could wear all-in-one spandex outfits, another offshoot of HM was emerging that despised all that hair metal stood for. It was Metallica coming out of L.A. who led this charge, and the young band were reacting to the glam metal that was more a subgenre of pop than metal in their eyes. Metallica's lyrics were dominated by alienation and rebellion, and the music was a loud, angry, and fast mixture of the NWOBHM sound and up-tempo aggressive punk. The term thrash was applied to this sound, and thus HM had been taken to the next level. This new, even heavier sound was driven by the Danish drummer Lars Ulrich, who gained a reputation for being the new heaviest and fastest drummer around. He literally threw himself at the drums, often leaping off his stool and into the air before crashing down with powerful effect. The fast thrash drumbeats are evident in tracks such as "Battery" from the 1986 *Master of Puppets* album. The tight sextuplet double bass drum patterns heard in the 1988 track "One" from the . . . *And Justice for All* album, which are played in close unison with the staccato rhythmic guitar riffs, are a good example of the direction that metal drumming was heading in the 1980s.

Although he started with Ludwig drums through the influence of his idol, Ian Paice, he soon became a Tama endorsee, appreciating the reputation of strength built by the Japanese. It can be clearly seen in the 1980s that whereas Bonham, Paice, and Ward started with American Ludwigs as per the trend in the late 1960s before changing to Japanese later (except Bonham, who passed away before this shift occurred), now we begin to see HM drummers starting their professional careers on Japanese drums, which reinforces that move toward durability.

Ulrich opted for a larger nine-piece kit in his earlier years, utilizing two 24-inch bass drums, 12-, 13-, 14-, and 15-inch rack toms at very steep angles similar to McBrain of Iron Maiden, and two floor toms. As his career progressed he omitted two rack toms and settled with a smaller seven-piece kit. He has two signature snare drums with Tama, both of which are 14 × 6.5, one a diamond-plate steel shell and the other a bell brass shell. With those he played two 22-inch bass drums, 10 × 8- and 12 × 10-inch rack toms, and 16 × 14- and 16 × 16-inch floor toms. He used Zildjian cymbals ranging from 17-inch crashes up to 20-inch china crashes. As a result of breaking wooden sticks too frequently, Ulrich became a user of the Ahead sticks made by Easton, which comprise aluminum and plastic components for greater durability. The focus was on power, stamina, and endurance rather than subtleties, nuances, or feel.

In a search for a bigger sound, rather than just louder and faster, Metallica enlisted producer Bob Rock and created the album that became known as *The Black Album*. The album was a grueling project over many months and with great tensions between band and producer, but the result was a very clinical and hugely powerful sound that sold over 15 million copies globally. It was around this time that Ulrich adopted a more spacious and precise style of playing, leaving behind his youthful, fast-thrashing rhythms and double bass drum phrases to some extent, although this style has been somewhat revived in later offerings. The development of Ulrich's drumming can be heard in stark contrast at this point when compared with the frantic and uneven semiquaver opening to the track "Motorbreath" from their debut studio album *Kill 'Em All* from 1983.

Metal is a progressive genre, and over time the main elements that define the genre have been stretched in an ongoing search to take the music beyond its current state. The result is that the sound has become louder, more distorted, and faster, taken to the extent that it may seem to be at the extreme of what is impossible, until another group arrives and pushes this further to the next level. This is helped by technology allowing for louder amplification systems at live gigs, more clarity, greater recording techniques on the studio albums, and better-quality drum equipment, which allows for greater power and speed. But it also involves placing the human body under greater demands. The guttural growls that often accompany modern-day heavy metal subgenres are far removed from the high-pitched but melodic screams of Ozzy Osbourne.

The drummer is also pushing the boundaries beyond what seems possible. This is most obvious when listening to the speed of the double bass drum playing. The thrash metal movement was responsible for the next progression in this evolution, and where Ulrich had helped bring thrash drumming to the masses, it was drummers such as Dave Lombardo in the band Slayer who were taking it to the extreme.

A particular drum rhythm that Lombardo helped popularize involves playing quavers on the hi-hat at speeds in excess of two hundred beats per minute with his right hand while playing a bass drum on the crotchet beat and a snare drum on every second quaver. This can be traced back to a basic polka pattern that was sped up in the punk genre and then developed to even greater speeds by thrash metal bands. In retrospect, it is also the forerunner to the blast beat that became so popular in later HM subgenres.

But his main talent is the incredible speed and stamina with which he can play on his two bass drums. The pinnacle of this playing and of Slayer's career is arguably the album *Reign in Blood* from 1986. With lyrics describing Nazi acts in Auschwitz concentration camp, Rick Rubin's higher-quality production, and such emphasized speed and heaviness, this album really set the benchmark for thrash metal on every level. Many of the songs are in excess of two hundred beats per minute, and for much of that Lombardo is playing semiquavers on his bass drums. A clear example of this is in the track "Angel of Death" and particularly the break after the guitar solo in which the whole band stops except Lombardo, who plays three bars of semiquaver bass drums at just over two hundred beats per minute.

Lombardo positions his beater much further back than many drummers and uses a heel-up technique with his toes positioned approximately halfway along the pedal, where he can achieve the greatest response with the effort he applies. The tuning is quite high on the bass drum so that he can achieve maximum rebound for the fast notes, although his toms are tuned lower for the desired tone. To achieve the necessary attack and definition when playing such quick notes, Lombardo uses the natural sound of his drum rather than relying on electronics and utilizes EQ techniques through the mixing desk, enabling more of the high frequencies. It is a far cry from the huge, boomy sound of John Bonham.

Lombardo is another heavy player who looked to Japan for equipment. It was a Tama Swingstar that he played in his earlier career before changing to the Tama Starclassic maple kit for such recordings as the seminal album *Reign in Blood*. Around this time he was using a huge kit, which extended from very small toms up to huge floor toms just as McBrain and Burr had done in the British movement. The whole kit consisted of a 14 × 5.5-inch hammered bronze snare, two 24 × 18-inch bass drums, 6 × 6, 8 × 8, 10 × 10, 12 × 11, 14 × 13, and 15 × 14 rack toms, and 18 × 16 with 20 × 16-inch floor toms. This was supplemented by Paiste cymbals, including the popular 15-inch Sound Edge hi-hats, and a collection of RUDE crashes and china crashes. Lombardo was an endorser of Tama for most of his career and looked set to stay loyal to them forever more until he made a surprise move in 2010 to Ddrum, who were rapidly making a name for themselves within the HM drumming community with their growing acoustic drum line and artist roster.

As well as Metallica and Slayer, two other bands were prominent in the thrash metal movement. These were the Californian band Megadeth, founded by ex-Metallica member Dave Mustaine, and the New York group Anthrax, which was formed in 1981 with drummer Charlie Benante. Benante has been a hugely influential drummer in the HM genre both with Anthrax and Storm Troopers of Death (S.O.D.). Just as Lombardo, he was known for his double bass drumming playing, but he is also credited with high significance in popularizing the rhythm that became known as the blast beat. This comes in various forms but generally involves an onslaught of sound at very high tempos in which a single stroke roll is played between the hi-hat or a cymbal and the snare drum, creating alternating voicing. The bass drum is then played in unison with the right hand on the hi-hat or cymbal. These are played as semiquavers or demisemiquavers at tempos in excess of two hundred beats per minute. Often the bass drum notes are doubled, with two bass drums used, or the hands may be played in unison on the snare and hi-hat/cymbal. The origins of this pattern may be found in earlier punk subgenres or earlier still in jazz patterns of the 1960s. It may be traced back to such styles as polka (as mentioned previously), but it was these thrash metal drummers that were playing them with such speed, ferocity, and power that they become the stuff of the HM elite. To achieve the rhythms at such speeds and power but with necessary accuracy became the ongoing goal for aspiring HM drummers. An example of Benante playing these can be heard as early as 1985 in the track "Milk" on the album *Speak English or Die* by S.O.D.

Although Benante began with a Gretsch, it may come as no surprise to hear that by the mid-1980s he had moved to Tama and soon had a kit that was comparable to Lombardo's. Benante's Tama Granstar included two 24-inch bass drums, a 14 × 6.5 Superstar snare drum, 10 × 10, 12 × 11, 13 × 12, and 14 × 13 rack toms, 16 × 16 and 18 × 16 floor toms, and a selection of Paiste cymbals, including RUDE crashes. He also used a second hi-hat on the right-hand side of his kit above the floor toms. This was becoming a popular feature, especially for double bass drum players who required a second hi-hat that could be set closed so that when they were playing with both feet on the bass drum pedals, they could still achieve the tight, closed hi-hat sound. Another aspect that became very popular was the modification of the bass drum's point of impact to achieve a more defined and "clicky" sound that would enable the incredibly busy notes to cut through the distorted guitars with definition. In the late 1980s Benante used a small piece of plastic that he covered in moleskin and positioned atop the black dot of his Remo skins. The beater would hit this point and give a more cutting click rather than the rumbling boom that had been in vogue with Bonham.

Toward the end of the 1980s some areas of metal had became stale and predictable, with a multimillion-dollar industry allowing expensive albums and a lazy approach. This overfed and stagnant genre was to receive a shock when all of a sudden grunge came along in the 1990s. With the Seattle band Nirvana at the helm they ripped the rug out from beneath these metal giants. Suddenly the big hair and latex outfits looked silly as Curt Cobain with Dave Grohl pounding the drums behind him brought a fresh sound and energy that was focused on the music and not the bloated excess of fame. Grohl's force and primal energy behind his stripped-down four-piece kit was the new vogue in the rock music world, and the metal bands were forced to evolve or fade away. This breathed new life into the industry and meant that only the strongest might survive.

One of the strongest to emerge was the Texas band Pantera and their powerful drummer Vinnie Paul. Although they had gone through glam metal and thrash metal phases, they really found their own sound with the 1990 album *Cowboys from Hell* and by 1992 had released the album *Vulgar Display of Power,* which gave them some mainstream success. The sound was termed as groove metal, and it displayed not only power in vulgar amounts, but also sheer aggression, hostility, and a heaviness that even surpassed what had been heard previously in HM. Once again, what seemed like the heaviest sound possible had just been leapfrogged by another, heavier sound. This time, however, the tempos had been decreased in comparison to the thrash metal era. Slower and heavier grooves were the order of the day, the vocals had reached a lower, gut-tural, almost animalistic growl and the drums had an even darker and more forceful sound than ever before. This was helped by two major factors. One was Vinnie Paul's recording technique, which involved eradicating the middle frequencies of the bass drum and toms while increasing the volume of the lower and higher frequen-cies. The second major factor was the sheer size of Paul's drums. As seen with earlier HM drummers, Paul used two big bass drums, which were very wide and long at 24 × 24 inches. He used a com-paratively small number of toms with 14 × 14- and 15 × 15-inch rack toms, and an 18 × 18-inch floor tom. The finishing touch, however, was his wildly deep 14 × 8-inch, eight-ply maple wood snare drum with a snakeskin finish. He was another fan of Japanese drums and endorsed Pearl for many years before making a move to

Ddrum, where he basically just transferred his configuration across, although Ddrum offer two Vinnie Paul signature 14 × 8-inch, six-ply maple snare drums, the difference between the two being the paint design, the rims, and the lugs.

Although the average tempos had slowed down since the thrash metal era, the notes played within the bars were still crammed in and Paul was certainly partial to filling the rhythms with fast double bass drum grooves. Whereas these grooves had been based on consistent semiquavers in the earlier days, drummers such as Vinnie Paul were now beginning to use triplet subdivisions more frequently and to break the patterns up, requiring more coordination between the limbs. A popular example of such a broken double bass drum pattern can be heard on the 1994 album *Far Beyond Driven* and the track "Becoming" where he employs semiquavers, semiquaver rests, and demisemiquavers into his bass drum part.

The basis of HM drumming had been well and truly cemented by the late 1990s, and not a great deal changed in terms of playing from this point onward. Drum kits became more diverse, of course, and the types of wood, shell sizes, and finishes increased dramatically, offering the drummer unlimited customization options. Drummers continued to push what was accepted as possible in terms of speed, and each brought their own styles and approaches to HM drumming, such as Mike Portnoy with Dream Theatre, who took progressive metal to new heights with constantly changing odd time signatures and intricate fills between the hands and feet; Derek Roddy with Hate Eternal, who came along and took blast beats to the next level of speed, often using only his right foot on the bass drum; Joey Jordison with Slipknot, who brought the intense speed and fused it with the industrial rhythmic sounds of the Slipknot percussionists while wearing masks and boiler suits and swearing at their fans, whom they describe as maggots; Chris Adler of Lamb of God brought an ambidextrous and unorthodox style as he played left-handed on a right-handed kit and with a highly tuned 12-inch snare drum; and Jason Bittner of Shadows Fall with his interesting two-handed ride cymbal patterns and four-stroke ruff bass drum applications. All of these players excel at playing double bass drum patterns at high tempos.

As mentioned with Pearl's introduction of the drum rack in 1983, it was no longer necessary for separate stands and multiple legs to get in each other's way. One of the most striking was the famous hard rock drummer Tommy Aldridge, who played with the likes of Ozzy Osbourne and Whitesnake. Aldridge's Yamaha kit in 1990 was made of carbon fiber and sat encased in a thick-tubed metal frame that positioned the kit upon a platform, meaning that the bass drums appeared to be floating. The cymbals hung down from the thick tubes high above the drummer. This particular rack was a Greg Voelker rack system. Shawn Drover, who went on to play for Megadeth, was another user of such a rack, and throughout the 1980s and into the 1990s, many courageous designs appeared in this genre, just as they have in pop with the likes of Jonathan Moffett.

Another, possibly surprising, significant equipment advance in HM drumming is the use of electronics. Although it would be reasonable to think of electronic drums in the professional environment as having pop or dance music connotations, with the advances in real-sounding drum samples, many professional players use them alongside their acoustic sounds. This is either achieved by supplementing the acoustic kit with electronic pads or, as is often the case in HM, using electronic triggers on the acoustic drums. The result of this is that every time a drum is hit, the natural acoustic sound is amplified via a microphone in the traditional manner while at the same time, a sampler or drum module is triggered, and this sound is also sent out through the PA system. This appeals particularly to HM drummers, as they are playing at such fast speeds and with such busy patterns, it is easy to lose the note definition and end up with a rumbling mess of noise. Triggering a sample can allow for a much tighter and defined sound so that the notes are not lost. As mentioned with Charlie Benante, many drummers experimented with different hard materials placed on the spot where the beater meets the bass drum skin. Plastic or metal plates allowed for a defined click to cut through the music. Hard beaters such as wood or plastic also aided this technique, and high tuning of the skin removed some of the boom. The front-of-house sound engineer for Metallica, "Big" Mick Hughes, also added more of the high frequencies into the mix to obtain more attack, as did Dave Lombardo with Slayer, as previously mentioned.

Another development that has aided the double bass drum player is that of the drop clutch. When the left foot is taken away from the hi-hat pedal to play the auxiliary bass drum pedal, the hi-hat is left in an open position, which is not always suitable when playing as a timekeeping rhythmic element in a pattern. The drop clutch enables the top hi-hat cymbal to drop down into the closed position by either hitting a lever with the stick, pressing a foot-operated lever, or by use of magnetic control, depending on the manufacturer of the clutch.

As with all genres, HM has many subgenres that fuse certain elements with other styles or give particular aspects more emphasis. One aspect, however, that has been constant through the emergence and evolution of heavy metal is the increased heaviness and speed, and drummers have been core to this progression. Boundaries are consistently pushed, which makes this genre exciting from the viewpoint of athleticism, stamina, and sheer brutality. It is almost as if the drummers are engaged in combat, each trying to outdo the next. What some of the drummers lack in variation, subtlety, and dynamics, they make up for in power, volume, and speed. How far this genre can be pushed is impossible to guess. Maybe one can speculate that it will implode. The soaring and highly talented vocals of Bruce Dickinson of Iron Maiden are now passé and are instead often replaced by guttural growls, which are far removed from the generally accepted definition of singing. The guitar sounds have been taken away from the melodic and harmonic lines of the 1980s, down tuned, turned up, and distorted until notes are barely recognizable in some cases. The drum patterns are so fast that there is no space in the music, no nuances, and as is often the case, no real drum tones as samples are triggered and notes shifted and quantized in recording software. Can that be taken any further until it stops becoming music and is simply just noise? The answer is probably yes. It may not be possible to see how, but somewhere out there in a dingy rehearsal room are a group of youngsters practicing hard to create the next phase in HM.

FUSION

The term fusion is incredibly ambiguous in music, but the fundamental definition is the merging of different musical genres to form something new, using preferential defining elements from each. This has been occurring in essence throughout the history of music. If we examine modern styles, we could argue that rock 'n' roll is blues/gospel/country fusion, or that disco is just soul/funk/Latin fusion, although a counterargument might be that these examples took the influences to a very new level that necessitated a new genre altogether.

Many fusion genres have had very little impact on drumming, as they simply involve the sensibilities of one style mixed with another. Blues/rock, for example, offers very little advance on the drum with regard to equipment or playing styles, and pop/rock takes the heavier rock drumming into a more commercial, pop-oriented setting. However, when the term fusion is used, the connotations are of a particular fusion of two musical styles: those of jazz and rock music.

Throughout the 1960s, the British rock explosion was exposing the likes of Ginger Baker and Mitch Mitchell to the world, and the sound of rock was exciting audiences wherever it was heard. These electrifying drummers were playing rock music with an influence of jazz evident in their playing style and with elements of free-form improvisation. When jazz/rock emerged, it was to explode out of the jazz world by taking on the rhythmic influences of rock. The two genres were to become fused into an exciting genre that gave rise to some of the greatest drum kit playing in musical history, attracting many of the world's elite performers to an arena in which anything was possible and creativity was never hindered by the need to conform to certain generic beliefs.

The evolution from pure acoustic jazz to electrified jazz/rock fusion didn't happen in one defining moment but, as with every other genre discussed in this book, over a period of time and as a result of different musicians and their reactions to the music that they were hearing at this time.

Musicians such as vibraphonist Gary Burton had already dabbled with the mixing of jazz and other popular genres such as rock 'n' roll or country as early as 1966 with the albums *Time Machine*,

Tennessee Firebird, and then *Duster* in 1967 with Roy Haynes on drums. However, it was Miles Davis who is best remembered for kick-starting the new craze that became known as jazz/rock and mentoring a host of other musicians to carry the flame.

The late 1960s were a very significant transitional phase for Davis, and evidence of this change can be heard on two albums that were released in 1968, both featuring Tony Williams on drums. These albums were *Miles in the Sky* and *Filles de Kilimanjaro,* both of which used a more electrified approach in a move away from the traditional acoustic jazz instrumentation with Herbie Hancock and Chick Corea playing electric pianos and Ron Carter and Dave Holland using electric bass guitars. Williams is also moving toward a funkier rhythm and leaving behind the traditional jazz swing pattern as heard on the track "Stuff" from *Miles in the Sky.*

A year later and Davis had released *In a Silent Way* with Joe Zawinul, Chick Corea, and Herbie Hancock on electric piano, Wayne Shorter on saxophone, Dave Holland on electric bass, John McLaughlin on electric guitar, and Tony Williams on drums. Each of these musicians went on to make a serious contribution to fusion music. The album put even more emphasis on electric instruments and with the producer Teo Macero cutting up and editing the structures of the recorded music, took Davis even further from the philosophies of traditional jazz.

Taking this new direction on further, Davis's album from 1970 *Bitches Brew* has been subjected to great criticism, acclaim, and analysis over the years but in retrospect has been accepted as undoubtedly one of the first jazz-rock fusion albums. One of the most unusual aspects of this recording was the size of the rhythm section, allowing immense interaction between musicians and creating an exciting foundation with two drummers over which the lead instruments could improvise. For much of the recording process Davis used Lenny White panned to the left and Jack Dejohnette panned to the right with the exception of a small number of tracks that substituted Billy Cobham or Don Alias to be recorded on the drums and panned to the left. On percussion were Airto Moreira, Don Alias, and Juma Santos. Other musicians who performed on this album included Chick Corea, John McLaughlin, Wayne Shorter, and Joe Zawinul.

The new direction had been set by Davis and his group, and the door was now open for others to move through and explore the unknown world before them. Just as John Mayall had inadvertently run an academy for British blues, which spawned many of the great players of that time from which many of the great groups were founded, Miles Davis was doing much the same for jazz/rock fusion. It was the musicians from Davis's groups that took the electrified sound on to the next level when Corea formed Return to Forever, Shorter and Zawinul formed Weather Report, and McLaughlin formed the Mahavishnu Orchestra with Billy Cobham.

However, the first Miles Davis alumnus to branch out into the fusion world was the drummer Tony Williams when he formed the Lifetime Trio. The trio with guitarist John McLaughlin and organist Larry Young recorded the double album *Emergency* and released it in 1969. Having teamed up with Davis at the tender age of seventeen, he had made a huge impact on the jazz world while being part of the much-celebrated Davis quintet of the time with Ron Carter, Wayne Shorter, and Herbie Hancock. He had demonstrated an unprecedented ability for polyrhythms and metric modulation and was therefore able to bring these talents and explore them further in this new setting. His playing was unpredictable, exciting, and spontaneous and transferred perfectly into his rock-infused trio. By the second album, *Turn It Over*, in 1970 Williams had drafted Jack Bruce on bass guitar, a former member of the English rock band Cream; a strong sign of where he was gaining inspiration at the time. The band went through several personnel changes and failed to achieve any great commercial success, but it did help carve the way for the emerging fusion style.

Although Williams had begun his career on the smaller four-piece drum kits that were standard in jazz at that time, he signed an endorsement deal with the American Gretsch in 1966 and soon found his preferred yellow kit with 24 × 18-inch bass drum, 14 × 6.5-inch snare, 12 × 9-inch and 13 × 10-inch rack toms, and then the unusual cluster of three floor toms in 14 × 14, 16 × 14, and 18 × 14 inches. In 1994 he jumped ship to another American company, DW, that had risen from the ashes of Camco. With them he retained his bright-yellow finish and personal tom configuration.

This was supplemented by a modest Zildjian *K* cymbal configuration with 15-inch hi-hats, an 18-inch and 20-inch crash, and a 22-inch ride.

John McLaughlin had left Tony Williams's trio and started his own group with drummer Billy Cobham, whom he had worked with on some of the *Bitches Brew* sessions. They formed the Mahavishnu Orchestra and released *The Inner Mounting Flame* in 1971. This provided an excellent vehicle from which Cobham could demonstrate his technical and creative prowess. He has crafted a very personal sound, achieved via a matched French grip. He is left-handed but plays on a right-handed setup with an open-handed playing style. He has tremendous command of dynamics, the ability to play very fast with excellent control, and an ambidextrous application aided by his open-handed approach.

In 1973 Cobham released his solo effort *Spectrum,* which was a great commercial success and employed the guitar work of guitarist Tommy Bolin, who later joined Deep Purple, a sign of the close link between jazz and rock of that period. This was a hard-edged and exciting album, giving the world some inspiring drumming. Not least was the track "Quadrant Four," which utilized a double bass drum shuffle.

Some left-handed players who play with an open-handed technique simply play on a right-handed setup, but Cobham has created some very unique configurations over the years with toms increasing in size from right to left and often not in a sequential order. He has used many different kits and setups during his long career and is always keen to try new ideas and push the boundaries.

He has been a user of Japanese drums for much of his career and has made a huge contribution to the development of the drum kit. He began with Tama when they were beginning to build a reputation in the West. After several years he left Tama and was replaced by Simon Phillips as the poster boy, and so he moved to Mapex. When they looked for new names in order to progress, Cobham went to Yamaha in 1997 and has enjoyed their high level of artist relations ever since, appreciating the fact that they could get the equipment to him as he took his music to some of the more remote regions of the globe.

However, his most interesting kit might be considered the Fibes acrylic set from around 1976, which had a striking clear crystallite finish, as well as a couple of North toms. At this time Cobham used Zildjian cymbals, although he later switched to Sabian. He used a 36-inch gong and brought back the china crash, which had been used in earlier big bands and known as a swish cymbal. Cobham simply turned it upside down and played it with more force. Due to his left-handed approach, he positions cymbals in slightly unusual ways, such as placing his ride cymbal above the hi-hats. The Fibes kit consisted of two 24 × 16-inch bass drums, two 12 × 8, a 13 × 9- and a 14 × 14-inch rack tom, 16 × 16-, 18 × 18-, and 20 × 20-inch floor toms, and then 22- and 24-inch gong drums. Added to this huge set was a 14 × 7-inch snare custom made by Al Duffy and Jeff Ochletree and 12- and 14-inch North toms set above the Fibes rack toms.

Billy Cobham is a very important figure in the development of the drum kit and as such was recognized in the Percussive Arts Society when they accepted him into their Hall of Fame. He has left a great legacy that all future drummers can draw upon.

There were also efforts to bridge the gap between jazz and rock from the other side. Notable rock musicians who incorporated elements of jazz in this period included Frank Zappa and Colosseum.

In 1969 Frank Zappa released his first solo album, having left the Mothers of Invention. The album was *Hot Rats*, and it turned out to be a pioneering album. Songs such as "Peaches en Regalia" really demonstrate the crossover from rock to jazz, and the use of new sixteen-track recording facilities allowed for many overdubs and extensive microphones to record the drums, making this a very cutting-edge record. In fact, over his long career, Zappa really embodied the spirit of fusion in general and amassed one of the most eclectic discographies in history, having experimented with styles from jazz to blues to rock to classical and many others. He used varied time signatures and often unusual phrasing within the beats, which meant that his expectations of his band members were incredibly high for them to be able to cope with the compositions. The drummers that played with him are some of the best in the world and include Aynsley Dunbar, Ralph Humphrey, Chester Thompson, Terry Bozzio, Vinnie Colaiuta, and Chad Wackerman.

Over in Britain yet more musicians had departed John Mayall's Blues Breakers and started a new band that would become successful in their own right. Jazz saxophonist Dick Heckstall-Smith and drummer Jon Hiseman founded Colosseum, which blended jazz elements tremendously with the rock and the blues that had brought them together initially. They released their debut album in 1969 titled *Those Who Are About to Die, We Salute You.*

Meanwhile the Miles Davis alumni were driving ahead, and it was Wayne Shorter and Joe Zawinul who teamed up and formed Weather Report with Alphonse Mouzon on drums and Airto Moreira on percussion to release their debut album *Weather Report* in 1971. Through a long career they went through many stylistic changes, but always keeping a strong emphasis on improvisation, and achieved great critical acclaim. The many great drummers that passed through the group included Eric Gravatt, Greg Errico, Ishmael Wilburn, Skip Hadden, Darryl Brown, Leon "Ndugu" Chancler, Chester Thompson, Narada Michael Walden, Alex Acuña, Peter Erskine, and Omar Hakim.

Shortly after Weather Report's formation, the next group to emerge from Davis's fusion incubator appeared led by Chick Corea on piano and keyboards. Return to Forever (RTF) released their self-titled debut album in 1972 with Airto Moreira on drums, Stanley Clarke on bass, Flora Purim on vocal duty, and Joe Farrell on saxophone. The debut and the follow-up album *Light as a Feather* in 1973 displayed a wonderful mix of jazz and Latin sounds, especially Brazilian influences. As well as playing with Corea, Airto Moreira also played with Weather Report and Miles Davis and through them developed a very unique drum and percussion setup that allowed him the dual role of drummer and percussionist. Having been sent back to his homeland Brazil by Davis with the finances to buy some interesting percussion, Moreira returned and gradually developed his current kit. With his table packed with various percussive instruments, he positioned a bass drum beneath it with a double pedal enabling him to play it while sitting off to the left-hand side of it. He had a snare and three single-headed toms custom built, and he sat straddling the floor tom with two rack toms above it and a snare to the left. The hi-hat was next to a rack tom and operated by a remote pedal. With this kit he could play drums and still reach his percussion table and cymbals.

By the third album, Moreira had moved on, and so Lenny White came in on drums, whom Corea knew from Davis's *Bitches Brew* sessions. The second phase of the band began. This new phase with Lenny White moved away from the airy, Latin-infused sounds and took a more jazz-rock approach that brought them closer to Mahavishnu Orchestra in sound.

Another influential drummer that Corea worked with was Steve Gadd, who was initially sought after for RTF but was reluctant to tour. However, Corea did manage to get him into the studio when in 1975 he had written some music outside of RTF, which became the album *The Leprechaun* with the outstanding drumming on the track "Nite Sprite." This album was the first of a number of recordings with the busy session drummer, including *My Spanish Heart* and *The Mad Hatter,* which occurred within three years of the first release. Corea's experimental jazz allowed Gadd to show his full creativity and demonstrate his unique personal style to its full potential.

Having entered the studio industry after three years in military band service, Gadd had excellent rudimentary skills, and he delved into this background regularly, applying these sticking patterns in a musical and wondrous manner with devastating effect. He also utilized the cowbell for authentic Latin patterns, which he orchestrated around the drum kit with sheer brilliance while crafting an instantly identifiable sound. Another big part of Gadd's sound was his use of linear phrasing. This afforded him a unique approach to drumming and exciting interplay between the different parts of the kit, especially the bass drum, snare drum, and hi-hat.

With his unlimited creativity he was able to take these influences from the jazz, Latin, and fusion genres and turn pop recordings into exciting drummer's records that would be studied for years to come. Such examples are the Mozambique rhythm that drives Paul Simon's track "Late in the Evening" from 1980 and the clever linear-based phrasing with all four limbs, entwined with rudimental rolls in "Fifty Ways to Leave Your Lover," also by Paul Simon in 1975.

Gadd began his recording career on a mismatch kit with a 20-inch Gretsch maple bass drum and Pearl fiberglass toms ranging through 10, 12, 13, and 14 inches. These were initially concert toms until he fitted bottom heads. But in 1976 he moved to Yamaha, where he has stayed ever since. He started at Yamaha with an all-birch kit but later decided that the maple bass drums had more bottom end and therefore used that wood for just the bass drum. He has also become synonymous with the famous Ludwig Supra-phonic 400 snare drum, which he used extensively during his 1970s and 1980s recording heyday. The Yamaha kit that he preferred in this period was the Recording Custom kit, or RC9000, which became very popular through the 1980s as a result. This was at a time when manufacturers were making the distinction between different woods for different scenarios. Whereas maple sounded more open and resonant, the birch drums were darker and more focused and therefore better suited for the recording studio. Where Yamaha called them Recording Customs, Pearl marketed their birch drums as Studio Drums. The RC9000 also used flush bracing in which the lug runs from the top of the shell to the bottom, thus spreading the stress along the drum. It also had highly lacquered finishes, similar to the pianos that they built.

He has helped develop the drum kit hugely via his tenure with Yamaha and popularized several concepts that have stayed in vogue ever since. For a start he often disregarded the normal 12- and 13-inch rack tom setup, instead choosing a 10- and 12-inch option. He then hung his floor tom from a clamp on the cymbal stand rather than sitting on the floor with legs. This set of 10-, 12-, and 14-inch hanging toms became known as fusion sizes as opposed to the rock sizes of 12-, 13-, and 16-inch toms. These are still the standard configurations on offer at music shops.

Gadd still uses these sizes today with a 22-inch bass drum, although he may substitute the 10-inch tom and go with 12 and 13 inch, while adding a 16-inch low tom, and even a 20-inch bass drum, depending on the musical situation. In 2006, Yamaha unveiled the Steve Gadd 30th Anniversary Drum Set, which was limited to only fifty units of the replica kit in piano black that Gadd is famous for playing. His choices of heads are the Remo Power-stroke 3 on the snare batter side and Pinstripes on the toms with clear Ambassadors on the resonant side. As well as a signature stick with Vic Firth, he also helped to develop the Zildjian K Session range of cymbals.

As well as showcasing Gadd's huge talents, Corea acted as a platform from which another great jazz drummer could leap into the world of greatness. That greatness came in the form of Dave Weckl, a drummer who rose up with many parallels to Steve Gadd. Just as Gadd had, Weckl burst onto the session scene in New York and did so via Simon and Garfunkel on their reunion tour in 1983, taking over the drum throne that had been held by Gadd in the past. By 1985 Corea had been suitably impressed with Weckl and employed him for the Elektric Band, which embraced the synthesized sounds of the 1980s and used them to further explore jazz, funk, Latin, and rock influences.

As well as incredible virtuoso technical and musical ability, Weckl really made his mark on the genre with his combination of acoustic and electric sounds while with Corea. An endorser of the Japanese Yamaha, Weckl embraced the 1980s technology and entwined it with his Yamaha Recording Custom setup. Weckl also took on Gadd's mounted low tom designs and added a second one to the left of his hi-hat. He also used the remote hi-hat pedals, which enabled a second hi-hat to be positioned on the right-hand side of the kit. This allowed a very ambidextrous approach. One signature aspect of Weckl's sound is his use of two snare strainers. Unable to achieve the desired sound with the traditional single strainer, he used both a tight strainer in regular steel for a precise sound and also a looser strainer in stainless steel to achieve the buzz. Yamaha produced his signature maple snare featuring the dual strainers in either a 13- or 14-inch diameter and 5.5 inches deep.

He was another player who recognized the difference between the types of woods used for drum shells, as shown by his use of the Yamaha Maple Custom kit for live work throughout the 1990s and his Yamaha Birch Absolute that he kept for studio work. He then moved on to the Yamaha PHX Phoenix Series, which mixes Japanese jatuba wood with Brazilian kapur and North American maple woods to form the nine plies of the shells.

His actual drum setup was nothing extraordinary once he returned to acoustic drums. In 2007 he was generally seen playing his Yamaha Maple Custom with a 22 × 16-inch main bass drum and an 18 × 16-inch bass drum positioned in front of the floor toms, played by way of a double pedal; his aluminum 14- and maple 13-inch signature snares; 10 × 7.5- and 12 × 8-inch rack toms; and 14 and 16 square-dimensioned hanging floor toms. However, he did incorporate a large cymbal set with a combination of two hi-hats, some crashes, and a ride, augmented with various sound effects such as the Sabian 17-inch Effeks crash, a 14-inch mini Chinese on top of an 18-inch crash, and a 7-inch splash inverted on top of a 12-inch splash. He has also continued to develop his sound by adding hand percussion such as bongos and djembes to his setup, as heard on many Dave Weckl Band albums such as the album *Transition* from 2000.

Weckl exemplifies the modern music business and the way in which a drummer might successfully remain employed in such a fickle industry by diversifying his skills. He works with his own band; drums as a sideman; runs his own studio from where he records, mixes, and produces; takes part in educational programs; performs at drum clinics; releases educational books and DVDs; and also collaborates with the likes of Yamaha, Sabian, and Remo to design new equipment. To this end, Weckl has helped design some muffling devices with Herbie May from the Remo drumhead company. The bass drum muffling system basically replicates a rolled-up towel, which can be adjusted to press against the inside of the batter head for varied muffling options. The second product was the Active Dampening System for the snare drum, which allowed a disc to fall into contact with the batter head soon after impact, thus allowing the natural feel of the head when playing it but stopped any unwanted resonance immediately afterward.

As Weckl continued to tour and record with his own fusion band and many others that he lent his mastery to, he constantly forged ahead as an ambassador for drummers worldwide. His influence has helped raise the game of the drum set player with regard to attitude, respect for others, and the history of the instrument, technique, musicality, education, and professionalism.

Returning to the subject of Miles Davis alumni, we are presented with the pianist Herbie Hancock, who left Davis and explored electronic music with the 1972 album *Crossings*, where Hancock failed to make a great mark. That was until he released the *Head Hunters* album in 1973 and brought a strong funk influence to the fusion genre, drawing on the psychedelic funk of artists such as Sly and the Family Stone. This first jazz/funk album of Hancock's became a huge seller and produced such tracks as "Chameleon," which is heavily based on funk sensibilities, with a strong bass line and drum pattern driving much of the fifteen-minute piece. The funky drum pattern was supplied by session drummer Harvey Mason and percussionist Bill Summers, giving Hancock an enticing foundation over which he could experiment with the newest sounds that technology had to offer. Mason left soon after, and the 1974 album *Thrust* featured drummer Mike Clark who demonstrated excellent interplay with bassist Paul Jackson's phrasing. This new style of funkier jazz was an exciting blend of the infectious groove from funk and the polyrhythms and interplay of jazz. The Head Hunters recorded several albums together, both with Hancock and without, before splitting in the late 1970s only to reunite in the late 1990s again.

Although this was exciting and fresh at the time, it led to the popularization of taking mainstream rhythms, such as disco, and overlaying jazzy solos and chord structures. While some areas of the genre began to sound insipid and bland, many of the originators briefly returned to their acoustic origins, such as Chick Corea's Acoustik Band, which was the predecessor to the aforementioned Elektric Band.

From these Davis alumni projects, other band leaders emerged. Weckl was one who enjoyed long success with the Dave Weckl Band and created a very distinctive sound, built around the pristinely tuned drums and exquisite drumming style. Another drummer to lead a fusion band was the former Journey drummer Steve Smith, who formed Vital Information in 1983 and continued successfully well into the next century.

Over in England the drummer Bill Bruford also experimented with his great love of jazz music, having moved away from his previous successes in progressive rock bands such as Yes and King Crimson. The group was simply called Bruford, and between 1977 and 1980 they recorded four studio albums. Also in the group was Jeff Berlin on bass, Dave Stewart on keys, and Allan Holdsworth on guitar, who had previously played with the New Tony Williams Lifetime group.

Bill Bruford was a great pioneer in drumming equipment and is most famous in this role for his use of electronics, but he also devised several interesting acoustic drum sets throughout his career. The experimentation with unorthodox drum configurations really began during the era of the fusion band Bruford. This comprised a 22 × 14-inch Ludwig bass drum, a 16 × 16-inch Ludwig floor tom, and a 14 × 6.5-inch Ludwig Super Sensitive chrome plated snare drum. To this he added a 12 × 8-inch Hayman rack tom and two Remo rototoms with diameters of 14 and 18 inches. He used Paiste cymbals, which comprised crashes, a ride, 15-inch Sound Edge hi-hats, an 11-inch splash above a crash, an 8-inch bell, a 20-inch china crash, and a 24-inch unturned gong. This was supplemented with a percussion rack containing triangles, unturned metal plates, woodblocks, finger cymbals, and two smaller rototoms in 6- and 8-inch diameters. From here he took an exciting leap into the world of electronic drums, which he successfully mixed with acoustic sounds throughout the 1980s and into the 1990s. Interestingly in the late 1990s when the second version of his jazz-oriented group Earthworks was mobilized, Bill Bruford returned to a purely acoustic drum set but still refused to sit behind a conventional configuration. By now he was using the Tama Starclassic maple drums with a 14 × 6.5-inch wood snare (later to be replaced by the Bill Bruford signature snare drum, which was half an inch shallower), 10 × 8-, 12 × 10-, and 13 × 11-inch rack toms, a 16 × 16-inch floor tom, and an 18 × 16-inch bass drum, which was sometimes substituted by a 20- or even 22-inch version. This was regular enough in itself, except that he positioned the toms in a vertically flat row and horizontally aligned in a gentle curve, mimicking the positions of a classical timpanist. The row ranged from the 11-inch tom on the far left and then moving right through the 8-inch, the snare, the 10-inch, and then the 16-inch floor tom on the far right. The cymbals were then positioned in a row in front of the drums with the hi-hat in front of the snare drum, operated by a remote hi-hat pedal. The

Bill Bruford behind his flat Tama configuration. From the Bill Bruford archive.

set was, in a way, symmetrical, with the central hi-hat and snare offering two toms and two cymbals to either side. This setup may look unusual to a drummer who is familiar with the conventional configuration, but it is actually very logical and perfectly suited to Bruford's economic playing style, which saw him moving around the drums effortlessly while creating very complex patterns.

However, it wasn't just the European and North American drummers that were fueling the fusion rhythms. As we saw in the early incarnations of Miles Davis's electronic jazz period, the Brazilian Airto Moreira was playing his part, as he did later with great effect in the Return to Forever and Weather Report bands. This helped promote the exciting influences of Latin rhythms to the Western world and spread the intrigue and wonder throughout the drumming world. Another drummer to follow in these footsteps and help promote his rhythmic culture further is the Cuban Horacio "El Negro" Hernandez. An interesting career has seen him journey to New York from Cuba via a spell in Italy and forge a sterling reputation along the way as a very versatile player with incredible limb independence.

Independence has always been an ongoing exploration for drummers, and particularly in the 1990s and beyond, this seemed to almost become an obsession with drummers dueling for independence supremacy. The extreme of this can be seen in Austrian drummer Thomas Lang and his instructional DVDs with lists of exercises involving different numbered groupings with each limb to achieve almost inhuman rhythms across the kit. However, Hernandez has built his reputation as an in-demand musician whose rhythms are drenched in pure Latin soul and send out a challenge to any human to resist the desire to dance or at least tap one's foot along with the grooves. It was through his diverse work with the likes of Michel Camilo, Steve Winwood, John Patitucci, Carlos Santana, and Michael Brecker that he built his name and then through performances at the Percussive Arts Society's International Convention, Modern Drummer festivals, NAMM music shows, and clinics for the companies that he endorses, such as Pearl drums and Zildjian cymbals, that he really showed off his talent to the wider drumming community.

He used a conventional drum kit consisting of a Pearl Reference 22 × 16 bass drum, 10 × 8 and 12 × 8 rack toms, 14 × 12- and 16 × 14-inch floor toms, along with a standard Zildjian cymbal collection of crashes, splashes, a ride, and hi-hats. What really identified his kit was the additional clave blocks, tambourines, and cowbells dotted around. He released his own signature range of five cowbells, which included a low and high cha-cha bell, a mambo bell that he attached to the bass drum hoop, and a timbale bell, which sat above the floor toms. The fifth bell was mounted to a foot pedal and sat beside his hi-hat pedal; this was the one that mystified many a drummer when he first hit the scene. He wasn't the first to do it, but he really brought this cowbell foot technique to the masses, demonstrating an unwavering clave with his left foot while using his other three limbs to layer complex grooves or improvised solos over the top. He is also very comfortable leading with either hand and has published many educational exercises to promote this practice to achieve ambidexterity and allow endless options around the drum kit.

The Latin and jazz influences proved to be very well suited and became enormously popular and successful for many artists. However, a less obvious fusion was brought to the world's attention thanks to Trilok Gurtu, an Indian percussionist. Gurtu developed a great fondness for jazz music and created a unique drumming style and instrument collection, which he used to great effect with a hugely diverse range of artists from pop artists such as Marti Pellow; rock players such as Jack Bruce; countless Indian musicians such as the violinist and composer L. Shankar and singer/composer Shankar Mahadevan; and fusion players like Joe Zawinul and John McLaughlin. It was with McLaughlin that Gurtu made his first big mark in this genre in 1989 and the live album *Live at the Festival Hall*. His personal style was an engaging mix ranging from the standard fusion drum sounds, which were expected from a Western kit, right across to traditional Indian percussion, and other effects. The other effects that could be commonly heard included dipping cymbals or shells into buckets of water in search of sonorous diversity and the impressively fast technique of vocalizing the mnemonic rhythmic sequence known in India as tala.

Gurtu helped bring this rich, diverse sound to the masses of the Western world and in doing so created music that transcended genres and cultures. He did this on an ever-changing percussion set that mixed Western and Eastern instruments sublimely from his squatting position, surrounded by drums and cymbals from the traditional Indian tabla and dhol drums to Western hi-hats, toms, and snare drums, as well as all manner of shakers, woodblocks, cowbells, and anything else that might please Gurtu when he strikes, rattles, or scrapes it. This man became well sought after as a result of his culturally rich and ever-impressive sound that created the unexpected.

Another country to offer a great drumming talent was Australia with their offering of Virgil Donati from Melbourne. He came to prominence in the 1980s, then through the 1990s with his 1995 solo album release Stretch, enabling him to forge a name for himself as one of the most technically gifted drummers on the planet. His command of the drum kit, demonstrating such high speeds and fluidity, was difficult to equal, and he used this to become a regular name at drum festivals and clinics. His career was varied, with musicals such as *Jesus Christ Superstar*, pop collaborations with the likes of Joss Stone and Mick Jagger, and work with renowned guitarists such as Steve Vai and Frank Gambale. But it is possibly his work with his own fusion project, Planet X, that really allowed his talent to shine through in an orgy of odd time signatures, polyrhythms, and improvisation that pushed fusion forward to the next level.

He made great use of double bass drum playing and in particular, double strokes on the foot pedals. He also furthered the development of breaking rhythms down into unusual phrases, such as the track "Moonbabies" from the 2002 album of the same name in which he divides bars made up of eleven semiquavers into smaller phrases of two crotchets, and a three-semiquaver grouping, or three lots of three semiquavers followed by two semiquavers. This approach is very mathematical and premeditated, in stark contrast to the improvised music of traditional jazz or even the funk-based fusion of Herbie Hancock and the Headhunters. It is certainly not designed for people to get up and dance to, but more likely watch with serious faces and nod in awestruck appreciation of the technical abilities on display.

Donati was an endorser of Sabian cymbals and Pearl drums, having switched from Premier in 2002. The setup was fairly standard for much of his career, often displaying a two-up, two-down tom configuration with an extra tom and snare drum to the left of the hi-hat. However, around the turn of the millennium, Donati could often be seen with an obscure setup sporting two "air toms," which involved suspending a 10 × 8- and 13 × 11-inch tom from a boom arm on a stand up high above his cymbals with one drum to each side in impossibly far-reaching positions. But when he improvised around the kit, he was able to flow effortlessly from snare, up to the first air tom, along the rack toms, and on to the floor toms via the second air tom as if they were in a perfectly straight line. This created interesting fills ideas that were pleasing to the ear but even more so as a visual demonstration.

And so it was that fusion had diversified greatly. Some had simply taken it down the road to commercial success by adding more mainstream rhythms and creating smooth jazz, some were mixing different cultural sounds in an effort to find a fresh perspective, and some were taking the rhythmic possibilities to new intellectual levels on a search for mind-bending music that was only accessible to people with a certain level of musical understanding. Fusion music may at times sound to some like a self-indulgent world where virtuoso musicians use the genre as a vehicle for meaningless extended solos. This could be viewed on the drum kit, where drummers may feel it appropriate to keep the band and crowd bound to watch them fly around the kit in an egotistical and self-satisfying manner. On the other hand, many of these solos by the masters of the instrument demonstrate a worthy and hugely respected act of high-caliber performance, employing great musicality and creativeness. Whoever is performing, and whoever is judging the worth of such music, it cannot be argued that this genre has opened the door, broken down barriers, and emancipated those who were bound by the conventions of a genre. It is also through the creative minds of these drummers that the drum kit has developed to such great extents to provide us with the options that we have today. And in the process, they have given the world some of the most technically gifted and intellectually rich music in history. As one avenue of exploration is exhausted of ideas, it is natural for the human being to look beyond it. It is human nature. The great musicians who have the creative and technical ability to do this will never be bound down; they will always be searching for something new to push music forward, and whatever they choose to do, we can be sure that it will be some of the most exciting music played on the planet.

Hip-Hop/Jungle/Drum and Bass

Although hip-hop may not necessarily stand out as a musical genre that has influenced the modern drummer in any significant way, the reality is that it has. It may have begun life as an underground art form that simply borrowed from previous recordings made by other musicians and recycled their ideas into something new, but it certainly inspired a large number of musicians and helped give rise to new subgenres. Ultimately it rose from the underground to the position whereby associated artists were ruling the pop charts and selling comparable numbers of records as other popular genres, if not exceeding them.

Hip-hop is not just about the music, but instead is an entire culture that developed in New York's Bronx during the 1970s, growing from the impoverished people of the area who had descended from many different cultures, although it has always maintained very strong roots in African culture. It varies from the traditional popular music forms in America such as rock 'n' roll, rock, pop, or jazz in which youngsters get together with their instruments and play covers of their favorite songs or possibly even dare to write their own material and invent something new. This interaction between school friends is the most common way for these art forms to spread through the generations. Instead, hip-hop music began at the hands of the disc jockey (DJ), who would play funk and soul records at the gatherings in the local area (block parties) and, in an effort to elongate the short percussion breaks in songs, would use two record turntables, set up with exactly the same vinyl record on each and with a mixer to control the relative volumes, allowing the DJ to alternate between the records. This was known as cutting. He would ensure that while one was playing, the other record was being queued up, ready to be played when the first record reached the end of the section. He would then use the mixer to amplify the second record and then he would queue up the original record while the second one was playing. With this method, a percussion break of only a few seconds could be played indefinitely by cutting between the two. These breakdown sections of music where the band stopped playing and allowed the drum kit, bongos, conga, or timbale to play on their own became known as break beats. While the audience danced to these break beats, they might have also heard a master of ceremonies (MC), who would speak in rhythmic, improvised rhymes, better known as rapping. The more gifted MCs required longer sections over which they could rap, and so the DJ would keep cutting between the two records to prolong these sections.

As a result of this practice, records with songs that featured a break beat were highly sought after, and it became desirable for a DJ to find a rare break beat that hadn't been used in this way before. In the mid-1980s, a DJ from New York's Bronx named Lenny Roberts compiled a set of tracks with popular breaks and released the collection on vinyl under the name *Ultimate Breaks and Beats*. This instantly usable collection was extended with twenty-four subsequent releases under the same title and numerous other imitators.

Previous to this release, rappers had taken their live improvisation into the studio to create recordings that would take the style to the wider, international audience and out of the poor urban areas of its origin. The first significant record of this kind was recorded by the Sugarhill Gang in 1979 and titled "Rapper's Delight" and became a hugely successful hit for the group. It consisted of very rhythmic rapping recorded over the backing track for Chic's "Good Times," which had been released in the same year. This was one of the early cases of copyright infringement in hip-hop, a subject that was to cause many problems throughout its history. Nile Rodgers and Bernhard Edwards were the original songwriters of "Good Times," and upon hearing the recycled version of their music, made a claim for the rights to the song, which was settled out of court, and they were subsequently credited on the record.

Despite stealing the backing music from a previous track, it did not utilize the traditional hip-hop approach of a DJ cutting between two records of "Good Times" to enable the drum and bass guitar pattern to continue for fifteen minutes. This track was not sampled and looped on studio machinery. In fact, this was actually rerecorded by session musicians from the group Positive Force to such a high standard that it is difficult to tell that it is not a sample. Some of the other backing instruments may have been sampled, but the drum kit and bass guitar line that forms such a prominent part of the song were not. The Sugar Hill Records label went on to form a house band that included Keith LeBlanc on drums, who subsequently worked with many artists such as Annie Lennox, Seal, and Peter Gabriel. Another great drummer to follow him into the Sugar Hill house band was the impressive Dennis Chambers, who forged a long and successful career with such artists as Funkadelic and Santana, among many others.

This practice of using live musicians was employed by some of the early recording rap labels, but part of the hip-hop sensibility for many purists is that the music must be created by a DJ using vinyl records. One of the early artists who maintained the traditional approach was Grandmaster Flash, who released "The Adventures of Grandmaster Flash on the Wheels of Steel" in 1981. It was con- structed purely from vinyl records in a performance that utilized many DJ skills, such as scratching (a technique involving spinning the record back and forth very quickly to achieve a rhythmic sound effect from the turntable needle) and frequently cutting between different records. This really took the art of the DJ and put it down for the general public to appreciate. By now hip-hop was really turning heads and forcing record companies to pay attention.

This emerging genre had necessitated little contact with actual drummers at this point, although the style had largely been built on the great feel of the early funk and soul drummers whose beats were being used as the basis for hip-hop tracks, as well as the warm and distinctive recorded sound of those genres and eras of recording. This was about to leap to the next level with the advent of a user- friendly sampling machine. Although sampling machines had been around since the 1960s, they were cumbersome and expensive.

As technology improved, the machines became much more obtainable and usable, and the hip-hop artists were quick to put them to use. Since those early days, hip-hop and the subsequent subgenres that were influenced by it have become a significant part of mainstream popular music, and it soon became commonplace to hear a sampled drum pattern or even an entire band that had become the main musical part of a new song over which another artist rapped or sang. Some of these samplers also offered a drum machine function that made it very easy for a producer to apply a hip-hop–type drum pattern over a sample of music such as a well-known, luscious string part. This became a very common sound with the typical computer-generated eight-beat drum pattern overlaid upon a well-known hook from a previous hit. One such sampler to offer this was the E-mu SP-1200, which was released in 1987 and became incredibly popular for its sampling capabilities.

But many producers longed after that human touch on the drums, and for this they continued to sample drum breaks. So why didn't they just record their own beats? This was due to a number of factors. One was the unique and highly desirable recorded sound of the 1960s and into the 1970s funk, soul, and R&B records from which many of the rhythms were taken. Those recordings captured a warmth and ambience that is still cherished today in this era of superior recording quality. Another factor was the incredible feel of the drummers in those tracks, such as Clyde Stubblefield and Jabo Starks for James Brown, who were very popular subjects for sampling. It was difficult to make a new recording and get that feel of playing without hiring a top-quality drummer and getting them to record a beat in a studio with the desired sound. It may have also been difficult for the nondrumming producers to know what they wanted before they had even heard it and therefore, difficult to instruct a drummer what to play in a studio. And from this point, it is easy to see that the factor of convenience is highly significant. Why would a producer spend lots of money and lots of time trying to get a drummer to play something that he can hear on a record, feel the rush of excitement as the groove inspires him, and then sample the pattern within a couple of minutes to be well on the way to creating a new track? The list of sampled drum patterns is endless today, but many grooves have become famous for their use in hip-hop. Some of these were a result of the *Ultimate Breaks and Beats* collections that made the process of finding suitable samples very easy.

One of the most famous sampled drum grooves is known as the "Amen Break," discussed in detail later in this section. This has been sampled countless times, but one such example is the title track from the 1988 album *Straight Outta Compton* by the group N.W.A., as well as "I Desire" from the 1986 album *Hot Cool and Vicious* by female rap group Salt and Pepa. Another example was the James Brown track "Funky Drummer," recorded in 1969 featuring Clyde Stubblefield on the drum kit playing a rhythm so funky that the track was named in homage to this. This has been sampled for many tracks, such as Ice Cube's track "Jackin' for Beats" from his 1990 album *Kill at Will* and LL Cool J's "The Boomin' System" from his 1990 album *Mama Said Knock You Out*. One other popular example was the track "Apache," released in 1973 by the Incredible Bongo Band, featuring the great session percussionist King Errisson, who has worked with many great artists, not least with his extensive playing for the Motown label. "Apache" also demonstrated the drumming of Jim Gordon, who was a very successful session drummer alongside Hal Blaine and Jim Keltner, as well as helping to compose such classic tracks as "Layla" before mental illness tragically led to him murdering his mother and subsequently being imprisoned. The use of this track can be heard in its most blatant form by the Sugarhill Gang in 1981, who released it for their album *8th Wonder* in its original form with the addition of structural editing alongside instrumental and DJ sounds as well as overlaying rapping. Grandmaster Flash also used a sample of it in the previously mentioned "The Adventures of Grandmaster Flash on the Wheels of Steel."

And so it was that these funk drummers from a decade or two ago were laying the foundations for another entirely different genre. However, their significant role in this creation of "new" work often went unaccredited and unpaid. Various treaties govern the use of artistic works, and it can be a difficult area of law. According to the Berne Convention for the Protection of Literary and Artistic Works, any creative work in a fixed medium is automatically protected for fifty years after the author's death. All of the above examples of drum breaks fall into that category and therefore, the usage without permission of these drum breaks was technically illegal. Initially this practice was not deemed as a problem, and the style of music that was doing this was considered underground and noncommercial. As a result, many original artists were happy for their work to be used, or at least accepted it. However, when these artists began to gain significant commercial success with records containing samples, people began to take notice. Suddenly hip-hop and rap were not confined to block parties in the Bronx. Suddenly they were appearing in the charts and gaining serious sales.

This began in the 1980s and rose steadily ever after, rising to a peak in October 2003 when for the first time since the beginning of the Billboard American Top 100 record charts, the top ten consisted of only African American artists and of those, all except Beyoncé Knowles were rap artists. This clearly shows the musical influence that these rap and contemporary R&B artists possess over the record-buying public at large, from middle class white youths to the black communities in the Bronx, where it all started many years ago. Of course with these successes came the large royalties, and when this began to happen, the people whose original recording had made a contribution to this money-earning single suddenly felt less obliging to hear their drumbeats on another record.

Artists were now being taken to court and faced huge fees, which had to be paid to the original author. However, it wasn't a black and white issue, and throughout the history of sampling there have been difficult cases with contrasting outcomes. A one-bar drumbeat that has been sped up, pitch shifted, and treated with reverb would be harder to prove as a sample of someone else's song than a top line chorus melody. However, most artists, and indeed their record companies, do not want to risk a day in court and substantial losses of earnings and therefore, the accepted practice was to obtain permission for any samples to be used. This may be granted free of charge or for a fee, which could vary dramatically.

The drummers responsible for the "Amen Break" and the "Funky Drummer" have not received any money for their contributions to hip-hop, drum and bass, or any other style that has delved into their legacy numerous times. Despite the fact that they are often unaccredited, they have since become well-known names within these industries, and general respect and admiration became widespread for their drumbeats and influence on the styles in question.

In an effort to help this relatively new practice of constructing drum patterns without owning a drum kit or being able to play the drum, the Sugar Hill Records house band drummer Keith LeBlanc released one of the first sampling albums with *Malcolm X: No Sell Out* in 1983. This soon took off as other companies looked to capitalize on the works of others' recordings. One such example is the UK-based company Zero G Ltd., who around the turn of the millennium were selling sample reconstruction collections called *Jungle Warfare* that could be bought for a one-off fee and used in new recordings without any copyright issues. They have offered a version of the "Amen Break," which is sped up to the speed usually preferred in drum and bass music. They claim that the recording is their own and is therefore theirs to grant permission for. However, it is difficult for the human ear to hear any difference between their version and the Winstons' original recording when sped up to the same speed. Some synthesizers also offer single hit samples of popular sounds, which can then be pieced together to create patterns. One example is the Korg Electribe Series of synthesizers, which include individual sound samples of a hi-hat, snare, and bass drum very similar to those of the "Amen Break." With the advent of such drumbeat sound libraries and synthesizer sounds, it is very easy for a person with very little musical ability to create a great-sounding drum part onto which they can build a track. This has undoubtedly had an effect on the session drummer industry. People can create drum parts at home for very little money with minimal equipment and in minimal time. As a result, people are less likely to spend money on a studio and a drummer to take the extensive time required to record a drum part. As these electronic styles became even more popular, it filtered through to other popular styles and even commercial music for advertisements or corporate films, compounding the loss of work for the live, skilled drummer.

Although the practice of using a house band of real musicians, adopted in the early days of hip-hop record labels such as Sugar

Hill Records, did wane considerably when the sampler became popular, it didn't die out completely. In the 1990s, during a period often cited as hip-hop's golden age, the sampler was used extensively, and yet Dr. Dre's multiplatinum 1992 album *The Chronic* featured drummer Cheron Moore. This element of live music hung on through the 1990s, and in the next millennium a resurgence in live drummers became apparent.

One such group is the Roots with their cofounder and drummer Ahmir "?uestlove" Thompson, who crafted a strong reputation as a formidable hip-hop drummer and producer. His approach was to play drums as metronomically perfectly as possible, leaving the listener guessing as to whether they are programmed or played by a human. This can clearly be heard on the track "You Got Me" from the 1999 album *Things Fall Apart.* The track, which won a Grammy Award a year after its release, features a very repetitive and clean-sounding drum pattern, which appears for all intents and purposes as though it is programmed until the final verse, when it breaks out into a more drum and bass–style pattern. Thompson achieves his drum rhythms primarily on a combination of Yamaha drums, but his fundamental sound philosophies dictate that he will always experiment in the search for new sounds. He is also a keen advocate of experimental recording techniques, sometimes recording drums through guitar amplifiers or positioning microphones in obscure positions in surrounding rooms and using the sound with high compression or equalization processing. His main band, the Roots, built up a loyal following over the many years since the inception in 1987.

Another, even longer-running hip-hop group was the hugely successful Beastie Boys, who began in 1979 New York and merged their rock, punk, and hip-hop influences with a mix of live playing and sampling. With Michael Diamond (Mike D) on the drums they have recorded a lot of drums from scratch, experimenting with different recording techniques such as building a tent structure over the drum kit for a very dry sound on the 2009 album *Hot Sauce Committee,* using tunnels made of cardboard boxes on the bass drum to enhance the boom qualities of the sound, and mixing in demo tracks, which were recorded as basic demos with only

PZMs (pressure zone microphones). They also experimented over the years with heavy sampling, most clearly observed on the 1989 album *Paul's Boutique,* which would cost a fortune to release in today's industry, where heavy royalties would be likely to be due to each author of each sample. Through their mix of live playing and sampling they achieved a very distinctive sound.

Many of the rap and contemporary R&B artists that have found success in the wake of hip-hop do not possess a drummer as part of the fundamental core, and therefore they have to bring in the session drummer who, in this field, needs to come ready with a number of different metaphorical hats to wear. One such drummer is Keith Harris, who was invited to power the record-breaking Black Eyed Peas in 2003. The group are renowned for their futuristic sounds, which are built around rhythms that often don't even sound like an actual drum. Harris was trained at Berklee College of Music following a background in church performance, but he had to learn quickly to forget the theory and technicality and simply play by feel. The real challenge for such a drummer is the discipline of playing very simplistic and repetitive parts with robotic accuracy and yet with great feel. The other aspect is the replication of drum parts that have been crafted in a studio from all manner of different sounds and treated by numerous effects. Up until the 2009 *E.N.D.* album, Harris was using an Akai MPC sampler into which he would load all the necessary drum sounds. Once edited in the sampler he would transfer the sounds to his Ddrum module from which he could trigger the sounds. As the sounds became more complex and demanding, so too did his electronic setup. Along with his electronics, he was an endorsee of Sabian cymbals and Tama drums, choosing to play with customized sizes for the *Monkey Business* period in 2005 and 2006 with a Maple Starclassic kit in diamond dust comprising a 20 × 18-inch bass drum, a 13 × 6-inch snare drum, 8 × 7 and 10 × 7 rack toms, as well as 12 × 12 and 14 × 14 floor toms. Harris is well aware of the royalties that can be earned as a result of a songwriting credit, and to that end he has worn the hat of composer for numerous tracks, such as a cowriter's credit on the 2009 single "Imma Be" from the Black Eyed Peas' *E.N.D.* album. Harris also founded a production company

called Harris Productions, which was an extension of his work as
a producer. Wearing his producing hat, Harris worked with many
artists, including Earth, Wind and Fire, as well as Michael Jackson
and Quincy Jones.

Another hip-hop drummer who plays well and truly in the
pocket for many big-name singers as well as writing and producing
is Nisan Stewart. Having played for such artists as Nelly Furtado,
50 Cent, Timbaland, and Busta Rhymes, Stewart was a fan of the
DW bubinga wood drums with a huge 24-inch bass drum, and 10-,
12-, 14-, and 16-inch toms. Just as Harris did, Stewart opted for
a 13-inch snare drum, which offers the pop that was so essential
in hip-hop drumming for an almost synthetic-sounding backbeat.
Despite the outwardly aggressive and offensive appearance of some
hip-hop artists, especially in the gangsta rap subgenre, many of the
musicians behind the music are deeply religious. Keith Harris and
Nisan Stewart are two such examples, having begun their drumming careers in church groups. Two others to follow such a path
are Aaron Spears, who played for such artists as Usher, and David
Haddon, who made his name with Rihanna.

Another interesting drummer who approached hip-hop from a
different angle than the gospel crowd Travis Barker, who rose to
fame in the punk band Blink-182 with his reputation for lightning-
fast punk grooves with an attack and ferocity to suit. During a break
from Blink-182, Barker began to experiment with hip-hop and how
the drum kit fit into this genre. Having begun a rap/punk project in
the early 2000s called the Transplants, Barker began remixing other
artists' tracks from Bun B (from the UKG hip-hop group) to Soulja
Boy, Rihanna, and Flo Rida, approaching them from his more punk/
rock-oriented point of view with very real, heavy-sounding drum
parts in contrast to the machinelike playing of traditional hip-hop
players. A good example of such playing can be heard on Barker's
remix of Soulja Boy's 2007 track "Crank This."

While hip-hop was evolving across America and spreading
throughout the world, other people in the United Kingdom were
finding new inspiration from the old funk break beats that had
been the foundation of the hip-hop genre. As briefly mentioned
previously, the "Amen Break" was an old favorite. It had originally

been recorded in 1969 by the Winstons and titled "Amen Brother."
It was only released as a B-side of the single "Color Him Father,"
which won a Grammy for the band. The B-side song didn't achieve
any great success in its entirety. It was the fact that the song contained this breakdown in which the very funky drum pattern was
exposed without any other instruments that made this song interesting. The drum pattern was played by drummer Gregory C. Coleman, and it would have been impossible for him to have known that
his six-second break was to have such a profound effect on music.
Unfortunately, as with so many others who were sampled in this
era, Coleman didn't receive a single penny for the use of his drum
pattern, nor did any other members of the Winstons. Over twenty
years later, inspired minds were excitedly working within the British
rave culture, which had reached a peak in the 1990s as improved
sampling technology was allowing producers to take their favorite
drum patterns in a new direction. In particular the beats were used
at a much faster tempo, often around 180 beats per minute. They
were also edited in greater depth, with each drum hit cut and then
reordered in endless combinations to create frenetic and inhuman
rhythms. They were often used beneath spatial synthesized sounds,
hi-tech sound effects, and sub bass lines, which use very low frequencies. This style of music became a genre of its own, which was
recognized as jungle and then later evolved into drum and bass.

The "Amen Break" was instrumental in this genre, along with
other popular breaks, many of which were released at tempos just
below two hundred beats per minute on sample libraries such as
the aforementioned Zero G Jungle Warfare collection. It didn't
take long before drummers became fascinated with these frenetic
and challenging rhythms and began to dissect them, assessing if
a human drummer could play them. One drummer who built a
reputation in this area was the London-based Chris Polglase, who
performed under the name the Jungle Drummer. Initially forging
his name with UK DJs such as Grooverider, he went on to play
with Timbaland and the group London Elektricity. His most notable work is arguably that with DJ Fu, which began in 2006 and
saw the drummer and DJ battling it out live on stage for rhythmic
supremacy just as MCs had done in the early days of hip-hop.

Another group to emerge from the United Kingdom was Tthe Bays with their drummer Andy Gangadeen. Having been inspired by Dave Weckl's electronic setup with the Chick Corea Elektric Band, Gangadeen found success with the Polish singer Basia, replicating the Linn 9000 drum machine sounds that were used on her album. From there he went on to play with Lisa Stansfield and the Spice Girls, which were both UK pop acts that required a good working knowledge of electronic drums. This experience helped him when he became a member of the Bays, who are unusual in that they don't record any albums, relying solely on their live performances to reach out to their audiences. The performances themselves are completely improvised, so that the music they play is a direct reaction to the audience and the energy in the room. This concept proved successful, and they took it a step further, playing with an orchestra whose parts were composed live on stage and sent to the orchestral players via electronic screens for them to sight read. The music played is a very diverse mix of electronic dance music but does involve strong themes of drum and bass. Through this work, Gangadeen built a formidable reputation as an incredibly precise drummer who could play effortlessly with metronomic accuracy when sequencing his mix of acoustic and electronic drums with samples, loops, and drum machines. The interesting mix of acoustic snares, bass drums, toms, and cymbals woven among electronic pads gave rise to the ingenious Pole-Kat setup in which two pads are placed one above the other, facing each other, only inches apart. With this setup Gangadeen can perform semiquaver notes with one hand at lightning speeds, achieving one note with his upstroke and another with the downstroke. Added to this are a series of Dauz trigger pads and two Fat Kat trigger pedals that are sent through a Yamaha DTS-70 trigger to midi converter. The midi signal is then sent to an Akai MPC3000 sampler, which triggers the custom samples that have been loaded into it.

Most drum and bass acts tend to stay underground or at least struggle to make any great impact on mainstream music. The use of the genre did become more diverse as it became more recognized and accepted into other formats such as TV commercials, but record sales have never achieved any great figures. One group to change that was the Australian band Pendulum, who relocated to the United Kingdom in 2003. A band rooted in drum and bass but adding a rock influence as heard on the 2008 album *In Silico*, they powered forward with their exciting blend of synthesizers and fast rhythms in a traditional live band format with Paul Kodish on drums.

Kodish used a Tama Starclassic with a 22 × 16-inch bass drum, a 10 × 6.5-inch rack tom, a 16 × 14-inch floor tom, a 10 × 6- and 12 × 6.5-inch bell brass snare, a 14 × 6.5 1979 Ludwig 402 snare, a 14 × 6.5 Slingerland Buddy Rich brass snare, and a 14 × 7-inch Gretsch maple snare. The small number of toms compared to the huge number of snares demonstrates the significance of diverse snare sounds that drive the rhythms of this genre, and the rarity of fills explains the smaller tom setup. The relatively shallow bass and tom sizes enable a faster attack and the avoidance of a rock drum kit sound when in search of the tight drum sound that is necessary. Although he doesn't use any electronic pads, Ddrum triggers are attached to the acoustic drums and sent through a computerized system for the more synthetic sounds. The recorded sound is a combination of Kodish's accurate and driving playing mixed with the band leader Rob Swire's scientific approach, in which he sends all the sounds through a spectral analyzer to make sure the frequencies of every drum and cymbal are well suited to each other and then to the track as a whole. The recorded drum sounds are then cut up and pasted into the song as the structure develops in the studio. This enables the human feel of a real musician to be coupled with a programmer's approach to song construction. Kodish was replaced in 2009 by the American drummer Kevin Sawyer, who had previously built a fierce reputation in his hometown of Seattle for his advancement of live drum and bass drumming, where he would sometimes perform alone, triggering all synthesizers, bass lines, melodies, and even the lighting show himself while playing the drum patterns.

Sawyer wasn't the only drummer in America to pick up this UK-led genre and take it to the next level. As previously mentioned, the Swiss-born drummer Jojo Mayer moved to New York in his younger years and played a very significant role in this field, having come to prominence in the jazz world with the Monty Alexander

Group, Dizzy Gillespie, and Nina Simone and then making the transition into drum and bass. His jazz-fused drum and bass style was best exhibited in his own project Nerve in which he demonstrated incredible aptitude in playing complex drum and bass rhythms, which would have been deemed possible only with a drum machine in previous years. He has used the term "reverse engineering" to describe this approach whereby a human strives to emulate a machine. During the late 20th century and into the 21st, he developed a strong reputation as a drum clinician, performing at many music events either solo or with a small group to demonstrate his abilities. This then led to educational material such as the popular 2007 DVD *Secret Weapons for the Modern Drummer*.

The education market was also enriched by the Chicago drummer Johnny Rabb, who came to fame in the drumming community after achieving the Guinness World Record for the world's fastest drummer in 2000 by playing 1,071 single strokes in sixty seconds. He then created a strong name for himself as a clinician and promoter for drum and bass drumming styles on the acoustic drum kit. Displaying excellent technical ability, Rabb constantly pushed the boundaries in much the same way as Mayer, always searching for new sounds and techniques with which to emulate complex programmed drum patterns. To help the wider drumming audience to do the same, he released his book *Jungle/Drum and Bass for the Acoustic Drum Set* in 2001, which detailed many different techniques, patterns, and approaches to this style, along with some stylistic background information and equipment guidance.

Emulating the up-tempo drum and bass patterns is as much about sound as it is about playing style. The funk beats of Coleman, Stubblefield, et al were sped up a great deal, and in doing so the pitch of the drums was raised. This sound therefore requires some careful drum selections and tuning options. The snare drum is central to the sound and as a result, many drummers in this field use multiple snare drums within their sets. Rabb is no different, and he often opts for a 14-inch main snare, augmented by a 10- and 12-inch snare. The smaller diameters are tuned highly to achieve the tight, high-pitched crack for the backbeat. He uses a 10-inch rack tom and a 14-inch floor tom in the conventional manner, as well as a single-headed, 16-inch floor tom with which he emulates an electronic bass sound by playing it with his hand.

Rabb has also worked closely with the Meinl cymbal manufacturers to create his own signature models. The Safari crash, ride, and hi-hats allow for some very unorthodox sounds, which help with the creation of electronic-sounding patterns. This line of cymbals featured an 8-inch brass cymbal mounted atop a larger nickel/silver flat cymbal. This provided two distinct playing surfaces and created trashy timbres such as the white noise that is often used in electronic loops. The cymbals also featured the Tension Tuning System, which allowed the wing nut to tighten or loosen to alter the decay of the cymbal. Rabb also designed the Drumbals with Meinl. These were two small cymbals of 8 and 10 inches, which had a small handle at the top so that they could be easily lifted by hand. They could be placed on top of a batter head and used to achieve various effects, either by hitting them with a stick or crashing them down on the drumhead for accents.

Rabb's kit was not too dissimilar from Mayer's, appearing like a small jazz set with auxiliary snare drums, extra cymbals, and an extra-strangely placed tom or electronic device. Where Rabb had endorsed the German Meinl cymbal company, Mayer was an endorser of the German Sonor drum company as well as Sabian cymbals, and his configuration often resembled a jazz kit with a 20-inch bass drum, a 10-inch rack tom, a 14-inch floor tom, and a 14-inch snare drum. This was usually augmented with a second snare, often of smaller diameter or a shallower depth, and other drums such as an 8-inch tom placed beside the floor tom. His Sabian cymbal setup varied and was always evolving to find new sounds, including the Fierce cymbals, which he helped design with the Sabian company. As well as cymbals, Mayer played a part in the design of Sonor's Jungle Kit, acting as a consultant with his vast knowledge of drum and bass drumming. The kit utilized small shell sizes with a 16 × 16-inch bass drum, a 10 × 8-inch rack tom, and a 14 × 12-inch floor tom, each made of nine maple wood plies. Sonor also produced a Jungle Snare drum, which boasted a 10-inch diameter and 2-inch depth. The drum was very limited in its application and didn't allow for individual head tuning, but it worked as a niche drum for styles such as drum and bass and obtained a unique sound with the sixteen jingles that were fitted into the side of the shell just as found on tambourines. The Sonor Jungle kit wasn't unique and had several rivals, its closest arguably being Yamaha's Rick Morrotta Hip Gig kit, which featured similarly small drums that are stored inside each other in the style of the Russian matryoshka dolls for incredibly easy transportation. These products reflected the growing interest in electronic music and the growing desire of drummers to play in such a way. An incredibly interesting full circle had occurred by this point in which earlier-generation players were sampled, edited, and processed to create new styles of music and ultimately replaced by machines to provide the rhythms. Real drummers then strove to replicate these rhythms, and the drum manufacturers reacted by designing equipment to help achieve this sound.

REGGAE

In the early 20th century, Jamaican music consisted of various musical influences from the American jazz that had infiltrated the island via radio waves, to the exciting calypso sounds, to their traditional mento music, which was a popular folkloric country music performed with rudimentary instruments. Drum kits were not practical for these rural and often impoverished musicians, but a single-hand drum was popular, often accompanied by maracas or a woodblock. This traditional music was experienced only through live performance due to the lack of recording facilities on the island. But then in the early 1950s, Federal Records Studios was opened in the capital city, Kingston, and Jamaican music was no longer restricted to local concerts. As the recording of mento and calypso tunes became popular, other producers and musicians became involved, and momentum really grew toward the 1960s, when the Jamaican music scene exploded onto the rest of the world.

As the Jamaicans grew tired of mento music, another style of their own emerged. By the early 1960s this style had become hugely popular, and this coincided with Jamaica gaining independence from Britain in 1962. The island had a new lease of life, and the soundtrack to this was ska music. Ska bands consisted of vocals, bass guitar, electric guitar, a horn section, and of course a drum kit. Ska was lively, it was fast, it was energetic, and it was filling the airwaves across the island as people danced away to the up-tempo rhythm that placed great emphasis on the offbeat. It began with a swung feel but later evolved with straight quavers. The standard ska drum pattern would feature a bass drum on beats one and three, a snare drum backbeat on beats two and four, accompanied by an unwavering hi-hat played on every offbeat. This offbeat hi-hat was played in unison with a staccato guitar chord (which became known as skanking) and sometimes a note from the brass instruments as well.

Lloyd Knibb was a major session drummer during this emerging period of ska and ended up as the drummer for the Skatalites, who were essentially formed from the island's studio session group that backed many of the hits at this time. They played a hugely significant role in forming the sound that became accepted as ska. During the 1940s when Knibb started to play drums in groups, there were no music shops in Jamaica, so a drum kit was made for him by a local craftsman. By the time the Skatalites were building a name for themselves, Knibb was laying down these iconic ska grooves on a simple four-piece kit, with a large bass drum, a very shallow, single-headed rack tom, and a single-headed floor tom. As well as the hi-hat, there was one crash cymbal attached to the bass drum and of course a shallow snare from which the distinctive, high-pitched, resonant snare fills came. His ska patterns came from a variety of sources such as the American R&B, American swing, calypso, and the burru rhythms. The burru drumming style involved three separate drum parts on three separate drums called the bass drum, the funde, and the repeater, but Knibb found a way to play all of the parts himself, which helped enrich his musical vocabulary. Knibb used interesting accented patterns on the bell of his ride cymbal as well as crash cymbal accents on the fourth beat of the bar. Both of these characteristics can be clearly heard on the 1964 Skatalites track "Occupation" and their later track "Fidel Castro." The "Occupation" ride bell accents use the same pattern as the Puerto Rican bomba rhythm, later made famous by David Garibaldi with Tower of Power.

Some of the groups who were popular in this ska period were the Wailers, the Maytals, Desmond Dekker, the Skatalites, Alton Ellis, and the Ethiopians. Such popular tracks from this time included Desmond Dekker's 1963 single "Honour Your Mother and Father," before he scored the international hits "Israelites" and "You Can Get It If You Really Want" in 1968 and 1970 respectively, and Toots and the Maytals' "Hallelujah," recorded for their 1964 debut album *I'll Never Grow Old* by producer Clement "Coxsone" Dodd at Studio One with the house band the Skatalites and drummer Lloyd Knibb. By 1967 ska was being replaced by rocksteady, although ska never died out completely. In the late 1970s and into the 1980s, ska enjoyed a revival in Britain with the second wave, also known as two-tone ska, which involved mixed Caucasian and African-American band members as well as fans. Popular groups in this wave were the Specials with John Bradbury on drums, and Madness with drummer Daniel Woodgate. A third wave then occurred in the late 1980s and early 1990s. This was primarily an American movement and embodied in groups such as the Mighty Mighty Bosstones.

Returning to the demise of the initial wave of ska's popularity around 1966, artists who had been popular in this field began experimenting with a different tempo. This new style of music was called rocksteady, and it was at a much slower speed than ska, lending itself to impressive vocal groups who had been influenced by the American R&B and soul groups. The rhythm still put great emphasis on the offbeats of the bar with syncopated guitar rhythms on the weaker beats and the bass guitar playing with a more broken pattern than the walking bass line often used in ska. The drum parts were generally very basic and simply reinforced the guitar rhythm with the hi-hat while filling in the stronger beats with an alternate bass and snare drum, thus acting purely as a timekeeping element. The snare drum often incorporated a laid-back cross-stick technique as opposed to the full snare sound of ska. Drum fills were minimal and often consisted of a simple drag on the snare drum, the accent often played as a rimshot for greater effect. This style also largely disposed of the horn section, which was popular in ska, opting instead for piano parts.

Desmond Dekker, the Heptones, the Melodians, and Alton Ellis were among the popular names in the rocksteady movement. In fact Alton Ellis was very significant in slowing the beat down to form rocksteady as heard on his 1967 track, which actually bears the title "Rocksteady," with another early track in this style being "Take It Easy," recorded by Hopeton Lewis in 1966 and released the next year. Another very influential figure in the rocksteady and reggae genres was the drummer Winston Grennan. Although he amassed an impressive CV working with Dizzy Gillespie, Marvin Gaye, Herbie Hancock, Aretha Franklin, Paul Simon, and the Rolling Stones, Grennan is best known as an innovator in Jamaica in the days of emerging rocksteady and reggae music. Throughout the 1960s and up until 1972 when he left Jamaica for the United States, Grennan was hugely significant in the music studios of Kingston, playing on countless tracks for artists such as Toots Hibbert, Jimmy Cliff, Bob Marley, and Peter Tosh. His grueling recording schedule bears similarities to that of Hal Blaine in Los Angeles of the same period. Many of these early albums did not credit the musicians on the album sleeves, and as a result his input into this style is sometimes overlooked. This is compounded by the fact that he left Kingston and the Jamaican reggae scene in 1972 to work in America and so faded from memories more quickly.

Grennan played on such tracks as Slim Smith and the Uniques' 1968 track "My Conversation," and the Melodians' 1968 track "By the Rivers of Babylon." Grennan performed these early rocksteady and reggae tracks on a very standard setup except for the unusual positioning of his crash cymbals, which were often positioned behind him.

It wasn't just Grennan who helped the rocksteady rhythms flourish. Several drummers were required to service the Jamaican studios, which were instrumental in spreading this music to the masses. Just as the Skatalites had been the house band for Clement "Coxsone" Dodd's Studio One recording facility, Duke Reid had his Treasure Isle recording studio with house band Tommy McCook and the Supersonics and drummer Lloyd Knibb, later replaced by

Hugh Malcolm. Meanwhile, at Federal Studios, the music was provided by Lyn Taitt and the Jets with drummer Joe Isaacs. Together they churned out many of the rocksteady hits in the late 1960s.

Throughout this rocksteady period, a new type of rhythm began to emerge, a rhythm that would be the bedrock of reggae. This rhythm was called the one drop, and it features an absence of sound during beat one. The pattern is generally used in four-four time and typically plays a hi-hat on beats two and four while the main downbeat is played on beat three. The generic reggae beat would place a bass drum on beat three and possibly double it up with a cross-stick snare note. This space during beat one and the single accent on beat three has become synonymous with reggae but can be heard on earlier rocksteady tracks such as the aforementioned "My Conversation."

However, just as quickly as it had emerged, by 1968 rocksteady was in decline after only two years in peak popularity. Times were changing in Jamaica following the independence and subsequent political unrest, especially within the unruly rude boy communities of the ghettos. As a result, the music was rapidly changing as well. It was time for the rocksteady tempo to slow down even further to allow the relaxed sounds of reggae to emerge. This slower style involved a slightly swung quaver groove, which was integral to the laid-back sound. Recording studio technology helped the rise of reggae, enabling the bass guitar to become more prominent and complex in arrangement. Reverb and delay effects were utilized, and the piano was relegated to make way for the electric organ, which often played the shuffle accents. The horns followed through from the rocksteady trend in becoming less important, and the guitar part became a muted and very rhythmic skanking sound. As the lyrical content became charged with political opinions and social comment, the drummer kept grooving with unwavering simplicity and incredible feel as the one-drop rhythm reigned supreme. Although the change happened gradually as new elements formed to make the distinction between reggae and rocksteady, the first track to reference reggae was "Do the Reggay," which was recorded in 1968 by the Maytals with Winston Grennan on drums.

Due to the short time frame between these Jamaican genres, many of the musicians involved in early reggae were also prominent figures in the ska and rocksteady movements, but there were also some new names that had floated to the top. Bob Marley was the best internationally known reggae star, and his songs have defined the genre to many listeners. His band the Wailers crafted an inspiring sound, which was founded upon the irresistible feel provided by the rhythm (or to use Jamaican slang "riddim") section. At the heart of this were bass player Aston Barrett and his brother on drums. Although the true creator of the one-drop rhythm would be hard to identify, it is true that Carlton "Field Marshall" Barrett helped to bring it to the masses. Having joined the Wailers in 1969, Barrett was soon regarded as a high-caliber reggae drummer throughout the world as his groove-drenched drumming promoted the art of playing for the song instead of trying to take center stage like many of the European and American rock drummers of the period. He used fills sparingly and often just opted for a simple but effective snare roll combining rim shots and cymbals with the occasional tom-tom. Reggae drumming doesn't rely on the almighty crash cymbal and bass drum on beat one after each fill as heard in rock, metal, funk, or most other popular Western styles of music. Due to the one-drop characteristic of leaving space on beat one, a crash cymbal, if played at all, was instead often played at the end of the bar containing the fill, most effective when doubled up with a snare drum accent. Barrett's most creative side was displayed through his hi-hat work, playing intricate patterns and using accents to help move the rhythm along. He tended to favor a simple five-piece drum kit, and although it varied through the years, he was a user of Ludwig drums, with a 20 × 16-inch bass drum, a 14 × 5.5 Supraphonic aluminum snare drum, 12 × 9- and 13 × 10-inch rack toms, and a 16 × 16-inch floor tom. The cymbal setup was also basic with some 14-inch hi-hats and two crashes of 16 and 18 inches. This very ordinary drum setup was responsible for a very distinctive sound, and that all came from Barrett's treatment of the drums. His toms were single headed, the batter head tuned high. His bass drum resonant skin was cut, leaving only a thin strip around the circumference, but the main feature of his sound was the snare drum. He often disengaged the snare strainer on this drum and tuned the skin very tightly, obtaining an almost timbale-like sound. The single-headed toms gave a drier sound, and this effect was heightened by the use of tape stuck to his black dot batter heads. Furthermore, Barrett placed cloth between the two hi-hat cymbals. Unfortunately, Barrett was shot in 1987 at his home by an assassin working on Mrs. Barrett's orders, but his influence on reggae drumming was huge and continues to inspire drummers today.

Another drummer to have a big impact in the direction of reggae drumming was Lowell "Sly" Dunbar, who was born in Kingston, Jamaica, in 1952. Having played on the Upsetters' track "Night Doctor" in 1969 and then Dave and Ansell Collins's successful 1969 album *Double Barrel* while only sixteen years old, Dunbar was soon to became a busy Kingston drummer by the time he met bass player Robbie Shakespeare at Channel One Studios, where they were session players in the house band known as the Revolutionaries. The name proved to be very apt, as the two musicians started their own record label and went on to play on hundreds of records for many of the big-name reggae artists; while doing so, they inadvertently changed the sound of reggae and helped to move it on to the next level. Sly and Robbie earned the nickname the "Riddim Twins" as they pioneered new ground for reggae and also worked with American and European names such as Sting, Sinead O'Connor, the Rolling Stones, Bob Dylan, Madonna, Britney Spears, and many more. Dunbar literally revolutionized the reggae rhythms that had become so popular and then, inevitably so overused. In a conscious effort to find new ground in reggae drumming, and having been listening to the Philadelphia sound, which was popularizing the disco beat, Dunbar created a rhythm for a track he recorded for the Channel One Studios engineer Ernest Hoo Kim. The 1976 recording became a hit under the name "When the Right Time Come." The rhythm in this track became very popular, sought after by many producers in Jamaica, and subsequently came to be known as the rocker beat. The rocker reggae beat was similar to the one drop except that it filled that empty space in beat one, often with a bass or snare drum. This particular example recorded by

Dunbar involved extensive use of a snare drum cross stick, creating the impression of a delay effect, which was popular in the genre, by repeatedly playing two subsequent hits. This more involved snare part became popular, another example of which can be heard in Peter Tosh's 1977 "Stepping Razor," which Dunbar contributed to. These patterns do display similarities to earlier drummers such as Lloyd Knibb, who had played a consistent, steady rhythm in 1965, which involved a very syncopated snare pattern on "Addis Ababa" by Don Drummond and the Skatalites. Back to the rocker beat, another example can be clearly heard on Gregory Isaac's 1982 hit "Night Nurse" courtesy of backing group Roots Radics and drummer Lincoln "Style" Scott, although this example uses a simple backbeat on beat three.

In a constant search for original rhythms, Dunbar embraced the move into digital sound and electronic drums, which helped him move reggae into the next phase of modern dancehall and then ragga. This shift generally relied on a drummer playing electronic drums or having them programmed into a drum machine. The Chaka Demus and Pliers 1992 track "Murder She Wrote" is an example of such evolution of reggae rhythm, which was recorded with use of an Akai *MPC 60* sequencer and sampler by Dunbar. Incidentally, a track from the same artist titled "Bam Bam" was recorded the very same day with the exact same backing drumbeat.

It was a fortunate and wise move from Dunbar to embrace this new direction. As other drummers who remained staunchly loyal to their acoustic drum heritage fell out of favor in the face of new, cheap technology, Dunbar thrived and enabled himself to spearhead the new sub ragga scene. From the early hits like Wayne Smith's 1985 "Under Me Sleng Teng," which enjoyed the rhythm of a preprogrammed Casio keyboard pattern, producers no longer had to pay session drummers. Instead they could plug in an electronic device and the rhythm track was already there; a familiar story throughout the drumming world during the 1980s. The genre took off and soon artists like Shaggy, Shabba Ranks, Maxi Priest, Beenie Man, and Chaka Demus and Pliers became international names. Ragga also influenced jungle music with its rapping vocal style and driving rhythms.

Having worked with all of the above while forging his immensely strong reputation in this field, Dunbar has not stayed loyal to one brand of drums, opting instead for diversity in order to push boundaries and stay ahead of the competition. As well as numerous brands of acoustic drums and cymbals, throughout his career Dunbar has used Syndrums, Simmons, and Roland electronic drums, as well as an Akai MPC 60 and 3000 sequencer/sampler, an Oberheim *DMX* drum machine, and an E-mu SP-1200 sampler, among many others. Furthermore, Dunbar used rototoms during his career, which have also been seen in other genres with Bill Bruford, Pink Floyd's Nick Mason during the drum solo intro to the track "Time" on their 1973 release *Dark Side of the Moon*, Terry Bozzio, Stewart Copeland, and Alex Van Halen.

These drums involved a standard drumhead mounted on a counter hoop with no shell. The counter hoop could be screwed up or down along a vertical thread, which pulled the head onto a metal ring sitting below it, thus altering the tension. This design was not original by any means, as strong resemblances can be seen over one hundred years earlier. Two examples are Johann Stumpff's 1821 rotary machine timpani, which used the screwing motion to tune the drums, while Adolphe Sax's timpani of 1846 used a concept devoid of any drum shells.

And so, moving forward with the idea, these rototoms were initially created in 1968 by the Chicago Symphony Orchestra percussionist Al Payson at the request of Michael Colgrass for his piece *Variations for Four Drums and Viola*. Another incarnation of the idea had been seen earlier that decade in Ludwig's Expando tunable bongos. Remo then released them with either a pressed wooden base for sitting upon a table, or a metal floor stand to allow them to be hung from a height. They then evolved to heavy aluminum castings and plated counter hoops as well as an option to have a shallow acrylic shell, which hung around the drum either fully encircling the drum or partially. These shells were called reflectors and allowed the sound to be focused either outward (half shell) or downward (full shell). The drums' fast tuning method allowed for different sonic effects, including a glissando. They were also popular as a training tool for timpanists, as they provided a smaller and cheaper alternative to the real thing.

Going back to reggae drumming, two of the three main patterns have been discussed in the form of the "one drop" and the "rocker," but one has thus far been omitted. This is the rhythm known as the stepper. Where the one drop favored a bass drum emphasizing beat three, and the rocker emphasized beat one and three, the stepper utilized a "four-on-the-floor" pattern. This type of pattern, which is most familiar in disco music, involves playing a bass drum on every quarter note in the bar. It drives the stepper beat with greater forward motion as heard in Burning Spears' 1975 track "Red, Gold and Green" as well as Bob Marley's "Exodus" from 1977 with Carlton Barrett on drums and "Is This Love" from Marley's 1978 album *Kaya*.

Thanks to international stars like Bob Marley exposing the style beyond Jamaica, many artists from the United States, Europe, and all over the world began to experiment with reggae rhythms, and some traveled to Jamaica to obtain these sounds, such as the aforementioned work that Winston Grennan did with Paul Simon on the track "Mother and Child Reunion" in 1972. Examples of Western songs that delved into this style are plentiful, but a listen to "Ghetto Defendant" by the Clash or "Ob-Li-Di, Ob-La-Da" by the Beatles instantly demonstrates this popular practice.

Countless other bands have successfully married or fused two distinct styles together to produce their own sound. One of the most successful and distinctive were the popular English trio the Police with Sting on bass, Andy Summers on guitar, and Stewart Copeland on drums. The band was hugely successful during the 1980s. Copeland is well known for his fiery relationship with Sting and his long partnership with Tama drums, but all of this comes second place to his incredibly and very personal playing style, which brilliantly fuses Jamaican reggae rhythm influences with English or American punk rock styles. This can be heard in tracks such as "Walking on the Moon," "Can't Stand Losing You," or "Message in a Bottle." As a result of his upbringing, which took him from America through Egypt, Syria, and Lebanon, the Arabic rhythms he had grown up around had a big influence on him and helped to develop his ability to displace the accent in drum patterns and to play interesting accented semiquaver patterns on the ride cymbal and hi-hat. This merged with his enjoyment of rock music, the popular punk and new wave styles at the time of the formation of the Police, and his energetic, driving style to form a sound that was instantly recognizable. The strong influence of reggae that imbued the Police's sound gave Copeland a platform from which to demonstrate some of the most creative and inspiring drumming in popular music of the 20th century. This great success and distinctive sound helped inspire listeners to explore the authentic reggae artists from which the Police had borrowed, and showed how different styles could be successfully mixed.

Copeland achieved this sound on his nine-ply midnight blue Tama Imperial Star, which was based around a fairly standard 22 × 14-inch bass drum, a 5 × 14-inch snare drum, 10 × 8-, 12 × 8- and 13 × 9-inch rack toms, and then a 16 × 16-inch floor tom. It was the use of extra toms to the left of his hi-hat, a rototom, four Octobans, a Roland 2000 digital echo machine that was triggered from certain drums, and woodblocks that helped his sound options to stand out. His intricate use of cymbals was also made possible with numerous crash and splash cymbals.

Since those early recordings in the 1950s, reggae has proven popular for its upbeat feel and infectious, laid-back groove. It continues to influence other genres whether it's via a revival in roots reggae, the programmed rhythms of raga, or the up-tempo ska patterns that have enjoyed several periods of popularity. As reggae continues into the future, the legacy left by original masters such as Barrett and Grennan will always be a constant source of inspiration to other drummers.

Chapter Thirteen

—————————○—————————

Rudiments

RUDIMENTS ARE A SERIES OF PATTERNS upon which all drumming techniques and sticking patterns are based. These are the basic foundation exercises that provide the ability to play anything and everything that a drummer will ever play. Even those who never formally learn these exercises will inadvertently use them; a self-taught punk rock drummer playing a fast snare roll to build up for the chorus will most likely execute a single stroke roll, which simply involves playing alternate hands at an even tempo. It is the proficiency of such rudiments and the technique with which they are played that is often the limit of how fast and how accurately a drummer can perform a specific pattern. In short, these are crucial for a drummer's progression on the instrument. It is also by use of these uniformed patterns that pieces of music can be taught to different drummers and they will know exactly how to play them. They are the vocabulary with which the musical phrases are communicated for consistent playing and accurate learning.

Rudiments have been in use for several hundred years in one form or another. As mentioned previously, the Swiss mercenary soldiers popularized the fife and drum, which triggered the demise of the pipe and tabor and the rise of the side drum. This larger drum needed a dedicated player as opposed to the pipe and tabor, which used one man simultaneously for both instruments. The side drummer now had two free hands to play, and so this was an instrument on which complex rhythms could be formed. These complex patterns made use of various techniques that had to be learned by rote for groups of drummers to play in unison. Battle signals needed to be learned accurately for soldiers to recognize the rhythms and understand the commands. Each exercise was learned with ono-matopoeic words such as da-da-ma-ma for the long roll.

With these early fife and drum corps the Swiss military, and in particular the Basel drummers, began using rudiments in the late 15th century and by 1620, a form of drum notation was being used in Switzerland to record these exercises. From here they migrated through France, Scotland, and then England, being adapted at each stage to suit each country's own needs, with Scotland especially developing a strong reputation in high standards.

By the 17th century, the British presence in America meant that the troops had brought their version across the Atlantic and the American military were adopting those rudiments into their culture. By 1812 Charles Stewart Ashworth had compiled a book with his set of rudiments primarily intended for use by the US army and navy. Throughout the 19th century, other drummers felt the need to publish their own instruction books for rudimentary drumming, and so in 1861 George Bruce and Daniel Emmett published such a book, followed by Gardiner A. Strube, who in 1869 published a book by order of the National Guard of the New England States, and then John Philip Sousa published a book called *Trumpet and Drum* in 1886 for the emerging US Marine Band and their drum and bugle corps before J.M. Flockton published his version in 1897. As the 20th century came and the role of the drum evolved with the advent of the trap set, rudiments became less important to many players. Nevertheless, many drummers still recognized their importance, but there was increasing frustration with the variations between different teachings. A standardized set of rudiments was needed, and it took a group of respected drummers with none other than William F. Ludwig at the helm to put this into action.

In 1932, this collection of drummers from across America congregated in Chicago and began to choose thirteen standard rudiments from the many that were available. These rudiments would be the standard at which a member must be able to perform in order to gain membership into their group. The group was to be known as the National Association of Rudimental Drummers (NARD). Beyond the thirteen rudiments necessary for entry into their group, they also planned to double that number with the second set intended for those drummers who had accomplished a sufficient level with the first group and saw the benefits of motivating themselves to learn the second. On December 10, 1935, NARD sent out a bulletin to the 246 members of the association asking for their votes on which rudiments should be included in the full twenty-six-rudiment list that they intended as the standard.

Ludwig sent out another bulletin on February 3, 1936, detailing the results of their votes. Here he noted that the principal difference between the existing rudiment studies was the placement of accents. This would now be a thing of the past. The options were drawn from several authors' lists, as seen below.

The Charles Stewart Ashworth Rudiments List that was copyrighted in 1812 in Washington was:

1. The long roll
2. The five stroke roll
3. The seven stroke roll
4. The nine stroke roll
5. The ten stroke roll
6. The eleven stroke roll
7. The flam
8. The flam and stroke
9. The single paradiddle
10. The flam paradiddle
11. The double paradiddle
12. The triple paradiddle
13. The flam paradiddle-diddle
14. The half drag (ruff)
15. The single drag
16. The double drag
17. The single ratamacue
18. The double ratamacue.

The Bruce and Emmett Rudiment List from 1861, also copyrighted in Washington, was:

1. The long roll
2. The five stroke roll
3. The seven stroke roll
4. The nine stroke roll
5. The ten stroke roll
6. The eleven stroke roll
7. The thirteen stroke roll
8. The fifteen stroke roll
9. The flam
10. The ruff
11. The single drag
12. The double drag
13. The single ratamacue
14. The double ratamacue
15. The triple ratamacue
16. The flamacue
17. The flam tap
18. The flam accent No. 1
19. The flam accent No. 2
20. The single paradiddle
21. The double paradiddle
22. The flam paradiddle
23. The flam paradiddle-diddle
24. The drag paradiddle No. 1
25. The drag paradiddle No. 2

The Gardiner A. Strube Rudiment List that was adopted by the US army in 1869 was:

1. The long roll
2. The single stroke roll
3. The five stroke roll
4. The seven stroke roll

5. The nine stroke roll
6. The ten stroke roll
7. The eleven stroke roll
8. The thirteen stroke roll
9. The fifteen stroke roll
10. The flam
11. The ruff
12. The single drag
13. The double drag
14. The single ratamacue
15. The double ratamacue
16. The triple ratamacue
17. The flam accent
18. The flamacue
19. The flam tap
20. The single paradiddle
21. The double paradiddle
22. The flam paradiddle
23. The flam paradiddle-diddle
24. The drag paradiddle No. 1
25. The drag paradiddle No. 2

The John Philip Sousa Rudiments List of 1886 was:

1. The long roll
2. The five stroke roll
3. The seven stroke roll
4. The nine stroke roll
5. The ten stroke roll
6. The eleven stroke roll
7. The flam
8. The flam accent
9. The flam tap
10. The ruff
11. The single drag
12. The double drag

13. The single ratamacue
14. The double ratamacue
15. The treble ratamacue
16. The four stroke ruff
17. The single paradiddle
18. The flam paradiddle
19. The drag paradiddle

The J.M. Flockton Rudiments List copyrighted in 1897 was:

1. The roll
2. The five stroke roll
3. The seven stroke roll
4. The nine stroke roll
5. The eight stroke roll
6. The ten stroke roll
7. The eleven stroke roll
8. The thirteen stroke roll
9. The fifteen stroke roll
10. The flam
11. The ruff
12. The single drag
13. The double drag
14. The single ratamacue
15. The double ratamacue
16. The triple ratamacue
17. The flamacue
18. The tap ruff
19. The flam accent
20. The flam tap
21. The single paradiddle
22. The double paradiddle
23. The flam paradiddle
24. The flam paradiddle-diddle
25. The drag paradiddle

And finally the Sanford A. Moeller Rudiments list from 1921 (revised in 1929) was:

1. The long roll
2. The single stroke roll
3. Roll of five strokes
4. Roll of seven strokes
5. Roll of nine strokes
6. Roll of eleven strokes
7. Roll of thirteen strokes
8. Roll of fifteen strokes
9. Roll of ten strokes
10. The flam
11. The ruff
12. The paradiddle
13. The double paradiddle
14. The flam paradiddle (flamadiddle)
15. The double flam paradiddle
16. The flam tap
17. The flam accent No. 1
18. The flam accent No. 2
19. The flamacue
20. The half drag
21. The single drag
22. The double drag
23. The single ratamacue
24. The double ratamacue
25. The treble ratamacue
26. The drag paradiddle

Of these many rudiment options, they were whittled down to thirteen that were adopted in 1934 to obtain membership to NARD. These were:

1. The long roll
2. The five stroke roll
3. The seven stroke roll

4. The flam
5. The flam accent
6. The flam paradiddle
7. The flamacue
8. The ruff
9. The single drag
10. The double drag
11. The double paradiddle
12. The single ratamacue
13. The double ratamacue

The second list of thirteen completes the twenty-six standard drummers' rudiments:

1. The single stroke roll
2. The nine stroke roll
3. The ten stroke roll
4. The eleven stroke roll
5. The thirteen stroke roll
6. The fifteen stroke roll
7. The flam tap
8. The single paradiddle
9. The drag paradiddle No. 1
10. The drag paradiddle No. 2
11. The flam paradiddle-diddle
12. Lesson No. 25
13. The double ratamacue

In 1928, the Swiss Basel drummer Dr. Fritz Berger concocted the monolinear notation system for rudiments. His system utilized a single line staff upon which he wrote the notes in the recognized form and note values. His input was to place the right-hand notes above the line and the left-hand notes below the line, thus enabling the reader to easily identify the sticking and concentrate on the notes rather than Ls and Rs for sticking instructions.

In 1985 the Percussive Arts Society (PAS) attempted to re-organize the work of NARD by whittling the thirteen essential rudiments down to just seven. They also added fourteen rudiments to NARD's total of twenty-six, which resulted in the forty PAS International Rudiments. The other development was to display them in their sticking groups in categories such as single-stroke rolls, multibounce rolls, double-bounce rolls, drag rudiments, flam rudiments, and diddle rudiments. The added rudiments were the single dragadiddle, the flam drag, the inverted flam tap, the pataflafla, the single flammed mill, the single paradiddle-diddle, the triple paradiddle, the fifteen-stroke roll, the seventeen-stroke roll, the six-stroke roll, the triple-stroke roll, the multiple-bounce roll, the single-stroke seven, and the single stroke-four. In fact, PAS released a DVD in 2008 titled *The Rudiment Project* with the intention of highlighting the benefit of studying rudiments in a variety of musical applications. Throughout the 20th century and into the 21st century, other drummers have continued to publish their own interpretations of rudiments and various applications for them so that others may continue to benefit.

Although the origins of rudiments lay in Europe, the Americans have really been at the fore of their development since the exercises crossed their shores with the British soldiers. Leading up to and beyond the American Civil War, the drum corps grew in competitiveness, and contests sprung up in which the musicians could compete for supremacy; although friendly competitive rivalry between the different companies' drummers had doubtlessly been in existence for many years before. Following the Revolutionary War in 1783, many army musicians returned to civilian life and set up fife and drum corps in their hometowns, and the popularity of such groups spread across the country. Some chose to play traditional pieces with traditional scoring at the traditional slower tempos of around 110 beats per minute. These groups were known as ancient corps and grew significantly in the state of Connecticut.

By the Civil War in 1861, rudimental drumming was hugely important for signaling, and the musicians had grown from initially having one or two drummers for each company, into large bands such as the Marine Band, which was established by an act of Congress in 1798. The fife had been largely replaced by the louder bugle by the Civil War, and many young boys in their early teens were enlisted to perform as military musicians. These more-modern drum and bugle corps also enjoyed a competitive nature, and they introduced baton twirling and began to incorporate intricate marches with complex choreography. These allowed for many different categories on which to judge each corps, but some, such as the First Individual Snare category, faced problems in light of the different nuances that were being learned from the different instruction manuals published since 1812. Contestants were bringing different interpretations of the same exercise, and the judges were not able to make fair assessments. One example of this is the long roll, which was sometimes written with an accented second note and sometimes not.

Associations were formed in the late 19th century to mediate this community, bring them closer together, and provide opportunities for competition, but it wasn't until NARD was formed in the 1930s that the rudiments became standardized to put an end to this confusion.

These military bands continued in popularity, although their practical use declined as louder artillery and better communication technology appeared in the battlefield. After World War I, civilian corps arose to continue the traditions under the posts of American Legion as well as Veterans of Foreign Wars. By the 1920s, they were organizing contests for their musicians, who consisted of snare drummers, tenor drummers, bass drummers, and cymbal players to make up the percussion sections. They also introduced a color guard, which consisted of baton majors or majorettes, flag carriers, saber squads, or rifle bearers.

In 1965 Drum Corps Associates (DCA) was formed as the governing body for senior drum and bugle corps in North America, taking over from the churches, communities, and veterans groups that had traditionally sponsored the classic drum and bugle corps. Drum Corps International was formed in 1972 as the junior version of DCA. These associations practice throughout the winter in readiness of the summer touring season culminating in the August World Championships. They operate with detailed marking schemes and instrumentation guidelines as the corps battle for supremacy in each category. Much more emphasis is now placed on the visual merit than before, thus detracting slightly from the musical elements as marks are given for the color guard and overall visual impact, with only a small percentage of marks allocated for percussion technique and playing ability. Liberated from the restrictive, old-fashioned marking schemes of the previous competitions, the 1970s modern corps took advantage of their new freedoms, incorporating greater range in tempo, highly elaborate costumes, and color guard props as well as new instrumentation. Multivalve brass instruments have also been allowed, causing the single-valve bugle to become obsolete. In 1982, a fixed stage area was adopted, and stationary percussion became accepted into the corps, known as front ensemble percussion. This involved orchestral percussion on a fixed stage area with instruments such as the glockenspiel, marimba, xylophone, vibraphone, gongs, timpani, and any other auxiliary percussion that is allowed by the organizers and required for the piece in question. Designers began to be employed to create themes for corps and then orchestrate their overall design as more points became awarded for these details. These designers came at a price, which added even more financial burden to the already large touring, staff, costume, and prop expenses. As well as the intricate choreography of the group's movements, the drummers, and particularly the snare drummers adopted many stick tricks, which were played between beats, and sometimes to actually play the beats, with stunning visual effect.

As rudiments are the rudimental drummer's vocabulary, it is only natural that this vocabulary should expand; just as our spoken language expands and evolves through time. Gradually new rudiments have appeared, which are known as hybrid rudiments. These are generally modifications of existing rudiments or are a fusion of two familiar rudiments, and the scope for new ones is limitless. They are being invented constantly, and new names are required to keep track of the most common types. One such example is the cheese, which is essentially a flam accent with the accented note of the flam played as a diddle. This can then be extended to become the chut cheese, which simply pushes the flammed diddle onto the second note while maintaining a regular flam on the first note.

Cheese

Chut Cheese

With the style, marking schemes, focus, instrumentations, and costumes changing so much, it was only natural that the actual instruments themselves would need to adapt to this modern style. This is very obvious with the snare drum, which has a long history. The calfskin heads had been replaced by Mylar after it became available post–World War II, but soon even they became outdated. This happened when the synthetic fiber known as Kevlar began to be used as a result of its performance under high tension. This enabled the snare drums to be tuned incredibly tightly, thus aiding the articulation of the very fast notes that were being played. This very durable material is also used by Remo drumhead company for their Falam Slam patch, which is stuck onto regular drumheads to provide added strength to the point of impact. This high-tension tuning in turn places extra tension on the drum itself, and so extra tension rods were added and rims were strengthened. This then transferred the tension onto the shell, causing damage to this important component of the drum. The solution was to place a metal ring around the circumference of the shell at the top and bottom end. The tension rods then attached to these rings with metal rods traveling up the length of the shell, connecting the two metal rings without anything making contact with the shell itself. The result is that the metal hardware takes the tension away from the shell and the drum can survive the high tunings. Cleland company in Canada (who now offer carbon-fiber marching snare drums) and Legato in Australia were at the fore of this innovation in the late 1970s.

Most marching snare drums now adopt this technique in varying forms. They also often have diecast aluminum rims and come much deeper than the drum kit snare drums, often around 12 inches deep for a 14-inch diameter and with metal wire (such as high-carbon steel) or synthetic gut snare strands below the resonant head as well as beneath the batter head. A sound projector is often used for outdoor performances, which allows a curved piece of plastic known as a scoop attached to the bottom of the drum to direct the sound toward the audience.

While this modernization was occurring, some rudimental drummers preferred the traditional approach. They chose to form "classic" style corps, which are sometimes known as alumni corps, although they don't necessarily have to involve members who have played previously for drum and bugle corps. These corps, who enjoyed a wave of popularity in the 1980s, do not play competitively, instead choosing to perform in public displays for pure entertainment. They opt to maintain the traditional values of this art form with details such as uniform, technique, repertoire, and drum types in a tribute to their drumming heritage.

Of course the rudiments are not exclusively for drum lines, and drum kit players apply themselves to rudiments with varying vigor. Notable drum kit players with a rudimentary background include session player Steve Gadd, who was in the Crusaders drum and bugle corps, and fusion pioneer Billy Cobham, who was in St. Catherine's Queensmen drum and bugle corps. Whatever genres and fashions come and go in the future, there will always be drummers who realize the value of these building blocks of the drummer's musical vocabulary and make it their duty to pass this knowledge on to the next generation. After all, with a continuing supply of drummers who feel they have something to say on the instrument, they need to make sure they know how to speak the language.

Chapter Fourteen

Women Drummers

IN THE WORLD OF MODERN DRUMMING, the instrument appears to be very much dominated by a male presence. The drum is often considered masculine, which is possibly a result of its evolution from an instrument of war. Seeing these drummers perform with such speed and power may be misconstrued as an act only possible by the dominant male of the species. This erroneous and outdated view is changing gradually as the years pass, but it will be a long time before the drum is considered equal between the two genders. This is unfortunate, as even for the heaviest and loudest styles, good technique can produce more volume than simply using brute strength. With modern amplification, even a gentle player can sound loud, and there can be no doubt, surely, that the female is capable of displaying the required aggression that these genres often demand. Even those men with the staunchest of prejudice against women in heavy metal and rock groups surely can accept that females are well suited to play pop, jazz, Latin, and other styles that require less force and more finesse. So if the physicality is not an issue, it remains that it is the unreasonable preconception embedded in many societies that this is a male instrument. Maybe it is not considered right and proper for one's darling daughter to play such an instrument. Maybe she should adopt a more feminine and dainty instrument; the violin, for example?

Interestingly this is a modern situation, or at least only present for two thousand years. In ancient civilizations, it was not so much a god who was the all-powerful creator of life, but the goddess. As the drum has always been considered a spiritual object that can communicate with or influence actions from deities, it was looked upon as a woman's instrument. Furthermore, the rhythm of life was always connected with the female, such as her menstrual cycle, which was closely connected to the lunar cycle. Drums were also associated with fertility, reproduction, and female sexual vitality. The rhythm of a drum was sometimes used to help women through the labor process or played over the fields of crops to help them achieve a greater yield.

This can be seen throughout history, exemplified in an ancient Turkish cave painting from 5600 BCE in which "a band of human figures, clad in leopard skins and playing various percussion instruments, dance ecstatically around a large stag. A second group of dancers ritually surround a gigantic bull. Among this group is a figure holding a horn-shaped instrument in one hand and a frame drum in the other."[1] It is likely that priestesses serviced the shrines in worship of their goddess, so it is very much a female entity.

The early-3rd-century-BCE statuette from Mesopotamia at the Louvre in chapter 3 shows a woman with a frame drum. Indeed in Mesopotamia we have records of a female drummer referred to by name. In the Sumerian city of Ur over four thousand years ago a priestess named Lipushiau is mentioned in texts describing ritualistic drumming in the time of the goddess Inanna. This spiritual leader was to have played the balag-di, known today as a frame drum. And so it was that the spiritual drum that carried such significant importance to humans' lives was usually played by the mystical female, who was gifted with the ability to create new life and communicate with the goddess. Females were the important gender in society, and the drum belonged to them.

However, in the post-Neolithic times from around 4000 BCE, the ensuing chaos that had occurred in the newly formed, over-demanding, and struggling major cities left them vulnerable to attack from violent aggressors who vanquished these civilizations

across Europe and Asia. The murdering of men and imprison-
ment of women relegated the female status from enhanced piety
and spiritual superiority to trophies of war. Now that militaristic
power had turned women into objects at the male's disposal, the
patriarchal society was free to develop, as it continued to do into
modern times.

Years later, after the formation of patriarchal Christianity, playing of music by women and even the frame drum itself were frowned
upon and in some cases banned, in an effort to diminish links with
the matriarchal worship. This misogyny that occurred as a result
of women's significance in the former pagan religions stopped the
frame drum from accompanying religious events as it had in the past
due to its links to goddess worship. The women had been silenced.

ORCHESTRA

If we now jump ahead several hundred years, it seems as though
the male invaders had really done a thorough job, as women were
still excluded from percussion-related pursuits, among many others
both within and beyond the world of music. The goddess seems
long forgotten now. In the orchestras, changes have always been
implemented gradually so the inclusion of females was never going
to be instantaneous. Throughout Europe and North America, the
number of female musicians was growing in the last part of the 19th
century and into the 20th century, but they were still not allowed
into the orchestras, whose doors were firmly closed to women with
the exception of harpists, who could join the orchestra with their
demure playing position and gentle style. As a result of this shun,
all-women orchestras became popular, although they weren't taken
as seriously as their male counterparts and the performance opportunities were therefore restricted. This often forced them to play
light music, which was unsatisfactory for the more talented female
members. These groups made it necessary for women to take on
male roles such as timpanist or conductor, which was a real step
forward. Interestingly, if a woman was taken ill and there were
no other women to deputize in that area of the orchestra, a male

musician might be drafted in wearing a dress and makeup so it would appear to be an all-female orchestra.

The great wars affected many areas of life and also gave women opportunities through necessity. With the men fighting abroad, many male roles were adopted by women. During the Second World War, women replaced missing male musicians. By the 1950s and 1960s, orchestras gradually started accepting women. It wasn't immediate; after all, thousands of years of conditioning had to be overcome before men could truly accept women stepping out of line and threatening this patriarchal society. Most German orchestras did not accept women until the 1980s, and the Vienna Philharmonic did not accept women until the late 1990s.

One woman who had total disregard for her assumed position within the patriarchal society was the Scottish percussionist Dame Evelyn Glennie. Born in 1965, Glennie has spent her life creating a reputation as one of the most incredible solo percussionists in the world, and in doing so has continually broken records and gained more than eighty various awards. Being the first person in musical history to sustain a full-time career as a solo percussionist is a huge achievement, especially for a female in this world. But to do so having being diagnosed as nearly deaf before reaching her teenage years is even more of an accomplishment. As a result of diminished hearing, Glennie instead uses other senses to a greater extent to hear the sounds. With the aid of touch, she can process the information gleaned from vibrations, as we all do, very acutely and adds to this the visual information of what she sees. Those three senses help her build a sound image in her mind just as people with perfect hearing do. The only difference is that her method of creating that image simply relies less on audio. With her unique approach to music and her incredible musicality, Glennie travels the world performing numerous concerts every year as a soloist or with various ensembles. Furthermore, she composes music under commission for many world-class composers as well as writing her own albums on both tuned and untuned percussion. Through her extensive and varied work, Glennie has inadvertently made it impossible for any male to argue that females are somehow intrinsically inferior as a result of their gender with regard to percussion.

DRUM KIT

It wasn't just in the orchestra where men were having trouble accepting women. The liberal world of rock 'n' roll was also facing the same struggles with their ingrained social beliefs. Although there may have been many closet female drummers and maybe even groups of females who met in secret throughout the centuries, drumming was firmly considered a man's instrument, and any woman who went against this widely held belief was not acting properly.

One woman to break free from these restraints was Mary McClanahan, who played the drum kit in Phil Spitalny's Hour of Charm All Girl Orchestra, which featured Evelyn and her magic violin.

He ran a strict regime for the girls that included six hours of practice a day and all members having to sign a contract pledging not to leave the band to marry without giving six months' notice. Having played their mix of light classical music and jazzy versions of classic songs in many concert halls, their big break came when they began a network radio show in 1935 called *The Hour of Charm*, where their all-female novelty visual impact was irrelevant. The band continued through the war and on into the 1950s before disbanding.

An all-girl orchestra of this type was unusual but not completely unheard of. Beginning around the same time in the mid-1930s was Ina Ray Hutton and her Melodears, in which even the conductor (Hutton) was a female, as well as the International Sweethearts of Rhythm with Pauline Braddy on drums. But it was Mary McClanahan that was making the real impression on the drum kit. Having built up a reputable name as a great drummer, in 1939 she achieved the unthinkable for a woman. She was featured in a Gretsch advertisement, printed in *Metronome* magazine in America endorsing her Gretsch Gladstone ensemble drum kit. This full-page advertisement included a large picture of the drummer proudly displaying her femininity, positioned behind the drum kit adorned in an elegant dress. Gretsch went even further by including her on their catalog covers in the early 1940s, among the greatly adored male drummers such as Papa Jo Jones. To be accepted as a female drummer in the 1930s would have taken grit, determination, and some great playing, but to actually feature on the front of Gretsch's catalog and advertisements when they were flying high as the kit to own in the jazz world was extraordinary.

With the onset of the 1960s and the rise of woman's liberation, these newly charged feminists started to realize that they could do anything they wanted just as well as men, drumming included. That didn't mean that men were ready to accept it quite so readily though, despite McClanahan's previous efforts.

One of the first to emerge in this period was Ann (Honey) Lantree of the Honey Combs and their 1964 UK number-one hit "Have I the Right." Seated behind her black four-piece Carlton kit, surrounded by four male musicians, Lantree really started the female audience's imagination and boosted the empowerment of women in that era.

Another significant event for women in music occurred in 1964 when Goldie and the Gingerbreads became the first all-female rock group to be signed to a major record label when the UK label Decca took them onboard as well as America's Atlantic label. With Ginger Bianco on drums, the group scored some chart success with "Can You Hear My Heartbeat" when it reached number twenty-five in the UK charts of 1965. After touring with bands such as the Yardbirds, the Rolling Stones, and the Kinks, Goldie and the Gingerbreads dissolved in the late 1960s after failing to enjoy any great commercial success.

Not far behind Lantree and Bianco was Maureen Tucker, who stumbled into the Velvet Underground aged nineteen in the mid-1960s, having been previously working as a data entry operator. She caught people's attention for being a female with sticks, but she also displayed a highly unconventional manner of drumming. Her style was simple and quite primal as she played in a standing position, the bass drum in an upturned position so that it could be beaten with sticks. She used a very simple setup with a snare drum and minimal toms alongside the bass drum. Staying focused on her role as a timekeeper, she chose to avoid cymbals, as they cluttered the music and detracted from the vocals, instead often riding on the bass drum with sticks or mallets. What she lacked in technical proficiency, she made up for with mesmerizing energy and an avant-garde approach, and in the process, made her mark on the history of female drumming.

And then we arrive at one of the most famous female drummers in history. Karen Carpenter began her musical life as a drummer, although became better known for her vocal talents that helped her and her brother Richard to become hugely successful throughout the 1970s. Their success was largely for soft ballad–type tracks such as "(They Long to Be) Close to You" and "We've Only Just Begun," but early recordings such as the 1966 Richard Carpenter Trio version of Duke Ellington's "Caravan" demonstrate an accomplished jazz drumming technique and soloing ability by the sixteen-year-old Karen. Furthermore, her love of Dave Brubeck and drummer Joe Morello is evident with such tracks as "All I Can Do" from their 1969 debut album. This jazz-based song flows very interestingly with its five crotchets in each bar. By the time "(They Long to Be) Close to You" was recorded in 1970, their recording label A&M insisted in bringing in the Wrecking Crew session musicians to create the perfect sound for their records with drummers like Hal Blaine and Jim Gordon taking over that role from Karen. Despite this recording process, Karen still played the tracks live, although this was tailored so that for slower songs she would sing from the front of the stage while the likes of Cubby O'Brien took over on drums. Karen enjoyed featuring a drum solo between herself and O'Brien at the shows, and by the 1973 album had returned to drumming in the studio with the album *Now and Then* and tracks such as "This Masquerade," which showed that she could play Latin rhythms as well as pop and jazz. Her chosen instrument was a silver sparkle Ludwig drum kit as influenced by her adoration of Joe Morello, who also actually instigated the silver sparkle color for Ludwig drum kits before it became a huge seller. Carpenter's untimely death in 1983 as a result of anorexia was tragic, and it took a great musician from this world, but a listen to recordings of her playing drum kit may offer a surprising treat for the inquisitive drummer.

Playing the lighter styles of swing and pop was a great achievement, but the raucous pinnacle of raw primal male power in music was a huge challenge. The world of rock music was synonymous with aggression, excess, strong physicality, and often degradation of women. One group who helped gain female acceptance in this patriarchal world was the 1970s band the Runaways with founding member Sandy West on drums. They were signed in 1976 while still teenagers and possessed a sufficiently raucous, aggressive, and powerful sound to equal their male counterparts. Their lyrical content also hit hard with references to drugs, casual sex, adolescent anarchism, and anger, leading many radio stations in America to belittle their creations by refusing to play them. Europe and Asia were more accepting, and the band enjoyed great success for four years before the group dissolved. With a strong character like West and her hard-hitting drumming style, the band proved that women could deliver power and aggression just as well as men. Further still their attitude was genuine, and the ensuing lifestyle of excess ultimately helped them on the downward slide from which they would never recover.

Following in their wake were bands such as the all-girl Los Angeles glam rock group Vixen with their classic lineup including drummer Roxy Petrucci throughout the late 1980s. This era also saw the formation of another LA rock band named Hole, fronted by Courtney Love, who was married to the Nirvana front man Curt Cobain until his untimely death. The Hole drummers were Caroline Rue, Patty Schlemel, and Samantha Maloney. Maloney also performed with Mötley Crüe and Peaches. The regular Mötley Crüe drummer, Tommy Lee, is well known for his tales of debauchery and mayhem, but less widely known for his drumming sister Athena, who has also made her mark in the band Kottak.

It wasn't just Sunset Boulevard that functioned as an incubator for female drummers. Nearly two thousand miles to the northeast in the late 1990s was a female drummer who was about make a big name for herself with a shy, unassuming personality that was far removed from her abrasive, hard-partying LA counterparts. Meg White was one half of the Detroit band the White Stripes, which was formed from a marriage in which Jack White was the guitarist with previous musical experience while Meg was relatively inexperienced, having only started playing the drums months before the band formed. Since 1997 White has displayed a very restrained, minimalistic but powerful sound, which has allowed Jack to write the songs that have proven so successful. This simple, driving style has garnered White many fans from both sexes as the perfect accompaniment to her former husband's blues- and punk-infused compositions.

Another wave of female drummers to emerge in the late 20th century brought an air of glamour and sophistication mixed with drumming technique and feel to silence any misogynists. One such lady was Sheila Escovedo, who grew up in a musical family with a father who was a respected timbalero named Pete Escovedo. While in her teens she began to develop a reputation and was soon touring with big names like Diana Ross, Herbie Hancock, Lionel Ritchie, Marvin Gaye, Gloria Estefan, and Stevie Wonder. Since the 1980s she has also released four solo albums, achieving a Billboard Number One, an MTV Award, and Grammy nominations. In this period, Sheila E caught the attention of the artist Prince and was soon touring as his opening act before becoming his touring band drummer. Amongst her many live, studio and even acting credits, Sheila E also became the first female band leader on a late-night television show when she was invited to become musical director of *The Magic Hour* with basketball player Magic Johnson hosting. She has managed to gain outstanding respect as a drummer while retaining an image of style and glamour.

Another glamorous lady who could excite the big crowds was Cindy Blackman, who came to fame in the early 1990s providing the drums for Lenny Kravitz. Having been taught by the renowned teacher Alan Dawson and been through the prestigious Berklee College of Music in Boston, she subsequently enjoyed a successful tenure with Kravitz and then toured with Carlos Santana, whom she married after he proposed to her live on stage in 2010. Despite these huge stadium bands that she has built a successful career with, Blackman's true love is jazz, and on that level she has released several solo albums throughout her career, with influences such as Tony Williams driving her forward. With such strong jazz connections, Blackman has favored Gretsch drums, which were so popular amongs jazz players in the 1940s and 1950s.

Taking over from these high-profile figures came a string of equally impressive women such as Cora Coleman-Dunham, who has also provided the rhythms for Prince; Kim Thompson, who has played with Mike Stern and in Beyoncé Knowles's 2006 all-girl band; Nikki Glaspie, who also played in the all-girl Beyoncé Knowles band along with percussionist Marcella Chapa; Stefanie Eulinberg. who plays in Kid Rock's Twisted Brown Trucker Band; Shauney Baby, who has played with Hilary Duff, Will.i.am, and Alicia Keys; Sudha Kheterpal, who plays for British electronic group Faithless as well as Kylie Minogue and the Spice Girls; and Hilary Jones, who came up through the US Navy Band, proving her worth within the testosterone-fueled military lifestyle before earning her place with names such as Robben Ford, the Mamas and the Papas, Lee Ritenour, Scott Henderson's Tribal Tech, Ray Obiedo, Eric Marienthal, Doc Severinson, Badi Assad, and Sheila E's father, Pete Escovedo. She has also released solo material since 2001 with her debut, *Soaring*.

Beyond the pop world where style is paramount and drumming complexities less so, the musical kudos often attributed to drummers in the jazz field have also been shared out with females. Some have played with the biggest names in the business, who are more than capable of employing any of the top drummers in the world, male or female. Such examples are Terri Lyne Carrington, who has amassed an impressive list of names on her CV such as Dizzy Gillespie, Stan Getz, Wayne Shorter, and Herbie Hancock; Vera Figueiredo, a Brazilian drummer who has created a strong reputation in the Latin drumming field playing with big-name Brazilian artists, releasing her own solo albums, performing at numerous international drum festivals, and releasing educational videos and books; Carola Grey, who has performed with Tower of Power's Rocco Prestia, Mike Stern, and Ravi Coltrane; Dr. Sherrie Maricle, who is a respected drummer and composer in jazz and orchestral settings and even leads her own big band called Diva; and Camille Gainer, who has performed with Roy Ayers, Chuck Mangione, and Christian McBride, as well as gaining many production credits.

Many of these women have had to endure sexism to some degree, or at least if not experiencing it overtly, have overcome the paranoia of gender judgments. This alone displays great strength of character, but not every woman who has a desire to beat a drum can, or should need to, experience that negative attitude.

In 1985 an organization called Women in Music was formed as a body to represent women in all areas of the music industry, be it a musician, producer, engineer, marketer, publisher, or songwriter. They provide seminars, one-to-one meetings, showcases, networking opportunities, and a newsletter to nurture the community of female musicians and provide a support network to help these embattled women become ready for the harsh patriarchal world that they might face in music. Another such group is Women Drummers International. They also have a presence to empower female drummers by providing tours, retreats, and a support network that focuses not only on the musical element but also on cultural and healing elements that are possible through the drum. Furthermore, an online monthly drum magazine emerged in the late 20th century offering articles that featured female drummer interviews, forums for networking, concert advertising, and equipment bartering services. It helped to maintain a close network between female drummers and give them confidence in the fact that they are not the only one out there among all those men.

It is thanks to such organizations and the single-minded determination mixed with unquestionable talent that has been demonstrated by women over the last century that new generations of women have felt freed from their musical shackles and gender-restricted instruments, enabling them to follow their hearts.

A sign of this growing movement can be quantified by looking at union memberships. In 1997 the British Musicians' Union membership consisted of 17 percent women. In 2010 the ratio had risen to 27 percent women. An extra 10 percent in thirteen years is an indication of the progress that women are making in music. Of that 27 percent of women, the largest numbers fell into the orchestra section (42 percent) and the teaching section (39 percent), while the smallest proportions were in the theater section (26 percent), the music writers section (22 percent), and the jazz section (21 percent). Not one single section consisted of 50 percent or more women, so the men still dominate every area of this organization.

As momentum grows and more women succeed in this area, the question that is left is, will the matriarchal drummer ever reign supreme again as she did thousands of years ago?

NOTE

1. Layne Redmond, *When the drummers were women: A spiritual history of rhythm* (New York: Three Rivers Press, 1997), 47–48.

Chapter Fifteen

---○---

Drumheads

THE FIRST DRUMHEAD DECOMPOSED WITHOUT a trace several thousand years ago. It is likely that it was a reptile or fish skin stretched over hollowed wood or even clay and may have been discovered by accident when drying a skin. A chance discovery of such a sound must surely have evoked great excitement and fascination, much as it still does today. Other skins were experimented with over time, and larger animals were used to accommodate larger drums. Up until the Middle Ages, the skins were attached by way of the counter hoop and rope tensioning, but this method was now being replaced by attaching the skin directly onto a separate flesh hoop.

As time went by, the quality and preparation of the skin improved. Expert tanners evolved who could prepare these animal hides to produce high-quality drumheads, and in the 19th century firms appeared who could supply these in large quantities as well as produce other products such as book bindings, lampshades, and sporting equipment. The heads were often priced as untucked with an additional fee for the service of tucking the head. Some drummers chose to carry out this task themselves, especially today, as it is a minority endeavor and many of the specialist companies have long since closed their doors. The task is quite laborious, as decisions need to be made that will greatly affect the end product. First of all a hide needs to be selected. Factors such as age, location, climate, diet, color, and quality of hide all affect the end result.

The thickness of the selected hide may be determined by intended style of use; the thicker heads suit reproduction of early music, for example. A choice of animal must also be considered, with calf and goat the two most common in Europe and North America. Once selected, the hides are soaked to loosen the hair and remove unwanted particles. They are then rinsed with water and the hair and flesh completely removed. At this point they are stretched and dried gradually, which increases durability. Once dried they are ready to be cut to size, and this is always a few inches larger than the circumference of the drum, to leave enough skin for tucking around the flesh hoop.

The hide is now ready to be tucked, or lapped, onto the wooden flesh hoop. The skin is laid on a flat surface and the flesh hoop placed centrally upon it. By use of a blunt steel blade with an upturned end, known as a lapping tool, the skin is brought up from the outside, over the flesh hoop, around it, and then tucked up underneath it, between the hoop and the hide. Once pushed up as far as it will go, it should be clamped in place while the procedure is repeated diametrically around the head, ensuring even tension throughout. The skin is now ready to be placed upon the drum shell and the counter hoop applied before screwing in the tension rods. This is a process that many have neither the time nor the inclination to become involved with, and to add to the inconvenience, throughout the mid-20th century the price of calfskin heads was rising dramatically, which left the market open for a cheaper alternative.

As mentioned previously, DuPont had been testing the synthetic polyester film Mylar during the early 1940s, and it soon began to be used commercially. Once found to be suitable for drumhead, many people began to experiment with it. Well-known drum manufacturers Ludwig and Slingerland were thinking along these lines, as were Hardies Highland Supplies in Glasgow, who were testing plastic heads with limited initial success for a company in Blackpool, England. As we now know, it was Remo and Evans who built the successful businesses that have supplied drummers since 1957 along with newer companies such as Aquarian.

Drumheads come in a vast array of options today. The first choice upon selection may be the number of plies. Single-ply heads are more sensitive and open sounding, whereas double-ply heads offer greater durability and less sustain. The thickness of head also affects the sound, with a thin head offering more sustain and less attack than a thicker head, although the thinner it is, the less durable it is. Some two-ply heads are available with products between the plies, such as Remo's Pinstripe series, which feature an epoxy ring bonded between the layers. Evan's Hydraulics series feature a thin film of oil between the layers, and their EC2 series features a control ring embedded between the plies to encourage low-frequency attack while subduing higher overtones. Many heads come with a fine material sprayed onto the batter surface to offer a coating that creates a warmer sound, slightly diffusing the brighter, harsh tones of plastic. It also enables wire brushes to create the popular swirling effect in jazz styles. Furthermore, some heads also include a center dot for greater durability at the point of contact with the stick and to control some of the overtones. This is simply a second layer of Mylar stuck onto the bottom or top of the batter head. Some heads offer a ring of added Mylar that runs around the circumference of the underside of the batter head, further taking away overtones. External muffling systems, such as Evan's EMAD bass drumheads, are also available to reduce resonance, offering a purpose-built version of the numerous improvised muffling techniques that have been used for decades by drummers such as gaffa tape, towels, cigarette packets stuck to the head, and whatever else is on hand at the time.

Manufacturers are aware of the desire for the original animal-skin sound and qualities for many drummers. To that end, products have been released to bridge the gap to some extent. For example, Remo's FiberSkyn 3 and Renaissance series heads are their attempt to replicate calfskin heads with synthetic materials.

Along with Mylar, aramid fibers were also experimented with, the most popular being the bulletproof Kevlar, and became common in marching snare drums as they offered greater strength and therefore tighter tuning options as well as better stick rebound, both of which are required for the staccato, up-tempo rudiments in this area of drumming.

Another type of drumhead that has become increasingly popular in the 21st century is the mesh variety. The woven mesh fabrics offer an excellent compromise for quiet practice while still offering the feel of a real drum kit, as well as being very effective when used in conjunction with electronic triggers.

Chapter Sixteen

Drumsticks

TO A DRUMMER, THE HANDS ARE AN EXTENSION of the mind. They may have the most advanced and innovative ideas in their heads, but unless this can be communicated through the hands and on to the drum, the idea is all but useless. Of course many drums are intended to be played with the hands, but the rest are best when struck with a beater. There have been many different beaters throughout the history of the drum, and many of these are discussed in the individual cultures' chapters where relevant. This chapter is concerned with the orchestral, military, and drum kit usage of the European and American cultures.

It could be speculated that wooden beaters have been used since the earliest drummers many thousands of years ago, but of course the wood would have vanished without a trace. It doesn't take a hugely imaginative mind to appreciate how early man may have picked up a nearby stick or bone and struck his recent invention: an animal skin stretched over a hollow vessel. In fact it's harder to imagine that he wouldn't have done so. Beyond speculation we have the Middle Ages depictions of pipe and taborers clearly showing the use of a stick from the 14th century CE. Before that the Mehteran's davul playing style utilized thick and thin sticks before reaching Europe.

But some of the earliest evidence might be that found in Kazakhstan and China, such as a "single-headed drum played gently by hand and drumstick as we see at Astana and Bazaklik (both dated to *c*. 7th to 8th century A.D).["][1]

Many different woods have been used over the years. In Europe during the 18th century, beef wood was a popular choice, and toward the end of the 19th century, ebony was used extensively for military side drummers who needed a heavy stick on their heavy calfskin heads. The wood and the size of the stick were also very dependent on their application. Orchestral sticks have always been lighter than military side drumsticks, although with synthetics the marching drummer's stick has been reduced somewhat. Kit drummers often use even lighter sticks than orchestral players, although this is again largely dependent on style. The heavy metal drummer is likely to opt for a much heavier stick, even using materials such as metal, and sometimes turning the stick around in their hand so that the larger butt end makes contact with the drumhead.

One major manufacturer of drumsticks is the American company Regal Tip and their innovative founder Joe Calato, who made his biggest mark on the industry in 1958 when he devised the nylon tip. Observing how drumsticks in good condition often suffered from damaged tips, rendering them useless, he used a nylon tip, which offered much-improved strength and a brighter, more articulate sound. This has since been adopted by most drumstick brands, although wood tip is still offered, as many drummers prefer the warmer, more organic sound. In 2003 Regal Tip released their 21st-century version of the nylon tip in the form of the E-Series stick. This stick involved a nylon tip with several grooves cut in around the circumference in an effort to maintain the benefits of a nylon tip but to offer a warmer, darker sound. Although the use of *E* in the name suggests an electronic element to the product, it is actually due to the profile of the stick resembling the letter E.

Another major American manufacturer is Pro Mark, founded by Herb Brochstein, a drummer and drum shop owner from Houston. After a chance meeting with a passing Japanese salesman, Brochstein bought several pairs of drumsticks made from an unknown Japanese wood. He was very impressed with the clarity of tone from this wood, as was an early endorser named Billy Gladstone. Brochstein soon began employing the responsible Japanese craftsmen to make his own designs with their highly skilled and consistent hand-carving technique. He became the first to import these Shira Kashi white Japanese oak sticks, and the company grew. Today they also offer American maple and hickory woods, cut with sophisticated machinery.

Such machinery has helped to overcome the problem of warped or inconsistent sticks. When purchasing sticks, most drummers will roll them along a flat surface to detect any imperfections and tap the sticks together in such a way as to determine the fundamental tone of each stick, ensuring that they are the same and therefore their notes on the drum will be consistent.

Another interesting design was conceived in the late 20th century when Leonice Shinneman of California filed a patent for his special-effects mallet in 1983. It consisted of a head made of soft vinyl in the shape of an ellipsoid rather than the spherical shape that many mallets are produced in. When dragged across a drum, the mallet was designed to produce an even drum roll, thus doing the work of two hands with just one.

Generally, however, drumsticks for the side drum and drum kit share the common design features that make up their shape. These are the butt (bottom end), shaft (straight area, which the hand grips), shoulder (tapered area), and tip (which strikes the drumhead). The tapered area could be very gradual on a lighter drumstick or very severe on a heavier stick.

As mentioned with Calato's bright-sounding nylon tip, the timbre can dramatically change, depending on the tip of the stick. Many different shapes and sizes are offered in this market, but the popular types are a round tip, olive tip, barrel tip, or pointed tip. The round tip is bright and focused; the olive tip offers full, low tones and increased durability; and the barrel and pointed tips both offer a medium tone, although the barrel has more focus due to its decreased contact area.

With so many stick options it can be confusing for a drummer to select a pair of drumsticks. Although many manufacturers use their own codes to label sticks, a universally recognized numbering system has been in place since the 20th century. Manufacturers still vary slightly on the sticks that they make within this system, but it does give the consumer a rough guide as to what they're looking for. A familiar name in the drumming community was instrumental in this numbering system: a Mr. William F. Ludwig. The system actually involves a letter and a number assigned to the stick. The letter refers to the intended application of the stick, and the options were S, A, and B. The A stood for orchestra and was chosen due to Ludwig's preference of the letter and displeasure at the aesthetic quality of the printed letter O. These sticks were the lightest and intended for big band–type group playing. The B stood for band, with the intended use of brass bands and symphonic concert bands. These were heavier than the A sticks but still able to play at softer dynamics. The third letter, S, stood for *street* and were the largest and heaviest available. Street uses included marching band and drum corps. The accompanying number simply refers to the circumference of the stick, and popular numbers are 5, 7, and 2. The larger the number, the smaller the circumference, and so 5A is a very popular choice as the standard beginner's drumstick for drum kit applications. For younger drummers who require a lighter stick, 7A is a popular choice.

In the late 20th century, ever more companies continued searching for a superior stick. The choice today is huge, but some of the popular woods that are used are rosewood, which is a very dense and hard wood; maple, which is light and soft; hickory, which is slightly harder and more durable than maple; while Japanese oak is very hard, durable, and heavy. Beyond wood, a drummer may also consider carbon fiber, graphite, aluminum, fiberglass, plastic, sticks with LEDs that illuminate upon impact, or ergonomic sticks, which fit the contours of the hand. There is also the market of signature sticks, of which just about every well-known drummer in the professional arena has designed to their personal specifications. Most just offer an alternative size, weight, or balance, but there are some more unusual sticks on offer. One example is Johnny Rabb's RhythmSaw, featuring a number of grooves carved into the shaft of the stick that can be used to scrape along a drum rim for an unusual sound effect: an innovative stick to complement his innovative playing. There are also quieter options that consist of a group of dowels bundled together. These are often marketed as hot rods and offer not only a different dynamic, but also a different timbre.

On the subject of quieter options, it would be relevant to mention the wire brush. The brush was adopted in the early years of the drum kit and gave the big, noisy drummers a softer option when playing in small groups and small venues. It was born from the humble flyswatter and may have begun life with straw brush strands before evolving into the wire version we know today. In fact, in 1913, a patent was granted to Louis Allis and Adolph Wiens of Wisconsin for a flyswatter with retractable wires. The telescopic handle enabled the wiry strands to retract into the handle so that the device might be carried upon the owner's person for convenient use if a swarm of flies engulfed them at any given moment. This bears an uncanny resemblance to the retractable brush that helps to protect the wires during storage.

Drummers of the 1930s such as Zutty Singleton, Papa Jo Jones, and Chick Webb were early pioneers of this playing style. Later, among others, Clayton Cameron emerged playing with many great artists such as Sammy Davis Jr., Frank Sinatra, Dean Martin, Tony Bennett, and Ray Charles, creating a reputation as the master of brushwork on the drum kit. In 1990 he released the video *The Living Art of Brushes,* which was an early instructional recording devoted to this art form, followed by the 2003 book *Brushworks.* Cameron's work has helped inspire new generations to take the delicate skill of brush playing further in a world full of noise and aggression. Although the humble brush hasn't changed a great deal since its inception, it has been successfully produced with plastic strands; although they don't sound as good as metal wire, they do offer greater durability and are less susceptible to bending. The handle has seen variation as well. The telescopic retractable versions do protect the wire strands, but solid handles offer other possibilities, such as Clayton Cameron's signature brush, which features a rubber handle for comfort and cymbal washes, a plastic butt for cross-stick playing, and a metal stud on the butt for cymbal-scraping effects. This helps the brush to become much more versatile.

As well as drumsticks and brushes, many drums require mallets to be played. Such instruments include timpani, bass drums, tenor drums or cymbals, and tuned percussion. These mallets have appeared in various guises throughout the history of these instruments, and popularity of certain materials has sometimes been determined by the preferred style at the time or the materials available. For example, in the 17th century wooden mallets were popular for timpanists, and then in the early 19th century sponge-headed sticks were used for their effectiveness at lower volumes. The spongy head allowed pianissimo but also had a firmness that was desired.

Today the handle is usually made of a wood such as beech, cherrywood, ebony, or ash. The head comes in a variety of materials, depending on the instrument. Even within each instrument, several sticks may be required. The timpanist will use different sticks for different pieces, or even parts of a piece to gain the optimum effect. The head may be covered with anything from leather, cloth, flannel, felt, cork, or sponge from the Mediterranean. The effect the mallet has on the sound of each note is so great, many timpanists chose to make their own sticks to their exact specifications rather than buy them, a practice that is still used today by some careful players.

The orchestral or military bass drum also offers several choices depending on application and chosen piece. These can be short or long handled, uncovered wooden beaters or beaters covered in lambskin, and have heads of varying sizes. There are also double-headed beaters, which allow for a continuous single-handed roll by way of a rotary motion. These have the unfortunate name of tampons.

NOTE

1. Udai Vir Singh, ed. "The late Harappan and other Chalcolithic cultures of India: a study in inter-relationship." (Papers presented at the 6th annual Congress of the Indian Archaeological Society and the seminar, Kurukshetra, 19–21 Nov. 1972), 135.

Chapter Seventeen

―――――――――○―――――――――

Practice Kits
and Education

SELLING EQUIPMENT TO FLEDGLING DRUMMERS is big business in the drum industry, and drum companies vie to sign up the most popular drummers to represent them. After all, how many drummers bought a Ludwig kit after seeing Ringo Starr playing Ludwig on *The Ed Sullivan Show* in 1964? These impressionable drummers are the ones who will spend the rest of their lives saving up for new drumming equipment, and many people develop an unnecessary loyalty toward a single company. This loyalty needs to be developed at the earliest stage as far as the drum companies are concerned. But it is not just a case of selling the same old kits that the pros use. The requirements of a child in a terraced house are clearly different from those of a rock drummer performing at an arena. To this end, many innovative products have been produced over the years to cater to these different needs.

One such product is the flat drum kit. An early example of this was the Flat Jacks that emerged from Indiana in the 1960s, bearing similarities to Adolphe Sax's 19th-century shell-less timpani drums. In an effort to create the smallest possible drum kit, designer Ralph Kester used 3-inch-deep metal shells with only a batter head attached. The tension screws didn't screw downward as they normally would; instead they screwed into the drum shell, pushing an internal metal ring up into the drumhead to alter tension. The snare and three toms connected to the 20-inch bass drum via elegant but flimsy-appearing metal rods with extra support from legs for the floor tom, and could fit inside each other for storage. These drums didn't sell well and soon disappeared, but they did make an impression on one man, who resurrected the design thirty years later. That man was the aforementioned Ivor Arbiter, who had designed the Autotune drum and was now producing the Arbiter Flats.

The Flats adjusted drumhead tension via a V-clamp, much the same as his Autotune design, which allowed for single-tension screw tuning. The drum sizes were available as 10-, 12-, and 14-inch toms, a 12-inch snare drum, and a 20-inch bass drum. These were all mounted via clamps and a frame made from a very durable plastic known as ABS. The whole kit folded up and fitted into a bag akin to a cymbal bag, while the hardware packed up into another bag. It also came with silent mesh drumheads and with the absence of shells, which allowed for a very compact setup so smaller children could play in the correct position. With such low volumes and easy transportation, this kit was perfect for many situations where an acoustic kit would normally not be a viable option. It also favored the peripatetic drum tutor who could show up at a student's house with his drum kit in his hands. Such a kit has also evolved into the Traps version, which is a reference to the early drum set "contraptions." The kit was produced by some of the Arbiter Flats team and really built on the positive attributes of that molded plastic kit, but using a standard multiscrew tuning system, chrome metal tubing, steel counter hoops, and Remo heads for a more realistic kit sound.

Drumhead manufacturer Remo longed for a share of the drum kit market and decided to begin with an innovative minimalist design. In 1982 Remo introduced the Pre-tuned Series (PTS) heads endorsed by Louis Bellson. These were tensioned on their own hoops and mounted on a specialized shell onto which they simply clipped rather than requiring conventional tension rods and lugs. Despite failing to achieve any commercial success, this design did begin Remo's foray into drum kit manufacturing, which continued with the late 1980s Encore product.

Of course, as an even smaller and quieter practice option we now have rubber practice pad kits, which enable a drummer to practice on the different drum pads in their correct positions with the minimal noise. This has been taken further by using electronic sensors so that a sound sample can be triggered when the pad is beaten and the produced sound listened to through headphones (see chapter 18).

In the actual acoustic drum market, the Japanese manufacturers Yamaha released a very appealing drum kit with the Manu Katche version of the hip gig kit, taken from the original Rick Morrotta kit but scaled down to accommodate younger drummers. This punchy kit consisted of a 16 × 16-inch nine-ply Philippine mahogany bass drum, a 10 × 7-inch six-ply rack tom, a 13 × 12 inch floor tom, and a 12 × 5 inch snare drum and gave younger drummers an excellent, albeit expensive, option aside from the usual toylike entry-level smaller kits.

Despite all this equipment, teaching in groups has always presented obvious challenges due to space and, more significantly, noise. The advent of quality electronic kits has enabled music colleges to furnish their drum classes with rows of electronic kits that are played with headphones and the added ability to amplify any chosen kit through a PA system for classroom monitoring. The teacher may also be able to use their own headphones to listen in to a particular student when required. A very innovative approach was adopted in 2009 in Teeside, Northeast England, which enabled several bands to practice in the same room. This seemingly impossible task has taken the drum class concept one step further and created band pods in which a drummer, guitarist, bass player, keyboardist, and percussionist all play electronic instruments within their pods using connecting headphones. Several other bands can also be doing the same thing simultaneously elsewhere in the room, and the teacher can work from their central pod by listening in to any pod and communicating via a microphone. It is this excellent use of the available technology that is making music, and in particular the noisy, heavy drum kit, more accessible to students at schools.

Equipment aside, drummers have been making money from the education market for many years. As mentioned, Charles Stewart Ashworth published his book *A New, Useful and Complete System of Drum Beating* in 1812 from his position of drum major for the US

Marine Corps Band with the intention of providing a concise guide to rudimental drumming and the techniques involved. This was followed by numerous similar books with varying interpretations of the fundamentals.

In the 20th century, a few drummers went into great detail to explain their techniques and approaches to drumming. Some of these men are still remembered and studied today, with their technique commonly known by their name, despite the fact that they did not invent anything new but simply explained old techniques in their own way. This is the case for most of what is taught, but it is those that publish the definitive explanations of such subjects that are remembered as the creators. An example of such a man is the Boston drummer and teacher George Lawrence Stone, who published several drum method books, such as *Stick Control for the Snare Drummer* in 1935 and *Accents and Rebounds for the Snare Drummer* in 1961. He was interested in the mechanics of the body and explained how a note should be played on the drum. He championed the use of loose, comfortable movements; using the natural stick rebound rather than preventing it; and that all the body's hinges should be free to move in order to play with varying dynamics. In other words, the shoulder, elbow, wrist, and fingers should be utilized rather than relying solely on wrists or fingers.

Another such drummer from the same era was New Yorker Billy Gladstone, who taught famous names in their formative years, such as Shelley Manne and Joe Morello, who subsequently went on to spread his teachings to the next generation. He taught concepts similar to Stone's, such as use of continuous movement instead of stopping and starting, as well as full-flowing motion of all upper-body joints, although Gladstone also treated the movement like a wave traveling down the arm. He taught that accents should be performed as relaxed notes at a louder dynamic level, focusing on playing them as loosely as possible to avoid stiff, tense muscles, which would inhibit articulation, accuracy, and speed. He also believed in a relaxed fulcrum point with an action that involved catching the stick immediately after impact as it rebounds, in an effort to allow the stick to do more of the work rather than the player.

A third significant teacher in the early years of the 20th century was another New Yorker named Sanford A. Moeller, who in 1925 wrote *The Moeller Book: The Art of Snare Drumming*. Using techniques that were popular throughout America's military drum history, he taught such future stars as Jim Chapin and Gene Krupa. He used more of a whipping motion in comparison to Gladstone, who focused more on finger usage. Moeller championed the relaxed, flowing motions that others promoted but also dissected the movements into different strokes, which enabled accents to be played fluidly. The downstroke, tap, upstroke, and full stroke allowed the stick to start in any position (high or low) and end in any position (high or low) to play any combination of accents or ghost notes smoothly.

Many more drummers released educational material of varying quality and practical use, and as television, video, and then DVDs became significant mediums, ever-increasing numbers of drummers and publishing houses felt a need to produce material. Some of these might focus on specific rhythms from specific songs. Chad Smith's 1993 *Red Hot Rhythm Method* video dissected drum patterns from his band the Red Hot Chili Peppers and particularly the 1991 album *Blood Sugar Sex Magik* while integrating technical and stylistic advice. This approach certainly appeals to fans of that band and the funk/rock genre with an entertaining and humorous atmosphere. Some others choose to provide a more formal and technique-heavy product, such as the drum and bass extraordinaire Jojo Mayer's 2007 *Secret Weapons for the Modern Drummer*, which explains the methods behind some of the well-renowned past drummers such as Gladstone and Moeller, as well as divulging his own views on how to develop speed, control, and accuracy. Others chose to get very conceptual, such as Gavin Harrison's approach in his books *Rhythmic Illusions* (1998) and *Rhythmic Perspectives* (2000), as well as the DVDs *Rhythmic Visions* (2002) and *Rhythmic Horizons* (2007), where he specializes in displacing beats and putting emphasis and phrasings within bars to create an unexpected or unusual result to great effect. Another conceptual DVD–producing drummer is the Austrian-born Thomas Lang, who released *Creative Control* (2004) and *Creative Co-ordination and Advanced Foot*

Technique (2007). His approach is one of incredible independence between all four limbs as well as extremely good technique, allowing movement around the kit at incredible speeds. This concept is nothing new, however. Jim Chapin, a student of Moeller, published *Advanced Techniques for the Modern Drummer* in 1948 and provided drummers of the 20th century with a challenging study in coordination and independence. Lang's approach in the 21st century is clinical and takes Chapin's work to the next level.

Another market has opened up for these players who have crafted a name for themselves on the drum circuit as clinicians. The drum clinic circuit is a significant part of some drummers' careers and is often a serious part of their endorsement agreement with equipment companies. Although drummers such as Steve Gadd and Greg Bisonette are known for their extensive live and studio work, they have still fulfilled clinic tours throughout their careers. Some other drummers are actually better known to the drumming community as clinicians than for any recorded body of work or live appearances with established artists. The aforementioned Lang is one such drummer. Although he does boast many high-level accomplishments on his CV, many drummers are aware of him for his performances for Sonor drums (and then DW) and Roland electronic drums at music shows around the world. It is here that he has the freedom to perform to his technical and physical limit, leaving audiences in awe of what can be achieved by a human on the drum set. The Australian drummer Virgil Donati is another such drummer who defies the limitations of what appears to be humanly possible at his one-man clinics for Pearl drums.

The German drummer Benny Greb brings a very unique approach to the table by exploring the full timbral options available, finding sounds that others may never have known were possible from a drum kit. In this exploration he plays with his hands, mutes drums by applying pressure to the skin with body parts such as his elbow, plays on the cymbal stands, and uses multipedal grooves where the feet dance between the pedals, creating intricate rhythms between bass drums, hi-hats, and other sound effect drums, a concept that featured in Lang's performances. Greb endorses his native Sonor drums and Meinl cymbals. As previously mentioned in the drum and bass section, American drummer Johnny Rabb has a very innovative approach using single-handed rolls, muting drums for pitch changes, using his signature Meinl Drumbals cymbals placed on the drumhead for various sound effects, and exploring an array of cutting-edge genres and drum patterns. He endorses DW drums, Meinl cymbals, and Roland V-drums. Many of these innovative drummers are involved in creating new products with their affiliated companies, with Lang, Greb, Mayer, Donati, and Rabb as such examples. And so with this increasingly popular area of performance, aspiring players are treated to numerous and varied insights into professional drummers' skills, ranging from the highly educational and the extremely entertaining to simple gladiatorial speed and technique competitions to ascertain who is the fastest and most physically impressive drummer alive.

With the live clinics, DVDs, books, CDs, and online lessons, there has never been such a wealth of educational material to whet the learning drummer's appetite. And as manufacturers dedicate increasing efforts into this area, there are ever more practice tools on which to learn how to play. With these aids, the quality of musical talent will continue to flourish and grow into the future.

Chapter Eighteen

---○---

Electronic Kits

THE DRUM IS A BEAUTIFULLY ORGANIC and natural instrument that allows us to connect with the earth, our gods, our primeval past, our inner consciousness, or whatever else the player allows themselves to experience. It is ancient and natural, made from the trees of our forests and bodies of our animals. This deep connection with the natural world and our civilization's history is one of the attractions of the drum. Another is the instant connection with the sound that is produced. The close contact with the instrument when struck, and the sound that is then created, means that the vibration is felt as much as it is heard. Drummers can feel and enjoy the impact upon the animal skin, the whoosh of air that is moved behind the skin, and the reverberations around the shell of the instrument.

It is therefore a slow and confusing process for some drummers when they are faced with the significant rise of electronics in the drumming market. While some may scratch their heads, unsure whether to embrace technology or run for the sanctuary of their tree house and frame drum, others push hard to discover what these futuristic gadgets can offer the drummer.

In the 1970s synthesizers were gaining increasing respect and enjoying wide use throughout the music industry as the new, modern sound of music. The greatest use of these synthesizers was keyboard instruments, which are ubiquitous today across a majority of musical styles. However, in 1971 Graeme Edge from the band

Moody Blues and Brian Groves, a professor from Sussex University, designed one of the first incarnations of the electronic drum kit. It consisted of rubber trigger pads that had a layer of silver paper on the back. Attached to this was a magnet, which housed a silver coil that moved up and down to create an electronic signal. It utilized sounds to create ten tom-toms, eight bass drums, five snare drums, and sixteen sequencers. It was a temperamental mass of transistors and wiring that was not robust enough to sell commercially, but it did warrant its place in history when it was used on the track "Procession" from the 1971 Moody Blues album *Every Good Boy Deserves Favor*.

Two years later and the Moog 1130 Percussion Controller had been released. It was not an electronic drum per se but a trigger that worked as an alternative to a keyboard. It consisted of a single-headed Ludwig drum casing with the Moog electronics housed inside the shell. Two voltage-output controls were positioned on the side, one for volume and one for pitch. The intention was to use it in conjunction with equipment such as a Moog modular synthesizer. This was often a huge modular monophonic analog synthesizer consisting of numerous buttons and patch cables like a telephone operator's switchboard, which could be moved around to alternate the sounds. The Percussion Controller was simply a device that controlled the signal sent to the synthesizer to trigger a sound.

The progressive and groundbreaking drummer Carl Palmer was involved in the early stages of drum sequencing. For the track "Toccata" from the 1973 *Brain Salad Surgery* album, Palmer used the drum kit to control synthesized sounds during his drum solo. The kit was made of stainless steel with engravings on the shell and set upon a revolving drum riser. Framed by two huge gongs and chime bars, Palmer would solo with a mix of rock drums and orchestral percussion. It was only when he introduced the cutting-edge modern electronics that he really broke new ground. The shells of the toms were rigged to trigger preset drum sequences whether it was a synthesized arpeggio or spaceship-type whooshes and screeches.

Then in 1976 the electronic drum market really opened up when the first commercial electronic drum was released by Pollard

Industries under the name of Syndrum. Joe Pollard and Mark Burton created this simple drum brain and released it with accompanying pads before it was bought out by Research Development Inc., who delivered the Syndrum 1, Syndrum Twindrum, and Syndrum Quad, each allowing a different number of pads with a Kevlar Duraline drumhead as the playing surface. The technology was basic with a waveform generator using filters to manipulate the sounds to achieve a sound that wasn't all that close to a drum. The laborious task of turning dials to find a suitable sound was alleviated slightly by the instruction manual that offered settings diagrams of popular noises. A budget model was also produced, called the Syndrum CSM, which housed the module inside the shell and sacrificed some of the sound-altering abilities. Big drumming names such as Jeff Porcaro, Terry Bozzio, Carmine Appice, and Keith Moon were associated with this cutting-edge drum equipment. Another early user was Michael Shrieve, who first came to prominence aged nineteen following his drum solo at the Woodstock festival in 1969 while playing for Santana. Experimenting with electronics since the early days of 1973, he was a user of Syndrum and of instruments made by Impact Percussion in Portland, Oregon. These were used in 1976 on the self-titled debut album of Shrieve's side project Automatic Man. Furthermore, in 1989 Shrieve recorded an album with David Beal titled *The Big Picture* in which he used electronic percussion exclusively, such as the Kat trigger pads.

A year after Syndrum, the Synare was released by Star Instruments as a self-contained unit with the pads built onto the edge of the module. It was similar to the Syndrum but also allowed for a ring modulator, a sequencer, and pink noise effects. It was very close to a keyboard synthesizer with melodic sounds that could be played across the four pads with twelve zones in total. Star Instruments released the Synare Two and then the budget Synare Three, which like the Syndrum CSM was housed within the UFO-shaped shell. Syndrum and Synare soon fell out of favor, but the electronic revolution wasn't over yet.

It wasn't just electronic instrument companies that saw the potential of this market; Japanese acoustic drum manufacturer Pearl wanted a piece of the action too. In 1979 they released the SY1

Syncussion unit, consisting of two separate channels, each with an oscillator that could produce basic waveforms, which could then be modified with an LFO, noise generator, or envelope generator. They were used in conjunction with two drums fitted with transducers and then placed around an acoustic drum kit to be used as an extra utility to the available traditional drum kit timbres. The unit was quickly picked up and used on a few unfavorable disco records and then had trouble disassociating itself from these tracks. It ultimately never achieved the sales that it might have otherwise achieved.

Another company working along the same line was Electro-Harmonix, who produced the Space Drum in the late 1970s. This small box had one playing surface and control knobs to alter the frequency of the produced note. However, with sounds bearing more similarity to a fictional spaceship laser gun than a drum, it never really threatened the acoustic drum kit too severely.

Many companies saw the potential here but had only managed a novelty auxiliary instrument to use alongside an acoustic kit. No one had yet produced a usable electronic drum kit to stand alone; that is, until Simmons arrived at the dawn of the 1980s. Founded in 1978, the English company had designed the SDS-3 with round real drumheads set on wooden shells, which were built by Premier. It had a brain with a noise generator and either two or four drum channels. These early models were experimented with but were really only part of the journey toward the big product. Simmons focused on the belief that a drum sound consisted of both a pitched and an unpitched sound. The pitched tone of the drum was to be tuned separately to the unpitched noise element, and a unique sound was achieved that other manufacturers had failed to create. With this in mind and help from Richard Burgess, the drummer from the jazz/fusion band Landscape, the SDS-V (or SDS-5) was released in 1981, and the world's first completely electronic drum kit had arrived. A revolution had now truly begun, and drumming would never be the same again. It has since become an icon of the 1980s with the hexagonal pads, which came as a snare drum, bass drum, and three toms. It featured a rack-mountable brain, which created the very distinctive and well-used sounds that epitomize

1980s pop music with controls to alter pitch bend, tone level, noise level, attack, and noise tone, as well as including a static filter. Each module enabled the same parameters, although they were each customized for optimum ability at their desired tasks. This allowed the bass drum to be distinguished from the snare drum and tom toms. It was by no means perfect, with wrist-damaging hard polycarbonate playing surfaces and incredibly poor cymbal sounds, which were often abandoned in favor of real cymbals. An early example of this drum kit can be heard on Spandau Ballet's "Chant No. 1," which Richard Burgess of Landscape produced. Another interesting early Simmons appearance came courtesy of sculptor Coleman Saunders, who produced a series of custom drum-pad casings in the shape of human heads. These fascinating and eerie drums were produced for publicity purposes but were also used in Landscape's 1981 video for the track "Einstein A Go-Go."

Other notable early users included Duran Duran, Rush, and Bill Bruford. In 1981 Bruford was using an interesting mix of acoustic Tama bass drum, snare drum, and gong drum; Remo rototoms; Paiste and Zildjian cymbals; six dragon drums; a slit drum; and six Simmons electronic pads. He then used electronic percussion in various electro-acoustic combinations, inadvertently acting almost as an ambassador for the instruments, until 1998 when he reverted to purely acoustic drumming.

Moving on from the SDS-V, Simmons then modified the SDS by making use of EPROM (erasable programmable read-only memory chips) in 1983, which were memory chips that allowed data to be stored on them even when the power was turned off. This technology was only around ten years old when Simmons used it in the SDS-7 to store sound samples on the chips, which could then be interchanged to quickly load different sounds into each drum pad. The pads were also made of rubber by now and therefore less damaging to the player's wrists. An EPROM Blower was then released alongside the SDS-7, which allowed the user to burn their own samples onto the chips with a maximum 128-kb capacity. The SDS-7 still used analog synthesis alongside this new digital technology, so it's an example of the transitional phase before digital took over.

Neil Peart of Rush was one fan of this technology, however, when he turned to electronic percussion in the 1980s to condense his huge set of drums and auxiliary percussion. By using MIDI trigger pads, he could dispense with the large instruments and use a single pad to trigger multiple instruments. The 1984 Rush album *Grace Under Pressure* saw him embrace the Simmons electronic drums as well as Akai samplers with an SDS-7 setup back to back with the acoustic set. He also used the EPROM facility to incorporate his own sampled sounds, such as African drums from the track "Mystic Rhythms" taken from the 1985 *Power Windows*, which was recorded after *Grace Under Pressure*. Just as Palmer experimented with unusual sounds for improvisation, Peart used many unique sounds during his extensive drum solos, including the "Malletkat Express," which replicated chromatic xylophone-type sounds by way of rubber pads instead of keys or bars. In his later kits, the triggers were built into custom DW shells that matched his highly personal kit designs.

As well as the introduction of the EPROM Blower, 1983 also saw Sweden enter the electronic drum competition with Clavia (better known today as the Nord synthesizer manufacturers) producing the Ddrum range. Hans Nordelius and Mikael Carlsson were the brains behind this venture, which hoped to knock Simmons off their perch. Unfortunately the hard playing surface and poor sounds dashed their dreams and Simmons stayed in control. But Ddrum wasn't finished yet.

Another occurrence in the early 1980s was for a musical instrument digital interface (MIDI) standard to be agreed on. This brought an end to manufacturers each using different connectors, and with a new standard connector, cross-manufacturer equipment setups could be utilized. In the early years, however, different manufacturers failed to designate the same sounds to the same channels. As a result, the bass drum that was programmed on one piece of equipment might play back as a ukulele on another. This was remedied in 1991 when General MIDI (GM1) was introduced; standardizing channel numbers for specific instruments, with channel 10 assigned to percussion sounds; later channel 11 was added with General MIDI Two (GM2).

Roland Octopads used this technology in 1985, consisting of eight touch-sensitive vinyl pads that could be connected to a drum computer or sampler to trigger sounds. Being only a MIDI controller allowed Roland to focus on the pad design without a need to develop the drum brain. This early incarnation was very popular and paved the way for later versions such as the SPD-S and SPD-20, while putting Roland on the map as a competitor in the electronic drums market.

By this 1980s midpoint, electronic drums were all the rage dominating music shows and drum catalogs with companies such as Dynacord, Maxim, Liss, GPMS, Klone Kit, Yamaha, Gretsch, Sonor, Pearl, Tama, Fishman, Barcus Berry, Trigger Perfect, Ddrum, K&K, and UP among the competition. Many of these companies simply copied the designs of Simmons, the market leader, and by the late 1980s most had dissolved or, in the case of Tama, Pearl, Gretsch, and Sonor, returned to what they were good at: acoustic drums.

In 1987 the Swedish Ddrum 2 was released, which improved on the hard plastic drumheads by using real drumheads. It allowed sounds to be changed via cartridges much more easily than their first effort had allowed and proved to be user friendly. But at around US$6,500 (£4,000), the price tag was too high for most drummers, and the electronic drum was not looking like a viable option.

By 1987, even Simmons was losing its grip on the market. In fact the market was disappearing quickly as acoustic drums were coming back into favor. It was at this point that Simmons released their most advanced and most expensive product to date. The SDX featured a huge synthesizer that wheeled in on a frame with a startling, futuristic, and sleek black plastic appearance, including a floppy disc drive and a large screen for easy use of the many sound manipulation functions that it had. The touch-sensitive playing pads were vastly improved, with different sound samples triggered by three different zones of the pads with three samples in each zone that afforded nine sounds per pad. Two hundred and eighty SDX kits were produced, but at a cost of around US$13,000 (£8,000), this equipment was even less attractive than the Ddrum 2 for the average drummer. Those that could afford it still faced serious issues when enduring system failures midconcert. Bill Bruford suffered this reluctantly even with the highly sophisticated SDX, of which he played two simultaneously at one point, and did so very publicly when he faced both modules crashing on him while performing at Madison Square Garden during a concert. During his time with electronics, Bruford pushed the capabilities forward, always searching for new mixes of rhythm with the newly available melody and harmony. But the unreliability proved too great ultimately, and even he steered back to the reliable and dynamically superior acoustic drums.

And so, with vast research and development expenses and numerous competitors at significantly lower costs (such as the Akai S900 at around US$3,250 [£2,000]), the SDX was a commercial mistake and ultimately ensured the company's demise.

As well as the huge price tag, another problem with electronic kits in general was latency. This is the time delay between striking the pad and hearing the sound. Add to this the fact that changing

Bill Bruford and his Simmons kit with A.B.W.H. in 1989. From the Bill Bruford archive.

between sounds could be awkward and lengthy and the user interface was often more complicated than many drummers wished to fathom when their trusty old acoustic drum just involved whacking it with a stick. And so with Simmons, the giant of electronic drums, dying, a fresh approach was needed for electronic drums to survive into the 1990s.

Following on from the disappointing Ddrum 1 and 2, Clavia changed tack in 1992 and introduced the AT-System. This new approach saw them introduce a brain and triggers that were to be used in conjunction with an acoustic drum kit. The triggers could be attached to the rims of acoustic drums to pick up the vibrations when the head was struck. These proved to be an instant success, and their striking red color, robust build, and ease of use has ensured that they are still popular well into the 21st century.

One company that was ascending in the 1990s was Alesis when they introduced the D4 drum module in 1992, with over five hundred drum sounds and a price tag under US$400 (£250). Among the sounds were acoustic representations, orchestral percussion, ethnic percussion, and a range of electronic sound effects, as well as twenty-one preset kits. Although the editing features were limited, this proved a popular sound module that could be triggered from a number of sources. By the early 1990s, Simmons had released the SDS 2000 as an attempt to salvage the company. This offering consisted of some of its bigger brother's features but at a cheaper cost. Unfortunately, other manufacturers were making more innovative products and the music scene had moved on from the 1980s synthesized drum sounds that Simmons was famous for. The company lumbered on until 1994, when Simmons ceased to function. In 2005 the American music chain Guitar Center bought the rights to the Simmons name and began to produce second-rate products that were nothing like the original designs; a sad end for such an iconic brand. However, many remember Simmons for their success and innovation in the 1980s, without which the pop world would never have been the same.

One of the said manufacturers that were muscling in on this marketplace was Roland. In 1992 they had released the TD-7, and the future of electronic drums had arrived. The compact drum system was the selling line for this product, and it was fully focused on emulating an acoustic kit. Of course it didn't succeed with its PD7 dual-zone round black rubber pads for all drums and cymbals alike, except for the bass drum, which used the trigger pad, forcing an adapted drum pedal to strike the beater downward toward an impact point on the floor. The pads felt unnatural and the response was poor, although some drummers found them suitable when augmenting their acoustic kits. The TD-7 module employed 512 samples and 32 programmable kits as well as a built-in digital reverb, delay, chorus, and flange effects. The compact kit had enabled people to furnish their homes and small studios with a playable electronic kit and, despite not breaking sales records, did show the way for the future.

In 1993 Clavia returned to the fold with the Ddrum 3. The pads were able to differentiate between different dynamics and impact positions on the head, triggering different sounds accordingly, and the module allowed onboard sampling and much more realistic sounds. This was a highly advanced piece of equipment but also carried a highly advanced price tag at around US$11,400 (£7,000), too much for the home user. Clavia followed with the Ddrum 4, a cheaper option with fewer features. It allowed extra sounds to be imported from an external source into the MIDI sample dump or downloaded from the manufacturer's website, just as its more expensive siblings had, as well as coming with 330 preset sounds inbuilt. But ultimately the inclination wasn't present at Clavia, and they left electronic drums to focus on synthesizers.

A year later Roland offered the TD-5 kit. With 210 preset instrument sounds, 32 programmable kits, and an onboard effects processor including reverb, it was the more modest sibling of the TD-7, and it gave the consumer an even cheaper option for home use. At the same time, another Japanese giant entered the arena with the DTX 1.0. That giant was Yamaha, and their first electronic drum offering was designed for home practice and small studio use. It incorporated many of the features of the Roland TD-5 and added play-along songs, a feature that had always proved difficult with the noisy acoustic drum kit and usually involved a very loud hi-fi system.

Three years after releasing the D4, Alesis introduced the DM5 module in 1995 with 540 drum sounds and 21 programmable kits. Despite features such as inbuilt reverb, ambience, and randomization of drum hits for a more realistic sound, it was still a fairly basic and limited product. However, its effectiveness as a box of samples that could be triggered by external sources in the studio or home environment was clear, and it stayed in favor until well into the 21st century. In fact, Alesis reissued it in 2006, accompanied by a full kit of pads. The pads were hard and insensitive compared to the top-end pads at that time, but by offering the same module as they had in 1995, Alesis cut costs dramatically and were able to offer the DM5 kit at a very cheap price, enabling many more people to afford one.

In 1996 Yamaha released the DTX 2.0, which surpassed any of Roland's current products with around a thousand instrument samples and sixty-four drum sets, half preset and half programmable. The polyphony sequencer allowed one hundred prerecorded songs with options for the user to add their own, and a "groove check" tool that helped the user to work on their timing when playing the kit.

Yamaha might have been enjoying this rise to the top, but it wouldn't last long as Roland's founder, Ikutaro Kakehashi, was determined to make the electronic drum work for him despite disappointing sales with his first attempts. In the wake of the space-age 1980s sounds and the subsequent demise of this market, as we approached the 21st century, manufacturers were well aware that what many drummers really wanted from an electronic kit was the ability to sound like an acoustic kit.

In 1997 Roland unleashed two major changes and yet again revolutionized the electronic drum market with the TD-10. This was the first of the drum kits to use the moniker V-drums, having followed on from other V products such as the V-guitar released in 1995. The first major change in this new V-drum was the modeling or alteration of sounds in a virtual environment that imitated how real acoustic instruments would be affected by all external factors. Such factors included the size of a room, the type of room, drum shell materials, drumhead types, tunings, microphone placement, and dampening. This offered seemingly unlimited options to create the drum sound that the user desired. The name for this technology was composite object sound modeling, and it set the V-drums high above any competitor.

The second major change was that of the drum pads. The cymbals were still round rubber PD-7 pads, but the drumheads were a world apart with the brand-new mesh heads. These mesh heads, which were inspired by a trampoline surface, were a huge achievement. The tunable mesh heads afforded much better playability and high-quality positional sensing. For the first time, electronic drum pads actually felt somewhere close to real drumheads, and they responded similarly as well. Positional sensing had been found on the Simmons SDX and Ddrum 3 to some extent, but Roland made it affordable. This was all patented, so no other company could clone the concepts as closely as had happened to Simmons' designs. Having employed Remo to produce these mesh heads, Roland also developed an interest in their Acousticon material, which they used for the V-drum shells to provide a result that looked something like an acoustic drum and was also robust. They then added a rubber rim to the shells, and the result was near-silent playing, even with rim shots. This product offered feel, playability, and expression at unprecedented levels, making this a kit that professionals might want to use rather than just the bedroom-practicing drummer.

Yamaha couldn't emulate the patented mesh heads, and instead of competing with this high-end product, they responded with an affordable DTXpress in 1999. Roland responded with the TD-8, a more affordable version of the TD-10, mesh heads included. By 2000, Yamaha had managed to fight back by releasing the DTX-treme. This offered a highly sophisticated drum brain but failed to offer competition to Roland's mesh heads. Their answer was to use real drumheads, as had been done in the past with the likes of Simmons' early efforts. Yamaha did apply muffling to their heads, but the result was inferior to Roland's mesh heads. With this admission, they overlooked one of the great attractions of these kits: near-silent playing. Outside of the headphones, a person practicing on the V-drums was only audible via a gentle patter on the mesh heads.

In 2001 Roland made efforts to bring their cymbals up to the standard of their drums. They dispensed with the old PD-7 round, plastic, multifunction pads and released the V-cymbals, which allowed for a natural feel as the cymbal swayed on the stand. These were made from a plastic base with a softer rubber playing surface.

In 2004 it was Roland that were again breaking new ground with the VH-12 hi-hat, which sat on a regular hi-hat stand with two separate cymbal pads just as a regular hi-hat has. Six research and design members worked on this product and decided on sensors that could detect the point of impact on the top cymbal and also motion sensors to determine when the hi-hat was open, allowing it to operate very closely to a real hi-hat.

And then in the same year Yamaha made their next move against Roland when they introduced the Yamaha DTXtreme II. With around two thousand drum samples, ninety preset kits, and 101 factory preset songs, as well as AIFF and WAV sampling facilities stored on a media card, this kit offered an interesting alternative to the V-drums. It even allowed for sound modeling just like Roland so that each voice could be altered individually. The pad playing surface was no longer a real drumhead but a soft rubber material that allowed quiet playing but still retained a realistic feel. The pads were sleek and the snare positioned on a separate snare stand for a more realistic feel. The module catered to eight triple zone pads along with eight other single zone pad inputs, and each pad had individual controls to alter pitch and pad selection, while the snare also incorporated dampening options. The hi-hat featured two cymbal pads set on an acoustic hi-hat stand, just as the Roland VH-12 had in the same year, although it struggled to achieve the full spectrum of open hi-hat sounds that are found on an acoustic hi-hat. The cymbals were round rubber pads complete with a choke facility, and the robust appearance of the curved rack system gave the kit an air of class and surrounded the drummer slightly so that they felt like they were playing a real kit. The marketing strategy for this product was to promote it as a professional standard kit at an affordable price, making it available even for the hobby drummer.

Meanwhile, Roland and Yamaha were still battling at the other end of the market with their entry-level kits, Roland with the TD-3 and Yamaha with the DTXplorer. But other companies had entered the race with no intention of competing with the TD-10 or

Yamaha DTXtreme III 950K, Yamaha Corporation of America.

DTXtreme. For under $300 (£184), a kit such as ION's Pro Session Drums could be bought, offering one hundred drum voices, fifteen preset kits, and forty-one music tracks to play along with, including a mute facility to hear a prerecorded drum part and then silence it so that the user can play. The drum and cymbal pads resemble those of Yamaha's flagship models, although on close inspection the build quality and playability is vastly inferior. Drum sounds can be edited and stored, and the user can also record themselves drumming for playback and assessment. This is one of many kits that emerged in the early 21st century to capitalize on this quickly growing market and make electronic drums affordable to everyone. These are often manufactured in China and sold under different brand names, even though some are actually the exact same product. They are playable, and an entry drummer would be able to learn the basics in near silence at home and have some fun with the variety of sounds. However, the brains of these kits are incredibly limited, but then at below US$300 (£184), few would expect the quality of a TD-10.

Unfortunately for Yamaha and their DTXtreme, Roland hadn't released the VH-12 hi-hat all on its own that year. It had been unveiled at the winter National Association of Music Merchants (NAMM) show as part of the TD-20 flagship drum kit; in doing this, they totally eclipsed all competition once again.

The TD-20 took the electronic drum to unbelievable levels with incredible dynamic and articulation capabilities as well as editing and recording facilities that helped convert many drummers who were previously loyal to the acoustic drum. The appearance was striking, with curved rack systems similar to Yamaha's DTXtreme and much of the cabling hidden inside the tubes. Now the kit looked even more like a real, solid piece of equipment and less like a whimsical toy. The TD-20 module boasted over five hundred drum instrument voices and 262 backing instruments. Added to the existing adjustable parameters were snare buzz level, strainer adjustment, sizzle effects on cymbals, cymbal sizes, and bass drum

Roland TD-20, Roland.

beater materials. The mesh head pads had also been updated with improved sensor mechanisms for even more accurate triggering, and by now they were offering the KD-120BK kick drum pad, which was a 12-inch mesh pad accommodating double bass drum pedals and offering a much more realistic feel. As well as being MIDI compatible, this module allows for ten analog outputs so that in studio recording situations, the individual instruments could be recorded as separate tracks. Expansion packs have been released for this module, allowing extra sounds and capabilities to be added, and new versions have been released, which again feature extra sounds and capabilities. In 2009 Roland updated the design with a brushed metal shell design and silver cymbals for an even less synthetic appearance, closer to acoustic drums.

Elsewhere in the market, having abandoned the pursuit of electronic drums many years earlier, Clavia sold the Ddrum name to the guitar manufacturer Dean in 2005, and Dean revived the brand and took it in a new direction. They kept on the successful triggers for use on acoustic drums (just as companies like Roland and Yamaha also produced), offering a Pro Acoustic range at a higher price and the Red Shot triggers for the smaller budget, but they also began manufacturing acoustic drums and attracted a number of high-profile endorsers.

Then in 2008 Yamaha fought back again at Roland with their DTXtreme III. Although it is very similar to its predecessor aesthetically, there were a number of important changes. The tom and snare pads, which featured a central zone and two rim zones each, were the same as the DTXtreme II, but the bass drum had a bigger 12-inch pad with a soft rubber playing surface. There were new cymbal pads with three playing zones and more realistic weighting and a sturdy hexagonal rack system to support it all. Crucially it boasted a brand-new brain with fifteen trigger inputs and sounds that range from high-quality samples of carefully recorded Yamaha acoustic drums, with the bonus of the Steve Gadd kit sound, to the synthetic sounds that would be expected of an electronic instrument. The number of these sounds has been reduced from over two thousand to just over one thousand to allow space for multilayered samples of each individual sound to allow greater dynamic and timbral options.

Extended articulation ensures that exactly the same sample is never triggered on two consecutive notes so fast rolls do not suffer from the familiar synthetic effect from past products that resembles a machine gun. It only has fifty preset and fifty programmable kits, but hundreds of extra kits can be stored on a USB device. The use of USB is another huge selling point, because samples could now be loaded via USB devices and altered or modified just as any other sound in the module. This could be sounds from other drum software, the user's own acoustic drum kit, or any other wacky sound they desire. Numerous sounds can be assigned to the different zones of each pad, creating vast possibilities beyond the preloaded options. This was expanded on in 2010 with the DTX950K. The main improvements included the textured silicone playing pads that allowed varied response characteristics between the drums so that the toms respond differently to the snare, as would be found on an acoustic kit. Furthermore, it was able to control a DAW (digital audio workstation) from the module's panel, meaning it could be used in conjunction with software such as Cubase and controlled from the drum throne via the Yamaha module rather than getting up and walking to the workstation and then dashing back to the drum kit. Once again the two Japanese companies were battling it out for the top spot.

Outside of this private war, other companies were aiming to corner their own part of the market. Despite impressive sales of their 2006 DM5 kit, which housed the module now approaching fifteen years old, Alesis were keen to advance their electronic drum catalog and bring it up to date. In 2009 they unveiled the DM 10 at the Nashville summer NAMM show, and rather than just copy the big players, they produced a new midrange product at around $1,500 (£920). This was a huge leap up from their previous foray into electronic drums and featured RealHead Mylar drum skins with steel triple-flanged counter hoops that were tension adjustable just like the Roland mesh heads. Dynamic articulation allowed the volume and timbre of the drum to alter according to the power of the stroke, and the sound samples were created from top brands of acoustic drums and cymbals. The brain boasted over a thousand sounds as well as the ability to import entire new kit setups via a USB lead linked to a computer, which also allows MIDI information to be transferred back to the computer. It had decent sound-editing capabilities, onboard sequencing, an advanced met-ronome for practice, and with the kit framed by a sturdy curved rack design, it looked like a serious product as much as it sounded like one. Maybe their most distinguishing feature was their Surge cymbals, which were made from a brass alloy and came in sizes as big as 16 inches. They had integrated piezo triggers and a laminated dampening ring on the underside. The intention was for them to look like real cymbals, move as real cymbals, and therefore feel like real cymbals to the person playing them. They were available in single-, dual-, and triple-zone options as well as having a choke feature. Although not quite the same as the countless nuances and colors available from a real cymbal, they were a definite step toward bridging that gap between the hard black rubber cymbals that other manufacturers have offered for many years.

ELECTRONIC KITS IN DISGUISE

By 2010 manufacturers were taking things in slightly new direc-tions once again. Competitors for the most real-feeling electronic drum set were still emerging, such as the Swedish 2-box and their Drumlt 5 product. Although a new company in this field, they came with personnel links to the old Ddrum series. But other companies had their own original ideas.

One such product was the e-Pro Live, created by Japanese acoustic drum manufacturers Pearl. The whole concept here was based on the word *real*. Pearl marketed this kit as the closest thing to playing real acoustic drums. The kit was instantly striking in appear-ance, as it simply looked like a well-manufactured acoustic drum kit. Rather than shallow plastic trigger pads, it featured real drum sizes in both diameter and depth. The standard toms were 10, 12, and 14 inch, with a 14-inch snare drum and a 20-inch bass drum. Just as with acoustic drums, extra drums could be added, such as a double bass drum set or extra toms. Added to this were the real Pearl hardware range and real acoustic drum finishes. The drumheads were TruTrac, featuring a coating applied to the playing surface that eliminated the slightly sticky quality that can be found on rubber pads while also providing a response similar to real acoustic heads rather than the bouncy mesh head response. Not only did they feel like acoustic drumheads, they were also able to detect a wide range of dynamics and handle buzz rolls. Their E classic cymbal range delivered aesthetically as well as being made from brass in a similar design to the Alesis Surge line. The triple zone cymbals offered bell, bow, and edge trigger areas with the ability to choke. The module was named the Red Box, with RED an acronym for real electronic drums. Just as the cymbals bore a resemblance to the Alesis Surge series, the Red Box module had an identical external design to the Alesis DM-10. Internally, however, Pearl marketed this as unique. It offered one thousand sounds, one hundred preset kits, and space for one hundred programmable kits. It also had a memory switch allowing the user to switch to flash memory and add kits from third-partner drum software companies such as Toontrack and BFD (discussed later in this chapter). Numerous effects can be applied, although only one effect can be applied to each entire kit, and it is very limited in comparison with its high-end Japanese competitors.

Pearl were by no means the first to conceive this idea. In 2009, Ddrum introduced a kit that they call the Ddrum Hybrid, which combined their knowledge of drum triggers with their more recent entrance into acoustic drum manufacturing. The result was acoustic drums with internal triggers, which was little more than an integrated version of what they had offered previously.

Several years earlier the English company Jobeky, founded in 2005, unveiled their electro-acoustic drum range. To an untrained eye their kits appear to be regular acoustic kits with well-crafted birch shells, regular metal lugs, and metal hardware. Shell sizes and finishes are chosen from set configurations or made to custom order, but they tend to stick with standard sizes as expected on an acoustic kit. However, hidden among these shells are electronic triggers positioned within a sandwich of two steel plates with a layer of foam between to diminish acoustic noise. A discreet jack socket is the only exterior evidence that there are electronics involved, and with the unique triggering system, the nuances of acoustic

drumheads are closely replicated on these mesh heads with satisfying dynamics, sensitivity, lack of crosstalk (accidental triggering of
another drum's trigger by way of vibrations), and response. The kit
can be used in conjunction with any manufacturer's drum brain to
acquire the sounds of the user's preference. Furthermore, they have
developed cymbals that range in size from 12 inches to 14 inches
and allow a choke feature. They are only available with a single
zone, which means that a ride bell sound cannot be achieved as it
can with the likes of Roland or Yamaha cymbal pads.

Even earlier than that, the American company Boom Theory,
who were founded in 1991, created the Spacemuffins kits, which
were electronic kits built into acoustic drum shells to offer the
player a viable option for live performance when typical electronic
kits were visually unsuitable.

These kits certainly offered a more acceptable option for live
performance, but as one of the great benefits of an electronic kit
has traditionally been the smaller size, by creating a kit as big as an
acoustic, that particular benefit has been negated.

While other companies clamber over each other for the most
advanced drum modules, several companies are happy to avoid all
of that and simply focus on the trigger pads themselves.

One such company was Pintech. With their lightweight but robust titanium boron alloy shells and mesh heads featuring their EZ
Tune System and dual zone triggers, they certainly had a distinctive
product. Alongside these drums were their colorful Visulite acrylic
cymbal pads.

In 1989, American company Hart Dynamics operated in a
similar way by offering a range of different drum pads, including
steel shells that were for all intents and purposes real drums with
inbuilt triggers with their patented Kontrol Screen Magnum mesh
heads on top. They also offered Ecymbal pads, which were made
of bronze metal with a piece of rubber to help dampen the sound.
These were fixed onto regular cymbal stands.

Across the Atlantic, English company Wernick offered their
notepad series, which consisted of small, brightly colored trigger
pads played with sticks or hands and positioned neatly around the
acoustic drum set.

SOFTWARE

The home studio market has never been as big as it is today. Technology is improving at an incredible speed, making the facilities to achieve professional recordings in the bedroom more affordable every year. One key feature of this is the numerous sound libraries available to help convert the basic MIDI recording patterns into high-end audio recordings. The drum kit is one of the most time-consuming, difficult, and expensive aspects of studio recording, and it is no surprise that companies have worked hard to eliminate the need for costly studio time and session drummers. Drum loop libraries have been around for some time, allowing producers to add prerecorded drum samples into their own music. These are useful but limited, as the pattern is fixed and little editing can be done. The sound libraries that really became popular in the late 20th century and beyond were produced to work in conjunction with MIDI and were a massive advancement, as now a producer could either play their pattern on a MIDI controller such as an electronic drum kit or a keyboard instrument; program a rhythm into their software using a mouse; or use prerecorded beats and edit them within the software. These patterns could then be assigned to any number of different drum kits and edited in many ways by using different microphones such as overhead or ambient room microphones or adding effects. The basic home budget electronic kit could now be used to play a rhythm using its substandard sounds. The recorded MIDI would then dispense with these sounds and assign its own sounds so that the recording could take on a very polished and professional end result.

Many of these sound libraries are recorded using the highest-quality drums in the highest-quality studios with high-quality session drummers performing the notes. They are sampled at a variety of dynamics and timbres so that the recording options for the end user allow a realistic result.

Such companies include Toontrack with their Superior Drummer range offering sound samples in many styles from metal, jazz, and funk to country. They also sell MIDI packs for users without the ability to record their own patterns, containing MIDI files of drum patterns that can be loaded into the chosen software. The user then assigns the kit of their choice to them. BDF is another similar product with a fifty-five-gigabyte sample library demonstrating just how many samples the user will command with this package as well as equalization, compression, and other crucial mixing effects. Others include Steinberg's Groove Agent packages, M-audio Premium Session Drums that also offer Afro-Cuban percussion and orchestral percussion, and many others of varying library size and quality.

DRUM MACHINES AND SAMPLERS

This massive growth in electronic drums would never have occurred if it wasn't for drum machines paving the way and showing people what could be achieved by electronics with regard to rhythm. After all, so many jokes and criticisms are aimed at the human drummer's inability to keep perfect time that it might often seem that band leaders would rather a mechanical drummer as opposed to a flawed human drummer. To this end, the drum machine may appear to be the perfect answer. Of course this isn't quite true, as the human nuances are what make the most-loved rhythms so lovable, and in fact great drummers can play as accurately as a machine but with the advantage of limitless adaptability and flexibility. However, the market has necessitated machines since their inception, and there is no sign of this need disappearing in the near future.

Drum machines have changed drumming dramatically since the late 19th century, when instruments such as nickelodeon roll pianos began adding other instruments within their mystical wooden cabinets and stained glass windows. Around the time of World War I, the extra instruments were expanding, and it wasn't long before percussion found its way in there with tambourines and snare drum rolls augmenting the popular foxtrots of the day. These mechanical instruments housed actual drums with mechanically operated beaters that struck them to make sound rather than the prerecorded or electronically made sounds that were to be heard in later drum machines.

The first electronically created drum machine came in the 1930s thanks to a Russian/American joint venture. The Russian inventor Léon Theremin, possibly most famous for his Theremin instrument that was used by such famous bands as Led Zeppelin and Aerosmith, also invented the Rhythmicon in collaboration with musician Henry Cowell and presented it in 1932 at the New School for Social Research, where Cowell was employed. The Rhythmicon could perform complex rhythmic and harmonic patterns as determined by the selected fundamental pitch and subdivision to be used. It was very limited and sounds totally unusable in today's developed electronic drum market, but it was groundbreaking in the 1930s.

The next step came in 1949 when Californian Harry Chamberlain created the Rhythmate, which utilized a 1-inch magnetic tape loop that was read by a movable tape head that could play back any of the fourteen tape loops of prerecorded acoustic drum patterns. Each tape loop consisted of three separate patterns that could be selected by use of a lever, providing a total of forty-two different patterns in total as well as volume and speed variation.

Moving on from the 1940s, it was the organ manufacturers who were pushing the drum machine forward in an effort to allow the organist to become the whole band with one instrument. This concept has carried on to this day with the producer increasingly able to make do without a drummer. Carrying on from the Rhythmate, organ manufacturer Wurlitzer produced the Sideman in the late 1950s. This small cabinet was operated by a control panel to set the speed at which a wheel would turn and therefore the tempo of the rhythm would play. This wheel made contact with a series of triggers, which were set to play a specific drum pattern by completing the electrical circuit for that particular sound. With each individual circuit connected in the preset order and timing, the desired rhythms were created. The available patterns included popular rhythms of the day such as the waltz, tango, cha-cha, samba, bolero, shuffle, rhumba, or march. Such a device may have sent a shudder of fear down the spine of the working drummer, and rightly so, although the sounds were far from realistic at this point and therefore, drummers' careers were in no immediate danger.

Interest in drum machines was growing in the 1960s, and inventor Raymond Scott produced the Rhythm Synthesizer in 1960 and Bandito the Bongo Artist in 1963, having experimented with other synthesized instruments previously. Close on his heels was a newly formed Japanese company who were destined to become a huge synthesizer force over the next several decades. In 1963 Keio Gijutsu Kenkyujo Limited, later known as Korg, produced the DA20 DoncaMatic Disc Rotary Electric Auto Rhythm Machine. Just as the Sideman had done previously, the DoncaMatic used a disc to trigger rhythms and had a built-in amplifier to generate the sounds.

Up until this point, many of the drum machines had been valve amplifiers, which utilized a vacuum tube to increase the sound signals. One of the earliest drum machines to make use of the new transistor technology was the R-1 Rhythm Ace released in 1964 by Acetone, who later evolved into Roland. This machine enabled drum sounds to be triggered when buttons were pressed but failed commercially, as it didn't offer any preprogrammed drum patterns. This was remedied with the FR-1 Rhythm Ace, released in 1967 and offering sixteen drum patterns that could be played simultaneously by pressing two buttons together. It also allowed for modifying of the patterns with four extra buttons that could mute the bass drum, cymbal, cowbell, and clave. This machine soon became incorporated into Hammond organs and helped to create a good reputation for Acetone.

However, the politics at Acetone were unfavorable for the founder, Ikutaro Kakehashi, and he resigned from Acetone before setting up Roland in 1972 and releasing the TR77 Rhythm Box as their first product. This was followed by the TR33 and TR55, which although quite similar to the Acetone Rhythm Ace products, did help the company to successfully launch and progress to become the electronic drum leader as discussed previously. Also that year a big step was taken by the Italian Eko with their Computerhythm, which allowed users to program their own beats as well as use preprogrammed patterns. This made the machine very appealing, and it can be seen in the early parts of Jean-Michel Jarre's video for his 1978 Equinoxe, Part Four. In 1975 Roland released the TR66 Rhythm Arranger, which was a simple unit to supply rhythms as an accompaniment to such instruments as the organ. It played a series of popular rhythms much like the earlier drum machines from Wurlitzer and Korg. Meanwhile the Programmable Drum Set from PAiA was released, allowing patterns to be programmed, as the name suggests, but it did use ringing oscillators to create the sounds, which bore only a passing resemblance to a drum sound. It was, however, a sign of the direction that people were heading, and uniquely programmable beats were to be crucial for other companies to keep up. In 1978 Roland released the CR68 Human Rhythm Player, which incorporated the newer popular rhythms such as rock and disco as well as allowing fills to be added to the rhythms when a button was pressed, but still missed out on programmable patterns. Then came the CR78 Compurhythm, which was a more advanced alternative to the CR68. It consisted of many of the same features but also enabled the user to create their own beats, as Eko and PAiA had previously achieved, and store them by using step programming that allowed a pattern to be built up one beat at a time. This proved to be very successful and was used by popular music groups such as Genesis on their 1980 single "Duchess," which even featured the unit in the video.

Up until now the drum machines had all been analog, which meant the sounds were either recorded patterns on tape or electronically generated through combinations of white noise and sine waves. The resulting sounds of the latter option were a far cry from authentic drum noises, but they did successfully create sounds that were unique to each manufacturer and model, and therefore became very desirable to fans of that particular sound throughout the late 1970s, into the 1980s, and beyond.

At the dawn of the 1980s the digital revolution took hold, and Roger Linn was poised to make his mark on the sound of the decade. The first digital drum machine was released in 1980, and the Linn LM-1 was upon us. This machine used twelve digital samples of acoustic drum kits with the facility to alter the pitch of each sample. Drum patterns could be programmed in real time by tapping the rhythm into the machine in sequence as it is intended to be heard, as if playing a drum kit via the buttons; or step time. It also allowed quantizing, which altered the timing of notes so they fit perfectly onto the time grid. Another Linn feature was the shuffle facility, which allowed semiquavers to be distanced by percentages. For perfectly even semiquavers, the distance from the first semiquaver to the second and the second semiquaver to the third would be 50 percent each. To delay the second semiquaver slightly and achieve a swung effect, the percentage could be adjusted in 4 percent increments, such as fifty-eight/forty-two for example. With such excellent sounds and editing facilities, the Linn LM-1 was used by many groundbreaking popular artists of the era and played a significant part in shaping the sound of the 1980s even though only five hundred units were ever produced. At a cost of around $5,000 (£3,100) it was generally an instrument for the professional musician and can be clearly heard in many tracks from the 1980s, such as Human League's "Don't You Want Me, Baby."

This was followed in 1982 by the Linn LM-2, a cheaper version with fewer options for sound editing but featuring cymbal sounds that were absent on the first version, as well as greater programming possibilities.

Other manufacturers sprung up looking to capitalize on this new technology, such as Oberheim's popular DMX, but it was Roland who created possibly the longest-lasting impact with an analog approach, which appeared to be a backward step at first. In 1980 they released the TR-808, offering sixteen instruments and the facility to completely program rhythmic patterns. This aspect was excellent, but unfortunately the unrealistic analog sounds appeared to be instantly obsolete in the face of the Linn LM-1. It did enjoy some mainstream use, such as Marvin Gaye's "Sexual Healing" from 1982, but it soon faded away into the shadow of the digital drum machine, especially with the Linn-2, which offered greater programming with digital acoustic drum samples. It cost approximately one-fifth of the price for a Linn LM-1, but even that price was too much for such dated technology to many potential buyers. However, the TR-808 wasn't finished yet, as many urban artists turned to it with its incredibly cheap price and inbuilt sequencer with highly accurate timing. As it appeared on increasing tracks in the emerging hip-hop, techno, and modern R&B genres, it soon grew a solid reputation for its distinctive character in sounds that

Roger Linn with (1) LM-1, (2) LinnDrum, (3) Lin9000, (4) Akai MPC60, and (5) Akai MPC3000. Courtesy of Roger Linn.

helped carve out the iconic rhythms for these styles and remained in demand for several decades. This product was followed up in 1984 by the TR-909, which had a combination of sound samples and analog-generated sounds. This still didn't offer the same quality of sounds as other drum machines on the market and didn't sell particularly well, although just like its older brother the TR-808, it has enjoyed greater success since it was discontinued. It also incorporated the brand-new MIDI capabilities, which made it more compatible than previous machines.

Roger Linn then made a move to eclipse the Roland products even further when in 1984 he released the Linn 9000, although these were only produced in small numbers, as Linn ceased to operate two years later. It combined a drum machine with a sampler, which was visionary and predated the shift that other companies made in the 1980s. However, the software was riddled with problems, and as a result it was unreliable. Forat have since replicated this device with improved software and sampling memory with the Forat 9000.

Other companies moved in this same direction, with very user-friendly samplers such as the 1987 E-mu SP-1200, which was both a drum sequencer and sampler. This equipment allowed for a beat to be programmed from the onboard drum sounds as well as sampling external sounds and storing them within the machine to be sequenced with the programmed drum patterns. This meant that large elements of entire tracks could be easily constructed and stored in one piece of equipment, and the hip-hop fraternity embraced this completely. The sampling times were short, with the E-mu SP-1200 only offering ten seconds in total, but this soon increased as the technology allowed it, with manufacturers such as Akai and Forat producing great products. The sampler became a key component for producers and songwriters, and subsequently drummers who needed to emulate these studio sounds on the live stage. The drum machine had become yesterday's news, replaced by the sampler and the electronic drum.

Taking this even further, some manufacturers produced sample pads that were specifically designed to enable drummers to trigger samples with drumsticks. One of the most effective products was the Roland SPD-S sample pad, which had six big rubber pads to strike as well as three rim triggers. This enabled the drummer to use it in conjunction with an acoustic or electronic drum kit and easily trigger the desired sample from either onboard sounds or external sounds that had been imported. One drummer who really took this to an interesting level was Tony Verderosa. Using keyboards, acoustic drums, acoustic triggers, electronic drum pads, synthesizers, and samplers he created a kit that allowed him to become a one-man band with numerous harmonic and melodic sequences, triggered when he hit specific pads. As a result he could trigger a range of harmonic sequences while playing the drum grooves beneath it, resulting in a rich and full sound. He has

taken something that initially looked like a threat to drummers a
turned it around so that he, the drummer, now has no need for ti
other band members.

MOVING WITH THE TIMES

Since the inception of electronic percussion, many drummers have
embraced the technology and seen their careers flourish. A large
number of these did so through choice and a desire to discover new
possibilities on this technology. However, others were forced into
this area of drumming either physically or through fear.

One drummer who has entered the world of electronic drums
through necessity rather than choice is Rick Allen of the English
rock band Def Leppard. In 1984 on New Year's Eve, Allen crashed
his car and lost his left arm. When most drummers would have
relinquished their drumming career, Allen set about designing an
electro-acoustic drum kit to maximize his remaining limbs and compensate for the missing arm. He first used the popular Simmons
kits of the 1980s until those sounds were considered passé, and
he began sampling his own real drum sounds to trigger them. His
21st-century configuration involved four pedals for his left foot with
a regular hi-hat pedal and three electronic triggers. He then had the
normal bass drum pedal for the right foot. Along the top level, he
had four hi-hats set at varying degrees of openness to achieve all
necessary sounds even when the left foot is being used elsewhere
and unable to control the hi-hat pedal. He had two crashes and a
ride cymbal positioned centrally with a cowbell above the snare. He
then used electronics with the hands via a Ddrum snare trigger on
the acoustic main snare drum and three Hart Dynamics electronic
trigger pads. Allen also developed short percussion loops that were
triggered by playing the hi-hat to help fill out the rhythm. Ability to
trigger the phrases manually allows this extra dimension to be used
without being tied to a sequenced track. The left foot was often
demanded to replicate the parts that would have been played with
his left hand before the accident, and through utter determination and hard work developing his limb independence, his career

continued incredibly successfully. By using the available technology to his advantage, he was a great inspiration.

Other drummers felt forced into the electronics world through fear. These drummers have feared for their career just as Rick Allen did, but it had nothing to do with an amputated limb. In 1980 Roger Linn was the antithesis of the living, breathing drummer ,and many were slain by his Linn LM-1, never to return to the big stage. Some other drummers realized the potential for this technology and decided to work alongside it rather than against it. It was primarily the session players who were at risk. Those without regular employment who always relied on constant phone calls to get their next paying job knew that they had to stay current and relevant. Session drummer Omar Hakim is one such player. Having enjoyed a long and illustrious career with the likes of Sting, Weather Report, Miles Davis, and Madonna, he is a master of adaptation, a chameleon who can blend in with any situation and make it feel natural. Having dabbled with Syndrums and other early electronics, he learned to program the Linn LM-1 as well as utilizing Simmons, Ddrum, and Dynacord electronics before settling with Roland in the 1990s. This enabled him to stay at the cutting edge of music for many years.

Allan Schwartzberg is another example of such a player. Being a busy New York session drummer, he either had to stay on top of technology or fade away with the declining industry. Much of the work for studio players is often centered on advertising jingles, and these jingles usually follow popular music trends. If popular music is rooted in synthesizer music, then so will be the studio work, and therefore the string orchestra, drummer, pianist, horn players, and guitarists may be replaced by a single programmer. Schwartzberg was meticulous in his work, always tuning his drums to perfection when others may not have bothered, and always striving for the perfect part for the song. To this end he embraced technology, often combining acoustic cymbals with electronic drums at first, as was the norm due to poor 1980s electronic cymbals. This enabled him to enjoy a long career playing with countless artists such as Stan Getz, Gloria Gaynor, Peter Gabriel, and James Brown.

Jeff Porcaro, who was a legendary session drummer, having played with such artists as Steely Dan, Dire Straits, Michael Jackson, and Toto, also embraced the technology and helped stay at the forefront of modern drumming. He used various electronics on many tracks, such as the Syndrum on Carly Simon's 1977 "Nobody Does It Better" as well as programming the Linn LM-1 for the George Benson track "Turn Your Love Around" in 1982 before his untimely death in 1992.

These examples demonstrate drummers using the earlier technology either alongside acoustic drums or as an obviously synthetic alternative. Since the inception of the Roland TD-10, and even more so with the TD-20 and various expansions of this product, drummers no longer simply augment their acoustic kits with electronics. They are now confident to arrive at a studio session or live performance with only their electronic drum kit. As mentioned with Hakim, he embraced electronic drumming from the beginning but only in later years with the high-end Roland products was he able to exclusively use V-drums on a tour, starting with Madonna in the late 1990s.

Despite this incredible evolution since the 1970s, the acoustic kit still retains some earthy, mystical magic that is irreplaceable to many drummers. No synthesis or electrical trickery can replace the natural resonance and instant connection that a drummer can enjoy with a drum. Steeped in thousands of years of history, it will be a difficult instrument to replace. Will the electronic kit ever replace it? It is impossible to answer. But with every passing year, engineers and designers are bridging the gap between the two, and with each success, more drummers become electronic converts. Maybe in years to come this book will serve as an insight to the long-discarded archaic acoustic drum that is spoken of in reminiscent stories by kids' grandfathers recalling their youth. It is unlikely that this will ever happen, though. The electronic kit is an alternative option to the acoustic kit rather than a replacement, and they will both surely prove invaluable for studio and live drummers alike for their own particular benefits well into the future.

Chapter Nineteen

───────────○───────────

Recording Drums

THIS IS A VAST SUBJECT: THE TECHNOLOGIES, the people, the genres, and the political history that have sped up certain research, which in time benefited the recording studio, is worthy of an entire dedicated book. Therefore this chapter simply attempts to outline and make sense of some key areas that have seen the recording environment develop to its present state, one where the drum, specifically the notoriously difficult multivoice drum kit, can be recorded to achieve the best results. As much as possible, the specifics of electrical recording equipment technology have been avoided, only mentioned when directly impacting the drum kit.

Recorded sounds are irreversibly woven into the fabric of developed countrymen's lives today to the point that we sometimes have to actively pursue silence if respite is desired. Blaring televisions, radios, PA system announcements, Muzak (elevator, shopping department, or telephone call waiting music), and the teenager in the next seat whose overly loud MP3 player is audible for every passenger on the bus, all contribute to the noise of our lives. But in the beginning it was a revolution. When music was first recorded, it was the first time the performer could hear himself in the same way that others hear him. It was the first time that the drummer could analyze every fill, every note on the hi-hat, every snare backbeat for consistent dynamics, and with that insight become incredibly self-critical. But also, for the first time the sound was detached from the performance, and that sound was different. However it sounded in that concert hall, or in the recording booth, it takes on its own life when amplified from a speaker in another room, another town, or another country. No matter how full and powerful the high-quality drum kit sounded to the naked ear in the live room, captured badly it can sound like nothing more than old cardboard boxes. And so the relationship between the drummer and studio technology had begun, and equally important that between the drummer and the sound engineer or producer. The drummer had to find a way to get the sound that they wanted on the recording in the face of other people's opinions and technological limitations.

It also meant that music could cross geographical boundaries with ease. Blues was not refined to the southern states' blacks, jazz to New Orleans, hip-hop to the Bronx. Anybody could now consume the music of any cultural group and feel a sense of belonging and understanding with that group, and this meant that drummers could draw on worldwide sounds, rhythms, and techniques when developing their own sound.

The notion of capturing sound is not a new one. The 16th-century monk Rabelais wrote into one of his stories the concept of words frozen in time, only to thaw in the future and be heard again, the moral being that our actions will come back to haunt us. In the same century the Italian scientist Giovanni Battista della Porta believed that he had captured words by speaking into lead piping and covering the ends, only for the words to be heard when the covers were later removed. But real progress was made three hundred years later when the dawn of sound recording was inspired and motivated by telecommunications. Men such as Oberlin Smith, Valdemar Poulsen, Alexander Bell, and of course Thomas Edison, with his tin foil wrapped around a cylinder in 1877 to create the phonograph, were instrumental in these advances. Electrical recording and the use of magnetic tape was developed in the late 19th century, and it wasn't long before people started experimenting with recorded music on these formats.

As time went on, the formats that were sold to consumers changed through wax and celluloid cylinders of the late 19th century, wax/shellac discs in the early 20th century, vinyl discs in the late 1930s, audio cassettes in the 1970s, and then digital recording with its 0s and 1s, including the CD (compact disc) in 1983 and the DAT (digital audio tape) 1986. As the technology changed, and the equipment and recording methods with it, the result inevitably changed too. These eras are often so distinct that it is generally discernible even to the untrained ear as to which decade a musical recording was made from the drum sound alone.

But this had less effect on the drummer. What really changed the drummer's job was that which was constantly evolving at the other end of the line: the recording studio.

In the early 20th century, music recording really got going, but it was very rudimentary at first, and the drummer didn't comfortably fit into this new technology. Restrictions were felt in the early jazz records of music-recording infancy, as songs were short by necessity of format length. In fact, until the 1940s, the 10-inch 78-rpm single side lasting three minutes was common (a time frame still adhered to today on radio singles despite technology advancing), but when subtracting time for the common jazz form with a head melody at the start and then again at the end, left little time for the improvised solos that were fundamental to the style. This forced concise, brief solos that had maximum effect within their allotted time frame. It also meant minimizing dynamic range due to technological limitations in dealing with such volume increases as heard from the live musicians. This affected the drummer a great deal, because the recordings were achieved by the musicians playing into an acoustic recording horn, the small end of which was attached to a cutting needle that formed grooves on a cylinder or disc. The loud sound of a drum could knock the needle off course, meaning that many recordings omitted drumming, or the drummer had to play quietly on a muffled drum kit. The concise playing of soloists also affected the drummer, who lost the opportunity to develop and experiment within the solos, instead playing more solidly and simply. This effective and concise playing was to become one of the main attributes of the recording session drummer and has pervaded commercial drum parts until this very day, spurred further since the introduction of radio in the 1920s.

The 1920s also saw the introduction of the electrical microphone, which would make the recording horn obsolete. This technological advance allowed greater flexibility, opening up recording
opportunities to quieter instruments, and would soon mean that the
drummer could be heard much more clearly as well. One such early
example came in the late 1920s, when recalling Louis Armstrong's
desire to hear Zutty Singleton's drums more prominently in the mix
than was usually expected, while recording the track "Muggles."
"This was achieved by the producer holding the snare drum in his
hand and Zutty playing it right beside the microphone."[1]

In the early 20th century the major record labels began using purpose-built large studios such as EMI's Abbey Road, which
opened in London in 1931. This recording studio complex was
the largest of its kind, able to accommodate large orchestras with
baffling to prevent leakage and multimicrophone recording capabilities, which became commonplace by the1940s. The studios
underwent different phases concerning the acoustic treatment of
the rooms, but initially a very dead sound was required to give the
engineer more control over the final mix.

In the smaller, independent studios, however, it was more common to find a much smaller live room with one, two, or three allocated vocal microphones and then a similarly small number to pick
up the musicians. They placed themselves at appropriate positions
from the microphone depending on the volume of their instrument,
playing live as a group and capturing the full excitement of their
performance.

By the late 1940s magnetic tape was introduced to the studios,
and editing became much easier by cutting and sticking together
again. This now meant that a mistake could be chopped out and
different sections stuck together. The search for the perfect performance hurtled onward.

Into the 1950s multitrack recording was being experimented
with and overdubbing became possible, a technique that was
adopted by guitarist Les Paul, who created tracks by layering up
instruments one at a time, a commonplace technique today. This
was actually following a trend set by the Hollywood film studios

that had already been doing this. The technique allowed musicians to record separately. They didn't even have to meet each other, as the drummer could record on Monday, the bass player on Tuesday, and so on. The musicians didn't even have to be in the same city or country, as the files could be transported to other studios. This was no longer a live ensemble performance. The distinction between live and studio had been pushed even further apart.

Of course, music was still often recorded with the musicians grouped together in one room, but things were changing. A sign of how quickly recording was evolving was demonstrated on the film music stage at 20th Century Fox, where Hal Blaine was the drummer for the 1961 recording of *Blue Hawaii's* soundtrack with Elvis Presley. The film studio technicians wanted to record with the traditional microphone method, whereas the rock 'n' roll music required for the film needed the latest multimicrophone setup with isolation baffles. Blaine had to teach them how to do this, which tested their equipment to the limit trying to set up extra microphones when they only had four track-recording machines. The film studios were now chasing music studios that had the upper hand, having developed these techniques for the burgeoning rock 'n' roll bands that were so popular.

One artist who made great use of the recent ability to record tracks individually to harness his great musical talent was Stevie Wonder. He used the studio environment in the late 1960s and 1970s to record many of the instruments himself, one track at a time. He was subsequently revered for his drumming ability and feel. Another well-known case in point was Mike Oldfield's "Tubular Bells" from 1973.

So now with microphones and multiple tracks at the engineer's disposal the sound could be evenly distributed across an orchestra or band, allowing the drums to have a greater prominence, which was desired, as their prominence was increasing with the ever more raucous music being produced. A band might be able to afford an entire microphone for the drums alone, but this still left a noticeable lack of the bass drum's low frequencies.

One popular remedy in the early 1960s was found in places such as Philadelphia's Cameo Parkway studios, which employed

Joe Tarsia, who later created Sigma Sound Studio, where such artists as Chubby Checker were creating hit records. House session musicians were employed, often with drummers Bobby Gregg and Ellis Tollin supplying the rhythms, and the drum sounds were captured by two microphones; one placed on the bass drum and one overhead to capture the overall kit sound. The recording sessions of this era could be intense, with several tracks recorded in a single day. The musicians had to read charts while playing with precision throughout the entire song without any correction in the postperformance stages.

Such an approach was used extensively during this time and has become popular again, with amateur drummers utilizing basic home recording equipment in an attempt to maximize the potential of limited microphones. A two-microphone technique has evolved to be known colloquially as the recorderman technique, from the user name of an advocate of this technique on recording chat Internet forums. In basic form it uses two condenser or ribbon microphones placed equidistantly from both the snare drum and the bass drum beater with one sitting slightly behind the drummer and one above them, the principle being to capture the drums as heard by the drummer.

Another technique that became famous was that of engineer Glyn Johns, who worked with the cream of rock bands in the 1960s and beyond, such as the Rolling Stones, the Who, Eric Clapton, the Beatles, and Led Zeppelin. Of course John Bonham is well known for his monstrous rock drum sound and the power it gave to Led Zeppelin's music. But someone had to capture that power and present it in all its glory with equipment that was basic by today's standards. Glyn Johns captured those sounds using just four microphones, and his technique is largely based on just two overheads to produce a very open drum sound. The overheads are positioned with one up slightly off center above the snare drum pointing down toward the bass drum pedal and one off to the right, just above and beyond the floor tom pointing back toward the hi-hats. Both of these microphones are equidistant from the center of the snare drum batter head, which eliminates phase cancellation problems where certain frequencies disappear in the mix. These are panned a certain degree in opposite directions to create a stereo image. Dedicated bass drum and snare drum microphones are then positioned to pick up the low bass frequencies and the clarity of the important snare drum. This technique records the drums in their true colors and leaves few options for postproduction fixes. This means that for the result to work, a great-sounding drum kit, played well in a great-sounding room, is more important than ever.

Glyn's brother, Andy Johns, also played a part in one of the most famous and experimental Led Zeppelin drum sounds. The 1971 track "When the Levee Breaks" was recorded at Headley Grange in Hampshire, England, with the help of the Rolling Stones' mobile recording studio. Andy had wanted to try an idea one evening using Page's Binson Echorec device and two other microphones with limiters over them. They positioned Bonham's kit in the hall of the former poorhouse, and he began to play it with his usual power and ferocity. The sounds thundered along the hall and into the microphones, creating the famously huge drum sound that has since become iconic. With the addition of Jimmy Page and John Paul Jones accompanying on guitars, and Robert Plant singing a 1920s Memphis tune, it soon became the piece of music we know today as "When the Levee Breaks," so the reverberating drum sound led the way for a classic rock track being created.

The previously mentioned Stevie Wonder was another example who used a similar three-microphone method to record himself on the drums with tracks such as the 1972 "Superstition," whose drums are instantly recognizable and actually start the track. The evidence that these techniques picked up the whole drum kit, warts and all, is seen on this track when the squeak from the bass drum pedal is audible. This is also evident on some of Bonham's tracks, such as the 1970 "Since I've Been Loving You." Although this is technically a recording faux pas by modern standards, it may also be viewed as part of the character of the track. These rudimentary setups achieved an instantly recognizable sound imbued with the performer's great feel but also a warmth that is enhanced by hearing the whole kit as it was, bass drum pedal squeaks and all, rather than a sanitized version that may have occurred in later eras.

We also find the same approach in the studios that created many of the hits that are still loved today, displaying the fact that a long-lasting classic track has much more to do with songwriting and performance than the technical aspects of sound production, although it would be foolish to discount the importance of good sound reproduction altogether. The Stax studio in Memphis was an old theater in which the likes of Al Jackson performed on a combination of Rogers and Ludwig drums with heads that were rarely changed. The drum and microphone positions were not altered or experimented with for a long period, possibly with the adage of "If it ain't broke, don't fix it" in mind. Jackson used a wallet resting on the snare to dampen the drum's resonance, and the whole sound was captured via an overhead and a bass drum microphone. The RCA capsule ribbon microphone sat around the hi-hat while the bass drum microphone, also an old RCA model, sat in front of the bass drum, which retained its resonant head. This evolved somewhat later when the technology improved, but not before many great hits were recorded like this.

Up in Detroit the Motown drummers were captured with a similar method, using minimal microphones and only a two-track mixing desk prior to 1961, before gaining three tracks and then eight tracks later in the decade before sixteen-track mixing came along. The drums were often sharing tracks with other percussion instruments, and leakage between different instruments was all part of the sound. The drummer's ethos was similar to that at Stax, with rarely tuned or changed drumheads. However, sound experimentation did occur, with blankets stuffed into the bass drum, the resonant head removed, and a microphone placed inside the drum. Snare drum microphone placement was trialled very close to the batter head as well as at the side by the airhole. The actual snare strands were taped to the resonant head of the drum to achieve a crisper sound, and tissue was stuck to the batter head to deaden the sound.

As mentioned previously, the KISS principle, "Keep It Simple, Stupid," was adopted, which encouraged the drummers to play sympathetically for the song and not personal adoration. In fact,

looking back at many great studio session drummers through Al
Jackson, Benny Benjamin, Earl Palmer, Hal Blaine, Jim Keltner,
Bernard Purdie, and Steve Gadd, to name just a few, they all have
impeccable timing, great feel, and the sympathetic ear. This enables them to play for the song and create simple yet magical drum
parts that make the song work to its optimum level.

Although many of the great songs that were churned out by
the artists mentioned above were recorded live with the band in
the room using entire takes, multitrack recording did offer another
technique as well as recording on separate tracks. The technique
known as "punching in" allowed musicians to rerecord imperfect
sections of their individual track by punching in to that particular
section to record over it. A poorly timed drum fill could be rerecorded while preserving the remainder of the drum track. This
enhanced the musician's desire for perfection, taking the recorded
result further away from a natural live performance. So with the
ability to layer extra drum parts on, add effects, and rerecord until perfection was achieved, music could now be recorded that
couldn't practically be performed live. This aspect has not gone over
the heads of drummers or producers.

However, one producer who went for that layered effect of extra
percussion and various other sounds but without necessarily relying
on punching in or overdubs was Phil Spector. In the 1960s Spector
famously created records that utilized what became known as the
wall of sound, in which he was aiming for a piece of pop music that
had a powerful, dramatic Wagnerian effect. But rather than record
individual parts and layer them up one by one, Spector would, to
the frustration of many seasoned session musicians, gather many
players in one room and painstakingly work until the perfect sound
was achieved. Everybody would sit waiting as he requested yet
another take, having asked for a drum to be repositioned several
inches to enable a superior capture of sound. The large ensembles
on some sessions included several guitars, upright basses, and even
drum kits with session drummers such as Hal Blaine and Earl
Palmer providing the rhythms. Interestingly the drums were often
omitted from his earlier recordings due to unsatisfactory results:
"I'd go out of my mind, spend five or six hours, trying to get a drum

sound, and it's really hard on the musicians because they're play-ing the same thing over and over. But I figured . . . I just tried to imagine one mike over everything, how it would be."[2] This is an interesting insight into the vision of the man who created such an innovative and huge sound at that time.

The wall of sound greatly inspired the Beach Boys' album *Pet Sounds*, which in turn inspired the Beatles' album *Revolver* at this time of studio innovation and experimentation. And so the Beatles were also to become instrumental in pushing the expectations of what could be achieved in the recording studio during the 1960s. As so much of their work was recorded at Abbey Road, they, or at least the engineers working with them, such as Geoff Emerick, had to cut through the endless red tape that was imposed on artists by EMI. Strict guidelines were enforced on such technical issues as the level of bass frequencies that were allowed on a recording and how close the bass drum microphone was allowed to be to the bass drum. Emerick's philosophy was to develop more focus on the sounds rather than a big, ambient overall wash of sound such as Spector's, and he was eventually granted permission from EMI to place the microphone three inches from the bass drumhead; but only for Beatles sessions.

The 1966 track "Paperback Writer" featured toms that had mi-crophones positioned above and below, large ribbon microphones as overheads, and an AKG D20 microphone to capture the bass drum, which had the front head completely removed. Cushions were placed inside to deaden the sound, a common technique today.

The 1966 track "Strawberry Fields Forever" also pushed boundaries, combining two tape recordings, one sped up and one slowed down, until the keys matched. Many effects were added to this track, such as reversed cymbals. By 1967 the revolutionary album *Sgt. Pepper's Lonely Hearts Club Band* was released and the studio environment would never be the same again. Emerick was under strict instructions to achieve a groundbreaking sound, and he did just that. Techniques such as removing the resonant bass drumhead to place a microphone right inside the drum nearer the beater to record more attack of the drum and less of the resonance were utilized, as well as moving the microphones closer to the other drums before processing the entire sound. The result was a focused and tight sound in contrast to those boomy, ambient Led Zeppelin recordings. He even added a microphone to the underside of the snare drum to pick up more snap from the snare strands. Sounds were also enhanced by draping tea towels over the drumheads for a very warm, muted sound, and adding compression to some of the drum kit sounds.

The Abbey Road facilities offered only four track recorders, but this limitation was partly sidestepped by using multiple machines to record four tracks, which were then mixed down to just one or two tracks on another machine, therefore leaving two or three tracks unused. Of course once the tracks were mixed down to one track, any mixing of that track affected every instrument on it. Therefore sounds were often panned to the left or right in groups, such as the rhythm section being mixed together. Incidentally Paul Mc-Cartney's bass guitar lines were often added to recordings toward the end of the process in this era to allow a more melodic and appropriate part to be created.

As technology continued to progress, the Beatles were using eight-track mixing for later albums such as *Abbey Road*, but back in America things had progressed even further.

The first stereophonic recording was made in 1943, but at that time the means to record was still limited by lack of channels, and so the drum kit felt little benefit of this. Techniques such as that of Glyn Johns allowed some panning or, as mentioned with the Beatles entire drum kits, would be panned to one side, but in the late 1960s the studio began to offer sixteen-track recording and close microphone techniques, meaning the drummer could have his kit panned across the speakers in such a manner as to allow the listener to hear him as if he was in front of them, with the hi-hats heard on one side of the room while the floor tom and ride sounded from the other side, and so on.

One of the first albums to be released utilizing this new sixteen-track technology was the Frank Zappa album *Hot Rats* in 1969, a hugely experimental album that enjoyed many overdubs, including drum fills and tape speed manipulation. Here the drummers, including John Guerin, were given the luxury of four dedicated tracks; not just four microphones, but actual individual tracks, which allowed the two overheads to be panned opposite sides as well as a bass and snare drum microphone to be treated individually.

This was a huge leap forward for drum sounds, as individual drums could be given greater or less prominence in the mix and even have effects applied to a single voice of the kit rather than the whole sound: a touch of reverb on the snare drum, the gating of tom-toms, or whatever was required within the seemingly limitless possibilities. However, this close-up analysis of each drum exposed some unwanted truths. A multitude of overtones, rings, and vibrations were audible, and anything but a well-tuned drum kit with recently fitted heads was a major offender in the overall sound. A new pressure was upon the drummer to treat their instrument as carefully as the other instrumentalists. No more could they hide beneath the cacophony of sound produced by the rock band in full flow. They were now subjected to intense analysis and had to rise to the challenge. Of course many failed on this part, or alternatively, many actively sought a less resonant sound to those mentioned earlier. And so sales of gaffa tape increased as drums were furiously taped and objects were stuck to the drumhead, such as tissue, tea towels (as with Ringo Starr), wallets, cigarette packets, and just about anything else that achieved the desired sound. Of course, this had been done before, but now with the closer examination of individual drum sounds it became more and more prominent. These were not entirely new ideas when considering the American composer William Russell, who in 1933 asked for "placing handkerchief over the head of a side drum, placing a piece of paper over the drumhead, and scratching strings (snares) lengthwise along winding, with a coin held like a banjo pick."[3]

Recorded drums were therefore sounding less and less like an actual drum, but it did help to spark an obsession in drummers to possess the perfect-sounding instrument, which led to a working knowledge of drum production that would have previously been reserved for drum manufacturers. Drummers were soon to become interested in the wood that their shell was made from, how many plies were involved, the type of rims used, and so on. This was a point taken up by the drum manufacturers, who began to market their products specifically for this market. One example was the Ludwig Octaplus concert toms, mentioned previously, which Hal Blaine instigated. With only a single head, these produced fewer overtones, which made them much more manageable in the studio. There was also a move in the 1980s to market the birch drum kits as studio kits due to their warmer and more focused sound, such as the Yamaha RC9000 played by Steve Gadd.

But back to the early 1970s, when equalization was being added to individual drums, the need arose to avoid leakage between each microphone. After all, if heavy compression was added to one drum, it might be undesirable for another drum to have been picked up in that microphone and received the treatment of compression inadvertently. The solution was to place the drum kit in a separate room that was acoustically treated to have very little natural reverberation. This left the drummer isolated and in a very unnatural situation. Of course, recording in this isolated way necessitated the use of headphones. This further added to the unnatural feeling during a drummer's performance, who was now hearing a processed, controlled sound of his drum kit rather than the unrefined, thunderous reverberations to which he was accustomed.

Playing in isolation, to a metronome, and possibly without any other instruments was an unfamiliar and clinical approach, far removed from the free-spirited mental state that was previously achieved when playing with other musicians in a comfortable environment allowing one's self to be emotionally moved. It can take great mental focus and discipline to achieve the precision required while maintaining a natural feel, although experienced studio professionals are in demand for this very attribute.

Unfortunately many drummers could not perform to the same standard in these conditions, but it also became evident that the ambience and room sound of the drum kit was a crucial factor in cementing the various voices as one whole instrument. This led to drummers returning to the main live rooms in studios but being packed into a fortress of screens to separate their sound from the other instruments.

Into the 1970s twenty-four-track recorders became common and the disco sound of Philadelphia benefited, as previously discussed, with Joe Tarsia at the fore. Here the wallet on the snare and tissue on the single-headed toms was well used, as well as removing the bass drum's resonant skin and placing pillows inside for a dead sound with a microphone positioned inside to capture it. The snare drum was subjected to a great deal of gate, an effect that is set to automatically control the length of a note, and snare buzz effects were manually added during the mixing process. And so the dead drum in a dead sounding room was at its peak, resulting in a very clinical and focused sound.

These advances showed the music world how good drums could sound in stereo with better microphone placement and individual treatment of drums. With whetted appetites the search continued for technology that allowed more control of each individual drum, and it wasn't long before two twenty-four-track recorders were being slaved together to offer forty-eight tracks. By the late 1970s thirty-two-track and even forty-eight-track recorders had been developed.

The 1980s arrived, and incredibly distinctive drum sounds were produced, many of which embraced electronic sounds and went further from a real-sounding drum kit. One very famous sound that really started on a session at London's Townhouse Studios for Peter Gabriel's *Intruder* was that of the Phil Collins/Hugh Padgham team who met during this recording. The session was immediately unusual for Collins, as Gabriel had opted for a sound free from any metallic percussion, so the cymbals were discarded. An SSL console was being used, which allowed a novel feature of compressors and noise gates on each individual track. It also offered reversed talkback to enable two-way communications between the band and producer in the control room via a hanging room microphone in the live room. This microphone was heavily compressed so as to pick up voices from all around the room. During an incident of Padgham/Collins conversation, Collins began to play the drums, which were picked up through the heavily compressed talkback microphone, and the resulting, albeit accidental, sound instantly got a reaction from Padgham.

The 1981 Collins track "In the Air Tonight" is immediately recognizable and famous for the distinctive fill that allows the drums
to take over from the Roland CR78 drum machine. Collins played
the fill spontaneously during the sixth take of the song and viewed
it with indifference, only keeping it because the rest of the take
was the best. The majority of the sound is taken from the ambient
Neumann U87 room microphones with the Shure SM57 snare
microphone, and Neumann U47 bass drum microphone allowing
just a little closer attention on those important drums. But what
we hear from those sessions are the ambient microphones heavily
compressed and gated to create a huge, barking drum sound, synonymous with 1980s Phil Collins.

Another big change in the same decade was the introduction of
MIDI in 1983 as discussed in greater depth in chapter 18. Drum
machines were now taking over as the ultimate in clean, sterile, and
precise drum patterns in a way that was hard for a human drummer to compete with. The rhythmic patterns that were perceived
as drum kits now rarely sounded anything like the sound produced
by a real drum kit as heard in the same room as the instrument.
The general consumers accepted this sound upon hearing the low-
frequency "thud" on beat one and three, as the bass drum, just as
they heard the higher-frequency "chit" sound across all the eighth
notes as the hi-hats.

But it didn't mean that drummers were obsolete. One interesting example of technology and performance living side by side is
found in the 1987 Michael Jackson album *Bad,* which saw session
drummer J.R. Robinson, who was by now playing Yamaha drums,
integrate his acoustic sound with this new technology. Quincy
Jones and engineer Bruce Swedien had plans for this album to mix
acoustic playing with programmed drums, so Robinson endured an
exercise of total discipline when he was asked to play the repetitive groove of some tracks for over ten minutes without any fills or
variations. This was all recorded to a skeletal backing track without
any real idea of the intended song melody or structure. Robinson's
loop of drums was now available for the producers to mix with the
programmed sounds to create a hybrid sound that proved very suc-

cessful. This was a long way from the band playing live in one room in the earlier days of recording.

Even further from the days of live recording, when several tracks might be recorded in a single day by prolific session musicians, successful rock bands were increasingly spending more time and money looking for the new perfect sound. The self-titled Metallica album from 1991 was an extreme example of a highly produced and studio-induced drum sound that was agonized over for days, with the room treated with hard surfaces to remove any soft, absorbing surface before extensive experimentation with microphone positioning, which resulted in around twenty separate tracks for the drum kit. The actual playing of Lars Ulrich was very broken into individual sections, or even specific bars of drumming recorded many times over before moving on to the next section. The resultant mass of drum parts could then be pieced together to form a whole part.

By the late 1980s computer recording software was starting to look slightly promising, and by the late 1990s it was finding its way into a majority of professional recording studios with Pro Tools becoming the standard shortly after the turn of the millennium. With the likes of Cubase, Logic, and Pro Tools, the possibility to manipulate both the sound of the drums and the actual performance itself became huge, with features such as Pro Tools' Beat Detective, which could automatically slice up a drum pattern and reorder the small segments into a perfectly timed sequence so as to clean up a messy drum part.

Of course, when something moves a long way from where it originally started, which might be considered progress by many, there will always be some who react, making a claim that the elements that made the original article so treasured have diminished to such an extent that it is now unrecognizable. In this case, the live musical performance involving real human musicians interacting with each other and creating something magical, which happened to be captured on a microphone, has been overanalyzed and disseminated to such a point that what we are often left with is a cold and sterile version, devoid of human emotion and excitement. It may be a valid point, and it certainly cannot be denied that some people today can become viewed as great musicians or vocalists that would never have been so in past decades thanks to studio technology allowing them to be corrected.

But a very positive aspect is that with digital files today, such as WAVs and MP3s, these compressed formats of high-quality sound have allowed many drummers to market themselves as session drummers from their own home studios with the finished drum track easily transferred through the Internet to the client. The drummer, who in many cases has also become sound engineer and producer, can record in their own specifically designed studio with complete control over the result and the manner in which it is achieved. Without the hiring of expensive studios and the staff that come with it, the cost is also dramatically reduced.

Furthermore, with the increased quality and ease of recording with MIDI drums through a USB connection used in conjunction with drum sample software, as discussed in chapter 18, the electronic drum kit is increasingly found at recording sessions, which is even more readily available to the budget or home studio.

So today with all the technology in the world to record the perfect performance with the perfect drum sound, the decision remains as to whether the desired effect is that of a musician or a machine, and that might come down to a choice made by either sonic or moralistic reasoning.

NOTES

1. Pekka Gronow and Ilpo Saunio, *An international history of the recording industry* (London: Cassell, 1998), 49–50.

2. Richard Williams, *Phil Spector: Out of his head* (New York: Outerbridge and Lazard Inc, 1974), 70–71.

3. James Blades, *Percussion instruments and their history* (London, UK: Faber & Faber, Ltd, 1970), 417.

Bibliography

BOOKS

Afolayan, Funso. *Cultures and customs of South Africa.* Westport, CT: Greenwood Press, 2004.

Ahlbäck, Tore, and Jan Bergman, eds. *The Saami shaman drum.* Abo, Finland: The Donner Institute for Research in Religious and Cultural History, 1991.

Aldridge, John. *Guide to vintage drums.* Fullerton, CA: Centerstream Publishing, 2000.

Allen, Matthew. *Identity and resistance in Okinawa.* Lanham, MD: Rowman and Littlefield Publishers, 2002.

Anyidoho, Kofi, and James Gibbs, eds. *FonTomFrom: Contemporary Ghanaian literature, theatre and film.* Amsterdam, the Netherlands: Rodopi B.V., 2000.

Ardinger, Barbara. *Pagan every day: Finding the extraordinary in our ordinary lives.* San Francisco, CA: Red Wheel/Weiser, LLC, 2006.

Austerlitz, Paul. *Merengue: Dominican music and Dominican identity.* Philadelphia, PA: Temple University Press, 1997.

Avila, Jose Francisco, and Tomas Alberto Avila. *Garifuna world.* Providence, RI: Milenio Associates, LLC, 2008.

Azadehfar, Mohammad Reza. *Rhythmic structure in Iranian music.* Tehran, Iran: Tehran Art University Press, 2006.

Bacus, Elizabeth A., Ian C. Glover, and Vincent C. Pigott, eds. *Uncovering South East Asia's past: Selected papers from the 10th international*

415

conference of the European association of South East Asian archaeologists. Singapore: NUS Press, 2006.

Badeau, John Stothoff, and John Richard Hayes. *The genius of Arab civilization: Source of renaissance.* New York: New York University Press, 1975.

Baines, Anthony. *The Oxford companion to musical instruments.* New York: Oxford University Press, 1992.

Baker, Mona, and Gabriela Saldanha. *Routledge encyclopedia of translation studies.* Abingdon, UK: Routledge, 1998.

Banham, Martin. *The Cambridge guide to theatre.* Cambridge, UK: Cambridge University Press, 1998.

Barthakur, Dilip Ranjan. *The music and musical instruments of North Eastern India.* New Delhi, India: Mittal Publications, 2003.

Bauer, Marion. *Music through the ages.* New York: G. P. Putnam's Sons, 1967.

Bebey. Francis. *African music. A people's art.* London: George G. Harrap and Co. Ltd., 1975.

Beck, John. *Encyclopedia of percussion.* New York: Garland Publishing, 1995.

Behnke, Alison. *Angkor Wat.* Minneapolis, MN: Twenty-First Century Books, 2009.

Ben-Ezer, Gadi. *The Ethiopian Jewish exodus: Narratives of the migration journey to Israel 1977–1985.* London, UK: Routledge, 2002.

Berhaus, Günter, ed. *New perspectives on prehistoric art.* Westport, CT: Praeger Publishers, 2004.

Berry, Mary Elizabeth. *Hideyoshi.* Cambridge, MA: President and Fellows of Harvard College, 1982.

Black, Jeremy A. *Sumerian grammar in Babylonian theory.* Rome, Italy: Editrice Pontificio Istituto Biblico, 2004.

Blacking, John, Reginald Byron, and Bruno Nettl. *Music, culture and experience: Selected papers of John Blacking.* Chicago: The University of Chicago Press, 1995.

Blades, James. *Percussion instruments and their history.* London, UK: Faber & Faber, Ltd., 1970.

Blades, James, and Jeremy Montagu. *Early percussion instruments.* Oxford, UK: Oxford University Press, 1976.

Blaine, Hal, and David Goggin. *Hal Blaine and the wrecking crew: The story of the most recorded musician.* Michigan: Rebeats Publications, 2003.

Blier, Susan Preston. *African Vodun: Art, psychology and power.* Chicago: The University of Chicago Press, 1995.

Blum, Stephen, Philip V. Bohlman, and Daniel M. Newman, eds. *Ethnomusicology and modern music history.* Champaign, IL: Illini Books, 1993.

Boland, Roy. *Culture and customs of El Salvador.* Westport, CT: Greenwood Press, 2001.

Booth, Janice, and Philip Briggs. *Rwanda.* Buckinghamshire, UK. Bradt Travel Guides Ltd., 2001.

Bordwell, David, Janet Staiger, and Kristen Thompson. *The classical Hollywood cinema: Film style and mode of production to 1960.* London: Routledge, 1988.

Bower, Harry A. *Imperial method for the drum.* Philadelphia, PA: John Church, 1898.

Bowles, Edmund A. *Timpani: A history in pictures and document.* Hillsdale, NY: Pendragon Press, 2002.

Bowman, Rob. *Soulsville U.S.A.: The story of Stax records.* New York: Schirmer Trade Books, 2003.

Bradley, Lloyd. *This is reggae music: The story of Jamaica's music.* New York: Grove Press, 2001.

Brock, Colin. *The Caribbean in Europe: Aspects of the West Indian experience in Britain, France and the Netherlands.* London: Frank Cass and Company, Ltd., 1986.

Broughton, Simon, Mark Ellingham, and Richard Trillo. *World music: Latin and North America, Caribbean, India, Asia and Pacific.* London, Rough Guides Ltd., 2000.

Buchner, Alexander. *Musical instruments through the ages.* London: Spring Books, 1961.

Budofsky, Adam. *The drummer: 100 years of rhythmic power and invention.* New Jersey: Modern Drummer Publications, 2006.

Burgh, Theodore W. *Listening to the artifacts: Musical culture in ancient Palestine.* New York: T & T Clark International, 2006.

Burkett, Delbert Royce. *An introduction to the New Testament and the origins of Christianity.* Cambridge, UK: Cambridge University Press, 2002.

Cai, Zong-qi. *Configurations of comparative poetics: Three perspectives on western and Chinese literary criticism.* Honolulu: University of Hawaii Press, 2002.

Camara, Ryan M., and Kalani. *West African drum and dance. A Yankadi-Macrou celebration.* Los Angeles, CA: Alfred Publishing, 2007.

Cameron, Clayton. *Brushworks.* New York: Carl Fischer, 2003.

Campbell, Murray, Clive A. Greated, and Arnold Myers. *Musical instruments*. Oxford, UK: Oxford University Press, 2004.

Candelaria, Cordelia Chávez, Arturo J. Aldama, and Peter J. García. *Encyclopedia of Latino popular culture*. Westport, CT: Greenwood Press, 2004.

Cangany, Harry. *The great American drums and the companies that made them, 1920–1969*. Cedar Grove, NJ: Modern Drummer Publications, 2000.

Carboni, Stefano. *Venice and the Islamic world, 828–1797 (English Ed.)*. Paris: Gallimard, 2007.

Chanan, Michael. *Repeated takes: A short history of recording and its effects on music*. London: Verso, 1995.

Chang, Chan Sup, and Nahn Joo Chang. *The Korean management system: Cultural, political, economic foundations*. Westport, CT: Greenwood Publishing Group, 1994.

Chang, Kang-i Sun, and Stephen Owen, eds. *The Cambridge history of Chinese literature, Vol. 2*. Cambridge, UK: Cambridge University Press, 2010.

Chang, Kevin O'Brien, and Wayne Chen. *Reggae routes: The story of Jamaican music*. Philadelphia, PA: Temple University Press, 1998.

Chapuis, Oscar. *A history of Vietnam: From Hong Bang to Tu Duc*. Westport, CT: Greenwood Press, 1995.

Ching-Chih, Liu. *A critical history of new music in China*. Hong Kong: The Chinese University Press, 2010.

Christensen, Thomas Street, ed. *The Cambridge history of Western music theory*. Cambridge: Cambridge University Press, 2002.

Cohan, Jon. *Star sets: Drum kits of the great drummers*. Milwaukee, WI: Hal Leonard Corporation, 1995.

Connor, Mary E., ed. *Asia in focus: The Koreas*. Santa Barbara, CA: ABC-CLIO, LLC, 2009.

Cooan, Michael D., ed. *The Oxford history of the Biblical world*. New York: Oxford University Press, 1998.

Cook, Rob. *The complete history of the Leedy Drum Company*. Fullerton, CA: Centerstream Publishing, 1993.

Cook, Rob. *The Rogers book*. Alma, MI: Rebeats Publications, 1999.

Crabtree, Philip D., and Donald H. Foster. *Sourcebook for research in music (2nd ed)*. Bloomington, IN: Indiana University Press, 2005, 1993.

Crane, Larry, ed. *Tape op: The book about creative music recording, Vol. 2*. Sacramento, CA: Tape Op Publishing, 2010.

Crawford, Harriet E.W. *Sumer and the Sumerians*. Cambridge, UK: Cambridge University Press, 1991.

Crook, Larry. *Brazilian music: Northeastern traditions and the heartbeat of a modern nation*. New York: ABC-CLIO, 2005.

Crook, Larry. *Focus: Music of northeast Brazil*. New York: ABC-CLIO, 2005.

Dagan, Esther A. *The heartbeat of Africa*. Montreal, Canada: Galerie Amrad African Art Publications, 1993.

Dales, George F., Jonathan M. Kenoyer, and Leslie Alcock. *Excavations at Mohenjo Daro, Pakistan: The pottery*. Philadelphia, PA: The University Museum, 1986.

Daniel, Eric D., C. Denis Mee, and Mark H. Clark, eds. *Magnetic recording: The first hundred years*. Piscataway, NJ: IEEE Press, 1999.

Davies, Carol Boyce, ed. *Encyclopedia of the African diaspora: Origins, experience and culture, Vol. 1*. Santa Barbara, CA: ABC-CLIO, 2008.

Davis, Richard H. *Worshipping Şiva in medieval India: Ritual in an oscillating universe*. Delhi, India: Motilal Banarsidass, 2000.

Davison, Julian, and Bruce Granquist. *Balinese temples*. Jakarta, Indonesia: Periplus Editions (HK) Ltd., 1999.

Dearling, Robert. *The ultimate encyclopedia of musical instruments*. London: Carlton Books, 1996.

Dechend, Hertha Von, and Giorgio De Santillana. *Hamlet's mill: An essay investigating the origins of human knowledge and its transmission though myth*. Jaffrey, NH: David R. Godine, Publisher, 1977.

Deva, Bigamudre Chaitanya. *Indian music*. New Delhi: New Age International (P) Ltd., Publishers, 1995.

Dillon, Michael. *China: A cultural and historical dictionary*. Richmond, Surrey, UK: Curzon Press, 1998.

Divekar, Pandit Hindraj, and Robin D. Tribhuwan. *Rudra Veena: An ancient string musical instrument*. New Delhi, India: Discovery Publishing House, 2001.

Doniger, Wendy, ed. *Merriam-Webster's encyclopedia of world religions*. Springfield, MA: Merriam-Webster, 1999.

Drake, Michael. *The shamanic drum: A guide to sacred drumming*. Salem, OR: Talking Drum Publications, 2002.

Droney, Maureen. *Mix masters: Platinum engineers reveal their secrets for success*. Boston, MA: Berklee Press, 2003.

Duncan, Andy, and Geoff Nicholls. *What drum*. London: Track Record Publishing, 1988.

Eberhard, Wolfram. *The local cultures of south and east China*. Leiden, The Netherlands: E. J. Brill, 1968.

Eberhard, Wolfram. *A history of China*. Los Angeles, CA: University of California Press, 1977.

Ebrey, Patricia Buckley. *Cambridge illustrated history: China*. New York: Cambridge University Press, 1996.

Ekrem, Inger, and Lars Boje Mortensen, eds. *Historia Norwegie*. Copenhagen, Denmark: Museum Tusculanum Press, 2003.

Eliot, Simon, and Jonathan Rose, eds. *A companion to the history of the book*. Malden, MA: Blackwell Publishing Ltd., 2007.

Elison, George, and Bardwell L. Smith, eds. *Warlords, artists and commoners: Japan in the sixteenth century*. Honolulu: The University Press of Hawai'i, 1981.

Elson, Louis Charles, ed. *Modern music and musicians*. New York: University Society, 1918.

Engel, Carl. *The music of the most ancient nations*. London: J. Murray, 1864.

Esses, Maurice. *Dance and instrumental diferencias in Spain during the 17th and early 18th centuries, Vol. 1*. New York: Pendragon Press, 1992.

Falola, Toyin, and Steven J. Salm. *Culture and customs of Ghana*. Westport, CT: Greenwood Press, 2002.

Farabee, William Curtis. *Indian tribes of eastern Peru*. India: Husain Press, 2008.

Farmer, Henry George. *A history of Arabian music*. New Delhi, India: Goodword Books, 2001 (1929).

Farmer, Henry George. *Historical facts for the Arabian musical influence*. New York: Arno Press, 1978.

Ferguson, John C. *Survey of Chinese art, chapter two, stone monuments*. Taipei, Taiwan: The Commercial Press, 1940.

Fernandez, Melanie, and Rayna Green. *The British Museum encyclopedia of native North America*. London: The British Museum Company Ltd., 1999.

Frédéric, Louis. *Le Japan: dictionnaire et civilisation*. Paris: Éditions Robert Laffront S.A., 1996.

Fridman, Eva Jane Neumann, and Mariko Namba Walter. *Shamanism: An encyclopedia of world beliefs, practices and culture*. Santa Barbara, CA: ABC-CLIO, 2004.

Frith, Simon. *Popular music*. London: Routledge, 2004.

Frith, Simon, John Street, and Will Straw. *The Cambridge companion to pop and rock*. Cambridge, UK: Cambridge University Press, 2001.

Gadkari, Jayant. *Society and religion: From Rigveda to Puranas*. Bombay, India: Popular Prakashan PVT, Ltd., 1996.

Galpin, Francis W. *The music of the Sumerians and their immediate successors the Babylonians and Assyrians*. Irvine, CA: Reprint Services Corp., 1937.

Galpin, Francis W. *A textbook of European musical instruments: Their origin, history and character*. London: Williams & Norgate, 1937.

Garstang, John. *Burial customs of Egypt as illustrated by the tombs of the Middle Kingdom*. London: Archibald Constable & Co, 1907.

Geertz, Hildred. *The life of a Balinese temple: Artistry, imagination and history in a peasant village*. Honolulu: University of Hawaii Press, 2004.

Ginsburg, Faye D., Lila Abu-Lughod, and Brain Larkin. *Media worlds: Anthropology on new terrain*. Berkeley, CA: University of California Press, 2002.

Godey, Louise Antoine, and Sarah Josepha Buell Hale. *Godey's magazine, Vol. 4*. Philadelphia, PA: L.A. Godey and Co., 1831.

Goodspeed, Edgar J. *The story of the New Testament*. Chicago, IL: The University of Chicago Press, 1916.

Gottlieb, Robert S. *Solo tabla drumming of north India: Its repertoire, styles and performance practices*. Delhi, India: Motilal Banarsidass Publishers Private Ltd., 1993.

Gray, Patrick. *Peoples of the Americas, Vol. 8*. New York: Marshall Cavendish Corporation, 1999.

Green, Lucy. *Music, gender, education*. Cambridge, UK: Cambridge University Press, 1997.

Gronow, Pekka, and Ilpo Saunio. *An international history of the recording industry*. London: Cassell, 1998.

Gunawardena, Charles A. *Encyclopedia of Sri Lanka*. Elgin, IL: New Dawn Press Group, 2005.

Guruge, Ananda W.W. *The society of the Rāmāyana*. New Delhi, India: Shakti Malik Abhinav Publications, 1991.

Gregory, Hugh. *A century of pop*. London: Reed Consumer Books,1998.

Green, Lucy. *Music, gender, education*. Cambridge, UK: Cambridge University Press, 1997.

Hamm, Charles. *Yesterdays: Popular songs in America*. New York: Norton, 1979.

Hammarlund, Anders, Tord Ollsen, and Elisabeth Özdalga, eds. *Sufism, music and society in Turkey and the Middle East*. Istanbul, Turkey: The Economic and Social History Foundation of Turkey, 2001.

Harris, Joseph, and Karl Reichl, eds. *Prosimetrum cross-cultural perspectives on narrative in prose and verse*. Suffolk, UK: Boydell & Brewer Ltd., 1997.

Harvey, G.E. *History of Burma.* New Delhi: J. Jetley, 1925.

Hastings, James, and John A. Selbie, eds. *Encyclopedia of religion and ethics, part nine.* Whitefish, MT: Kessinger Publishing, 2003 (reprint).

Hatch, David, and Stephen Millward. *From blues to rock: An analytical history of pop music.* New York: Manchester University Press, 1987.

Hernandez, Horacio. *Conversations in clave.* Miami, FL: Warner Bros. Publications, 2000.

Hernández, Jo Farb. *Forms of tradition in contemporary Spain.* Jackson, MS: University Press of Mississippi, 2005.

Herrman, J., and E. Zurcher. *History of humanity, Vol. 3. From the seventh century B.C. to the seventh century A.D.* London: Routledge, 1996.

Hesselink, Nathan. *P'ungmul: South Korean drumming and dance.* Chicago, IL: The University of Chicago Press, 2006.

Higham, Charles. *Encyclopedia of ancient civilizations.* New York: Facts On File, 2004.

Higham, Charles. *The bronze age of Southeast Asia.* Cambridge, UK: Cambridge University Press, 1996.

Hillier, Sir Walter Caine. *The Chinese language and how to learn it: A manual for beginners.* London: Kegan Paul, Trench, Trubner & Co, Ltd., 1907.

Horn, Gabriel. *The book of ceremonies: A native way of honoring and living the sacred.* Novato, CA: New World Library, 2000.

Houtsma, M. TH., and A.J. Wensinck. *E. J. Brill's first encyclopaedia of Islam 1913–1936.* Leiden, the Netherlands: E. J. Brill, 1993.

Hurtig, Brent. *Multi-track recording for musicians.* Van Nuys, CA: Alfred Publishing, 1988.

Icon Group International. *Ancestry: Webster's quotations, facts and phrases.* San Diego, CA: Icon Group International, 2008.

James, Billy. *Necessity is: The early years of Frank Zappa and the Mothers of Invention.* London: SAF Publishing Ltd., 2001.

Jameson, Robert, and Ian Shaw, eds. *A dictionary of archaeology.* Oxford, UK: Blackwell Publishers, 1999.

Jasper, Tony, and Derek Oliver. *The international encyclopedia of hard rock and heavy metal.* New York: Facts On File, 1987

Johansen, Claes. *Procol Harum: beyond the pale.* London: SAF Publishing Ltd., 2000.

Johnson, Paul Christopher. *Diaspora conversions: black Carib religion and the recovery of Africa.* Berkeley, CA: University of California Press, 2007.

Julien, Olivier. *Sgt. Pepper and the Beatles: It was forty years ago today.* Aldershot, Hampshire, UK: Ashgate Publishing Ltd., 2008.

Junod, Henri. A. *Life of a South African tribe, social life, 1926, part 1*. New York: Macmillan, 1927.

Kalani. *Together in rhythm. A facilitator's guide to drum circle music*. Los Angeles, CA: Alfred Publishing Co., 2004.

Kartomi, Margaret J. *On concepts and classifications of musical instruments*. Chicago, IL: University of Chicago Press, 1990.

Katz, Mark. *Capturing sound: How technology has changed music*. Berkeley, CA: University of California Press, 2004.

Kemp, Herman C. *Oral traditions of Southeast Asia and Oceania: A bibliography*. Jakarta, Indonesia: KITLV-Jakarta, 2004.

Kempers, A.J. Bernet. *The kettle drums of Southeast Asia: Modern quaternary research in Southeast Asia, Vol. 10*. Rotterdam, Netherlands: A.A. Balkema, 1988.

Kent, Harold Winfield. *Treasury of Hawaii words in one hundred and one categories*. Honolulu: University of Hawaii Press, 1986.

Klein, Herbert S. *The Atlantic slave trade, New Edition*. Cambridge: Cambridge University Press, 2010.

Klokke, Maryjke J., and Pauline Lunsingh Scheurleer. *Ancient Indonesian bronzes*. Leiden, the Netherlands: E. J. Brill, 1988.

Klöwer, Töm. *The joy of drumming: Drums and percussion instruments from around the world*. Havelte, the Netherlands: Binkey Kok Publications BV, 1997.

Koskoff, Ellen. *Music cultures in the United States: An introduction*. New York: Routledge, 2005.

Kramarae, Cheris, and Dale Spender. *Routledge international encyclopedia of women: Global women's issues and knowledge, Vol. 1*. London: Routledge, 2000.

Kramarae, Cheris, and Dale Spender. *Routledge international encyclopedia of women: Global women's issues and knowledge, Vol. 3*. London: Routledge, 2000.

Krauss, Beatrice H. *Plants in Hawaiian culture*. Honolulu University of Hawaii Press, 1993.

Krauss, Richard. *The party and the arty in China: The new politics of culture*. Lanham, MD: Rowman and Littlefield Publishers, 2004.

Kubik, Gerhard. *Theory of African music, Vol. 1*. Chicago, IL: The University of Chicago Press, 1994.

Kuss, Malena, ed. *Music in Latin America and the Caribbean: Performing the Caribbean experience*. Austin, TX: The University of Texas Press, 2007.

Lackowski, Rich. *On the beaten path. Metal: The drummer's guide to the genre and the legends who defined it*. Van Nuys, CA: Alfred Publishing, 2008.

Lackowski, Rich. *On the beaten path. The drummer's guide to musical styles and the legends who defined them.* Van Nuys, CA: Alfred Publishing, 2008.

Lameer, Joep. *Al-Fārābī and Aristotelian syllogistics: Greek theory and Islamic practice.*

Lavezzoli, Peter. *The dawn of Indian music in the west: Bhairavi.* London: Continuum International Publishing Group, 2006.

Lee, Ki-baik. *A new history of Korea.* Seoul, Korea: Ilchokak Publishers, 1984.

Leith, Denise. *The politics of power: Freeport in Suharto's Indonesia.* Honolulu: University of Hawaii Press, 2002.

Lemprière, John. *A classical dictionary: Containing a copious account of all the proper names mentioned in ancient authors.* New York: Evert Duyckinck, Collins and Co, 1827.

Levine, Laurie. *The drumcafé's traditional music of South Africa.* Johannesburg, South Africa: Jocana Media, 2005.

Lewis, Bernard, vol. ed. *The encyclopaedia of Islam, Vol. 3.* Boston, MA: Brill, 1986.

Li, Yongxiang. *The music of China's ethnic minorities.* Beijing: China Intercontinental Press, 2006.

Lindqvist, Cecilia. *China, empire of living symbols.* Indianapolis, IN: Addison Wesley, 1991.

Lonely Planet. *Rio de Janeiro.* Victoria, Australia: Lonely Planet Publications, 2004.

Lonely Planet. *Tahiti and French Polynesia.* Victoria, Australia: Lonely Planet Publications, 2006.

Long, David E. *Culture and customs of Saudi Arabia.* Westport, CT: Greenwood Press, 2005.

Louis, Dr. André. *Voodoo in Haiti: Catholicism, Protestantism and a model of effective ministry in the context of voodoo in Haiti.* Mustang, OK: Tate Publishing & Enterprises, LLC, 2007.

Malm, William P. *Traditional Japanese music and musical instruments, Vol. 1.* Tokyo: Kodansha International Ltd., 2000.

Manuel, Peter. *Caribbean currents: Caribbean music from rumba to reggae.* Philadelphia, PA: Temple University Press, 2006.

Manuel, P., and Marshall, W. *The riddim method: Aesthetics, practice, and ownership in Jamaican dancehall.* Cambridge, UK: Cambridge University Press, 2006.

Mar, Norman Del. *Anatomy of the orchestra.* Berkeley, CA: University of California Press, 1981.

Marshall Cavendish Corporation. *World and its peoples: India and its neighbours.* Tarrytown, NY: Marshall Cavendish Corporation, 2008.

Marshall Cavendish Corporation. *World and its peoples: Myanmar and Thailand.* Tarrytown, NY: Marshall Cavendish Corporation, 2008.

Martels, Zweder Von, and Arjo Vanderjagt, eds. *Pius II, "el più expeditivo pontifice": Selected studies on Aeneas Silvius Piccolomini (1405–1464).* Leiden, The Netherlands: Koninklijke Brill, 2003.

Marvin, Elizabeth West, and Richard Hermann, eds. *Concert music, rock, and jazz since 1945: Essays and analytical studies.* Rochester, NY: The University of Rochester Press, 1995.

Mason, Bernard Sterling. *How to make drums, tom toms and rattles: Primitive percussion instruments for modern use.* New York: Dover Publications, 1974.

Mason, Peter. *Bacchanal!: The carnival culture of Trinidad.* Philadelphia, PA: Temple University Press, 1998.

Massey, Reginald. *India's dances: Their history, technique and repertoire.* New Delhi, India: Abhinav Publications, 2004.

Massey, Reginald, and Jamila. *The music of India.* New Delhi, India: Abhinav Publications, 1996.

Matusky, Patricia, and Tan Sooi Beng. *The music of Malaysia: The classical, folk and syncretic traditions.* Aldershot, Hampshire, UK: Ashgate Publishing Ltd., 2004.

May, Elizabeth, ed. *Musics of many cultures: An introduction.* Berkeley and Los Angeles, CA: University of Californian Press, 1980.

McEvilley, Thomas. *The shape of ancient thought.* New York: Allworth Press, 2002.

McGowan, Chris, and Ricardo Pessanha. *The Brazilian sound: Samba, bossa nova, and the popular music of Brazil.* Philadelphia, PA: Temple University Press, 1998.

McIntosh, Jane. *The ancient Indus Valley: New perspectives.* Santa Barbara, CA: ABC-CLIO-Inc., 2008.

McLean, Mervyn. *Weavers of song: Polynesian music and dance.* Honolulu: University of Hawaii Press, 1999.

Mehta, Tarla. *Sanskrit play production in ancient India.* Delhi, India: Motilal Banarsidass Publishers Private Ltd., 1995.

Merriam, Alan P. *The anthropology of music.* Evanston, IL: Northwestern University Press, 1964.

Midgley, Ruth, ed. *Musical instruments of the world.* London: Paddington Press, 1976.

Millard, Andre. *America on record: A history of recorded sound, second edition.* New York: Cambridge University Press, 2005.

Miller, Barbara Helen. *Connecting and correcting: A case study of Sami healers in Porsanger*. Leiden, the Netherlands: CNWS Publications, 2007.

Miller, Terry E., and Andrew C. Shahriari. *World music. A global journey*. New York: Routledge, 2009.

Miller, Terry E., and Sean Williams, eds. *The Garland encyclopedia of world music: Southeast Asian*. New York: Garland Publishing, 1998.

Miller, Terry E., and Sean Williams, eds. *The Garland handbook of Southeast Asian music*. New York: Routledge, 2008.

Mittler, Barbara. *Dangerous tunes: The politics of Chinese music in Hong Kong, Taiwan, and the People's Republic of China since 1949*.Wiesbaden, Germany: Otto Harrassowitz, 1997.

Monelle, Raymond. *The musical topic: Hunt, military and pastoral*. Bloomington, IN: Indiana University Press, 2006.

Montagu, Jeremy. *Timpani and percussion*. New Haven, CT: Yale University Press, 2002.

Moore, Brian L. *Cultural power, resistance, and pluralism: Colonial Guyana, 1838–1900*. Montreal and Kingston, Canada: McGill-Queen's University Press, 1995.

Moore, R.I., ed. *The Hamlyn historical atlas*. London, UK: The Hamlyn Publishing Group, 1981.

Moore, Wendy. *West Malaysia and Singapore*. Singapore: Periplus Editions (HK) Ltd., 1998.

Moorefield, Virgil. *The producer as composer: Shaping the sounds of popular music*. Cambridge, MA: Massachusetts Institute of Technology, 2005.

Morton, David. *The traditional music of Thailand*. Berkeley, CA: University of California Press, 1979.

Moskowitz, David. *Caribbean popular music: An encyclopedia of reggae, mento, ska, rocksteady and dancehall*. Westport, CT: Greenwood Press, 2006.

Mudimbe, V.Y. *The idea of Africa*. Bloomington, IN: Indiana University Press, 1994.

Muller, Carol A. *Focus: Music of South Africa*. New York: Routledge, 2008.

Muller, Stephanus, and Chris Walton, ed. *Gender and sexuality in South African music*. Stellenbosch, South Africa: SUN ePReSS, 2005.

Munro, Martin. *Different drummers: Rhythm and race in the Americas*. Berkeley, CA: University of California Press, 2010.

Mudge, William. *Tabernacle of Moses*. Whitefish, MT: Kessinger Publishing, (1842) 2003.

Mutwa, Credo Uusa'mazulu. *My people, my Africa*. New York: John Day, 1969.

Nannyonga-Tamusuza, Sylvia A. *Baakisimba: Gender in the music and dance of the Buganda people of Uganda.* New York: Routledge, 2005.

Nariman, J.K. *Literary history of Sanskrit Buddhism: (from Winternitz, Sylvain Levi, Huber).* Delhi, India: Montilal Banarsidass, 1972.

Neciosup, Professor Hector, and Professor Jose Rosa. *World music survey: The history of music from Cuba, the Caribbean, South America and the United States.* Orlando, FL: Contemporary Latin Music Educators, LLC, 2008.

Newell, Philip Richard. *Recording spaces.* Oxford, England: Focal Press, 1998.

Nicholls, Geoff. *The drum book.* London: Balfon Books, 1997.

Nidel, Richard. *World music: The basics.* New York: Routledge, 2004.

Nketia, Kwabena. *African music in Ghana.* Accra, Ghana: Longmans, Green and Co. Ltd., 1962.

Oldenburg, Hermann. *The religion of the veda.* Delhi, Motilal Banarsidass Publishers Private Ltd., 1988.

Oliver, Paul, Tony Russell, Robert M.W. Dixon, John Godrich, and Howard Rye. *Yonder come the blues: The evolution of a genre.* Cambridge: The Press Syndicate of the University of Cambridge, 2001.

Olsen, Dale A., and Daniel E. Sheehy. *The Garland handbook of Latin American music, Vol. 2.* New York: Garland Publishing, 2000.

Ooi, Keat Gin, ed. *Southeast Asia: a historical encyclopedia, from Angkor Wat to East Timor.* Santa Barbara, CA: ABC-CLIO, 2004.

Pandey, Ashish. *Encylopaedic dictionary of music, Vol. 1.* India: Isha Books, 2005.

Panikkar, Raimundo. *The Vedic experience: mantramnjari: An anthology of the Vedas for modern man and contemporary celebration.* Delhi, India: Motilal Banarsidass Publishers Private Ltd., 1977.

Parmeshwaranand, Swami. *Encyclopaedic dictionary of the Purānas.* New Delhi, India: Sarup and Sons, 2001.

Payne, Jim. *The great drummers of R&B, funk and soul.* New York: Face the Music Productions, 2006.

Payne, Jim. *100 famous funk beats.* New York: Face the Music Productions, 2006.

Peek, Philip M., and Kwesi Yankah. *African folklore: An encyclopedia.* New York: Routledge, 2004.

Pellicer, Sergio Navarrete. *Maya Achi marimba music in Guatemala.* Philadelphia, PA: Temple University Press, 2005.

Penyeh, Tsao, ed. *Tradition and change in the performance of Chinese music.* London: Routledge, 2002.

Perani, Judith, and Norma Hackelman Wolff. *Cloth, dress and art patronage in Africa.* New York: Berg, 1999.

Peregrine, Peter N., and Melvin Ember, eds. *Encyclopedia of prehistory, Vol. 3: East Asia and Oceania.* New Haven, CT: Published in conjunction with the Human Relations area Files at Yale University/Springer, 2001.

Perry, Richard, and Rosalind W. Perry. *Maya missions: Exploring colonial Yucatan.* Santa Barbara: CA: Espadana Press, 1988.

Peters, Mitchell. *Fundamental method for timpani.* Van Nuys, CA: Alfred Publishing Company, 1993.

Picken, Laurence. *Musica Asiatica, Vol. 1.* Oxford: Oxford University Press, 1977.

Picken, Laurence. *Musica Asiatica, Vol. 4.* Cambridge: Cambridge University Press, 1984.

Picken, Laurence, and D.R. Widdess, eds. *Music and tradition: Essays on Asian and other music presented to Laurence Picken.* Cambridge: Cambridge University Press, 1981.

Pinksterboer, Hugo. *The cymbal book.* Milwaukee, WI: Hal Leonard, 1992.

Pinn, Anthony. *African American religious cultures.* Santa Barbara, CA: ABC-CLIO, LLC, 2009.

Possehl, Gregory L. *The Indus civilization: A contemporary perspective.* Walnut Creek, CA: Rowman and Littlefield Publishers, 2002.

Prahlad, Anand. *Reggae wisdom: Proverbs in Jamaican music.* Jackson, MS: University Press of Mississippi, 2002.

Prakash, Om. *Cultural history of India.* New Delhi, India: New Age International (P) Ltd., Publishers, 2005.

Pratt, Christina. *An encyclopedia of shamanism, Vol. 1.* New York: The Rosen Publishing Group, 2007.

Pratt, Keith, and Richard Rutt. *Korea: A historical and cultural dictionary.* Richmond, Surrey, UK: Curzon Press, 1999.

Pruthi, R.K. *Indus civilization.* New Delhi, India: Discovery Publishing House, 2004.

Pruthi, R.K. *The epic civilization.* New Delhi, India: Discovery Publishing House, 2004.

Quintana, José Luis, and Chuck Silverman. *Changuito: A master's approach to timbales.* Van Nuys, CA: Belwin-Mills Publishing, 1998.

Rabb, Johnny. *Jungle/drum 'n' bass for the acoustic drum set.* Miami, FL: Warner Bros. Publications, 2001.

Randel, Don Michael, ed. *The Harvard dictionary of music (Fourth Edition).* Cambridge, MA: Harvard University Press, 1986, 2003.

Randel, Don Michael, ed. *The Harvard concise dictionary of music and musicians.* Cambridge, MA: Harvard University Press, 2002.

Reader, Lesley, and Lucy Ridout. *The rough guide to Bali and Lombok.* New York: Rough Guides Ltd., 2002.

Redmond, Layne. *When the drummers were women: A spiritual history of rhythm.* New York: Three Rivers Press, 1997.

Roads, Curtis. *The computer music tutorial.* Cambridge, MA: Massachusetts Institute of Technology, 1996.

Roe, Derek Arthur. *Prehistory: An introduction.* Los Angeles: University of California Press, 1970.

Romanowski, Patricia, and Otis Williams. *Temptations.* New York: G.P. Putnam's Sons, 1988.

Rosenthal, Franz. *The classical heritage in Islam.* Los Angeles, CA: University of California Press, 1965.

Rossing, Thomas D. *Science of percussion instruments.* Singapore: World Scientific Publishing Co. Pte. Ltd., 2000.

Roy, David T., and Tsuen-hsuin Tsien. *Ancient China: Studies in early civilisation.* Hong Kong: The Chinese University Press, 1978.

Ripinsky-Naxon, Michaël. *The nature of shamanism: Substance and function of a religious metaphor.* New York: State University of New York Press, Albany, 1993.

Ruan, Xing. *Allegorical architecture: Living myth and architectonics in Southern China.* Honolulu: University of Hawai'i Press, 2006.

Ruiz, Ana. *The spirit of ancient Egypt.* New York: Algora Publishing, 2001.

Sachs, Curt. *The history of musical instruments.* New York: Norton, 1940.

Sadie, Stanley, ed. *The new Grove dictionary of music and musicians.* London: Macmillan, 1980.

Saint-Lot, Marie-José Alcide. *Vodou, a sacred theatre: The African heritage in Haiti.* Coconut Creek, FL: Educa Vision, 2003.

Sanyal, Ritwik, and Richard Widdess. *Dhrupad: Tradition and performance in Indian music.* Aldershot, Hampshire, UK: Ashgate Publishing Ltd., 2004.

Sartwell, Crispin. *Political aesthetics.* New York: Cornell University Press, 2010.

Scaruffi, Piero. *A history of rock music: 1951–2000.* Lincoln, NE: iUniverse, 2003.

Schloss, Joseph G. *Making beats: The art of sample based hip-hop.* Middletown, CT: Wesleyan University Press, 2004.

Schuessler, Axel. *ABC etymological dictionary of old Chinese.* Honolulu: University of Hawaii Press, 2007.

Sharma, Shubhra. *Life in the Upanishads*. New Delhi, India: Shakti Malik Abhinav Publications, 1985.

Shashi, S.S., ed. *Encyclopedia Indica: India, Pakistan, Bangladesh, Vol. 100*. New Delhi, India: Anmol Publications PVT, Ltd., 1997.

Sheets, Payson D. *Archaeology, volcanism, and remote sensing in the Arenal region, Costa Rica*. Austin, TX: University of Texas Press, 1994.

Shepherd, John. *Continuum encyclopedia of popular music of the world, Volume 2: Performance and production*. Continuum: London, 2003.

Shiloah, Amnon. *Music in the world of Islam*. Detroit, MI: Wayne State University Press, 1995.

Shively, Donald H., and William H. McCullough, ed. *The Cambridge history of Japan, Vol. 2*. Cambridge, UK: Cambridge University Press, 1993.

Simanjuntak, Truman, M. Hisyam, Bagyo Prasetyo, and Titi Surti Nastiti, ed. *Archaeology: Indonesian perspective*. Jakarta, Java: Lipi Press, 2006.

Simmonds, Jeremy. *The encyclopedia of dead rock stars: Heroin, handguns and ham sandwiches*. Chicago, IL: Chicago Review Press, 2008.

Singh, Bilveer. *The Talibanization of South East Asia: Losing the war on terror to Islamic extremists*. Westport, CT: Praeger Security International, 2007.

Singh, Upinder. *A history of ancient and early medieval India: From the stone age to the 12th century*. Delhi, India: Dorling Kindersley (India) Pvt. Ltd., 2008.

Singhal, K.C., and Roshan Gupta. *The ancient history of India, Vedic period: A new interpretation*. New Delhi, India: Atlantic Publishers and Distributors, 2003.

Smedley, Edw. *Encyclopaedia Metropolitana; or, universal dictionary of knowledge, Vol. 18*. London: J.J. Griffin, 1845.

Solomon, Anne. *The essential guide to San rock art*. Claremont, South Africa: David Philip Publishers (Pty) Ltd., 1998.

Somervill, Barbara A. *Empire of the Aztecs*. New York: Chelsea House, 2010.

Spiller, Henry. *Gamelan: The traditional sounds of Indonesia*. Santa Barbara, CA: ABC-CLIO, 2004.

Stanley, Henry M. *How I found Livingstone in Central Africa*. London: Sampson, Low, Marston & Co., 1895.

Stevenson, Robert. *Music in Aztec and Inca territory*. Berkeley, CA: University of California Press, 1968.

Stevenson, Robert. *The music of colonial Spanish America*. Cambridge, UK: Cambridge University Press, 1984.

Strein, Burton. *A history of India: second edition*. Chichester, West Sussex, UK: Blackwell Publishers, Ltd., 2010.

Sublette, Ned. *Cuba and its music: From the first drums to the mambo, Vol. 1*. Chicago, IL: Chicago Review Press, 2004.

Sutton, Richard Anderson. *Traditions of gamelan music in Java: Musical pluralism and regional identity*. Cambridge, UK: Cambridge University Press, 1991.

Swangviboonpong, Dusadee. *Thai classical singing: Its history, musical characteristics and transmission*. Aldershot, Hampshire, UK: Ashgate Publishing Ltd., 2003.

Tarling, Nicholas. *Cambridge history of Southeast Asia. Volume one, part one. From early times to C. 1500*. Cambridge, UK: The Press Syndicate of the University of Cambridge, 1999.

Taylor, Eric. *Musical Instruments of South East Asia*. Oxford, UK: Oxford University Press, 1989.

Taylor, Keith Weller. *The birth of Vietnam*. Berkley, CA: University of California Press, 1983.

Te Nijenhuis, Emmie. *Sangitasiromani: A medieval handbook of Indian music*. Leiden, the Netherlands: E. J. Brill, 1992.

Thakur, Upendra. *Some aspects of Asian history and culture*. New Delhi, India: Shakti Malik, 1986.

The Toledo Maya Cultural Council, Toledo Alcaldes Association. *Maya atlas: The struggle to preserve Maya land in Southern Belize*. Berkeley, CA: North Atlantic Books, 1997.

Thurston, Edgar. *Castes and tribes of southern India*. New Delhi, India: Asian Educational Services, 2001.

Titon, Jeff Todd, ed. *Worlds of music: An introduction to the music of the world's people*. Belmont, CA: Schirmer Cengage Learning, 2009.

Tripathi, Rama Shankar. *History of ancient India*. Delhi, India: Motilal Banarsidass Publishers Private Ltd., 1942.

Turner, Edith L.B. *Experiencing ritual: A new interpretation of African healing*. Philadelphia, PA: University of Pennsylvania Press, 1992.

Uribe, Ed. *The essence of Brazilian percussion and drum set*. Los Angeles, CA: Alfred Publishing Co., 1994.

Vennum, Thomas. *The Ojibwa dance drum: Its history and construction*. St. Paul, MN: Minnesota Historical Society Press, 2009.

Vernon, Paul. *Ethnic and vernacular music, 1898–1960: A resource and guide to recordings*. Westport, CT: Greenwood Press, 1995.

Villepastour, Amanda. *Ancient test messaging of the Yorùbá Bàtá drum: Cracking the code*. Farnham, UK: Ashgate Publishing Ltd., 2010.

Wade, Bonnie C. *Imaging sound: An ethnomusicological study of music, art and culture in Mughal, India*. Chicago: The University of Chicago Press, 1998.

Wade-Matthews, Max. *The world guide to musical instruments*. London: Lorenz Books, 2000.

Wadhams, Wayne. *Inside the hits: The seduction of a rock and roll generation*. Boston, MA: Berklee Press, 2001.

Wanasundera, Nanda Pethiyagoda. *Cultures of the world: Sri Lanka*. Tarrytown, NY: Marshall Cavendish Corporation, 2004.

Wang, Oliver. *Classic material: The hip-hop album guide*. Toronto, Ontario: ECW Press, 2003.

Warner, Timothy. *Pop music—Technology and creativity*. Aldershot, Hampshire, UK: Ashgate, 2003.

Watsky, Andrew Mark. *Chikubushima: Deploying the sacred arts in Momoyama Japan*. Seattle, WA: University of Washington Press, 2004.

Welch, Patricia Bjaaland. *Chinese art: A guide to motifs and visual imagery*. North Clarendon, VT: Tuttle Publishing, 2008.

Welsh, Kariamu. *African dance, second edition*. New York: Infobase Publishing, 2010.

Williams, Charles. *Chinese symbolism and art motifs*. Boston, MA: Tuttle Publishing, 1974.

Williams, Joanna Gottfried, ed. *Kalādarśana: American studies in the art of India*. Leiden, The Netherlands: E.J. Brill, 1981.

Williams, Richard. *Phil Spector: Out of his head*. New York: Outerbridge and Lazard, 1974.

Williams, S. Wells. *A history of China: Being the historical chapters from the middle kingdom (1897)*. Whitefish, MT: Kessinger Publishing, 2008 (reprint).

Williamson, Alexander. *Journeys in North China, Manchuria and Eastern Mongolia*. London: Smith, Elder and Co., 1870.

Witzleben, John Lawrence. *"Silk and bamboo" music in Shanghai: The Jiangnan Sizhu Instrumental Ensemble Tradition*. Kent, OH: The Kent State University Press, 1995.

Yifa. *The origins of Buddhist monastic codes in China: An annotated translation and study of the Chanyuan Quinggui*. Honolulu: University of Hawaii Press, 2002.

Young, Richard. *Music, popular culture, identities*. Amsterdam, the Netherlands: Rodopi B.V., 2002.

ARTICLES

Boesche, Christophe. "Symbolic communication in wild chimpanzees," *Human Evolution* Volume 6–N. 1 (1991): 81–90. http://www.eva .mpg.de/primat/staff/boesch/pdf/Boesch_Symbolic%20comm%20 in%20wild%20chimps%201991.pdf (2 December 2010).

Hornbostel, Eric M. von, and Curt Sachs. "Classification of musical instruments." Trans. by Anthony Baines and Klaus P. Wachsmann. *Galpin Society Journal* 14 March 1961: 3–29. First published in 1914.

WEBSITES

Allen, Robert, ed. *Pocket Fowler's Modern English Usage. Oxford Reference Online. Oxford University Press,* 2008. http://www.oxfordreference .com/views/ENTRY.html?subview=Main&entry=t30.e2970 (8 February 2010)

Aluede, Charles. O. *The anthropomorphicattributes of African musical instruments: history and use in Esan, Nigeria.* http://www.krepublishers .com/02-Journals/T-Anth/Anth-08-0-000-000-2006-Web/Anth-08-3- 147-214-2006-Abst-PDF/Anth-08-3-157-160-2006-303-Aluede-C-O/ Anth-08-3-157-160-2006-303-Aluede-C-O-Text.pdf (3 August 2010). Ekpoma, Nigeria: Department of Theatre and Media Arts, Ambrose Alli University, Ekpoma, Nigeria, 2006.

Arcadi, Adam Clark, Christophe Boesch, and Daniel Robert. http://www .fas.harvard.edu/~kibale/pdfs/Arcadi2004_Primates.pdf (10 September 2010).

Randall, Jan A. "Evolution and function of drumming as communication in mammals." *Department of Biology, San Francisco State University.* 2001. http://intl-icb.oxfordjournals.org/cgi/reprint/41/5/1143 (23 August 2010).

Saoud, Rabah. *The Arab contribution to music in the Western world.* Manchester, UK: Foundation for Science, Technology and Civilisation (FSTC) Ltd., 2004. http://www.muslimheritage.com/uploads/Music2.pdf.

DISSERTATION

Yew, Christopher. *The Turk on the opera stage. A history of a musical cliché. Thesis (M.A.).* Norderstedt, Germany: Druck und Bindung. Books On Demand Gmb H, 2009.

Conference Paper

Singh, Udai Vir, ed. "The late Harappan and other Chalcolithic cultures of India: a study in inter-relationship." Papers presented at the VI annual congress of the Indian Archaeological Society and the seminar, Kurukshetra, 19–21 Nov. 1972.

Index

CONTENTS

ALBUMS

8th Wonder, 303

90125, 257, 258

The Adventures of Grandmaster Flash on the Wheels of Steel, 301, 303

. . . And Justice for All, 273

Autobahn, 253

Bad, 253, 254, 412

The Big Picture, 369

Bitches Brew, 283, 285, 288

The Black Album, 274

Blood Sugar Sex Magik, 364

Brain Salad Surgery, 368

The Chronic, 306

Cowboys from Hell, 278

Crossings, 292

Dangerous, 254

Destiny, 254

Dark Side of the Moon, 322

Double Barrel, 320

Duke, 258

Duster, 283

Emergency, 284

E.N.D., 307

Every Good Boy Deserves Favor, 368

BANDS/ENSEMBLES

DRUMS

PIECES

PLACES

About the Author

Matt Dean is a busy professional drummer both in live performance and studio recording sessions in nearly every style of contemporary music throughout London and Europe. An active instructor, Dean shares his passion for the drum through his writings on Matt Dean's Drum Blog and his contributions to *Modern Drummer, Making Music, Music Teacher*, and *Drumscene*.